Impler

MW01046091

Estate Freezes

2nd Edition

David Louis, B.Com., J.D., C.A.

with Contributors

Samantha Prasad, B.A., LL.B.

Yosef Adler, Sharona Ishmael, students
of Minden Gross*

*Minden Gross Grafstein & Greenstein LLP, Toronto,
a member of MERITAS law firms worldwide

Published by CCH Canadian Limited

Important Disclaimer: This publication is sold with the understanding that (1) the authors and editors are not responsible for the results of any actions taken on the basis of information in this work, nor for any errors or omissions; and (2) the publisher is not engaged in rendering legal, accounting or other professional services. The publisher, and the authors and editors, expressly disclaim all and any liability to any person, whether a purchaser of this publication or not, in respect of anything and of the consequences of anything done or omitted to be done by any such person in reliance, whether whole or partial, upon the whole or any part of the contents of this publication. If legal advice or other expert assistance is required, the services of a competent professional person should be sought.

ISBN 1-55367-557-6

Acknowledgements

This edition of *Implementing Estate Freezes* features a number of material changes from the first edition. Notably, Estate Freeze from Hell, a case study pertaining to the 21st anniversary of a freeze into a discretionary family trust is considerably expanded — from less than 20 pages in the first edition to nearly 80.

I would like to thank the contributors for both their materials and participating in several live presentations: from outside of our firm, Howard Carr, Joel Cuperfain, Ed Northwood[1]; and from Minden Gross, Joan Jung, Samantha Prasad, Daniel Sandler, Stephen Witten, and most particularly Michael Goldberg, who coordinated the materials and presentations. We also feature a number of external articles, by Allan Tiller[2], Robert Spenceley, as well as Michael Goldberg and Samantha Prasad.

While I have also expanded the discussion on family trusts, for me, the most difficult part of the book was the expansion of the materials on asset freezes in Chapter 2, the big issue being how far should I go in terms of section 85 commentary. My answer is endemic of my general compulsive approach to taxation — a nearly 70 page chapter, excluding several Appendices. I figure that if you're not interested, you don't have to read it!

I would like to thank those who assisted me in various portions of the book, particularly Samantha Prasad. I am also grateful for the assistance of students Yosef Adler and Sharona Ishmael — and to our CCH editor Heather Egger.

---

[1] Michael Atlas reviewed various parts of the materials.

[2] Allan Tiller is from Chamberlain Hrdlicka, our MERITAS affiliate in Houston

Table of Contents

Chapter 1

Introduction

TOPICS DISCUSSED

The Basics

What is an Estate Freeze?

An estate freeze refers to the transfer of the future growth in value of a business, investments, or other assets into the hands of subsequent generations (the "Children"). The current owners (the "Parents") are effectively divested of this future growth. An estate freeze typically limits the value of the Parents' estate to the value at the date the freeze is implemented (the freezor typically retains the current value of the asset, although often in a different form). Accordingly, capital gains and other tax exposure on the future growth that would otherwise arise when the assets pass from Parents to Children are avoided.

Why is an Estate Freeze Implemented?

The main reason to implement a freeze is to maximize the value of the estate that will ultimately pass to the freezor's beneficiaries. The avoidance of capital gains and other tax that would otherwise be incurred on the transfer of appreciated assets to a subsequent generation means that the beneficiaries will receive more (and the CRA[1] less). An individual is generally considered to dispose of his or her capital property on death at fair market value. Reducing the value of one's property that will be subject to these "deemed disposition" rules serves to maximize the value of the assets received by the beneficiaries. For this reason, an estate freeze is implemented when the assets of the freezor are expected to appreciate. If the assets are expected to depreciate, it is usually preferable not to implement an estate freeze.

In addition to avoiding capital gains tax upon the death of the Parent, an estate freeze may serve a number of other purposes:

Income splitting

Income and capital gains might be taxed in the hands of family members who are in a lower marginal tax rate than that of the Parents. There are a number of income tax rules (the "attribution rules") which are designed to thwart this objective. It is, however, quite possible to implement successful income-splitting strategies within the context of a freeze, notwithstanding these rules. In the corporate context, income-splitting also refers to the ability to have corporate distributions, as well as gains from the sale of shares themselves, taxed in the hands of lower-bracket family members. In the latter case, multiple recourse to the enhanced ($500,000) lifetime capital gains exemption may also be an objective of the freeze. We will return to the attribution rules below, as well as the "kiddie-tax" (originally announced in the 1999 federal budget).

---

[1] Readers will be aware that the CRA (Canada Revenue Agency) was formerly known as Revenue Canada, and afterward the CCRA (Canada Customs and Revenue Agency). References are generally made to the CRA, one exception being the *Revenue Canada Round Table*, which continues to exist in electronic form as a CCH publication with this title.

Creditor protection

It may be possible to afford a degree of protection from creditors with respect to shares held by Children (or better still by a discretionary family trust in their favour). Shares held by Parents might be subject to claims as a result of personal guarantees, judgment creditors, etc. Depending on the circumstances and the structure of the estate freeze, this may not be the case with respect to shares held by Children.

Probate planning

Because an estate freeze limits the future growth of assets, it also limits the value of the freezor's estate at death — probate tax being imposed in accordance with the magnitude of the latter. Probate tax is highest in Ontario and British Columbia and, in these provinces, probate planning has become an integral part of estate planning.

Marital considerations

In addition to limiting the future growth of assets with respect to Parents, an estate freeze will often be designed to limit marital claims *vis-à-vis* the growth assets.

Incorporation tax benefits

The tax benefits of incorporation may also be obtained or enhanced by implementing an estate freeze. This may include creating a second small business base — i.e., by creating a new corporation to be frozen which is not associated with a pre-existing operating company.

How is an Estate Freeze Implemented?

In its most basic form, an estate freeze is simply the transfer of appreciating assets to a subsequent generation. It can be as simple as transferring ownership of an asset (by sale or gift) to a child or grandchild. Although this will achieve the objective of shifting capital gains tax liability from one generation to the other, such simple transfers may involve immediate tax exposure because of the deemed disposition rules. Further, a straightforward transfer may undermine the desire of the Parents to maintain a degree of control over the assets.

For these reasons, the most common form of estate freeze involves the transfer of assets to a corporation with a freeze configuration (see Fig. XX below) or the reorganization of an existing corporation into such a configuration, typically combined with a family trust. The corporate vehicle usually permits the implementation of the estate freeze on a tax-deferred basis. Furthermore, corporate equity structures allow economic and legal rights in respect of the underlying property to be specifically defined and carved out. The trust affords additional degrees of control and protection against mismanagement by the beneficiaries and may enable the trustees to actually determine the beneficiaries themselves.

In this book, the primary focus is on the corporate/trust freeze vehicle. Simpler forms of freezes are discussed briefly.

Basic Configuration of an Estate Freeze

Achieving the basic objectives of estate freezing with respect to an incorporated business usually involves a corporate reorganization such that Parents have shares with either limited or no participation in the future growth of the corporation. Children have shares which carry rights to future appreciation, and in many cases income-splitting advantages, notably the ability to distribute dividends such that they are taxed in the hands of the Children.

Figure XX depicts a "typical" corporate estate freeze and income-splitting configuration. This configuration can be achieved in a number of ways, including the transfer of personally held assets to be frozen into a corporation — i.e., in consideration for freeze shares, with common shares representing the future growth of the corporation. (For further discussion, see Chapter 2.)

Where the assets to be frozen are already held by a corporation, the configuration can be achieved through an "internal freeze", whereby the pre-existing shares are converted into freeze shares, with common shares representing the future growth of the corporation. An offshoot of the foregoing is a holding-company freeze, whereby the shares of an existing corporation are transferred into a Holdco, which is the freeze vehicle. (For further discussion, see Chapter 3.)

Figure XX

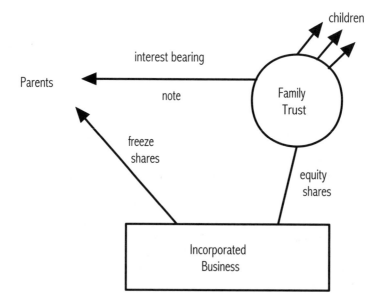

Parents' Shares

Once this configuration is achieved, the Parents will typically hold freeze shares with most or all of the following attributes:

- *redeemable* at the value of the pre-existing shares at the time of the freeze, or can otherwise be repurchased (subject to corporate-law solvency requirements);

- *retractable* (i.e., redeemable at the option of the holder) at the same amount;

- *preference on liquidation* and possibly redemption;

- *price adjustment* mechanism in effect in the event of a dispute with the CRA as to the correct value of the freeze shares (relative to the value of the pre-existing shares) at the time of the freeze;

- *dividend feature* — non-cumulative or other;

- *voting features*, as desired. It appears that, with the proper design, Parents' shares can maintain effective control without presenting a valuation problem;[2]

- *non-impairment feature*, i.e., no dividends can be declared on any classes of shares if the ability to retract would be interfered with (such provisions are often inserted notwithstanding corporate law remedies which might be available to shareholders in such event).

In addition, a number of other provisions are typically inserted with respect to the freeze shares. For example, the articles might specify that dividends can be paid on Parents' shares without participation by the common (growth) shares and vice versa (i.e., so that a waiver would not be required in the event that common shareholders are to receive a dividend).

Several of the attributes described above are, in fact, essential to ensure that the value of the shares received by the Parents on the reorganization is equal to the fair market value of the assets in question at the time of the freeze. These include retractability, the price adjustment mechanism, dividend features, provisions that no dividends can be declared if the ability to retract is interfered with, as well as the preference on liquidation or redemption. For further discussion, see Chapter 4.

 If, at the time of the freeze, the fair market value of the freeze shares is not equivalent to that of the transferred assets or pre-existing shares (as the case may be), various provisions of the *Income Tax Act* may be triggered, resulting in taxable benefits being attributed to the parties of the reorganization.

---

[2] See *Re Mann Estate* [1972] 5 WWR 33 (B.C.S.C.), affirmed [1974] 2 WWR 574 (S.C.C.).

Children's Shares

The Children typically receive "equity" or "growth" shares. These shares will convey rights to residual equity growth and dividend participation, that is, after the rights of Parents' shares are satisfied. Since the existing value of the corporation is typically reflected in the freeze shares, the growth shares would initially have a relatively low value (arguably, nominal)[3]. As a result, a nominal subscription or transfer price is normally involved. It should be noted that it may well be possible to use common shares in this respect (accordingly, in this context, the terms "common shares" and "growth shares" are often used interchangeably).

In most cases, the subscription or purchase is structured in a manner so as not to trigger the attribution rules; this allows income-splitting objectives to be achieved. For example, the acquisition of growth shares could be funded by a promissory note that bears interest at prescribed rates, so as to come within one of the exceptions to the attribution rules. However, in Ontario at least, an alternative is to have another individual subscribe to the growth shares and then gift them to the Children/family trust. If there is a gift after marriage, a degree of protection of the assets in respect of marital claims might be obtained.

Family Trust

In the configuration shown in Figure XX, the Children's shares may be held through a family trust. The purpose of the trust is to afford a degree of control and protection against mismanagement by the beneficiaries and, often, to determine who the beneficiaries will be.

Trusts are vehicles through which property is managed and administered for the benefit of the trusts' beneficiaries. Trusts are established for tax and non-tax reasons. Some non-tax reasons for the establishment of trusts include providing individuals with the benefit of property ownership where they are unable to manage the property personally. Trusts are implemented for beneficiaries who lack business experience or knowledge, for infants, mentally disabled and incompetent persons who lack the capacity to manage their affairs, and for those persons who are not legally incompetent but merely lack judgment. Some tax reasons for the establishment of trusts include the saving of income tax through income splitting and the deferral of income tax on capital gains. However, such tax benefits can be achieved without the interposition of a trust — i.e., the tax planning arrangements could be made directly with family members. Accordingly, even though trusts may, in a sense, be tax motivated, in another sense, it is the protective element that usually dictates the interposition of a trust.

However, trusts are a particularly effective tool in estate and business succession planning, and estate freezes in particular. They are a means by which an owner-manager can slowly ease into various succession phases. Trusts are predominantly used in the estate planning area to allow individuals to transfer assets to family members (or others), while maintaining some form of control over the transferred

---

[3] Of course, it might be argued that these shares have a significant value because they are effectively an option on future growth. The premise that growth shares have a nominal value has been tacitly accepted by the CRA as well as tax and estate planning practitioners.

assets. In a direct transfer to such persons (as opposed to a trust), the transferees acquire full title to the assets and the transferor may relinquish all control over the assets. The use of a trust allows for a degree of flexibility as to whom the transferor may want to give eventual control of the business if she or he so chooses. Through the use of a trust, the transferor retains some control, either as a trustee of the trust or by choosing the trustees, and by dictating the terms of the trust. (It should be noted though, that he or she could personally retain voting control of the corporation by holding thin voting shares.)

Accordingly, the typical estate freeze in an owner-manager context would normally use a trust so that any future accrued gain is passed on to the trust, for the benefit of his or her children/issue. The same result could be obtained were the growth shares transferred directly without the use of a trust to the spouse and children, but, in such a case, the transferor would have to decide immediately as to the percentage of ownership to go to each child. The use of a trust allows the transferor to maintain control and flexibility, while at the same time, setting up the scenario for the eventual succession of the business to the next generation.

Discretionary Trusts

A discretionary trust's main advantage is its inherent flexibility. Although the trust specifies the beneficiaries, the beneficiaries are not necessarily entitled to the trust property. Subject to applicable trust law, discretionary trust allows the trustees to direct income and capital of the trust to select beneficiaries as well as to direct the timing of distributions, as they may choose in their discretion. This also allows for effective tax planning by distributing to certain tax beneficiaries in the most tax efficient matter, from year to year.

Assuming that the trust indenture confers upon the trustees a power which they may exercise at their own discretion, the trustees may transfer the trust property to any of the beneficiaries, or any combination thereof in any proportion they see fit. If, in their discretion, they choose to transfer the shares only to a subset of the beneficiaries that would be within their power as set out in the trust indenture, subject of course to fiduciary obligations imposed on trustees under trust law.

Provisions of Family Trusts

Some of the provisions typically found in a discretionary family trust include the following:

Discretionary as to income and/or capital: The allocation and distribution of income and capital is at the discretion of the trustee as between the children (and other beneficiaries, if applicable). The discretionary clauses would typically seek to provide the trustees with the widest possible powers in respect to the allocation and distribution of capital and income.

Replacement of trustees: In many cases, one or both Parents (or perhaps a nominee or trusted person) will be given the power to dismiss trustees, so as to effectively maintain an added degree of control over the trust.

Irrevocable: The trust is irrevocable (i.e., in view of the attribution rules and subsection 75(2), which may otherwise apply).

Family law: A clause may be inserted which attempts to exclude distributions from net family property subject to division in the event of a marital breakdown.

The following are some other provisions that may be inserted in a trust:

Power of Appointment

This is the power to transfer part or all of the trust fund to another trust.

Payment to trust/corporation

This clause specifies that a payment or distribution may be made to a trust in favour of a beneficiary or a corporation owned by the beneficiary, rather than directly to the beneficiary.

Anti-nuisance clause

Provides penalties if beneficiaries commence or threaten litigation against the trust/trustees.

Subsection 75(2) — Special protection

As will be seen, subsection 75(2) of the *Income Tax Act* (Canada) (the "Act")[4] can be a fundamental complication to an estate freeze. Besides the trust being irrevocable, special provisions may be inserted to guard against the application of subsection 75(2); for example, a trustee from whom property has been received may not participate in decisions relating to its disposition.

Residence clauses

Generally, the cessation of Canadian residence of a trust gives rise to a number of tax problems. Accordingly, provisions may be inserted to ensure that the trust continues to be resident in Canada, e.g., by precluding a majority of trustees from being non-resident, or preventing the resignation of a trustee if this would be the effect. Similarly, the trust may provide that all meetings of trustees must occur within Canada.

Anti-corporate attribution clause

The corporate attribution rules may not apply to a trust that has a clause which is in accordance with subsection 74.4(4). For further discussion of the corporate attribution rules, and this clause, refer to Chapter 4.

---

[4] R.S.C. 1985 (5th Supp.) c.1 as amended. Unless otherwise indicated, all statutory references herein are to the Act.

Beneficiaries

The starting point of a discretionary trust is that the beneficiaries are "issue" (basically lineal descendants). If they are the issue of the freezor and spouse, then children of a different marriage will not be beneficiaries. Beneficiaries may (or may not) specifically include adopted children or children who become adopted by others. As will be seen, in a properly designed "bail-out freeze" (a.k.a. "gel") a beneficiary may include the freezor.

The possibility of a catastrophe which leaves the trust devoid of beneficiaries should not be forgotten. For example, it might be prudent to include the spouses of issue, more remote relatives, or charities as beneficiaries.

When selecting beneficiaries, income tax issues should not be forgotten. For example, according to paragraph 55(5)(e), a person who is related to every beneficiary of a trust (other than a registered charity) who is or may (otherwise than by reason of the death of another beneficiary of the trust) be entitled to share in the income or capital of the trust is deemed to be related to the trust. Meeting this requirement may later permit a spinout reorganization (other than a true "proportional butterfly"), where the trust is a shareholder of the corporation to be reorganized.

Protection against trustees

A trustee may be deemed to have resigned if he or she becomes mentally incapacitated, bankrupt, or ceases to be resident.

Protection to trustees

It is customary to insert an indemnity to the trustees. This has become even more important because of the possibility of joint and several personal liability for a trust's tax, pursuant to subsection 159(1) of the Act. It should be noted that this is not limited to distributions without clearance certificates, per subsection 159(2), but is an ongoing joint and several liability. An important example of where this could be problematic is if the 21st anniversary of a trust is missed, and there are adverse tax consequences by virtue of a deemed disposition of trust property, e.g., growth shares. While the property itself is available to satisfy the liability, it is possible that there could be complications in respect of liquidating the property, e.g., in a freeze situation, corporate and trust-law barriers to liquidation could be asserted. If so, theoretically at least, the CRA could turn to the trustees rather than pursuing the trust assets themselves.

An issue is whether the indemnity should be limited. While it is likely that an indemnity should not extend to fraudulent actions, should it exclude ordinary negligence or gross negligence? Also, should an indemnity be limited to trust assets, or should Parents give an additional indemnity?

Illegitimate children

A trust may provide that an illegitimate child is deemed not to be a beneficiary of the trust.

Majority decision rule

A trust may provide that decisions can be made by a majority of trustees. In Ontario at least, the absence of this clause means that decisions must be unanimous.

Other

Compensation, trustee powers and so on may also be contentious, depending on the circumstances. Although this is more common in respect of "offshore trusts", some trusts contain so-called "flee clauses" — which give the trust the ability to change jurisdictions. Finally, the provisions pertaining to investments should be considered, particularly where statutorily required to diversify.

Letter of Wishes

If the intentions of the Settlor are not expressed in the trust document itself, it is usually a good idea to prepare a "letter of wishes" for guidance of the trustees. In most case, the letter of wishes is a non-binding document; however, the trustees should not lightly disregard it. The letter of wishes can also protect the trustees against actions by the beneficiaries, especially if an "asymmetrical" distribution is to be made.

 In Doc. No. 2000-0023997, November 3, 2000, the CRA suggested that a letter of wishes, particularly if prepared contemporaneously with the trust, might be considered to form part of the terms of the trust, in the situation in question, resulting in the application of subsection 75(2). The CRA indicated that, based on the letter of wishes, it appeared that the trust company in question was acting as agent for the Settlor; even of a valid trust existed, the inclusion of a letter of wishes as part of the terms of the trust would result in the application of subsection 75(2). The position was expressed in respect of a non-resident trust set up by a Canadian immigrant.

Settlor

The settlement of a trust is the contribution of property to a trust to formally establish it. This is usually done with a nominal initial contribution, e.g., a gold coin. (There are "three certainties" required to establish a trust: certainty of property, certainty of intention (i.e., to create a trust), and certainty of objects (i.e., beneficiaries). For tax purposes, the availability of the preferred beneficiary election was dependent on the relationship between the settlor and the particular beneficiary, but with the preferred beneficiary election no longer available (except in the case of incapacity), this relationship is no longer critical.

The significance of a settlor is now by virtue of the fact that he or she has transferred property to the trust. Accordingly, the significance of the identity of the settlor as a transferor of property is determined by reference to the attribution rules, including the reversionary trust rules in subsection 75(2).[5] It is usually important that the identity of the settlor should not result in tripping off these rules.

Besides resulting in the attribution of income and capital gains, a "rollout" of trust property may be denied pursuant to subsection 107(4.1) where at any time subsection 75(2) has applied to a trust. Given that there is normally a deemed disposition of trust property on the 21st anniversary of the trust, this could obviously be a significant problem, since it is usually advisable to roll out the property to beneficiaries prior to this time.

Very basically, subsection 75(2) may apply in circumstances where the property may revert to the transferor; the transferor may determine who gets the property; or, the transferor has a "veto" over the disposition of the property.

Although subsection 75(2) is often said to apply to the settlor of the trust, it potentially applies to anyone who transfers property to the trust.

These problems are discussed in much greater detail in Chapter 4.

Trustees

Trustees are subject to a fiduciary duty to the beneficiaries, a duty of utmost good faith. Obviously, the ability to carry out this duty is the most important factor in the choice of a trustee. For tax purposes, the reversionary trust rules in subsection 75(2) may also be significant in respect of the choice of trustees. It is important that the trustee not contribute property to the trust, or in any event, he or she should not be in a position to get the property back or determine the disposition of property transferred to the trust (which could also be as a result of a negative veto).[6]

The choice of trustees involves some thought to various issues.

In order to plan around any potential subsection 75(2) or 107(4.1) problems, it may be advisable to appoint three trustees. (See discussion of subsections 75(2) and 107(4.1) in Chapter 4.) Potential candidates often considered include family members, close friends, close business associates or professional advisors. However, when setting up a discretionary family trust, the trustees will typically include the father, mother (or other immediate family member) and a third person who is a close friend of the family, and who would be capable of exercising the discretion afforded to him or her objectively. Thought should also be given to the potential situation of both

---

[5] Where an individual has settled more than one trust, another consideration (at least theoretically) is the possible application of subsection 104(2). Under this provision the Minister can treat a number of trusts as a single trust where:

    (a) substantially all of the property of the various trusts has been received from one person, and

    (b) the various trusts are conditioned so that the income thereof accrues or will ultimately accrue to the same beneficiary, or group or class of beneficiaries.

While an *inter vivos* trust is taxed at top marginal rates, the application of this provision could have unintended consequences.

[6] See Chapter 4 for a discussion of recent administrative developments in respect of the application of subsection 75(2).

parents dying prior to the distribution of the trust property. Accordingly, planning for potential replacement trustees would be recommended.

It is also possible to appoint certain beneficiaries of the trust as trustees. However, this may lead to potential problems down the road (i.e., when trust property is to be distributed) between such a beneficiary/trustee and the other beneficiaries of the trust, such as conflicts of interest issues and fiduciary duties owing to the beneficiaries by the trustees.

Due to the fact that trusts will most likely stay in place at least until their 21st anniversary, due regard should also be given to the age of the trustees to be chosen. As it is quite likely that the trust property will remain in the trust until the 21st anniversary, an elderly trustee may not be the appropriate choice.

In the event that there is a vacancy among the trustees, the trust should provide for a mechanism by which new trustees are to be appointed. (Otherwise, the appointment is governed by applicable trustee legislation. See, for example, sections 3–8 of the *Trustee Act* (Ontario), R.S.O. 1990, chapter T.23.) Conversely, this mechanism should also provide for the removal of a trustee should it be appropriate. The appointment of a protector of the trust (also referred to as "Person Entitled to Appoint Trustees") could provide a mechanism whereby the protector would be given the discretion to demand the resignation of a trustee, and appoint a replacement trustee. As noted above, the protector would usually be the parent who is implementing the estate freeze, thereby giving him or her a greater degree of control over the trust.

A trust can, however, provide for a deemed removal of a trustee in certain circumstances, without the protector having to ask for a resignation. These circumstances would normally include the following:

- where a trustee refuses or becomes unable to act or to continue to act or becomes mentally incapable of managing his affairs. For the purposes of this deeming provision, the trust may provide, for example, that a trustee must be found to be mentally incapable by two separate medical doctors licensed to practice in Canada;

- a trustee is declared bankrupt; or

- a trustee ceases to be a resident of Canada, thereby resulting in an equal number of or a majority probably of trustees not being resident in Canada. This provision would prevent against the trust from becoming a non-Canadian trust, as a residency of a trust is determined largely by the residency of a majority of its trustees. (See *Thibodeau Family Trust v. The Queen*, 78 DTC 6376 (F.C.T.D.), and IT-447, *Residence of a trust or estate*.)

Powers of the Trustees

The trust will usually provide certain powers available to the trustees, such as powers to invest, to borrow or to lend. However, where a trust is silent on an issue, a trustee's powers will be governed by the applicable provincial statute.

The provisions of the *Trustee Act* (Ontario) include certain clauses outlining specific powers of trustees, such as the power to invest trust funds, the ability to deal with certain types of assets which may be the subject of trust property, and others.

A trust instrument may contain certain specific clauses that confirm, alter, add to or attempt to effectively supersede the statutory provisions noted above. Where the document creating the trust contains such specific provisions, they will generally take priority over the clauses included in the legislation, if any.

The statutory powers are fairly limited in scope, not contemplating the variety of situations with which a trustee may be faced in the administration of a trust and often not contemplating the potential variety of asset types which may be represented in the particular assets which form the trust property. It is for these reasons that expanded powers, far beyond those contained in the statute, will often be, and ought to be included in the documentation creating the trust.

A number of individual trustee powers may already be provided for in the list of statutory powers included in the *Trustee Act* but nevertheless should also be included in the trust for greater certainty and particularity. The following are some examples of certain powers relating to trustees to be included in a trust agreement (this list is not an exhaustive list):

1. Power to Invest: Certain Canadian jurisdictions (New Brunswick, Nova Scotia, Manitoba, Prince Edward Island, Yukon, N.W.T., Ontario, and Newfoundland) have adopted the prudent investor rule pursuant to which a trustee may make any investment that a prudent investor would make; in so doing, the trustee must "exercise the judgment and care that a person of prudence, discretion and intelligence would exercise as a trustee of the property of others". In Ontario, rather than merely allow a trustee to make any investment that a hypothetical prudent investor would make, the Ontario legislation sets out specific criteria that a trustee must consider in making an investment. The criteria that must be considered are as set out in subsection 27(5), which provides as follows:

> A trustee must consider the following criteria in planning the investment of trust property, in addition to any others that are relevant to the circumstances:
>
> - General economic conditions.
> - The possible effect of inflation or deflation.
> - The expected tax consequences of investment decisions or strategies.
> - The role that each investment or course of action plays with the overall trust portfolio.
> - The expected total return from income and the appreciation of capital.
> - Needs for liquidity, regularity of income and preservation or appreciation of capital.
> - An asset's special relationship or special value, if any, to the purposes of the trust or to one or more of the beneficiaries.

As to the question of diversification, subsection 27(6) provides that a trustee must diversify the investment to an extent that is appropriate (subject to anti-diversifications clauses if effective). It is interesting to note that subsection 27(8) provides that it is not a breach of trust for a trustee to rely on advice obtained if a prudent investor would rely on the advice under comparable circumstances. It is, therefore, advisable that a trustee should seriously consider obtaining advice in relation to the investment of trust property. The choosing of an advisor and the advice received should be documented as a further support of the prudent investment decision-making process.

2. Power to Pay Debts, Taxes: A clause is usually inserted that provides for the payment of debts and taxes, often specifying the order in which certain assets of the estate should be charged.

3. Power to Retain or Convert and to Distribute In Specie: At common law, trustees were prohibited from disposing of certain assets and, yet, were under an obligation not to postpone the conversion of other types of assets. These common-law principles are usually ousted by the inclusion of a provision in the trust which permits the trustees to either retain the assets in the form in which they exist or to convert them into a liquid form, all at the discretion of the trustees.

4. Power of Sale: This clause provides the trustees with broad powers to deal specifically with any real estate comprising part of the trust property.

5. Power to Borrow

6. Power to Lend

7. Power to Incorporate

For a discussion of fiduciary duties of trustees, see Chapters 5 and 7.

Alterations and Variations on the Basic Configuration

There are various alterations that can be made to the basic freeze/income splitting mechanism, in order to achieve particular objectives. For example, it may often be desirable to effect a partial freeze whereby the Parents receive some residual equity participation, e.g., by receiving some equity (growth) shares. Also, despite certain technical issues, it has become common for a Parent to be included as a beneficiary of a discretionary trust. This adds bail-out capabilities — which is to say, the shares could be distributed to a Parent thereby unwinding the freeze. This is referred to in the vernacular as a "gel". In addition, the Children's shares could be made redeemable by the company at fair market value, so that the transaction could be unwound in the event of altercations. Notwithstanding the *Mann Estate* case[7], many prudent practitioners insert a clause that the freeze shares taken back by the Parents would lose the voting rights immediately before the death of the Parents.

In many cases, a freeze may involve the use of a holding company. Accordingly, the above configuration would be with respect to the shares of the holding company, which would in turn hold the shares of the operating company. One key advantage of a holding company is that the operating company could distribute dividends to it to limit the operating company's exposure to creditors. The dividends could then be lent again to the operating company on a secured basis.

For further discussion, see Chapters 3 and 5.

---

[7] *Supra.*

Partnership Freezes

Another possible estate planning structure involves the use of a partnership. "Freeze units" could be designed to have attributes similar to freeze shares, with growth units held by Children/family trust. There could be material advantages to such a structure, especially where the assets to be frozen are held personally rather than by a corporation, notably, the avoidance of land transfer and capital taxes. However, perhaps because the CRA has provided little in the way of assurance in respect of subsections 103(1) and (1.1) (which deal with the reallocation of partnership income), partnerships have not become mainstream freeze vehicles.

For example, pursuant to a question at the 2004 STEP Conference CRA Round Table, the CRA indicated that it had never issued a favourable ruling on a partnership freeze. The CRA reiterated its response to Q.13 of the 1992 Revenue Canada Round Table: the allocation of income within a partnership should recognize the capital contributions of the partners, as well as the non-monetary contribution of each partner; otherwise subsections 103(1) or (1.1) of the Act may apply to alter the allocation. The CRA concluded by stating that, in order to provide any definitive comments on a particular arrangement, and in particular, whether subsections 103(1) or (1.1) would apply, it would need to review all of the facts and documentation related to the transactions. Such a review would normally only be undertaken in the context of an advanced ruling request, with respect to which, the CRA indicated earlier in the question, it had never actually issued a favourable ruling on a partnership freeze — so the prospects of such a process would not appear to be fruitful.

Having said this, freeze-type structures are starting to become more commonplace, at least in certain areas of tax planning (e.g., capital tax structures). In addition, partnership freeze structures have been put in place whereby, to avoid the section 103 issue, all of the income would accrue to the freeze units, so that the growth would be attributable to appreciation of the frozen assets.

When Should a Freeze be Implemented?

Before proceeding to implement a freeze, a practitioner should review the pros and cons with his or her client. Do not presume that a freeze will always be advantageous.

Traditionally, several non-tax factors have been put forward in this respect. First, it is important to ensure that the effects of inflation do not leave Parents without sufficient assets to meet their personal needs.

Also consider whether the capital gains exemption would be available to shelter tax exposure when shares eventually pass from Parents to Children. Attention must be paid to matters such as the asset composition and thereby the eligibility for the exemption. (For further discussion of the capital gains exemption and related strategies, see page 121.)

In addition to the shares themselves qualifying for the exemption, note that recourse to the exemption could be restricted if an individual has a Cumulative Net Investment Loss ("CNIL") account. Capital gains will be non-exempt except to the extent that the taxable amount of the qualifying capital gain exceeds the amount of the CNIL account. Furthermore, a taxpayer's allowable business investment losses for the year or a previous year (after 1984) will reduce the extent to which capital gains for the year may qualify for the exemption. Conversely, previous years' capital gains exemption claims will reduce the ability to claim allowable business investment losses.

The psychological (not to mention legal) effects of income splitting as well as estate freezing should be considered carefully, as the outcome may be to place substantial assets in the hands of Children. These effects should be considered carefully, both from the point of view of the Parents and Children. (There may be a significant element of control available through the use of a family trust; however, it is normally advisable to distribute the growth shares before the 21st anniversary of the trust. After this, it might be possible to obtain a significant degree of protection if a shareholders' agreement can be implemented.)

Family law and creditor protection considerations should be addressed.

If the assets to be frozen are likely to be sold after the death of the Parents, there may not be too much point in an estate freeze, since the Children will have to pay tax on the sale of the assets in any event.

In other words, a freeze is for a long-term hold only. For example, a freeze should not be necessary if there is a mandatory sale of shares on death resultant from a buy-sell. In such cases, consideration should be given to the effective utilization of corporate-owned life insurance to reduce death tax exposure. Often, assets which are looked on by Parents as long-term holds may not in fact be such once the Parents pass away. A vacation property might not be perceived to be as desirable to the Children/Grandchildren as it was to the Parents (or may be undesirable due to psychological factors after the Parents pass away). Children may have a very different view of marketable securities which were perceived by parents to be long-term family assets.

In recent years, a more fundamental issue has arisen in terms of preservation of family wealth: The presumption — valid in previous generations — that Children will be motivated to carry on a family business or otherwise continue to hold assets may no longer be well-founded. In many milieus, the work ethic taken for granted by previous generations may be eroded by decades of affluence, resulting in a very different mindset of Children. Far from wishing to take over the family business, or pursue a lucrative, but demanding career, Children's financial prospects may be based on the affluence of their Parents. Real estate and other assets that were treasured by Parents may be used to finance the lifestyle of a succeeding generation. A family business — with all its pressures and responsibilities — may be put up for sale once the Parents are out of the picture. It may not be the happy situation parents envisioned for their kids years ago — but it's a growing fact of life.[8]

In the new millennium, for some, the assumption of a continual build-up of family wealth may no longer be valid. If not, an estate freeze takes on a new rationale

---

[8] One fairly recent trend, at least in North America, is the "family office" in which service providers offer affluent families a full range of services — everything from financial planning to paying personal bills, so that family members are free to pursue a carefree lifestyle.

— if the prospects of succeeding generations are tied to that of the Parents, the drain on wealth resulting from death tax can be all the more crippling. An estate freeze can preserve the asset base, pending a more gradual liquidation as assets are sold off to finance lifestyles. In addition, if the financial prospects of Children are limited, it may even be possible to reduce the tax impact from a gradual liquidation as a result of low marginal tax rates.

The following are some other considerations as to whether or not a freeze should be implemented:

Very generally, to the extent that future growth of a corporation would generate refundable tax (or capital dividend) balances, e.g., where investment-type assets are involved, it may not be necessary to undertake a freeze. Although it is true that the shares of the corporation would continue to grow in value and thus increase the tax exposure from a deemed disposition at death, it may be possible to undertake post-mortem procedures to mitigate this result. If, for example, all of a corporation's growth generates refundable tax balances, it should be possible to liquidate the corporation within the first year of death. This should result in a capital loss (due to the high cost base resulting from the deemed disposition on death) which can be applied to the terminal-period capital gain pursuant to subsection 164(6) of the Act. There should also be a corresponding dividend (deemed or actual) to the estate, but this could be largely "tax paid" by the dividend refunds to the corporation. Note, however, that there are a number of issues in respect of post-mortem reorganizations, especially when a complete liquidation of the corporation is not desirable.

Having said this, build-ups of refundable tax and capital dividend balances in a frozen corporate system will be available to redeem freeze shares on a tax-effective basis, including when the build-up occurs after the freeze. Thus, in a standard corporate freeze (e.g., of a business or real estate) it is desirable to inject assets which facilitate the build-up of investment profits and therefore future refundable tax balances. While, in a sense, such refundable tax balances "should belong" to the holders of the growth shares, dividend refunds will, of course be generated as freeze shares are redeemed, by and large tax-paying such redemptions (either prior to death or through post-mortem redemptions) that would otherwise be exposed to capital gains tax on death. Of course, one subset of this effect occurs with corporate-owned life insurance which generates capital dividend accounts which can reduce taxes through post-mortem redemptions, subject to certain stop-loss rules which could have the effect of limiting the tax reduction by up to (about) $1/3$ of the terminal period tax exposure, depending on the province. In addition, if the business has been successful, it will tend to generate cash which, if not needed in the business, would presumably be used for investment purposes, thus increasing refundable tax and (possibly) capital dividend accounts. In fact, recent (and proposed) reductions in corporate tax rates tend to encourage such corporate investment, and therefore accelerate the build-up of these accounts.

Some practitioners mistakenly believe that if the underlying assets held by a corporation decline in value after a freeze, the freeze value will, nevertheless, hold. Although the freeze shares would normally be retractable by the holder based on fair market value at the time of the freeze, if there are insufficient assets to fund the retraction, then the shares would be worth less than the retraction amount. Having said this, the executors could find themselves in an uphill battle to refute the ostensible value of the freeze shares. One alternative is to refreeze at a lower value — i.e., whereby the freeze shares would be changed into similar freeze shares, but redeemable/retractable at a lower amount. At one point, the CRA took the position that such reorganizations raised "benefit" issues; however, this is no longer the CRA's position.

Income Splitting

In the corporate context, the primary advantage of income-splitting is the ability to divert dividends to low-bracket shareholders. Practitioners should ascertain the tax and financial advantages of such distributions, and whether there are alternatives available to achieve this effect. For example, it may be possible to pay low-bracket family members a salary if the amount is not unreasonably large in relation to the business-related services performed.

However, if funds are not required for personal and living expenses, the advantages of paying dividends to low-bracket family members may be limited. For example, for a corporation which earns active business income well in excess of $300,000 per year, the normal salary and bonus mechanism (that is, down to the $300,000 small business limit) may enable sufficient funds to be distributed for personal and living expenses. If so, the primary advantage of distributing dividends to low-bracket family members may be the ability to reduce the corporation's net assets and thus keep the value of the corporation at a relatively low amount, but the ultimate tax benefits of this objective will be deferred. However, increasing disparities between top personal and corporate rates have caused owner-managers and their advisors to reconsider the advisability of bonusing down to the small business limit (in Ontario, the disparity is greater than 10% counting EHT). This, of course, restores the desirability of income splitting by means of dividends.

☞ **On November 23ʳᵈ 2005, the Liberal government proposed reductions to the effective tax rate for eligible dividends paid after 2005. Besides those paid by public corporations, eligible dividends will generally include dividends paid after 2005 by Canadian-controlled private corporations, to the extent that their income (other than investment income) is subject to tax at the general corporate income tax rate (currently 36.12% in Ontario). Also eligible are non-CCPCs that are resident in Canada and subject to the general corporate income tax rate. Assuming, first, that the proposals (as well as reductions in corporate tax rates which are also proposed by the Liberal government) are ultimately implemented and second, that similar provincial changes are enacted, this would largely eliminate underintegration and thus encourage the retention of business earnings at the corporate level.**

The advantages of income splitting in respect of an estate freeze were greatly restricted by the introduction of the so-called "kiddie tax" (applicable as of 2000).[9] While the advantages of "dividend splitting" with minor children are restricted, such restrictions do not apply to adult children. As mentioned earlier, the possibility of limited financial prospects of many adult children may make this area more important.

Complications

An estate freeze can turn out to be a relatively complicated manoeuvre in some situations. Accordingly, there is always the possibility of a tax misadventure.

Where an estate freeze involves the transfer of assets to a corporation (or a partnership, for that matter), it should be noted that there could be potential for double taxation, especially on death. Since the corporation is a separate taxpayer, the deemed or actual disposition of the shares of the corporation and the underlying assets that give the shares their value may result in tax complications because of the potential for double taxation in this instance — i.e., once on the actual or deemed disposition of shares, and a second time when the underlying assets themselves are sold.

Mechanisms are available to avoid the double taxation resulting from the deemed disposition on the death of a shareholder. However, in many cases, such post-mortem procedures must be taken within the first year of the estate, and may turn out to be surprisingly complex. If the assets are already held by a corporation (or a partnership), although an estate freeze may change to some extent the post-mortem procedures, it might not materially complicate post-mortem tax planning of this nature (at least, relative to the tax benefits of a freeze).

The "Kiddie Tax"

The advantages of income splitting in respect of an estate freeze were greatly restricted by the introduction of the so-called "kiddie tax" (applicable starting in 2000).

Section 120.4 applies a special tax — at the highest rate — to individuals who have not turned 18 in the year. Included are taxable dividends (and other shareholder benefits) on private-corporation shares.

However, the kiddie tax does not apply to individuals 18 and over in the year, nor does it apply to spouses or parents.

The types of income taxed under this provision include:

- Taxable dividends and other shareholder benefits on unlisted shares of Canadian and foreign companies (including those received through a trust or partnership). This, of course, is intended to eliminate dividend splitting for private corporations.

---

[9] Applicable to individuals who have not reached the age of 18 in the year. Another significant barrier to dividend splitting is the so-called "corporate attribution rules" which cease to apply at the age of 18. See Chapter 4 for a detailed discussion of the corporate attribution rules.

- Income from a partnership or trust which is derived from providing property or services to a business carried on by a relative of the child or in which the relative participates, e.g., as a major shareholder. This is designed to clampdown on so-called management partnership/trust arrangements — e.g., where a minor receives income from a partnership or trust which renders services to a firm in which the minor's relative is a member

Dividends from Canadian companies continue to be eligible for gross-up and credit. However, the income subject to the kiddie tax is not reduced by personal exemptions or graduated tax rates.

Of course, section 120.4 has no effect on the taxation of the corporation itself; for example, the ability to obtain the small business deduction will be unaffected. Accordingly, in an estate freeze structure, it may be advantageous to pay out retained earnings as dividends once the children are no longer minors. If the growth shares are held by a discretionary trust, it should be possible (subject to any issues regarding fiduciary duty) to stream dividends to adult children to the exclusion of minors.

Also, section 120.4 does not affect the ability to multiply the capital gains exemption on the sale of shares of a private corporation.

Although section 120.4 will detract from the advantages of an estate freeze, the loss of the ability to income split with minors may not be a critical issue in the decision to effect a freeze. If a business is successful, necessary funds could be obtained by "dividend sprinkling" to low-bracket family members not subject to the kiddie tax, if possible (e.g., adult children in university). Of course, another alternative is to bonus down to the small business limit. However, this will typically result in an increase in tax, since top personal rates exceed corporate rates; in other words, the element of tax deferral that is available by retaining earnings at the corporate level will be lost.

Tax and Other Statutory Considerations

There are no provisions of the *Income Tax Act* which specifically address the implementation of an estate freeze. However, it should also be noted that a number of provisions (particularly sections 85 and 86) are commonly used in implementing a freeze. In addition, there are quite a number of other provisions dealing with various technical aspects of estate freezes.

While there are no definite legal steps that must be taken (i.e., prescribed under the Act) in conjunction with a freeze, the CRA has delineated a number of policies on certain aspects of estate freezes, notably in respect of attributes of freeze shares which would avoid benefit provisions. A number of Revenue Canada/CRA Round Table Questions which delineate policies in these and other areas are reproduced in Appendix B.

The appropriate provisions of the Act to be considered, and the corresponding legal steps to be taken, will depend on the nature of the assets being frozen, and how the freeze is to be carried out. The following are some provisions of the Act that may need to be considered when implementing an estate freeze:

Issues	Applicable Provisions of *Income Tax Act*
Capital or income gains or losses, where the freeze involves the transfer of property	section 69, "superficial loss rules" (paragraph 40(2)(g), section 54)
Income attribution rules, where the freezor has a continuing interest in the property or where the freezor's spouse or a minor has or may acquire a direct or indirect interest in the property or a substituted property	sections 74.1 to 74.5; subsection 56(4.1)
"Kiddie Tax"	section 120.4
General Anti-Avoidance Rule	section 245
Transfer of property to a corporation, if a corporation is to be used as an estate freezing vehicle	section 85, 84.1
Corporate reorganization provisions, where an existing corporation is involved in the freeze	sections 86, 87, 51
Taxation of trusts and trust distributions, where property is transferred or held by a trust as part of the freeze	subdivision k
Taxation of an individual in the year of death and taxation of an estate	sections 70–72
Conferral of benefit	subsections 15(1), 15(1.1), 51(2), 56(2), 86(2), 246(2); paragraph 85(1)(e.2)
Capital Gains exemption — i.e., lifetime ($500,000) exemption	section 110.6
Association Rules — where freezes involve the formation of a second corporation	section 256
Taxation of the income of a corporation and corporate distributions, where a corporation is involved, including Taxable Preferred Share Rules	section 82–84, 125, 129, Parts VI.1/IV.1, etc.
Other Technical/Statutory Considerations	
Family Law	N/A
Capital Tax	Part I.3; applicable provincial legislation
Fraudulent Preferences/Conveyances/Bankruptcy	N/A
Accounting Considerations	N/A
Land Transfer Tax	N/A

Where the property to be frozen is located in a foreign jurisdiction, or where the freezor or a beneficiary is not a Canadian resident or is a citizen of another country, the legal and tax consequences of the foreign jurisdictions will also need to be considered. These are largely beyond the scope of this book; however, some U.S. considerations are discussed in Appendix C.

Simple Estate Freezes — Some Examples

As stated above, apart from the usual corporate configuration, it is possible to effect an estate freeze in a more simplistic manner. However, these types of freezes may be suboptimal because they trigger one of the following rules:

- deemed disposition at fair market value — paragraph 69(1)(*b*);

- personal attribution rules — section 74.1 *et seq.*

The following are examples of various types of such transactions which may involve the avoidance of capital gains tax at death by the transfer of future value to a subsequent generation. As will be seen, simple freezes may or may not involve the retention of current value.

Gift of Cash

Parent gives a sum of money to Child, which is to be used for reinvestment purposes.

Issue	Effect
Deemed disposition	Irrelevant — no tax exposure
Applicability of attribution rules to capital gains	No
Attribution of income	Depends on age of Child (i.e., whether Child has turned 18 in the particular year)

Loan of Cash

Parent lends a sum of money to Child, which is to be used for reinvestment purposes.

Issue	Effect
Deemed disposition	Irrelevant — no tax exposure
Applicability of attribution rules to capital gains	No
Attribution of income	If Child has not turned 18, interest should be charged at prescribed rate; if Child is 18 or over in the year, a main purpose cannot be income splitting unless prescribed interest charged[10]

Gift in Kind

Parent gives a specific investment asset to Child.

Issue	Effect
Deemed disposition	Yes
Applicability of attribution rules to capital gains	No
Attribution of income	Depends on age of child (i.e., whether Child has turned 18 in the particular year)

Sale for Consideration

Parent sells a specific investment asset to Child.

Issue	Effect
Deemed disposition	Yes
Applicability of attribution rules to capital gains	No
Attribution of income	If child has not turned 18 in year, full value must be paid

---

[10] Or a reasonable rate, if less; see subsection 56(4.1) *et seq.*

In addition, section 69 may apply to reduce the tax cost of the transferred asset unless full value is paid.

One candidate for a gift-in-kind or sale-for-consideration freeze is a second home. With the principal residence exemption available to only one home at a time per family, growth in value of a second home can be exposed to capital gains tax when it passes between generations. Accordingly, if ownership of the home is transferred to children/grandchildren (or a family trust in their favour), this death tax exposure can be escaped. This strategy can apply if an individual is about to purchase a second home or to transfer an existing home. But in the latter case, if the home has already appreciated in value, there is a potential capital gains exposure when the transfer is effected. It is possible to shelter this by using the principal residence exemption claim, but because this exemption is, in essence, restricted to one home at a time, this may eventually leave the first home exposed to capital gains tax.

Chart YY shows the interaction between the attribution and deemed disposition rules for these and other common types of transfers of investment assets. Of course, the first columns are not relevant if cash or other assets that do not have a "deferred tax exposure" are transferred:

Chart YY
Summary of Deemed Disposition/Attribution Rules

Transferee	Capital gain triggered?	Terminal loss triggered?	Capital loss triggered?	Income taxed to transferee?	Capital gain taxed to transferee?
Child, grandchild under 18	Yes	Yes	Yes[3]	No[5]	Yes
Child, grandchild 18 or over in year; parent	Yes	Yes	Yes[3]	Yes[1]	Yes
Spouse	Optional	Yes	No[3]	No[5]	No[5]
RRSP	Yes	n/a	No	Yes[4]	Yes[4]
Controlled corporation	Yes[2]	Yes	No[3]	Yes	Yes

Notes:

1. Income from low-interest loans made by family member may be taxable to the lender if one of the main purposes of the manoeuvre is to reduce tax — see subsection 56(4.1).

2. Unless Section 85 procedure is followed. If shares of a "connected" corporation are transferred, a "deemed dividend" may be triggered — see section 84.1.

3. Similar rules apply to property held as an "adventure in the nature of trade", etc. See subsections 18(14) and (15).

4. Tax is deferred until assets are distributed from the RRSP.

5. Unless property is transferred for "full-value consideration" and certain other prerequisites are met — see subsection 74.5(1).

Intergenerational Transfers: Some Common Technical Issues

The following is an overview of some income tax and other provisions as they apply to intergenerational transfers in general.

Deemed Dispositions

Paragraph 69(1) deals with a situation where a taxpayer disposes of property by way of sale to a person with whom he is not dealing at arm's length at an amount which is less than the fair market value, or by way of a gift *inter vivos* to any person. It provides that in these circumstances, for the purpose of determining the taxpayer's income, the fair market value shall be deemed to have been received as proceeds of disposition.

Exceptions to deemed disposition rule

The following are exceptions to the deemed disposition rule:

Specific rollovers: Section 69 can be overridden by various rollover provisions. Rollovers that are commonly used in estate freezes involve sections 85 and 86, and to a lesser extent, sections 87 and 51.

Spousal rollovers: The deemed disposition rules do not apply if an asset is transferred to a spouse (see subsection 73(1)). In this case, there will be no capital gain and the transferee spouse will inherit the original tax cost of the property (i.e., on a rollover basis). It is possible to opt out of these rules and purposely trigger a capital gain (or other tax exposure).

Affiliated persons — stop-loss rules: If property in a loss position is transferred to an "affiliated person", capital losses will generally be disallowed under several sets of stop-loss rules. For example, the superficial loss rules may apply to transfers by individuals (see paragraph 40(2)(g) and section 54). If so, the would-be tax loss will generally be added back to the transferee's tax cost of the transferred asset. In the case of a transfer by a corporation, subsection 40(3.4) may apply. If so, the would-be loss will remain with the transferor, but would not be triggered until certain events occur, notably the sale of the loss item to a non-affiliated transferee.[11]

Income Attribution

The various income attribution rules are of concern when an estate freeze is carried out, as the nature of a freeze involves the transfer of property to someone else who often will use the property to create income. Where the attribution rules apply, the transferor of the property, rather than the recipient of the income, may be

---

[11] "Affiliated persons" is defined in section 251.1 to include, for example, a spouse or controlled corporation, but not a child.

the person who is required to report the income for tax purposes. The following is a brief description of a number of attribution rules.

Property that can Revert to the Transferor

Where an individual transfers property to a trust, but continues to control the property as if it were his or her own, the income from the property may be attributed to the transferor. More specifically, subsection 75(2) imposes attribution of income and capital gains where property is transferred to a trust and the property (or substituted property) is held on condition that it:

- may revert to the person from whom the property was (directly or indirectly) received (subparagraph 75(2)(a)(i));

- may pass to a person determined by the transferor after the creation of the trust (subparagraph 75(2)(a)(ii)); or

- may not be disposed of during the transferor's existence without the consent or in accordance with the transferor's direction (paragraph 75(2)(b)) — i.e., the transferor has a veto power over the transferred property.

Where any of these conditions exist, the income from the property is included in the transferor's income. For example, the Parent settles a trust with cash. One of the beneficiaries of the trust is the Child whom the Parent wants to receive the income. The Parent is the trustee and has complete control over the trust funds, including the right to transfer the funds back to him- or herself and the right to allocate the income or distribute the capital to beneficiaries he or she chooses. The result is that subsection 75(2) would apply, and the income from the property transferred to the trust, or from substituted property, would be included in the Parent's taxable income.

The application of subsection 75(2) is a consideration in estate freezes where trusts are used to hold property. The onerous consequences of the provision can be avoided, however, with careful planning. The trust should be irrevocable. Where the trust is discretionary — i.e., the trustee(s) can decide who will receive the income or capital from the trust — many practitioners ensure that the settlor of the trust (or other person who transfers property to the trust) is not a trustee.

Attribution Rules — General Application

In addition to the situations discussed above, attribution of income can result where property is loaned or transferred to a spouse or to a minor who is not at arm's length with the transferor. The rules in question are found in sections 74.1 to 75. The income attribution rules can also apply where property is transferred directly or indirectly to an individual and encompasses transfers of property to a trust or to a corporation. Since estate freezes often involve the transfer of property to corporations, these rules will generally be of concern.

Where the rules apply, income from the transferred property and substituted property is generally attributable to the transferor. In the case of a transfer of property to, or for the benefit of, a spouse, capital gains are also attributable. Capital gains realized by a minor are not attributable and income from a business is not attributable from a spouse or from a minor.

Example ──

Mr. X lends Mrs. X $1,000. The loan is invested in a term deposit for one year and earns $90. After one year, Mrs. X purchases shares of XYZ with the $1,000 and earns dividends of $60. The shares of XYZ are sold for $1,000 and shares of ABC are acquired with the funds. No dividends are earned on the ABC shares; however, they are sold for $1,500. The income attributed to Mr. X is the $90 interest on the term deposit, the $60 dividend on the XYZ shares, and the $500 capital gain on the ABC shares.

There is an exception to the rules where there is a loan or transfer of property for value (see subsection 74.5(1)). For example, Mr. A sells shares of XYZ Corporation to Mrs. A, who pays fair market value for the shares. Mrs. A has worked and accumulated funds in her bank account that are used to pay Mr. A for the XYZ Corporation shares. Provided that Mr. A treats the transfer as a sale for fair market value and therefore pays tax on the gain (if any), the dividends Mrs. A receives on the XYZ Corporation shares are not attributed to Mr. A. If Mrs. A sells the XYZ Corporation shares and realizes a capital gain, the gain would not be attributed to Mr. A.

───

Trusts and corporations are commonly used in estate freeze transactions and the estate planner must be aware of the attribution rules when planning the freeze.

Where property is transferred to a corporation, or funds are loaned to a corporation, and "one of the main purposes of the transfer or loan is to reduce the income of the individual and to benefit ... a designated person", the individual may be deemed to have received an amount as interest under the so-called "corporate attribution rules" in section 74.4. The amount included in the lender's income is based on the prescribed rate of interest, which is adjusted quarterly. To the extent that interest or dividends are received, however, the amount included in income is reduced. A designated person is the spouse of the individual or a minor who does not deal at arm's length with the individual (e.g., is the niece or nephew of the individual).

A more detailed discussion of the attribution rules can be found in CRA Interpretation Bulletins IT-369RSR, *Attribution of trust income to settlor*; IT-510, *Transfers and loans of property made after May 22, 1985 to a related minor*; and IT-511R, *Interspousal and certain other transfers and loans of property*.

For further discussion of the personal and corporate attribution rules, with specific reference to corporate estate freezes, see Chapter 4.

Interest-free and low-interest loans, related persons, and arm's length

Subsections 56(4.1) to 56(4.3) may apply to low interest/interest free loans made to an adult child/grandchild (etc.). The provisions apply where an individual, the creditor, has made an interest-free or low-interest loan to a person, the debtor, with whom the creditor does not deal at arm's length and where "it can reasonably be considered that one of the main reasons for making the loan" was to reduce or avoid tax by causing the income from the loaned property to be included in the income of the debtor. Like most of the attribution rules, subsection 56(4.1) applies where there are indirect transactions, such as where a trust is interposed. If subsection 56(4.1) applies, the income from the loaned property, or property acquired with the loan, is included in the income of the creditor.

For example, the Parent lends $1,000,000 to an adult child who invests the money in term deposits and earns $50,000 in interest. The $50,000 of interest may be the Parent's income and not the Child's. For subsection 56(4.1) to apply, one of the main purposes of making the loan must be to reduce the Parent's income by having the amount included in the Child's income. This is a question of fact.

Other conditions must also exist for subsection 56(4.1) to apply. The loan must be to a person with whom the lender does not deal at arm's length and generally one of the other attribution provisions in the Act cannot apply. Non-arm's length persons include those related to the transferor (spouse, children, grandchildren, parents, etc.) and entities over which the transferor has control. For example, a corporation controlled by the transferor (refer to Interpretation Bulletin IT-419R2, *Meaning of arm's length for additional discussion*). Related persons are defined in subsection 251(2) of the *Income Tax Act*, and subsection 251(1) deals with persons who do not deal at arm's length. It should be noted that, under paragraph 251(1)(*b*), "it is a question of fact whether persons not related to each other were at a particular time dealing with each other at arm's length".

The following comments of the court are worth considering when faced with a determination as to whether two or more parties are dealing at arm's length:

> In my view, the basic premise on which this analysis is based is that, where the "mind" by which the bargaining is directed on behalf of one party to a contract is the same "mind" that directs the bargaining on behalf of the other party, it cannot be said that the parties are dealing at arm's length. In other words where the evidence reveals that the same person was dictating the terms of the bargain on behalf of both parties, it cannot be said that the parties were dealing at arm's length.

> *M.N.R. v. Estate of Thomas Rodman Merritt*, 69 DTC 5159 (Exch. Ct.)

> To this I would add that where several parties — whether natural persons or corporations or a combination of the two — act in concert, and in the same interest, to direct or dictate the conduct of another, in my opinion the "mind" that directs may be that of the combination as a whole acting in concert or that of any one of them in carrying out particular parts or functions of what the common object involves.

> *Swiss Bank Corporation et al. v. M.N.R.*, 71 DTC 5235 (Exch. Ct.)

General Anti-Avoidance Rule

The general anti-avoidance rule ("GAAR") is found in subsection 245(2) and may apply to determine the tax consequences or deny a tax benefit that would result, directly or indirectly, from a transaction or series of transactions. GAAR does not apply unless there is a misuse of a provision of the Act or an abuse having regard to the provisions of the Act read as a whole.

When GAAR was introduced, the 1987 White Paper on tax reform indicated that "estate freezes would not ordinarily result in misuse or abuse given the scheme of the Act". The CRA's comments on estate-freeze transactions in paragraph 10 of Information Circular 88-2 dealing with the general anti-avoidance rule confirms this:

10. Estate Freezes

Facts

Under a typical estate freeze arrangement a parent transfers to a newly-formed corporation all of the shares of an operating company and elects under subsection 85(1) in order to defer recognition of the gain on the transfer. The consideration for the transfer is preferred shares retractable at the option of the parent for an amount equal to the fair market value of the shares of the operating company transferred. The preference shares carry voting control. A trust for minor children of the parent subscribes for common shares of the new company for a nominal amount.

Interpretation

The Explanatory Notes state that estate freezes would not ordinarily result in misuse or abuse given the scheme of the Act including the recently enacted subsection 74.4(4). Section 74.4 was enacted to deal with income splitting and could have application to certain estate freeze arrangements.

Subsection 74.4(2) may apply to deem an amount to be received as interest by an individual who loans or transfers property to the corporation and one of the main purposes of the loan or transfer may reasonably be considered to be to reduce the income of the individual and to benefit a designated person. A designated person is the individual's spouse or a person under 18 who does not deal with the individual at arm's length or who is the individual's niece or nephew.

Subsection 74.4(2) will not apply to "attribute" income to the individual throughout a period throughout which the corporation is a small business corporation as defined in subsection 248(1). In addition, as provided in subsection 74.4(4), the rule will not apply where the only interest which the designated person has in the corporation is a beneficial interest in the shares of the corporation which are held through a trust and the terms of the trust provide that the person may not obtain the use of any income or capital of the trust while the person is a designated person.

Subsection 245(2) will not apply to the transfer of the shares to the corporation where subsection 74.4(2) applies to deem the parent to receive an amount as interest. Similarly, subsection 245(2) would not apply where, for the reasons stated above, subsection 74.4(2) does not apply to deem the parent to receive an amount as interest.

Similar considerations would apply to other types of estate freezes involving a transfer of property by a parent to a corporation. For example, in an estate freeze carried out pursuant to section 86 of the Act, the parent would dispose of the shares of the operating company and receive preferred shares of the company having a redemption amount equal to the fair market value of the shares disposed of. The disposition of shares by the parent would constitute a transfer of property to the operating company for the purposes of subsection 74.4(2) of the Act and the application of subsection 245(2) to the transfer would be determined in the manner described above.

The application of GAAR has been the subject of numerous papers and panel discussions and a comprehensive discussion is beyond the scope of this reporter. Based on the comments in the CRA's information circular, there is a certain amount of comfort that estate freezing transactions would generally not be caught. However, if there is any doubt (due to the particular structure or fact situation), it would be prudent to request a tax ruling from the CRA on the estate freeze transactions and to include GAAR as one of the ruling issues.

Chapter 2

Asset Freezes

Overview

There are three basic types of estate freezes involving corporations:

- **freeze of assets,** wherein previously unincorporated assets are transferred to a corporation in return for freeze shares (redeemable and retractable based on the value of the pre-existing assets);

- **holding company freezes,** whereby the corporation's shares are transferred to a holding company in return for such freeze shares (these are discussed in Chapter 3); and

- **internal freezes,** whereby the shares of an existing corporation are reorganized into a freeze configuration (usually pursuant to section 86 of the *Income Tax Act*, but there are other methods as well — see Chapter 3).

From an "evolutionary standpoint", perhaps the starting point for discussion is an asset freeze, since business and investment endeavours usually start from an unincorporated state. However, more often than not, the incorporation of such endeavours will usually not involve a freeze, which comes later in the "life cycle" of a business.

However, the centre point of an asset freeze, section 85 of the Act, is relevant to all three types of freezes, so we will start here.

The transfer of assets, particularly of an ongoing business, is a complex matter. Some commentary is fairly dismissive of the many issues that can arise on such a transfer. However, if one is to implement an asset freeze — or any incorporation of an ongoing business, for that matter — these issues cannot be ignored. Even though our discussion is extensive, many areas have been deleted or dealt with only briefly. Examples include provisions pertaining to farms, a number of areas pertaining to pre-1972 property (e.g., pre- and post-pools of shares), paid-up capital deficiency and debt limit (section 84.2), and so on.

Basic Principles

Because the concept of a corporation as a separate legal entity from its shareholders extends to income tax law, the incorporation of a business, and in particular the transfer of assets to the corporation, results in a number of tax and other consequences that must be reckoned with. If the transaction involves the transfer of assets, a disposition for tax purposes will be involved, with a variety of tax consequences resulting therefrom. Taxable gains or losses could be triggered and where the transferor and transferee corporation do not deal at arm's length, section 69 of the Act may impose various tax penalties unless the transfer is made in return for consideration from the corporation equal to the fair market value of the assets transferred. In addition, the attributes of the assets for tax purposes may not "flow through" to the transferee corporation unless various specific income tax prerequisites are met.

Of course, the transfer could also result in consequences unrelated to the Act itself. For example, it may be necessary to comply with other statutes; to comply with restrictive covenants relating to the divestiture of assets; and permission to assume a liability may have to be granted by a creditor; etc.

Finally, there will be capitalization considerations to be dealt with. Should shares and/or debt be issued in return for the assets being transferred? What should the characteristics of the shares be? These considerations are discussed in detail in Chapter 6.

Section 85

Although the considerations specified above will necessitate the examination of a variety of income tax and other provisions, the incorporation of a business typically involves the utilization of section 85, particularly subsection 85(1). This subsection (and a number of closely related provisions) is designed to alleviate a number of adverse tax effects which might otherwise occur as a result of a disposition of assets to a corporation.

Subsection 85(1) itself has two main functions:

1. To allow the transferor and transferee corporation to choose ("elect") an amount as the proceeds of disposition and cost for tax purposes of most assets ("eligible property" — see page 35) which are transferred to the company. This will, of course, alleviate various untoward tax consequences that might otherwise occur pursuant to the normal rules of the Act.

2. To provide a method of allocating the cost for tax purposes of any consideration (such as shares, debt, etc.) received from the corporation as a result of the transfer.

The rules in subsection 85(1) envision the transfer of various assets in return for consideration, which can be in the form of shares issued by the transferee corporation, as well as non-share consideration (e.g., cash, debt, or the assumption of the transferor's liabilities). Although subsection 85(1) does not preclude taking back consideration in excess of the cost for tax purposes of an asset transferred to a corporation, the amount of non-share consideration received may effectively be limited, to the extent that tax deferral is desired. Also, subsection 85(2.1) may restrict the paid-up capital of the transferee corporation.

The rules of subsection 85(1) provide for certain limits within which the elected amount can be chosen. One of the most important of these stipulates that the elected amount cannot be less than the value of non-share consideration received on the transfer. In the majority of cases, the elected amount will be chosen so that the deemed proceeds of disposition are equal to the cost amount for tax purposes of the property being transferred. However, other results may occur. For example, a gain may often be purposely triggered to use up prior years' tax losses. In addition, subsections 13(21.2), 14(12), 40(3.3) to 40(3.6) and the "superficial loss rules" (section 54 and paragraph 40(2)(g)), may restrict the ability to claim a tax loss on a transfer, even though subsection 85(1) may not, itself, present a restriction.[1]

---

[1] See section on superficial loss rules on page 68 *et seq.*, for further discussion.

The mechanics of subsection 85(1) stipulate that the elected proceeds of disposition of property transferred to the corporation will also be the cost for tax purposes of the property which is transferred to the corporation, as well as (generally speaking) the cost base of the consideration received by the corporation. Because of this, any untoward tax consequences which might have been avoided by the election itself may be recognized in a subsequent disposition of the transferred property or the consideration received from the corporation.

Subsection 85(1) is a very flexible provision. The ability to take advantage of such a provision extends to any "taxpayer", including a non-resident, a trust, another corporation, or a partnership (by virtue of subsection 85(2), a complementary section), etc. The transfer must involve the receipt of shares, or at least a portion of a share; otherwise the provision will not be operative.

However, the transferee corporation must be a "taxable Canadian corporation", as defined in subsection 89(1) (the definition is partly based on subsection 89(1)). Effectively, a taxable Canadian corporation means a corporation that was resident in Canada at a particular time and was either incorporated in Canada or resident in Canada throughout the period commencing June 18, 1971 and ending at the particular time. In addition, the corporation must not be exempt from Part I tax under a statutory provision of the Act. This means, for example, that a section 85 election cannot be made where assets are rolled into a foreign incorporated corporation which carries on business in Canada.

In order to take advantage of section 85, it is necessary to file a prescribed form with the CRA. In the case of a transfer from a partnership, form T2058 must be filed; otherwise form T2057 is required. Among other things, the forms involve designating the elected amount of assets transferred. Although, technically, this must be done on an asset-by-asset basis, the CRA administratively allows certain assets to be grouped together.[2]

As mentioned above, the elected amounts potentially form the cost for tax purposes of consideration received on the transfer. However, pursuant to section 85 itself, there are restrictions on how the cost is allocated. Generally, the cost will first be allocated to debt received; then to preferred shares (as defined in the Act), and lastly to common shares.

In addition, a number of provisions within the Act may have an important bearing on the consideration received from the transferee corporation. For example, the following provisions should be considered carefully:

- Subsections 15(1) and 84(1) may result in adverse tax consequences where the value of the consideration, including any increase in paid-up capital of shares resultant from the transfer, exceeds the value of the assets transferred into the company.

- Section 84.1 could result in either an immediate deemed dividend or a reduction of paid-up capital where a non-corporate Canadian resident taxpayer transfers shares of a closely held corporation to another corporation with whom the taxpayer does not deal at arm's length (this section will be of

---

[2] See "Formal Requirements," page 42.

particular importance where the transferor or a non-arm's length person has claimed the capital gains exemption or a V-Day increment — i.e., on shares held prior to 1972).

- If a non-resident transfers shares of a Canadian corporation to another Canadian corporation with which the non-resident does not deal at arm's length, the transferor could be deemed to have received a dividend pursuant to section 212.1 where the non-share consideration exceeds the paid-up capital of the transferred corporation.

- Where there is more than one shareholder of the corporation, and the fair market value of the assets transferred exceeds the value of all consideration received, there could be a number of untoward consequences as a result of paragraph 85(1)(*e*.2), where the excess may reasonably be regarded as a benefit desired to be conferred on a person related to the transferor.

- Subsection 85(2.1) restricts the paid-up capital for tax purposes of shares taken back on a section 85 transfer, essentially to the cost base of the property transferred to the corporation, less any non-share consideration received by the transferor.

These provisions will be discussed later.

Eligible Property

The section 85 rollover applies on an asset-by-asset basis. There is no requirement of any "relationship" between assets. For example, a single asset or one or more businesses may be transferred. However, practitioners should ensure that each type of asset transferred is eligible for the election. Eligible property is defined in subsection 85(1.1) to include the following:

- Capital property — other than real property, an interest therein, or an option in respect thereof, owned by a non-resident person (paragraph 85(1.1)(*a*)).

- Canadian resource property (paragraph 85(1.1)(*c*)).

- Foreign resource property (paragraph 85(1.1)(*d*)), subject to an anti-avoidance rule in subsection 85(1.11) which provides that foreign resource property is not an "eligible property" where:

  — the taxpayer and the corporation do not deal with each other at arm's length; and

  — it is reasonable to conclude that one of the purposes of the disposition, or series of transactions or events of which the disposition is a part, is to increase the extent to which any person may claim a deduction under section 126.

- Eligible capital property (paragraph 85(1.1)(*e*)).

- Inventory, other than real estate or an interest or option therein, (paragraph 85(1.1)(*f*)).

- Property that is a security or debt obligation used or held by the taxpayer in the year in the course of carrying on the business of insurance or lending money; however, excluded are a capital property, inventory or, where the taxpayer is a financial institution in the year, a "mark-to-market property" for the year — paragraph 85(1.1)(g).

- Where the taxpayer is a financial institution in the year, a specified debt obligation, other than a "mark-to-market property" of the taxpayer for the year (paragraph 85(1.1)(g.1)).

- Capital property that is real property, an interest in or an option in respect of real property, owned by a non-resident insurer where that property and the property received as consideration for that property are "designated insurance property" (paragraph 85(1.1)(b)).

- Capital property that is real property, an interest in real property or an option in respect of real property, owned by a non-resident person (other than a non-resident insurer) and used in the year in a business carried on in Canada by that person (paragraph 85(1.1)(h)).[3]

- A NISA Fund No. 2 — this refers to a farmer's Net Income Stabilization Account (paragraph 85(1.1)(i)).

- Inventories other than real property include work in progress of a professional who has elected pursuant to the provisions of paragraph 34(1)(d), as well as inventories of cash basis taxpayers.

The following assets are not eligible for transfer under section 85:

- Real property (or an interest therein, or an option in respect thereof) where the transferor is a non-resident person or a non-Canadian partnership (subject to the above).

- Real property (or an interest or option therein) which represents inventory to the transferor. This means that real property must be eligible for capital gains status in order for section 85 to be applicable.

☞   **Real property, at common law, includes buildings and fixtures.**

- Prepaid expenses; however, most prepaid expenses are of a current nature and could be treated as a closing adjustment in respect of the purchase price under an agreement of purchase and sale.

---

[3] However, subsection 85(1.2) sets out conditions to qualify for the rollover. These conditions are intended to ensure that only those transfers that are part of the incorporation of a Canadian branch are allowed on a tax-deferred basis under subsection 85(1). First, the transfer must be to a corporation controlled by the taxpayer, persons related to the taxpayer or the taxpayer together with those persons. Second, all or substantially all of the property used in the course of carrying on the business in Canada in which the real property is used must be transferred by the taxpayer to the corporation. Third, the transfer cannot be part of a series of transactions in which control of the corporation is acquired by a person or group of persons. In this respect, subsection 256(7) of the Act provides that certain acquisitions of control, including those involving related persons, will not be considered to be an acquisition of control for the purposes of subsection 85(1.2).

- "Mark-to-market" property of financial institutions. Paragraphs 85(1.1)(*g*) and (*g*.1) deny financial institutions the ability to use subsection 85(1) for "mark-to-market" property.

- Life insurance policies are excluded as they are not "capital property" under subparagraph 39(1)(*a*)(iii), except in limited circumstances, although it is conceivable that they could qualify as inventory. "Rollovers" are available in section 148 of the Act, but only under limited circumstances, for example, in situations where a policy is transferred to a spouse or a child. Of more relevance is subsection 148(7), which provides that, where an individual and transferee corporation do not deal at arm's length, the transferor is deemed to have received proceeds equal to the "value" of the policy and deems the transferee to acquire the policy at the same amount. For the purposes of section 148, "value" essentially means cash surrender value of the transferred life insurance. Accordingly, if this is in excess of the policy's "adjusted cost basis", as calculated under section 148, the excess will be taxable to the transferor under subsection 148(1) (see also subsections 148(8), (8.1) and (8.2)).[4]

See Appendix B at the end of this volume for a reproduction of various CRA Round Table questions and answers relating to eligible property.

In addition, a number of CRA Technical Interpretations (some of which are summarized in Appendix B) have dealt with non-eligibility or rollover treatment in respect of rights to income, such as a dividend receivable. These rights are generally not capital property and there is no provision in subsection 85(1.1) that allows eligibility under subsection 85(1.1).

> ☞ **The October 30, 2003 Notice of Ways and Means Motion in respect of the taxation of FIEs and non-resident trusts (also reflected in the July 18, 2005 draft legislation) proposes rules designed to restrict section 85 rollovers of FIEs, by adding a "specified participating interest", as defined in subsection 248(1) to subsection 85(1.11), applicable to taxation years that commence after 2002. Similar restrictions are proposed in respect of a number of other rollovers, including sections 51, 73, 85.1 and subsection 86(3).**

In respect of non-eligible assets, an issue has arisen in respect of the eligibility of a partnership interest where the underlying assets do not qualify for the rollover. For example, will an interest in real estate that is inventory be eligible for a subsection 85(1) transfer if the interest is held through a partnership? Similarly, one may question whether a non-resident's interest in a partnership, the assets of which are primarily real property, qualifies as an eligible asset for a subsection 85(1) rollover.

In the 1990 Revenue Canada Round Table, at Q.35, the CRA confirmed that, for the purpose of section 85, an interest in a partnership is not considered to be an

---

[4] For further discussion, reference should be made to Glenn R. Stephens' "The Valuation of Life Insurance for Canadian Income Tax Purposes", *Canadian Tax Journal*, 1992, Issue 4 at p. 957 *et seq.*

interest in its underlying assets. Therefore, an interest in a partnership held by a non-resident as capital property would qualify as "eligible property" under paragraph 85(1.1)(*a*), notwithstanding the fact that the assets of the partnership consist primarily of real property.

The CRA warned, however, that if a partnership is formed as one of the steps in a series of transactions designed to circumvent the provisions of subsection 85(1.1), the General Anti-Avoidance Rule ("GAAR") (subsection 245(2)) could apply.[5] However, in *Loyens v. The Queen*, 2003 DTC 355 (T.C.C.), the CRA was unsuccessful in this assertion. The taxpayers transferred land inventory into a partnership under subsection 97(2) and then transferred their partnership interest to a corporation with losses, pursuant to subsection 85(1). The CRA argued that subsection 97(2) was used to effectively transfer land inventory into a corporation, in circumvention of the definition of eligible property in paragraph 85(1.1)(*f*) — which excludes land inventory — resulting in a misuse of these provisions. The court found instead that the policy behind paragraph 85(1.1)(*f*) is to prevent conversion of inventory status to capital gains status by rolling land inventory into a corporation and subsequently selling the shares thereof; accordingly, GAAR did not apply to the transaction.

In the case of accounts receivable, it may be more advantageous to utilize the election contained in section 22 rather than section 85. Otherwise, a number of untoward results may occur, such as the inability of the transferor to claim appropriate discounts on the transferred receivables, etc.[6]

One potentially eligible property is a share of the transferee corporation itself, since "eligible property" is determined with reference to the transferor rather than the transferee. Such shares can be transferred to the transferee in consideration for other shares of the transferee corporation or, perhaps non-share consideration. Although either section 86 or 51 would generally apply on such a reorganization, subsections 86(3) and 51(4) provide exceptions to these "automatic rollovers" where a section 85 election is filed.

These "internal reorganizations" can be used to achieve different results and effects than the automatic rollovers, including the following:

1. It is, of course, possible to elect into a capital gain so as to crystallize the capital gains exemption (if the transferred shares qualify) or utilize capital losses.

2. The allocation of cost base to the consideration received may differ. For example, the section 86 rollover allocates cost base in accordance with the fair market value of the different classes of shares received, whereas the section 85 mechanism would allocate the cost base to preferred shares to the extent of their value, with the remaining cost base going to common shares.

3. An internal section 85 reorganization may be available in cases when section 86 does not apply. For example, section 86 requires the transferor to dispose of all of the transferor's shares of a particular class and will not be applicable unless such shares are capital property. It should be noted, however, that if a reorganization

---

[5] For similar questions, see 1989, Q.10; 1986, Q.50; 1984, Q.48.

[6] See "Receivables Election" on page 78 *et seq.* for further commentary.

will not qualify under section 86, it may qualify under section 51. For further discussion, see Chapter 3.

Although shares held pursuant to a share purchase agreement qualify under section 85, it appears that the transfer of shares subject to the benefits under subsection 7(1.1) to an employee's holding corporation (pursuant to subsection 85(1) of the Act) would potentially trigger the taxable benefit that would otherwise be deferred pursuant to subsection 7(1.1). This is because the incidence of the benefit is governed by section 7 rather than section 85.

This appears to occur despite the fact that section 85 allows a taxpayer to elect the proceeds of disposition of the shares, since the effect of subsection 7(1.1) is to delay the incidence of the taxable benefit, based on the difference between value at time of acquisition and amount paid to the point of disposition or exchange of the shares. In other words, it would appear that the taxable benefit is triggered on this disposition as it is not based on the proceeds of disposition as elected under section 85 (section 85 allows one to elect the proceeds of disposition but there is, nevertheless, still a disposition). It further appears that this adverse effect could occur whether or not the two-year holding period, after which a favourable tax status would be applicable pursuant to paragraph 110(*d*.01), has expired.

Subsection 7(1.5) provides an exception that might apply in a section 85 rollover situation; however, it is required that the corporation issuing the "new shares" must be in a non-arm's length position in relation to the corporation issuing the "old shares" (i.e., the shares originally acquired under the share purchase arrangement). This would generally not be the case for employees who have previously qualified for the subsection 7(1.1) benefit, since they must be at arm's length with this corporation at the time the shares are received. It also appears that, for similar reasons, the tax consequences pertaining to the disposition of "stock options" is similarly governed by section 7, particularly subsections 7(1) and 7(1.4).

Common Pitfalls

Although the transfer of assets to a corporation may sometimes be a simple matter, there are a number of common pitfalls involved, especially where a transfer under section 85 is involved.

In all probability, the most common pitfall is failure to file the section 85 election itself within the time limit specified in the Act (see "Formal Requirements" on page 42 *et seq.*). It is recommended that, where a transaction involving a section 85 election is involved, responsibility for the filing of the election be affixed in writing.

Other common pitfalls are noted below:

1. Failure to comply with the formal requirements of section 85, including mechanical filing defects, failure to elect on all assets, failure to take back shares, late filing, etc.

2. Violation of the parameters of section 85, within which the elected proceeds of disposition, etc., may be chosen, including failure to allocate liabilities assumed by the corporation properly to various assets involved in the section 85 transfer.

3. The creation of a taxable benefit to a shareholder in the course of a transfer pursuant to subsection 15(1), or 84(1), paragraph 85(1)(*e*.2), etc.

4. Failure to consider the so-called "stop-loss" provisions, including subsections 13(21.2), 14(12), 40(3.3) to 40(3.6), and the "superficial loss rules" (section 54, paragraph 40(2)(*g*), etc.), which deal with transfers of depreciable, eligible capital and capital properties in loss positions — that is, where the value is less than the cost for tax purposes applicable to the asset.[7]

5. Failure to consider sections 84.1 and 212.1 or subsection 85(2.1) which may restrict paid-up capital or trigger deemed dividends (see above).

6. Failure to consider various capitalization alternatives which could be beneficial for tax or other purposes. For example, the selection of the capitalization may affect the continued ability of the transferor to deduct business or investment-related loans; also, the transferor should be able to extract the cost base inherent in the transferred assets in the future with a minimum of untoward tax or legal consequences.

7. Failure to consider non-tax-related legislation which may be relevant.

Shares Required

In order to take advantage of the section 85 election procedure with respect to any eligible property, the consideration must include shares of the capital stock of the transferee corporation. However, since (per the subsection 248(1) definition) a "share" includes a fraction of a share, it is possible to satisfy this requirement by allocating portions of a single share. (Practically speaking, it is important to show shares being received in each entry on the schedule on page 3 of the election forms T2057 and T2058.)

Although the issuance of shares in respect of particular assets transferred is a necessary precondition of the section 85 rollover, it is not, in itself, sufficient to achieve the tax objectives desired, e.g., in respect of the elected proceeds of disposition or the allocation of cost base to the consideration received. As a simple example, an individual might transfer capital property to a new corporation with a cost base of $100 and a fair market value of $200. If the consideration received were, say, $199 in debt and one common share (worth one dollar), paragraph 85(1)(*b*) would automatically increase the elected amount to $199,[8] for a gain of $99.

If for some reason, the shares are not actually issued at the time the transfer occurs, there is, at time of writing, authority that the section 85 rollover may, at least in some cases, still be valid, provided that the shares are issued within a reasonable time. It should be noted that the preamble to subsection 85(1) requires that the

---

[7] See section on superficial loss rules in this chapter for further discussion.

[8] See "Section 85 Limits on Elected Amounts" in this chapter.

consideration for the transfer includes shares, but does not itself impose any specific time limit on the issuance thereof.

In *Peter Dale and Bernard Dale v. The Queen*, 97 DTC 5252 (F.C.A.), the taxpayers transferred assets to a corporation in 1985 and filed elections under section 85 whereby the transferree corporation purportedly issued preference shares to the taxpayers. However, the corporation did not have authorized capital to permit the issuance of the shares. Steps were taken to rectify the authorized capital on a retrospective basis under corporate law. In 1992, the corporation obtained a court order from the Supreme Court of Nova Scotia declaring that its authorized capital had been amended retroactively and that the shares in question had been validly issued and were outstanding at the time of the rollover. However, the Minister reassessed on the grounds that the shares had not been validly issued, therefore disallowing a rollover, as well as denying a capital dividend election which was purported to have been made on the preference shares. The Tax Court of Canada allowed the taxpayers' appeal in respect of section 85, but found that the capital dividends were not validly declared.

The Federal Court of Appeal allowed the taxpayers' appeals on both issues, holding that the preference shares in question were never a nullity. The court order obtained in 1992 had never been reversed and had been made under valid statutory authority. Heretofore, the CRA's administrative practice has been that, where shares have not been issued at the time of the transfer, a section 85 election will be valid only if there is an agreement to do so, the transferee acts immediately to authorize the shares and, once the necessary authorization has been obtained, the transferee issues the shares.[9]

It should also be noted that in the *Dale* case, the transfer agreement itself provided for the receipt of shares as consideration for the transfer. This may differ from a situation where the transfer agreement does not provide for the issuance of shares to begin with (e.g., through oversight) and the shares are subsequently issued.

In *Juliar et al. and Attorney General of Canada et al.*, 2000 DTC 6589 (Ont. C.A.),[10] the applicant taxpayers (a husband and wife) transferred their shares of a holding corporation ("Holdco") to a second corporation ("Juliar Holdings"), taking back as consideration a promissory note rather than shares of the second corporation. This was done on the advice of the taxpayers' accountant (although such advice had been based on certain misinformation given to the accountant by one of the taxpayers concerning the cost of the Holdco shares). As a result of the way in which the transaction was structured, it did not fall within section 85, but constituted a disposition of property falling within section 84.1. This gave rise to an immediate liability to pay tax, which formed the subject matter of reassessments issued to the taxpayers in January 1997. On May 7, 1998, the taxpayers applied to the Ontario Superior Court of Justice for an Order rectifying the transaction in order to transform it into an exchange of shares of Holdco for shares of Juliar Holdings,

---

[9] See "Exchanges of Property for Shares: Section 85 — Part I", Andrew W. Dunn and Kimberly A. Nielsen, *Canadian Tax Journal*, Volume 43, Issue 1 at p. 203.

[10] Supreme Court of Canada refused leave to appeal on May 24, 2001.

rather than an exchange of shares of Holdco for a promissory note of Juliar Holdings. The taxpayers also appealed to the Tax Court of Canada in December, but did not proceed with such appeal, pending the outcome of the rectification proceedings. Cameron, J. of the Ontario Superior Court concluded that rectification should be allowed. He found that the taxpayers had intended, from a date prior to March 1993, that the transaction would not trigger an obligation to pay income tax immediately. He also found that the structure of the transaction would have been in accordance with section 85 had the mistake in determining the cost of the Holdco shares not been made.

The Crown's appeal to the Court of Appeal for Ontario was dismissed. Mr. Justice Austin, on behalf of the Court, noted that in the lower court, evidence was provided that the taxpayers had a common and continuing intention from the outset to transfer their interest in Holdco to Juliar Holdings "on a basis which would not attract immediate liability for income tax on the transaction". He also noted the lower court's finding that the structure of the transaction would have been in accordance with section 85 had the mistake in determining the cost of the Holdco shares not been made. The Court of Appeal repeated the following comments from the lower court:

> Denial of the application would place on the Juliars a heavy burden which they were entitled to avoid and which they sought to avoid from the inception of the transaction. It would yield to Revenue Canada a premature gain solely because of an error in understanding or communication between Paul (Juliar) and Fast (the Juliars' accountant).

Accordingly, the Ontario Court of Appeal held unanimously that it was appropriate for the trial judge to permit rectification in a manner that would not attract immediate liability for income tax because this reflected the true intention of the parties. The Supreme Court of Canada refused leave to appeal on May 24, 2001.

Should an Election Be Made to Begin with?

In some cases, it may not make sense to make an election. Consider, for example, a professional who is incorporating his or her practice, but expects to need significant funds from the corporation. Instead of rolling goodwill into the corporation, a better course of action could be to transfer it at fair market value. The transfer would be taxable at about 23% to an Ontario resident. Although the "bump" on which the goodwill can be amortized is restricted to the taxable portion of the gain (by virtue of the December 20, 2002 draft legislation), there would still be a material "tax shield" in the corporation. The taxable sale would allow the professional a "pipeline" to extract the value of the goodwill (e.g., if sold for a promissory note). Tax on a dividend distribution, by comparison, would exceed 31%.

Formal Requirements

The transferor and the transferee corporation must jointly file the section 85 election in the forms prescribed — either Form T-2057, or Form T-2058, where a partnership transfers assets to a corporation. The following formalities should be noted:

1. Where a transferred property is beneficially held in a tenancy-in-common by two or more taxpayers, a separate election is required for each taxpayer.

2. The filing deadline is the date on which any party to the election is required to file an income tax return for the taxation year in which the transaction occurred.[11]

3. Subsection 85(2) provides for a tax-deferred transfer from a partnership to a corporation. Where this subsection is involved, all members of the partnership must jointly elect. For a partnership, the filing deadline relates to the taxation year of the partners, rather than the partnership itself.

Further filing requirements are indicated on Forms T2057 and T2058 themselves.[12]

Late-Filed and Amended Elections

Subsection 85(7) allows for a late-filed election, provided that it is filed within three years of the due date (as described above). The late-filed election must, of course, be made in the prescribed form; an estimate of the penalty (see below) in respect of the late-filed election must be paid when the election is made.

Subsection 85(7.1) empowers the Minister to accept elections filed after the three-year deadline where, in his opinion, it would be "just and equitable" to do so. Under the same criteria, the Minister is also empowered to accept *amendments* to elections already filed.

In both cases, the late-filed or amended elections must be made in prescribed form and an estimate of the penalty, as described below, must be paid when the election (or amended election) is made. If the Minister accepts the election or the amended election, it shall be deemed to have been made at the normal deadline. In the case of an amending election, the original election shall be deemed not to have been "effective".

It should be emphasized that the provisions in subsection 85(7.1) depend on the exercise of ministerial discretion, whereas an election which is late filed within the time limits specified pursuant to subsection 85(7) may be filed as of right.

---

[11] See subsection 85(6).

[12] In some cases, where there is a large number of transferors, the filing of section 85 elections can be an onerous requirement. However, it appears that the CRA will sometimes consent to the bulk filing of section 85 elections. Where a public share-for-share exchange is completed pursuant to subsection 85(1), the CRA may be willing to accept the filing of a single Form T2057, provided that each offeree tendering shares to the offeror and desiring to make an election duly authorizes either the offeror or a person designated by the offeror as his or her lawful attorney for the purpose of executing the form. A schedule to Form T2057 will set forth the name and other particulars of each offeree making the election. In addition, information on the elected amount will be required by the CRA. Obviously, arrangements along these lines should be worked out in advance. See D.S. Ewens, "New Considerations in Structuring Share-for-Share Exchange Offers", *Canadian Tax Journal*, March 6, 1988, p. 449.

In the case of late-filed or amended elections, subsection 85(8) provides for penalty taxes equal to the lesser of:

- $\frac{1}{4}$ of 1% per month, based on the difference between the fair market value of the transferred property and the agreed amount, and

- $100 per month, to an $8,000 maximum.

In either case, the amounts are calculated based on the number of months each of which is a month or part of a month during the period commencing at the normal filing deadline (in accordance with subsection 85(6)) and ending on the day the election (or amended election) was made.

At the CRA Round Table presented at the 1984 Canadian Tax Foundation Conference, a CRA official indicated that it was anticipated that, as a result of the amendments, late-filed and amended elections would be accepted under the "just and equitable" criterion, provided that the requirements of section 85 have been met and there is no evidence that the parties to the elections intended to avoid taxes.

Omitted Assets

Practitioners should attempt to ensure that all assets with a value exceeding the cost for tax purposes have been included in the election. Particularly troublesome assets are those which have been fully depreciated (for example, Class 12) as well as goodwill, licences and trademarks — which may not have a tax cost, but may have a significant value. In these cases, the CRA will accept a nominal amount as the elected proceeds of disposition if the constraints of section 85 are otherwise met. However, a "nil" election amount is not considered to be a "nominal" amount.[13] If property has been omitted from an election, it is, of course, possible to file a late-filed election in respect of the omitted property, provided that the procedures outlined above are adhered to.

In addition, in order for the election to apply, it is necessary that shares be taken back for each property transferred. However, technically, a "share", as defined in subsection 248(1), can mean a share or fraction thereof. Therefore, the CRA allows the requirement to be satisfied if the transferor receives one share for a number of different assets transferred.

Description of Property

Although section 85 requires that the election be made on an asset-by-asset basis, the CRA will allow the following aggregations of assets:

1. If all depreciable properties of a class are transferred, they may be described in an aggregate form.[14]

---

[13] See IC 76-19R3, paragraph 5.

[14] For further details, see IC 76-19R3, paragraph 3.

2. Where identical properties are involved (e.g., shares of a corporation), they may be aggregated. However, if some properties were acquired prior to 1972, the pre-1972 "pool" must be subject to a separate election.

3. In addition, the CRA allows a taxpayer to use "some discretion" where many properties are transferred.[15]

Valuation Issues

The election forms require the disclosure of the fair market value of property transferred to a corporation at the time of the transfer, as well as the fair market value of the consideration received. In many cases, a precise valuation will present practical difficulties.

Price Adjustment Clauses

In many cases, and in particular, where undertaking an estate freeze, it will be critical to attempt to ensure that the value of shares and other consideration received in return for the transfer of the assets accurately reflects the fair market value of the property transferred. This equivalence is reflected in the redemption/retraction amount of freeze shares. If this equivalence is not maintained, there is the spectre of various benefit provisions, particularly the application of paragraph 85(1)(e.2).[16] As a result, it is customary in an estate freeze to obtain a written formal valuation by a qualified valuator, e.g., an accredited real estate appraiser or business valuator. In the latter case, particularly where the valuation is relatively straightforward, many practitioners will be content to rely on the valuation of the business's existing accountant.

In order to assure the required equivalence, it is prudent to include a price adjustment clause in respect of the shares issued. Price adjustment clauses are discussed in more detail in Chapter 6.

Price adjustment clauses are used in the context of section 85 transfers where there is more than one shareholder of the transferee corporation. In a situation where there is only one shareholder, a benefit should not be considered to have been conferred irrespective of the form of shares taken back on the transfer, since the transferor's interest in the corporation would be 100% both before and after the transfer. Practitioners should bear in mind that, if a price-adjustment clause becomes operative, it would change the economic rights as between the shareholders of a corporation. Accordingly, price adjustment clauses which are automatically triggered as a result of tax considerations may be more appropriate in a non-arm's length situation.

---

[15] See IC 76-19R3, paragraph 3.

[16] See, for example, commentary on sections 15, 84, and paragraph 85(1)(e.2), in "Other Income Tax Restrictions" at page 57 *et seq.*

Other Valuation Issues

In the 1981 Revenue Canada Round Table, CRA officials indicated that where, as a result of a disagreement on the fair market value of properties subject to section 85 election, subsection 84(1) comes into play and the tax consequences so triggered are "extremely harsh", the CRA may be prepared to consider granting administrative relief on a case by-case basis.

Valuations also may come into play where property owned prior to the end of 1971 is transferred and parties intend that the agreed amount should be the adjusted cost base of the property. In those cases, it is usually necessary to estimate the fair market value at Valuation Day ("V-day").

In paragraph 14 of Information Circular 76-19R3, the CRA has stated that where taxpayers make a reasonable effort to determine the V-day value and specify on the election form that the elected amount is the estimated adjusted cost base, it will be prepared to adjust the elected amount to the proper figure should it subsequently be determined that the adjusted cost base of the property differed from the estimated amount because of an erroneous estimate of the V-day value. In the 1980 Revenue Canada Round Table, it was indicated that the only circumstance in which an adjustment to the elected amount will be made is that set forth in paragraph 14 of Information Circular 76-19R.[17] It should be noted, however, that this statement is not included in the current version of the Circular.

The CRA will not, however, adjust the agreed amount to an amount less than the fair market value of consideration other than shares received in respect of the properties transferred.[18]

Where the cost amount of a transferred asset is in doubt, whether by virtue of a valuation issue or otherwise, it may be prudent to include an adjustment clause in respect of the elected amount. This clause may be included in addition to a price adjustment clause. Because there are two different adjustments, a traditional price adjustment clause is designed to avoid tax liability by virtue of the conferral of a benefit[19] and would typically adjust the redemption/retraction amount of special/preferred shares taken back on a transfer, whereas this clause would adjust the elected amount.

Another valuation issue is whether there should be a tax discount for assets transferred to a corporation under section 85, i.e., in view of the fact that the corporation will assume the deferred tax liability. This issue is addressed at paragraph 24 of IC 76-19R3, which indicates that the potential deferred tax liability in the hands of the transferee does not reduce the fair market value of the transferred property. The rationale for this policy is described in Q.53 of the 1981 Revenue Canada Round Table. In essence, the fair market value of a property is the value available in an open and unrestricted market between informed prudent parties (i.e., a "willing buyer" and a "willing seller"), acting at arm's length and under no compulsion to act. Since an arm's-length buyer would not inherit a deferred tax liability, a

---

[17] See 1980 Revenue Canada Round Table, *Canadian Tax Foundation Conference Report*, at p. 603.

[18] See IC 76-19R3.

[19] For example, pursuant to paragraph 85(1)(e.2), subsections 15(1), 56(2) or section 246.

discount should not be attached to transferred assets. However, the situation would differ where shares of another corporation are transferred, since there would be an inherent tax liability in respect of the disposition of corporate level assets, so that a "willing buyer" may well attach a discount to the shares.

Section 85 Limits on Elected Amounts

The section 85 election process involves electing an amount to be the proceeds of disposition and cost for tax purposes to the transferee corporation.

However, there are certain parameters within which the elected amount must fall, as follows.

(1) Elected amount must not exceed value of property transferred

The maximum elected amount must not exceed the fair market value of the property transferred to the corporation. In some cases, the cost for tax purposes may exceed the fair market value of the asset, in which case the restriction would become applicable if an election at cost is attempted. This will force a "loss election" in which the stop-loss rules, discussed later in this chapter, will apply.

(2) Elected amount must not be less than "boot"

Paragraph 85(1)(*b*) requires that the elected amount must not be less than the fair market value of non-share consideration (usually referred to as "boot") received from the company on the transfer. Otherwise, the elected amount will automatically be increased to the fair market value of the non-share consideration. In this case, the proceeds of disposition and the cost for tax purposes of the "boot" will be increased by a like amount.

It should be noted, however, that in the event of a conflict between this constraint and constraint (1), the former constraint will apply, according to paragraph 85(1)(*b*).

Liabilities assumed by the transferee corporation will constitute non-share consideration. Accordingly, it is essential that such liabilities be allocated so as not to exceed the amount otherwise elected. Otherwise, the upward adjustment will apply, the result of which could be a taxable gain.

Generally, the CRA permits the allocation of consideration at the discretion of the taxpayers.[20] Specifically, the CRA has indicated that where a property to be transferred is subject to a mortgage which exceeds the adjusted cost base of the property, paragraph 85(1)(*b*) will not apply if the amount of debt assumed is allocated among several assets to be transferred and the amount allocated to each asset is no greater than the agreed amount in respect of the particular asset.[21]

---

[20] See Information Circular 76-19R3.

[21] See Q.47, 1984 Revenue Canada Round Table.

Furthermore, the CRA indicated that paragraph 85(1)(*b*) will not apply if the excess is assumed by the transferee in consideration of the delivery by the transferor of a promissory note in the amount of the excess.

Suppose, for example, that a taxpayer wishes to transfer assets to a corporation having an adjusted cost base of $100,000; however, the liabilities that the taxpayer wishes to have assumed by the transferee corporation have a principal amount of $150,000. It would appear that subsection 85(1)(*b*) could be avoided if the transferor delivered a promissory note in the amount of $50,000 in consideration of the transferee assuming $50,000 of indebtedness. The remaining indebtedness could be assumed on the roll-in of the asset having an adjusted cost base of $100,000, without violating paragraph 85(1)(*b*). Of course, the indebtedness of the transferor could result in other income tax problems, particularly if the transferor was an individual, since this would presumably trigger shareholders' loans provisions. These provisions would not normally be a problem if the transferor were a corporation. This position was confirmed at the 1996 Corporate Management Tax Conference; however, the CRA indicated that its position was under review.

The CRA has now completed its review of paragraph 85(1)(*b*) and has amended its position on the application of the provision with respect to transfers after 2000, as follows:

where, after 2000, a property (the "First Property") is transferred pursuant to the provisions of section 85, and:

(a) the purchaser assumes an obligation of the vendor as consideration for the acquisition from the vendor of a second property (for example, a note of the vendor) and the purchaser subsequently disposes of that property to the vendor;

(b) the purchaser assumes an obligation of the vendor as consideration for the redemption or acquisition by the purchaser of its shares held by the vendor; or

(c) the purchaser subscribes for shares of the vendor,

the obligation so assumed or the property so contributed will be regarded as consideration for the First Property. Thus, if the total non-share consideration so considered to have been given by the purchaser for the First Property exceeds the amount agreed upon by the vendor and purchaser in their election under subsection 85(1), paragraph 85(1)(*b*) will apply to increase the amount agreed upon.[22]

The previous position regarding the allocation of non-share consideration, including the allocation of liabilities, among several properties transferred to the corporation continues to apply, providing the properties are retained by the purchaser and the amount allocated to each asset is not greater than the amount elected in respect of that asset.

---

[22] See Technical Interpretation Document Number 2000-0039335, September 27, 2000, reported in CCH *Tax Topics* No. 1511, dated February 22, 2001.

Note issued by vendor

Sellco has a capital property with a cost amount of $200, a fair market value of $1,000, and a $700 mortgage on the property. Sellco transfers the property to Buyco for $1,000, pursuant to section 85, and issues a promissory note to Buyco for $500 (the difference between the $700 mortgage and the $200 cost amount of the property). The consideration for the property is $200 of the mortgage liability, redeemable preferred shares with a fair market value of $500, and common shares with a fair market value of $300. As consideration for the $500 promissory note, Buyco agrees to assume $500 of the mortgage liability. Subsequently, Buyco redeems the preferred shares by surrendering the promissory note. In this situation, the non-share consideration received by Sellco is $700, which is the minimum amount that can be elected under section 85.

Transfer of debt as consideration for share redemption

A variation of the transaction involves the issuance of redeemable shares as consideration for the transfer of property under section 85 and the assumption of debt as consideration for the redemption of those shares. Assuming the same facts as above, Buyco issues redeemable Class B shares with a fair market value of $700 and redeemable Class A shares with a fair market value of $300 as consideration for the property. The Class B shares are redeemed and as consideration, Buyco assumes the $700 mortgage. It is the CRA's view that the mortgage assumed by Buyco is consideration for the transferred property and $700 is the minimum elected amount under section 85.

Subscription for shares

In another variation of the transaction, Buyco borrows $700 and uses the funds to subscribe for shares of Sellco. Sellco uses the $700 to repay the mortgage on the property. Sellco then transfers the property to Buyco and elects at $200 under section 85. Buyco purchases $700 of its shares held by Sellco and Sellco pays $700 to Buyco as a return of capital on the shares issued to Buyco. In this situation, the $700 capital contribution by Buyco is regarded as consideration for the transferred property, and paragraph 85(1)(*b*) would apply to deem the elected amount to be $700.[23]

(3) Specific minimum limitations

Besides the foregoing limitations, there are other minimum limitations with specific reference to the type of property transferred:

For *inventory*, paragraph 85(1)(*c*.1) effectively provides that the transfer price must be at least as great as either the fair market value or the value of the inventory for the purpose of computing income for tax purposes, whichever is the lesser amount.

For *capital property* (other than depreciable property of a prescribed class) or a *NISA Fund* No. 2, paragraph 85(1)(*c*.1) specifies that the elected amount must be at

---

[23] See Technical Interpretation, Document Number 2000-0039335, September 27, 2000.

least as great as the adjusted cost base, or the fair market value of the property, whichever is the lesser amount. [24]

For *eligible capital property*, e.g., goodwill, etc., paragraph 85(1)(*d*) provides that the elected amount must be at least as great as the least of:

- $^4/_3$ of the amount of the cumulative eligible capital in respect of the business immediately prior to the disposition (the $^4/_2$ inclusion rate, occasioned by tax reform, is subject to certain transitional rules.);

- the cost of the eligible capital property; or

- the fair market value of the eligible capital property at the time of the disposition. (See Note 4, below.)

For *depreciable property* of a *prescribed class*, paragraph 85(1)(*e*) specifies that the elected amount must be at least as great as the least of the following amounts:

- the undepreciated capital cost of all depreciable property in the class immediately before the disposition;

- the cost to the taxpayer of the property; or

- the fair market value of the property at the time of the disposition.

In the event that any of the specific limitations mentioned above are not met, the elected amount of the property will be adjusted so that it meets the minimum amounts specified above.

Technical Notes:

1. Paragraph 85(1)(*e*.3) provides for a conflict between these parameters: Where the amount determined pursuant to specific limitations described above is greater or less than the elected amount pursuant to paragraph 85(1)(*b*), subject to paragraph 85(1)(*c*), the elected amount is deemed to be the greater of the two amounts.[25]

2. Paragraph 85(1)(*c*.2) applies when the taxpayer, who carries on a farming business and uses the cash method of computing income, disposes of inventory under section 85.

3. Paragraph 85(1)(*d*.1) is intended to prevent an overstatement of the amount to be included in income by virtue of paragraph 14(1)(*b*) in computing the income of a corporation in a taxation year as a result of the disposition by the corporation of eligible capital property subsequent to the transfer. Specifically, this provision ensures that the proportionate 20(1)(*b*) deductions taken by the transferor prior to the "adjustment time", as defined by subsection 14(5), flow through to the transferee corporation for the purposes of calculating its cumulative eligible capital under subsection 14(5).

---

[24] For *property that is a security or debt obligation* used or held in the year in the course of an insurance or lending business, paragraph 85(1)(*c*.1) specifies that the elected amount must be at least as great as the fair market value of the property or the "cost amount" (as defined in subsection 248(1)) of the property at the time of disposition, whichever is the lesser amount.

[25] For an example of the application of this paragraph, see paragraph 19 of IT-291R3.

4. An anomaly arises in respect of paragraph 85(1)(*c*.1), pertaining to receivables denominated in a foreign currency. This is because paragraph 85(1)(*c*.1) states that the relevant agreed amount cannot be less than the lesser of the fair market value of the property at the time of the disposition and the cost amount of the property to the transferor at that time. However, the cost amount of the foreign currency denominated receivables appears to be the Canadian-dollar equivalent at any point in time — i.e., at the moment of transfer. Accordingly, to the extent that the ACB — which reflects the *historical* Canadian dollar equivalent — is different, a gain or loss can arise.

The following example is taken from "Exchange of the Property for Shares: section 85 — Part I" by Andrew W. Dunn and Kimberley A. Nielsen (*Canadian Tax Journal*, Vol. 43, No. 1, at p. 215):

> Consider ... a receivable for US$100 held as a capital property and issued when the U.S. dollar was at $1.25. Currently the U.S. dollar is at $1.40. Paragraph 85(1)(*c*.1) limits the agreed amount to its cost amount, $1.40, even though the adjusted cost base of the receivable would be $1.25. If the receivable is transferred, the disposition appears to result in a $15 gain to the transferor, even with subsection 85(1) "protection".

5. Paragraph 85(1)(*e*.4) puts a limit on the elected amount where the property being transferred is a passenger vehicle (as defined in subsection 248(1)). There are special rules (in sections 67.2 and 67.3) that restrict the deductions, including capital cost allowance, that may be claimed in respect of the operation of a passenger vehicle. Paragraph 85(1)(*e*.4) is designed to prevent these rules being circumvented by the use of a corporation.

Ordering

A technical problem arises with respect to the specific limitations mentioned above, which are applicable to eligible capital property or depreciable property. This arises because the lower limits on the elected amounts refer to the cumulative eligible capital in respect of the business, or the undepreciated capital cost of the class, respectively, and could therefore apply to more than one asset. However, the section 85 transfer applies on an asset-by-asset basis. Because of this conflict, the simultaneous transfer of a number of assets at the lowest possible amount could still result in a minimum aggregate elected amount in excess of the undepreciated capital cost of the class, or the cumulative eligible capital of the business.

This problem can be corrected if the order in which the assets are transferred is designated.

Paragraph 85(1)(*e*.1) allows such a designation to be made by the transferor. Failing such a designation, the order of assets would be that designated by the Minister.

Example: ——

Consider the following example of two depreciable assets within a class, where ordering would be relevant.

	Asset A	Asset B
Cost	$100,000	$120,000
Fair market value	120,000	130,000
Undepreciated capital cost — Applicable to both assets	$170,000	

If the undepreciated capital cost is applicable to both assets, the minimum transfer price will be $100,000 for Asset A, and $120,000 for Asset B, thus exceeding the undepreciated capital cost of the class by $50,000 and creating recapture on the transfer.

However, if Asset A were designated to be transferred first, it could be transferred at $100,000. Because the undepreciated capital cost of the class would then be relieved, this would leave $70,000 remaining in the class. This amount could be elected with respect to Asset B (since it would be the least of the cost, fair market value, or undepreciated capital cost remaining in the class).

It should be noted, however, that where only some of the assets of a depreciable class are transferred, even with the ordering provisions of paragraph 85(1)(e.1), there could be inappropriate allocations of undepreciated capital cost as between the transferred and retained assets.

———

Example: ——

Consider the following example of three assets within a depreciable class which have identical characteristics in respect of cost and fair market value.

	Asset A	Asset B	Asset C
Costs	$100,000	$100,000	$100,000
Fair Market Value	150,000	150,000	150,000
Undepreciated capital cost — Applicable to all three assets		180,000	

Suppose that Asset A and Asset B are to be transferred pursuant to subsection 85(1) of the Act, but Asset C is to be retained by the transferor. Intuitively, one would assume that two-thirds of the undepreciated capital cost should carry over to the transferee corporation, with $60,000 of undepreciated capital cost ("UCC") remaining in the hands of the transferee.

However, even with the ordering provisions of paragraph 85(1)(e.1), the transferor would find that all of the undepreciated capital cost would carry over to the transferee, as follows:

UCC	$ 180,000
Asset A — minimum elected amount (least of $100,000, $150,000, $180,000)	(100,000)
	80,000
Asset B — minimum elected amount (least of $100,000, $150,000, $80,000)	(80,000)
UCC — Asset C	Nil

It would appear that this inequitable result might be avoided if the transferred asset were considered to be part of separate businesses and therefore constitute separate classes pursuant to Regulation 1101(1) of the Act.

A related difficulty which may be remedied by paragraph 85(1)(e.1) may arise where consideration other than shares is received on the transfer; for example, cash and shares are included in the consideration. This is illustrated by the example in paragraph 15 of IT-291R3.

Assumptions:

Cost of Property A	$100
Fair market value of Property A	80
Fair market value of non-share consideration in respect of Property A	80
Cost of Property B	500
Fair market value of Property B	400
Fair market value of non-share consideration received in respect of Property B	NIL
UCC of the class	300

The taxpayer stipulates that the properties are to be transferred at the minimum allowable amounts and designates the order to be Property A followed by Property B. To achieve the best result, the taxpayer should elect in respect of Property A $80 which, when deducted from the UCC of the class, leaves a balance of $220. Property B would then be transferred at an elected amount of $220 and no recapture of capital cost allowance results. If the order of transfer was Property B followed by Property A, Property B would have to be transferred at an amount of $300 and the UCC of the class would be reduced to "nil". Property A cannot be transferred at an elected amount of "nil" because of the non-share consideration of $80 received in respect of it. Property A must therefore be transferred at an amount of $80 pursuant to paragraphs 85(1)(b) and 85(1)(e.3) and recapture of capital cost allowance of $80 results.

Cost Base Allocation and the Ability To Extract Assets

As previously mentioned, the cost base of shares and other assets received by the transferor in return for the assets transferred into the company is a reflection of the elected proceeds of disposition of the transferred assets.

It is often important that, if possible, the cost base be allocated among the considerations received in a manner that allows assets to be distributed from the corporation so that the cost base can be effectively and expeditiously liquidated without accompanying untoward tax consequences or complicated corporate restructuring. For example, rather than receive a distribution from the corporation in the form of salary or dividends, an owner/manager may be allowed to "drain out" his cost base through the repayment of debt or redemption of shares received from a previous transfer of assets.

Paragraphs 85(1)(f) through (h) provide for the allocation of the cost base amongst non-share consideration, preferred shares, and common shares, respectively.

The cost base of assets transferred is allocated to consideration received on the transfer in the following order:

- First, to non-share consideration received, to the extent of its fair market value.[26]

---

[26] See paragraph 85(1)(f).

- To the extent that there is remaining cost base, it is then allocated to preferred shares receivable, to the extent of their fair market value.[27]

- Any remainder is allocated to common shares receivable.[28]

Technical Notes

1. The meaning of common and preferred shares is defined in section 248, rather than under corporate law. Accordingly, care should be exercised to ensure that the income tax definitions are met; otherwise, distortions in the cost base may result. A common share is defined to mean a share, the holder of which is not precluded, upon the reduction or the redemption of capital stock, from participating in assets of the corporation beyond the amount paid-up thereon, plus a fixed premium and a defined rate of dividend. Preferred shares are defined to mean a share other than a common share.

2. In the case where the fair market value of property transferred to a corporation is less than the fair market value of the non-share consideration received, subparagraph 85(1)(f)(ii) specifies that the cost base of the non-share consideration will be the lesser amount. (If more than one property is received, the cost base will be *pro-rated* according to fair market value of properties received.) Under these circumstances, however, the shareholder will be deemed to have received the taxable benefit equal to the excess,[29] which would then be added to the cost base of the non-share consideration pursuant to subsection 52(1). Therefore, the cost base would be restored to the fair market value of the non-share consideration received.

3. The elected amount allocated to preferred shares will be equal to the lesser of:

- the fair market value immediately after the disposition of the preferred shares; and

- the excess of the elected proceeds of disposition for the particular asset over the fair market value of non-share consideration received.

4. In the event that the transferor receives more than one class of preferred or common shares in consideration for the transfer, the cost base allocable to the preferred or common shares (as the case may be) will be allocated according to the fair market value of the class, relative to the total fair market value of preferred or common shares receivable (as the case may be).[30]

5. Because the allocation of cost base to non-share consideration and preferred shares is limited to the fair market value of such consideration, it may be important to receive at least one common share on the transfer, since the cost base allocated to common shares is, by definition, the remaining unallocated cost base. It should also

---

[27] See paragraph 85(1)(g).

[28] See paragraph 85(1)(h).

[29] See subsection 15(1).

[30] Note that because of the definition of common shares, it is possible to receive more than one class of common shares on the transfer. See Note 1 above.

be noted that if the transferor does not receive common shares on the transfer, any residual cost base will not be allocated to pre-existing common shares owned by the transferor.

6. Where cost base is to be extracted through the redemption of shares or the reduction of paid-up capital in respect thereof, practitioners should ensure that sufficient paid-up capital is available in respect of the particular shares. In this respect, it should be noted that the paid-up capital is calculated based on the average applying to the issued class of shares.[31] Furthermore, pursuant to subsection 248(6), where shares have been issued in series, the paid-up capital would be calculated in accordance with the average within the particular series.[32]

For example, if shares are redeemed with respect to which the paid-up capital is deficient relative to the adjusted cost base, there will be a tendency to create deemed dividends and offsetting capital losses to the extent of the deficiency. The usefulness of the latter in terms of tax relief may, of course, be limited.

Restrictions on Paid-Up Capital — Subsection 85(2.1)

Subsection 85(2.1) of the Act is a specific anti-avoidance rule that is consequential to the introduction of the capital gains exemption. As stated previously, it is intended to prevent the removal of taxable corporate surpluses on a subsequent redemption or other return of capital as an exempt capital gain, under circumstances where the share transfer provisions of section 84.1 and 212.1 do not apply.

This provision applies where property is transferred to a corporation pursuant to subsection 85(1) or (2) and paid-up capital of the share consideration exceeds the cost (as elected under section 85) to the corporation of the property, less the fair market value of any non-share consideration received. It should be noted that, whereas the capital gains exemption is only available to individuals, subsection 85(2.1) applies to limit the paid-up capital of all "persons and partnerships" (including corporations).

In any such case, paragraph 85(2.1)(*a*) requires the paid-up capital of the shares of the corporation to be reduced by the amount of the excess described above. The paid-up capital reduction is allocated among those classes of shares that include the shares issued as consideration for the property, based on their legal paid-up capital increases.

---

[31] See subsection 89(1).

[32] See also "Restrictions on Paid-Up Capital", below, for instances in which the paid-up capital may be restricted.

In formulistic terms, the paid-up capital reduction required by subsection 85(2.1) in respect of any class of shares is calculated as follows:

$$(A - B) \times (C \div A)$$

where:

A   is the increase in the paid-up capital of shares of all classes in the transferee corporation, due to the acquisition of the transferred property.

B   is the transferee corporation's cost of the transferred property (as elected under section 85), less the fair market value of non-share consideration received by the transferor from the corporation for the transferred property.

C   is the increase in the paid-up capital as a result of the transfer, with respect to the particular class of shares.

It should be noted that section 85(2.1) does not affect pre-November 21, 1985 transactions where high paid-up capital has been taken back. Accordingly, a current redemption can trigger tax-exempt capital gains.

Note also that the operation of subsection 85(2.1) is to restrict the paid-up capital for tax purposes of the transferee corporation. The paid-up capital for corporate purposes ("stated capital") will not be affected by subsection 85(2.1). However, it may be prudent to limit the paid-up capital for corporate purposes to correspond with the tax amounts, for example, so that the income tax effect described above will not be forgotten.

Pursuant to subsection 24(3) of the *Ontario Business Corporations Act* (the "OBCA")[33] the paid-up capital of shares may be limited where a corporation issues shares in exchange for:

- property of a person who immediately before the exchange does not deal with the corporation at arm's length within the meaning ascribed by the *Income Tax Act*; or

- shares of a corporation that immediately before the exchange or by virtue of this exchange does not deal at arm's length with the issuing corporation.

The *Canada Business Corporations Act* contains similar provisions.[34]

In addition, where there is more than one class of shares taken back on a transfer of assets, there may be distortions in the allocation of cost base and paid-up capital to such shares.

In this respect, it should be noted that the cost base of shares taken back will be calculated in accordance with paragraphs 85(1)(g) and (h), whereas the paid-up capital will be determined in accordance with the formula described above. Where preferred and common shares are taken back, the cost base would first be attributed to preferred shares taken back, with any residual going to the common shares. The formula in subsection 85(2.1), on the other hand, would *pro-rate* the paid-up capital

---

[33] R.S.O. 1990, Chapter B.16

[34] See subsection 26(1.2) of the *Canada Business Corporations Act*, R.S. 1985, c. C-44.

decrease in accordance with the paid-up capital of the shares (computed without reference to subsection 85(2.1)).

It appears that such distortions can be eliminated by limiting the paid-up capital to correspond with the tax amounts.

Pursuant to paragraph 85(2.1)(*b*), there is an addition to the paid-up capital of any class of shares of the transferee corporation where dividends are subsequently paid. The addition is equal to the amount of a deemed dividend paid on the redemption or reduction of the paid-up capital, less the amount of the dividend that would have been paid if there had been no paid-up capital reduction under paragraph 85(2.1)(*a*). However, the addition is restricted to the amount of the previous paid-up capital reduction.

The purpose of paragraph 85(2.1)(*b*) is to ensure that the paid-up capital reduction will be reversed to the extent that dividends are subsequently deemed to be paid on the shares of the class of shares subject to the previous paid-up capital reduction.

Other Income Tax Restrictions

There are a number of other specific provisions in the Act which may come into play on the transfer of assets into a corporation. Some of these may effectively restrict the form and amount of capital that can be received in the course of a transfer to a corporation. These restrictions are not necessarily contained in section 85 itself; rather, they are general application provisions that may arise on any transfer to a corporation. The most important of these is described below.

The Corporate Attribution Rules

The corporate attribution rules may apply when assets are transferred or loaned (directly or indirectly) by an individual to a corporation, and one of the main purposes of the transfer or loan may reasonably be considered to have been to reduce the individual's income and benefit (directly or indirectly) as a "designated person" in respect of the individual. For further discussion, reference should be made to "Corporate Attribution Rules" in Chapter 4.

Subsections 15(1) and 84(1) — Receiving More than is Transferred

The paid-up capital of a particular class of shares should not exceed the increase in the value of the company's net assets as a result of the transfer; otherwise, there will be a deemed taxable dividend in the amount of the excess pursuant to subsection 84(1). The amount of the deemed dividend will be added to the cost of the shares on which the dividend is deemed to have been paid, pursuant to paragraph 53(1)(*b*).

If the increase in non-share consideration received as a result of the transfer exceeds the value of property transferred into the corporation, subsection 15(1) will be operative, with a resultant taxable benefit to the transferor. The amount of the benefit will be added to the cost base of the non-share consideration, under the provisions of subsection 52(1).

It should be noted that the subsection 15(1) benefit will not be treated as a dividend but as a fully taxable benefit where the transferor is a Canadian resident; however, paragraph 214(3)(*a*) would result in a deemed dividend in the case of a non-resident transferor, so that withholding tax will be exigible under Part XIII of the Act.

If both shares and other considerations are received in respect to property transferred to a corporation, a deemed dividend will arise under subsection 84(1) to the maximum possible extent. Any remaining excess will be taxable under subsection 15(1).

The following is a numerical example of the interaction between subsections 15(1) and 84(1):

Assumptions:

Fair market value of assets transferred	$ 500
Paid-up capital of shares issued	1,000
Fair market value of non-share consideration	1,200

84(1) Deemed Dividend:

Paid-up capital increase	1,000
84(1) net asset increase, if any ($500-$1,200)	NIL
84(1) deemed dividend	$ 1,000

15(1) Income Amount:

Fair market value of non-share consideration	$ 1,200
Fair market value of assets transferred	$ 500
15(1) income account (the net asset decrease)	$ 700

Benefit on Related Person — Paragraph 85(1)(e.2)

Where there is more than one shareholder of the transferee corporation, paragraph 85(1)(*e*.2) may impose some harsh tax consequences where the value of the assets transferred to the corporation exceeds the value (immediately after the disposition) of all consideration received as a result of the transfer. In addition, it must be "reasonable" to regard any part of such excess as a benefit that the transferor desired to have conferred on a related person, other than a corporation that was a wholly owned corporation of the taxpayer immediately after the disposition.

For the purposes of this provision, the meaning of "wholly owned corporation" is defined in subsection 85(1.3) as a corporation all of the issued and outstanding shares of the capital stock of which (except for directors' qualifying shares) belong to the taxpayer, a corporation that is a wholly owned corporation of the taxpayer, or any combination thereof.

If the provision is operative, the amount that is elected to be the proceeds of disposition under the section 85 election will be increased by the amount that could reasonably be regarded as the benefit. Consequently, an immediate gain could result. The cost amount of the transferred asset will also be increased by the same amount;

however, a corresponding increase in the adjusted cost base of the share consideration received by the transferor will not occur. As a result, there will be additional exposure to a taxable gain on the subsequent disposition of such shares.

As noted previously, paragraph 85(1)(*e*.2) may apply where it is reasonable to regard the discrepancy between the fair market value of property transferred to the corporation over the consideration received as a benefit the taxpayer desired to have conferred on a person related to the taxpayer. In many or most situations, of course, the transferee corporation will be such a related person. Therefore, if the value of the consideration taken back on the transfer is inadequate, it is arguable that the provision may be triggered. The Technical Amendments to the Act of July 13, 1990 allow an exception in respect of a corporation that was a "wholly owned corporation" of the taxpayer immediately after the disposition. Accordingly, it would appear that anything less than 100% ownership (ignoring directors' qualifying shares) could result in the potential application of this provision.

Generally speaking, if the corporation is solvent and issues retractable preferred shares which may be redeemed at any time (and the corporation is precluded from making distributions to its shareholders that would render the corporation unable to redeem the preference shares), the shares are usually considered to have a value equal to the redemption amount. However, a prudent practitioner may wish to take further steps to assure a fair market value equivalent, rather than relying on the retraction feature alone.[35]

In addition, it will, of course, be desirable to substantiate the value of the transferred assets via a *bona fide* valuation. Furthermore, the shares taken back (which, for the reasons mentioned previously, will typically be retractable at the fair market value of the transferred assets) should be the subject of an adjustment clause whereby, in the event of a dispute with the CRA, the retraction amount would be varied accordingly.[36]

At the Revenue Canada Round Table presented at the fall 1985 Canadian Tax Foundation Conference, the CRA expressed its views on the efficacy of independent valuations and, inferentially, price adjustment clauses, as follows:

> Where the fair market value of a transferred property is ultimately determined to be in excess of the fair market value of the consideration received in exchange therefor, the provisions of paragraph 85(1)(*e*.2) may apply notwithstanding that the taxpayer had obtained an independent valuation.

> The Department will only consider the application of paragraph 85(1)(*e*.2) if its valuation was significantly different from the taxpayer's valuation.

> Whether the taxpayer intended a gift is a question of fact and while an independent valuation may be an indication that no gift was intended, all factors would have to be considered. A price adjustment clause is usually employed by taxpayers to ensure that their intention of transferring the property for fair market value consideration is in fact achieved and paragraph 85(1)(*e*.2) will not apply.

---

[35] For a discussion of the issues related to a valuation of preferred shares in this context, see Richard M. Wise, "The Valuation of Preferred Shares Issued on a Section 85 Rollover", *Canadian Tax Journal*, March-April 1984, page 239.

[36] Adjustment clauses providing for the issuance or a cancellation of additional shares should be avoided, at least in the eyes of the CRA; for an example of a price adjustment clause, see the "Asset Sale Indenture" at p. 215.

It should be noted that the views expressed above related to the former terminology contained in paragraph 85(1)(*e*.2), in which the application of the provision depended on there being a "gift" rather than a "benefit" to a taxpayer.[37]

Capital Gains Anti-Avoidance Rules

Consideration should be given to subsections 110.6(8) and (9) which could result in the denial of the capital gains exemption on shares of the corporation. Subsection 110.6(8) will be operative where it may reasonably be considered that a significant portion of the capital gain is attributable to the fact that dividends were not paid on a share (other than a prescribed share) of a corporation or that dividends paid on such a share were less than 90% of the "average annual rate of return" for the year or any preceding taxation year. Subsection 110.6(9) specifies rules with respect to the "average annual rate of return", by reference to the annual return that a "knowledgeable and prudent investor" would expect to receive in the particular year under certain circumstances. (Reference should be made to the exact wording of this subsection.)

As will be apparent from an examination of these anti-avoidance provisions, the rules in this respect are somewhat vague and ill-defined. It is possible, however, that they could apply in a wide variety of circumstances in which shares are taken back on a transfer of assets to a corporation.

An exception to these rules applies in the case of a so-called "prescribed share" as defined in Regulation 6205. It should be noted, however, that most types of shares with restrictions or special features would not likely be prescribed shares, and therefore not eligible for the exception to the anti-avoidance rules.

Regulation 6205 contains exemptions in respect of estate freeze situations. (For further discussion, reference should be made to Chapter 3.)

Regulation 6205 also contains exceptions whereby prescribed share status may be achieved with respect to certain rights relating to retraction, redemption, or loss protection, or minimum earnings may be exempted if they arise by virtue of a qualifying shareholder's agreement. This refers to an agreement amongst shareholders of a private corporation who own more than 50% of its issued and outstanding share capital having full voting rights under all circumstances, provided that the corporation is a party to such an agreement.[38]

If "prescribed share" status is to be achieved, so as to pre-empt the application of the anti-avoidance rules in subsections 110.6(8) and (9), it is recommended that the provisions of Regulation 6205 be reviewed in detail.

Subsection 69(11)

Subsection 69(11) is an anti-avoidance rule that is intended to prevent a vendor from disposing of property on a tax-deferred basis as part of a series of transactions

---

[37] For discussion on price adjustment clauses, see "Valuation Issues" above at p. 45 and later in Chapter 6.

[38] See Regulation 6205(3)(*d*).

or events, one of the main purposes of which is to obtain the benefit of tax-loss deductions or other entitlements (including any balance of undeducted outlays, expenses or other amounts) available to a "non-affiliated" person in respect of a subsequent disposition of the property with respect to which arrangements are made within three years of the original disposition.[39] In general terms, one corporation will only be "affiliated" with another corporation if that other corporation is controlled by the same person(s) and/or the spouse(s) of the person(s) who control the other corporation. The provision will be applicable where a taxpayer disposes of property as part of a series of transactions for proceeds of disposition of less than fair market value, included by virtue of deemed proceeds pursuant to a rollover, and it may reasonably be considered that one of the main purposes was to obtain the benefit of such tax accounts from a non-affiliated person; if so, the vendor is then deemed to have disposed of the property at fair market value.

For example, if not for this provision, a property might be rolled into a non-affiliated corporation (e.g., under section 85), followed by the triggering of the accrued gain after the roll, which would then be sheltered by the non-affiliated corporation's tax losses. Where the provision applies, subsection 69(11) denies the benefit of the rollover on the original disposition by deeming the vendor's proceeds of disposition to be equal to the fair market value of the disposed property.

Tax proposals originally announced on April 25, 1995 amended subsection 69(11) as follows:

- to deny the rollover on the original disposition where one of the main purposes of the series of transactions is to use the *tax-exempt* status of any person to shelter from tax, under Part I of the Act, any income arising on a subsequent disposition of the property;

- by removing the three-year limitation for the subsequent disposition of the property and replacing it with a provision which permits the subsection to apply if arrangements for the subsequent disposition have been made within the three-year period;

- to delete the reference to "specified person" (which in turn was based on the "related person" majority-interest-partner concepts) and to use instead the concept of "affiliated person" in proposed section 251.1.

The last-mentioned amendment is quite significant because "affiliated person" is considerably narrower than "related person". For example, a transfer to a parent or child's corporation would be to a related corporation but not an affiliated corporation. Accordingly, the amendments to this provision materially restrict the utilization of loss companies (and so on) in related party situations.

---

[39] For detailed commentary on the meaning of the term "affiliated persons" see p. 71.

For further discussion, reference should be made to "Don't Get Burned by Revised 69(11) When Utilizing Corporate Tax Losses Within the Family!" by Michael I. Atlas, C.A.[40] As noted by that author:

- The relevant time for determining whether or not the transferor is affiliated with the transferee corporation is immediately before the beginning of the series of transactions or events aimed at utilizing the corporation's tax accounts. Furthermore, under subsection 248(10) of the Act, a series of transactions or events includes "any related transactions or events completed in contemplation of the series".

- Subsection 69(11) will only apply if one of the main purposes of the transfer is to obtain the benefit of the transferee's tax accounts to shelter income that arises in connection with a disposition of the transferred property. It will not apply if the only purpose is to gain the benefit of such tax losses to shelter income generated from the ownership of the property (e.g., rents).

- Certain comments made by the CRA officials at a forum held as part of the annual tax conference of the Canadian Tax Foundation in November 1996 suggest that the changes to subsection 69(11) of the Act will have a bearing on interpreting whether or not the GAAR might be applied in general to loss utilization within affiliated rather than related groups.[41] In particular, according to the CRA, a transaction that results in a transfer of the benefits of tax losses between corporations not affiliated will generally be considered to be an abuse and be subject to attack under GAAR. Whether or not this interpretation is correct is another matter.

Subsection 69(13) provides special rules for the purpose of determining whether subsection 69(11) is applicable in respect of amalgamations or mergers.

Effect of Distribution from Surplus

The effect of the limitations on paid-up capital described previously will be to create additional surplus. This, of course, will enable further distributions to individual owner/managers as dividends, so as to provide an alternative to remuneration via salary or bonuses.

Where a corporation is a shareholder, such dividends will not usually give rise to a tax liability under Part I of the Act. However, there are a number of complications to be considered, including the following:

(a) Part IV tax liability may apply to the dividend unless the corporations are "connected". In addition, even if the corporations are connected, Part IV tax may arise if the payor corporation receives a dividend refund.

(b) Where a taxable dividend is received as part of a transaction or a series of transactions to effect a significant reduction in the capital gains that would have otherwise occurred on a sale or other disposition of assets to an

---

[40] *Tax Topics*, No. 1302, February 21, 1997.

[41] See, for example, paragraph 8 of IC 88-2.

unrelated person, the inter-corporate dividend could be transmogrified into a capital gain pursuant to subsection 55(2).

Deductibility of Financing Costs

If the transferor has previously incurred deductible financing costs which are related to the assets transferred to the corporation, care should be taken that the consideration received on the transfer is not in a form that may jeopardize the continued ability to take these deductions. (For further discussion, reference should be made to Chapter 6.)

Tax Characteristics of Assets Transferred and Consideration Received

When transferring assets to a corporation, it is important to examine the effect of the transfer on the assets transferred and received. Because there is an acquisition by a separate legal entity, the transfer could affect the future ability to claim capital-cost allowance, the transitional rules for pre-1972 property, the cost base, etc.

In this regard, the following provisions of the Act should be noted:

Effect of Transfer on Capital Gains Status

If a capital property is to be transferred to a corporation, followed shortly by another sale, it might be argued that the short holding period of the transferee corporation may jeopardize the asset's status as a capital property.

This issue has been addressed in a number of CRA (Revenue Canada) Round Table questions. Generally, the CRA's response has been fairly reassuring. For example, Q.49 of the 1984 CRA Round Table canvassed the CRA's then-current policy with respect to the treatment to be afforded to the income generated in the hands of a corporation that acquires capital property from an individual, who is its controlling shareholder, pursuant to section 85 of the Act, and within a very short time thereafter disposes of the property. The question went on to ask whether the property so acquired would constitute capital property to the corporation so that, in consequence, the gains incurred by the corporation upon the disposition of the property would be treated as capital gains.

The CRA indicated that it was prepared to accept the transfer pursuant to subsection 85(1) of the Act and to accept that the nature of the property transferred would not have changed solely as a result of the transfer. The Agency indicated that it is prepared to accept this general position with respect to an individual who transfers capital property to his or her corporation. However, the Agency went on to indicate that whether or not anti-avoidance provisions would be applicable to any such transfer could only be determined with respect to the facts of each particular case.[42]

A closely related issue arises from several cases, notably *Fraser v. M.N.R.*, 64 DTC 5224 (S.C.C.), wherein it has been indicated that, where non-capital assets are

---

[42] For similar questions, see 1980, Q.8; 1983, Q.24; and 1986, Q.20.

transferred to a corporation, the consideration received may not qualify as capital property, notably where the transferor intends to sell the consideration received shortly after the transfer, claiming capital gains status on the sale.

The CRA's position on this issue was canvassed in Q.20 of the 1986 Revenue Canada Round Table. The Agency responded by indicating that generally, if the sale of the capital property would have been on account of capital, then similarly the sale of the shares will be on account of capital. The nature of the property transferred and the reason for the transfer may, however, indicate that the gain on the share sales is not a capital gain. The CRA gave an example where a transferred property is depreciable property, and under these circumstances, indicated that the gain on the sale of shares may, depending on the circumstances, be on account of income, citing *Fraser (supra)*, *Bell-Isle v. M.N.R.*, 66 DTC 5100 (S.C.C.) and *Gibson Bros. Industries Ltd. v. M.N.R.*, 70 DTC 6190 (F.C.T.D.).

As noted in "Transfer of a Business for Shares" below, capital gains status is now deemed to occur where section 54.2 applies. Pursuant to this provision, where a person disposes of all or substantially all of the assets used in an active business to a corporation, the shares of the corporation received as consideration shall be deemed to be capital property of that person.

Transfer of a Business for Shares — Deemed Capital Property

Section 54.2 of the Act provides that where a person disposes of "all or substantially all" of the assets used in an active business to a corporation, the shares received in consideration shall be deemed to be capital property of that person. The purpose of this rule is to ensure that the sale of the business through the sale of the shares of a corporation to which the business was recently transferred is not treated as a sale on income account.

Accordingly, a parent corporation may transfer a separate business to a subsidiary and subsequently sell the shares of that subsidiary. If so, section 54.2 would normally apply, such that capital gains treatment would be available in respect of the corporation's shares. As a further example, an individual proprietor of an unincorporated business might transfer the business assets to a newly formed corporation in contemplation of a subsequent sale of all of the shares of that corporation. In that case, section 54.2 will generally apply to ensure that the shares received as consideration for the business will obtain capital gains treatment, and thus will be eligible (provided other conditions are met) for the lifetime capital gains exemption for shares of a small business corporation.

It should be noted that a prerequisite for the application of section 54.2 is that the shares must be issued in consideration for "all or substantially all" of the assets used in an active business. Section 54.2 is not intended to apply where a taxpayer sells indirectly, through the sale of the shares of a corporation, non-business assets or only some of the assets used in a business.

It should also be noted that the definition of "business" contained in subsection 248(1) has been amended to ensure that the disposition of assets used in adventure or concern in the nature of trade will not qualify for the application of section 54.2.

Stop-Loss Rules

The Act contains various "stop-loss" rules, which are designed to prevent the creation of tax losses through the transfer of assets within a "closely related" milieu. In 1995, the stop-loss rules were overhauled to make their application more consistent, as well as to prevent certain perceived abuses to the pre-existing regime. As a result of the changes, the stop-loss rules now potentially apply where there is a transfer to an "affiliated person". This definition is discussed at page 71; however, in the context of transfers to a corporation, the test relates to control (legal and *de facto*). Generally (but with exceptions), the thrust of the rules is that when loss property is transferred to an affiliated person, the potential loss "sticks" to the transferor to be crystallized when certain events occur.

Subsections 40(3.3)–40(3.5)

Subsections 40(3.3) and (3.4) set out rules that defer losses on certain dispositions of non-depreciable capital property.

Under subsection 40(3.3), these rules apply where:

- a corporation, trust or partnership has disposed of a non-depreciable capital property;

- the transferor or a person "affiliated" with the transferor acquires the transferred property or an identical property (either of which is termed the "substituted property") during the period that begins 30 days before and ends 30 days after the disposition; and

- at the end of that period, the transferor or an affiliated person owns the substituted property.

Where these conditions are met, subsection 40(3.4) provides that no loss may be recognized on the transfer. Instead, any loss is deferred until the earliest of the following events:

- a subsequent disposition of the property to a person that is neither the transferor nor a person affiliated with the transferor (provided that, for 30 days after that later disposition, neither the transferor nor an affiliated person owns the substituted property or an identical property acquired after the beginning of the 61-day period described above);

- a deemed disposition of the property under section 128.1 (change of residence) or subsection 149(10) (change of taxable status);

- in the case of a corporation, an acquisition of the corporation's control;

- where the substituted property is a debt or a share, a deemed disposition under section 50; or

- where the transferor is a corporation, a winding-up of the transferor (other than a winding-up to which subsection 88(1) applies).

Further rules relating to subsections 40(3.3) and (3.4) are:

- They do not apply to transfers by individuals other than trusts, but can, as a result of the adoption of the definition of "affiliated persons" in section 251.1, have application to transfers of non-depreciable capital property transferred to individuals, corporations and partnerships in cases where former subsection 85(4) would not have applied.

- The denied loss is not added to either the cost of any shares held by the transferor or the transferee after the disposition, or to the cost to the transferee of the transferred property. Instead, the loss is preserved in the transferor's hands to be deducted as a loss from the transferred property under the circumstances described earlier, e.g., when it is no longer owned by an affiliated person, when it is deemed to have been disposed of under other provisions of the Act, or when control of a corporate transferor is acquired. (An exception arises in the case of shares of a corporation's capital stock that are disposed to that corporation.[43])

Subsection 40(3.3) and (3.4) apply to dispositions of property that take place after April 26, 1995, subject to certain grandfathering exceptions. Subsection 40(3.5) sets out certain special rules that apply for the purposes of the loss-deferral rule in subsection 40(3.4). For example, a right to acquire a particular property is normally deemed to be identical to the property itself.

Subsection 40(3.6) — Dispositions of a corporation's shares to the particular corporation

Although subsection 40(3.4) applies to most dispositions of non-depreciable capital property to affiliated persons, subsection 40(3.6) (which potentially applies to any taxpayer, as opposed to corporations, trusts or partnerships) applies special rules where the property is a share of the capital stock of a corporation and is disposed of to that corporation. Provided that the corporation acquiring its own shares is affiliated with the shareholder immediately after the acquisition, any loss that would otherwise arise with respect to the transaction is denied. Instead, the amount of that loss is added by paragraph 40(3.6)(b) to the adjusted cost base to the shareholder of other shares owned by it in the acquiring company.

One important instance in which subsection 40(3.6) may apply is where there is a *post-mortem* redemption/reacquisition of a corporation's shares that were formerly held by the decedent and are now held by the decedent's estate. It may be advisable to effect such a reacquisition within the first year of the estate in order to eliminate potential "double tax" exposure, i.e., there would be a deemed capital gain on the decedent's death if shares do not pass to a spouse or qualifying "spouse trust" and a second incidence of tax when the corporate level assets are sold/distributed.

[43] See subsection 40(3.6).

The reacquisition of shares, which would have a stepped-up cost base as a result of the deemed gain on death, would potentially allow a capital loss to the estate, which could be applied to the decedent's terminal period capital gain, pursuant to subsection 164(6).

Because subsection 40(3.6) could have unintended adverse consequences in such situations, new subsection 40(3.61) has recently been brought into force, providing that subsections 40(3.4) and (3.6) will not apply to any portion of an estate's capital loss carried back under subsection 164(6). (However, at time of writing, there has not been an analogous change to address the situation when the shares are held by a spouse trust, since subsection 164(6) would not be applicable in this instance (in this situation, there would, of course be an ordinary loss carryback instead). In this situation, subsection 40(3.6) may continue to have adverse results in some circumstances.) This new provision applies in respect of dispositions occurring after March 22, 2004. Subsection 40(3.6) applies to dispositions that take place after April 26, 1995, subject to certain grandfathering exceptions.

Subsection 14(12) — Stop-Loss for Eligible Capital Property

Subsection 14(12) is a provision similar to subsections 40(3.3) and (3.4) that applies where a corporation, trust or partnership has disposed of eligible capital property and would, but for this provision, have been entitled to claim a deduction under subsection 24(1) for any undeducted amounts remaining in its cumulative eligible capital pool in respect of that business. (In general terms, subsection 24(1) ordinarily permits such a deduction where the taxpayer has ceased to carry on the business and no longer owns any eligible capital property of value with respect to that business.)

Where these conditions exist, and a person affiliated with a transferor (or the transferor himself or herself) acquires the transferred property (or an identical property) within the period beginning 30 days before and ending 30 days after the disposition, and the transferor or an affiliated person owns the property at the end of the period, no deduction may be recognized on the transfer. Instead, such a deduction is deferred until the earliest of the following events:

- a subsequent disposition of the property to a person that is neither the transferor nor a person affiliated with the transferor (provided that, for 30 days after the subsequent disposition, neither the transferor nor an affiliated person owns either the substituted property or an identical property acquired after the beginning of the period described above);

- a change whereby the property no longer constitutes eligible capital property of a business of the transferor or an affiliated person;

- a "deemed disposition" of the property under section 128.1 (change of residence) or subsection 149(10) (change of taxable status);

- in case of a corporation, an acquisition of the corporation's control; or

- where the transferor is a corporation, a winding-up of the transferor (other than a winding-up to which subsection 88(1) applies).

Where subsection 14(12) applies, the transferor will be treated as continuing to own the eligible capital property of the business in respect of which the transferred property was used, thus enabling the transferor to continue to claim a deduction under paragraph 20(1)(*b*) in respect of the remaining eligible capital property pool, and to claim a loss for any portion of the pool that remains undeducted when any of the events described above occur.

Transfers by individuals — The "superficial loss rules"

The foregoing provisions do not pertain to transfers of loss items by individuals (except for subsection 40(3.6)). In the case of capital properties, however, the "superficial loss rules" may apply.

Pursuant to section 54, a "superficial loss" in respect of a particular capital property potentially arises where:

(a) during the period that begins 30 days before and ends 30 days after the disposition, the taxpayer or a person who is affiliated with the taxpayer acquires a property ("substituted property") that is or is identical to the particular property (an identical property normally includes a right to acquire the particular property); and

(b) at the end of that period, the transferor or an affiliated person owns or has a right to acquire the substituted property.

There are a number of exceptions to the application of the superficial loss definition, including where subsection 40(3.4) applies. In other words, the application of this provision will pre-empt the "superficial loss rules". However, as stated previously, subsection 40(3.4) does not apply to a transfer by an individual. Accordingly, where an individual transfers a capital loss item to an affiliated person, the "superficial loss rules" would potentially apply.

The significance of the application of the superficial loss rules is that — unlike most of the other stop-loss rules that may apply — the disallowed loss is added to the cost base of the transferred property, pursuant to paragraph 53(1)(*f*), rather than "sticking with" the transferor pending the occurrence of certain events.

This tax treatment would apply, for example, where a non-depreciable capital property in a loss position is transferred by an individual to a corporation controlled by the transferor individual or a corporation controlled by the spouse of the transferor, since the transferor and the corporation would be "affiliated persons" under these circumstances.

☞ **Another stop-loss rule may apply to the disposition of a debt obligation where the transferor, transferee, and debtor are in related party circumstances.**[44]

---

[44] See paragraphs 40(2)(*e*.1), 53(1)(*f*.1) and (*f*.11).

Subsection 13(21.2) — Stop-loss for depreciable property

Subsection 13(21.2) applies on the transfer by a person or partnership of a depreciable property whose tax cost (see below for further discussion) is greater than the amount that would otherwise be the transferor's proceeds from the transfer. Where these conditions exist, and a person affiliated with the transferor (or the transferor itself) holds or has a right to acquire the property 30 days after the disposition, no loss can be recognized on the transfer.[45] Instead, such a loss is deferred until the earliest of the following events:

- a subsequent disposition of the property to a person that is neither the transferor nor a person affiliated with the transferor (provided that neither the transferor nor an affiliated person acquires or has a right to acquire the property within 30 days after that later disposition);

- a change in the property's use from income-earning to a non-income-earning purpose;

- a "deemed disposition" of the property under section 128.1 (change of residence) or subsection 149(10) (change of taxable status);

- in the case of a corporation, an acquisition of a corporation's control; or

- in the case of a corporation, a winding-up of the transferor (other than under subsection 88(1)).

The tax cost of a depreciable property is, for the purposes of this rule, treated as being the proportion of the undepreciated capital cost of the class to which the property belongs, so that the value of the property is of the value of all properties in the class.

When subsection 13(21.2) applies to deny the loss, the amount by which that tax cost exceeds the amount that would otherwise be the transferor's proceeds of disposition of the transferred property is treated as the capital cost of a property, of the same class as that from which the property came, and acquired by the transferor before the taxation year in which the transfer took place. This new property will be treated as being owned by the transferor until the earliest of the events described above. As a result, the transferor will be permitted to claim capital cost allowance (CCA) after the transfer on the difference between the transferred property's tax cost and the transferor's proceeds of disposition otherwise determined. As well, any portion of the difference not claimed as CCA may be eligible for recognition as a terminal loss, when any of the events described above occurs, provided the transferor has no other properties of the same class.

Subsection 13(21.2) replaced subsection 85(5.1) of the Act and differs from the latter in the following material respects:

- Subsection 13(21.2) can, as a result of the "affiliated person" definition (see below) have application to depreciable property transfers to individuals,

---

[45] For the meaning of "affiliated persons", see section at p. 71.

corporations and partnership in cases where section 85(5.1) would not have applied.

- Subsection 13(21.2) does not pass the excess of tax cost over a property's value on to the transferee but instead retains this excess in the transferor's hands, to be "amortized" as CCA and (to the extent of any "unamortized" portion) deducted as a terminal loss.

Paragraph 13(21.2)(f) clarifies the result where a transferor partnership ceases to exist after a disposition but before any of the events that put an end to its deemed ownership of the notional depreciable property have occurred.

Paragraph 13(21.2)(g) provides that the "subsequent owner" of the transferred property, i.e., the transferor or a person affiliated with the transferor, is treated for the purposes of determining any potential recapture with respect to the transferred property as having the same capital cost of the property as it had to the transferor, and as having deducted, as CCA in previous years, the amount by which the capital cost of the transferred property exceeds the property's value at the time of disposition.

Subsection 18(13)–(16) — Stop-loss for adventures in the nature of trade and money lenders

Subsections 18(13) and (14) respectively set out the conditions under which certain losses of money lenders and adventurers in trade are deferred. Subsection 18(15) of the Act describes the loss deferral itself.

Pursuant to these provisions, any loss that would otherwise be deductible with respect to a property will be deductible by the transferor upon the first occurrence of any of the following events:

- a subsequent disposition of the property to a person that is neither the transferor nor a person affiliated with the transferor (provided that for 30 days after that subsequent disposition neither the transferor nor an affiliated person owns either the substituted property or an identical property acquired after the beginning of the period described above);

- a "deemed disposition" of the property under section 128.1 (change of residence) or subsection 149(10) (change of taxable status) of the Act;

- in the case of a corporation, an acquisition of the corporation's control; or

- where the transferor is a corporation, a winding-up of the transferor (other than a winding-up under subsection 88(1) of the Act).

The subsection applies where the taxpayer is "affiliated" with the transferee — using the tests set out in section 251.1 of the Act.[46]

See Appendix C at the end of this volume for a more detailed discussion of the stop-loss rules in an article by Michael Goldberg and Samantha Prasad of Minden Gross LLP.

---

[46] For further discussion, reference should be made to the "Affiliated Persons" section on p. 71 in this chapter.

"Affiliated persons"

As mentioned previously, the stop-loss rules will apply where there is a transfer to an "affiliated person". This term is defined in section 251.1 and is somewhat reminiscent in its complexity to the association rules. Paragraphs 251.1(1)(*a*) and (*b*) provide that affiliated persons include:

- an individual and spouse or common-law partner of the individual. It should be noted that the "affiliated persons" concept includes a spouse, but does not include a child;

- a corporation, and:

  (i) a person by whom the corporation was controlled;

  (ii) each member of an affiliated group of persons by which the corporation is controlled; and

  (iii) a spouse of a person described in (i) or (ii) above.

Two or more corporations

According to paragraph 251.1(1)(*c*), two corporations will be affiliated if:

- each corporation is controlled by a person, and the person by whom one corporation is controlled is affiliated with the person by whom the other corporation is controlled;

- one corporation is controlled by a person, the other corporation is controlled by a group of persons, and each member of that group is affiliated with that person; or

- each corporation is controlled by a group of persons, and each member of each group is affiliated with at least one member of the other group.

Corporation and partnership

Paragraph 251.1(1)(*d*) provides rules whereby a corporation and a partnership will be affiliated. This will be the case if the corporation is controlled by a particular group of persons, each member of which is affiliated with at least one member of a "majority interest group of partners" of the partnership, and each member of that majority-interest group is affiliated with at least one member of the particular group.

According to subsection 251.1(3), "majority interest group of partners" means a group of persons, each of whom has an interest in the partnership such that:

- if one person held the interests of all members of the group, that person would be a majority interest partner of the partnership; and

- if any member of the group were not a member, the test described in paragraph (*a*) would not be met.

Partnerships and partners

Paragraphs 251.1(1)(e) and (f) pertain specifically to affiliation between partnerships and partners. Pursuant to paragraph 251.1(1)(e), a partnership and a majority-interest partner of the partnership will be affiliated.

Two or more partnerships

Paragraph 251.1(1)(f) affiliates two partnerships, if:

- the same person is a majority interest partner in both partnerships;

- the majority interest partner of one partnership is affiliated with each member of a majority interest group of partners of the other partnership; or

- each member of a majority interest group of partners of each partnership is affiliated with at least one member of a majority interest group of partners of the other partnership.

Definitions

Subsection 251.1(3) includes the following definitions:

"Affiliated group of persons" means a group of persons each member of which is affiliated with every other member.

"Controlled" means "controlled directly or indirectly in any manner whatever". This is the so-called *de facto* control test per subsection 256(5.1).

According to subsection 251.1(4), for the purposes of section 251.1:

- persons are affiliated with themselves; and

- a "person" includes a partnership.

☞   Subsection 251.1(2) provides a special rule for the affiliation of corporations in relation to an amalgamation or merger. Where two or more corporations amalgamate or merge to form a new corporation, that new corporation and a predecessor corporation will in certain cases be treated as having been affiliated with one another. This deemed affiliation will arise where the new corporation and the predecessor would have been affiliated if the new corporation had existed before the amalgamation or merger, and if it had the same shareholders at that time as it had after the merger.

Trusts

Prior to 2005, the above rules applied to individuals, corporations and partnerships, and did not deal comprehensively with trusts. As a result of proposals introduced in the 2004 Budget that have now become law, subsection 251.1(1) has been expanded to deal more fully with trusts.

The new definition of "affiliated persons" now sets out general rules to determine when persons are affiliated with trusts and when trusts are affiliated with each other. These provisions state that a person will be affiliated with a trust if the person is a "majority interest beneficiary" of the trust or is affiliated with a "majority interest beneficiary" of the trust.

A "majority interest beneficiary" is defined as a person whose beneficial interest in the income (or capital) of the trust together with other affiliated persons has an aggregate fair market value that is greater than 50% of the fair market value of all the income (or capital) interests in the trust at that time.

Moreover, two trusts will be affiliated with each other if a "contributor" to one trust is affiliated with the "contributor" to the other trust; and

- the majority interest beneficiary of one trust is (or is affiliated with) a majority interest beneficiary of the other trust;
- a majority interest beneficiary of one trust is affiliated with each member of a majority interest group of beneficiaries of the other trust; or
- each member of a majority interest group of beneficiaries of each trust is affiliated with at least one member of a majority interest group of beneficiaries of the other trust.

A "contributor" includes a person who has made a loan or transfer of property, whether directly or indirectly in any manner whatsoever, to or for the benefit of a trust. However, where a person who deals at arm's length with a trust and is not a majority interest beneficiary makes a loan at a reasonable rate of interest or where the transfer is made for fair market value, the person will not be a contributor for these purposes.

A "majority interest group of beneficiaries" means a group of persons, each of whom is beneficially interested in the trust such that if one person held all of the interests of the group, that person would be a majority interest beneficiary of the trust and if any member of the group were not a member, the above requirement would not be met.

In addition, there are certain deeming rules to make certain determinations. In the case of a discretionary trust, the affiliated person rules will apply as between a person and a trust as if any discretion of any person in respect of the trust had been fully exercised (or not exercised as the case may be) in determining the rights of the person. Further, for purposes of applying these rules, a person's beneficial interest in a trust will be disregarded in determining whether such person deals at arm's length with the trust if, in the absence of such interest, the person would be considered to be at arm's length with the trust.

Subsection 85(5) — "Inheritance" of Original Cost For Depreciable Property

Subsection 85(5) applies where the transferor's capital cost exceeds the proceeds of disposition otherwise determined. Where the subsection is operative, the original capital cost of the depreciable property will be the same amount as applicable to the original transferor. The excess is deemed to have been taken by the transferee as capital cost allowance, leaving the transferee corporation with exposure to recaptured capital cost allowance.[47] Subsection 85(5) is potentially applicable to any situation covered in subsections 85(1) and 85(2).[48] (See, however, subparagraph 13(7)(e)(iii), discussed below.)

Paragraph 13(7)(e) — Non-Arm's Length Transfers of Depreciable Property

Paragraph 13(7)(e) of the Act sets out special rules that limit the transferee's cost of depreciable property (and thus the depreciation base) where such property is transferred between persons not dealing at arm's length.

In general, the transferee's capital cost of the property is deemed to be equal to the aggregate of the cost (or capital cost) of the property to the transferor plus the taxable portion of the transferor's capital gains — currently $1/2$ of the amount by which the transferors' proceeds of disposition exceeds the cost (or capital cost) of the property — to the extent that a capital gains exemption related to the gain was not claimed under section 110.6.

Subparagraph 13(7)(e)(iii) provides a special rule where a taxpayer acquires depreciable property in a non-arm's length transaction and his capital cost of the property at the time of the acquisition is less than the vendor's cost or capital cost (as applicable). In this case, for the purposes of computing recapture on a subsequent disposition, the difference between the purchase price and the vendor's capital cost of the property is treated as having been claimed by the purchaser as capital cost allowance. Accordingly, the transferor's original cost is potentially subject to recapture.

As can be seen in the discussion of subsection 85(5) above at page 73, the provision is very similar to subsection 85(5) whereby the transferee will "inherit" the transferor's original cost for recapture purposes in any situation covered by subsections 85(1) or (2). Accordingly, the "cost inheritance" rule for depreciable property will apply to non-arm's length situations as well.

---

[47] Subsection 85(5.1) provides a similar concept, applicable to apprentices' tools transferred to the corporation.

[48] Subsection 85(5) does not apply to the calculation of capital gains. While this gives rise to a double tax exposure when the property is disposed of by the corporation, the CRA appears to have adopted a lenient assessment policy in this respect. See "Double Tax Issues on Section 85 Rollovers" by Stuart Bollefer that appeared in CCH's *Tax Topics*, Number 1532, July 19, 2001.

Eligible Capital Grinds

Similar provisions in respect of eligible capital are contained in the December 20, 2002 technical amendments.[49]

Paragraph 85(1)(i) — Taxable Canadian Property

Paragraph 85(1)(*i*) provides that where property transferred to a corporation on the section 85 election is taxable Canadian property, all of the shares of the transferee corporation received as consideration for the transferred asset shall be deemed to be taxable Canadian property.

In this context, however, this provision has limited significance since, pursuant to the definition of taxable Canadian property in subsection 248(1), a share of a non-public corporation resident in Canada will be taxable Canadian property in any event. (It would be more significant if assets are transferred into a public company.)

Preservation of the Tax-Free Zone — ITARs 26(5.2) and 20(1.2)

Subsections 26(5.2) and 20(1.2) of the *Income Tax Application Rules* preserve the tax-free zone in respect of pre-1972 assets for non-depreciable capital property and depreciable property of a prescribed class, respectively, when these assets are transferred via section 85.

Although the benefit of the tax-free zone carries forward to assets transferred under section 85, there is no analogous rule that applies to the consideration received from the transferee corporation on the transfer of these assets. In other words, the assets received will be considered to be post-1971 property.

Assume, for example, that a taxpayer transfers capital property having an original cost of $20, a V-day value of $100, and a value of $140 at the time of the transfer in return for common shares of the transferee corporation. In this case, the maximum elected amount which would avoid a taxable gain will be $100; this is the adjusted cost base to the transferor, taking the special V-day rules into account. Thus the shares received on the transfer would have a cost base of $100. If the value of the transferred asset were to decline below $100, the transferee corporation's adjusted cost base on a subsequent disposition would also fall below $100, by virtue of the V-day rules. Nevertheless, the $100 cost base of the consideration received on the transfer would continue to be applicable.

Loss of V-day Protection — Pre-1972 Depreciable Property

Where real estate and other depreciable property acquired before 1972 is transferred to a corporation, practitioners should be aware that the result of the transfer could be the loss of the V-day protection with respect to the shares of the corporation to which the transfer was made.

The reason is that if the depreciable asset's V-day value (i.e., at the end of 1971) has increased over its original cost, the elected amount may nevertheless have to be

---

[49] Variable A of the definition of cumulative eligible capital in subsection 14(5) is subject to grandfathering relief.

restricted to the undepreciated capital cost of the asset; otherwise, there would be recaptured depreciation with respect to the transferred asset. The elected amount would then form the cost base of the shares taken back on the transfer. There is no provision to "flow through" the V-day value of the transferred property to the shares of the transferee corporation.

Example:

Consider a situation where a building was purchased for $500,000 prior to 1972 and is now to be transferred to a corporation pursuant to subsection 85(1) of the Act. The UCC of the building at the time of the transfer is $100,000. The fair market value of the building at the end of 1971 is $1,000,000 and the current fair market value of the building is also $1,000,000.

In order to avoid recaptured depreciation, it would be necessary to elect at $100,000 under subsection 85(1). This would then form the adjusted cost base of the shares taken back on the transfer. Although the V-day protection would flow through to the transferee corporation under these circumstances,[50] this would not be the case with respect to the shares of the transferee corporation received by the transferor.

Accordingly, a subsequent disposition of the corporation's shares would carry tax exposure based on the difference between the deemed or actual proceeds and the elected amount of $100,000, thus effectively eradicating the V-day protection with respect to the shares.

Obviously, this result can be a significant deterrent to estate freezes involving personally held pre-1972 depreciable property which has appreciated in value to V-day. In this case, the benefits of the freeze would have to be weighed against the increased tax exposure due to the effects described above.

Retention of CCA and Other Characteristics

Because of the fact that the transferee corporation will be different from the transferor, depreciation and other characteristics of the transferred asset may be altered in the process. In order to ameliorate such effects, a number of Regulations are directed toward the preservation of pre-existing CCA characteristics, including the following:

Regulation 1102(14) preserves the pre-existing classes of assets transferred from a person with whom the acquiring taxpayer was not dealing at arm's length (otherwise than by virtue of a right referred to in paragraph 251(5)(*b*)); the Regulation will also apply to property acquired in the course of a "butterfly" reorganization (i.e., to which paragraph 55(3)(*b*) applies). If the property was considered to be a "separate prescribed class", this too will carry over to the transferee corporation.

Regulation 1101(1)(*ad*) provides that where a rental property was exempt from the rules creating separate classes for rental properties costing $50,000 or more, the property will continue to be so exempt if it is transferred from a person with whom the acquiring taxpayer was not dealing at arm's length (otherwise than by virtue of a right referred to in paragraph 251(5)(*b*)), or acquired in the course of a "butterfly" reorganization (i.e., to which paragraph 55(3)(*b*) applies).

---

[50] See ITARS 26(5) and 26(5.2)

If the same prerequisites are met, if the property acquired would otherwise be a "leasing property" of the taxpayer (and therefore subject to the "stop-loss" rules in respect of leasing property), Regulation 1100(19) stipulates that it shall be deemed not to be a "leasing property" if, immediately prior to the acquisition, it was exempt from the stop-loss rules by virtue of Regulation 1100(18) to (20).

If the same prerequisites are met, Regulation 1100(2.2) may preserve the rapid write-off if available to assets in certain classes as well as ameliorate the effect of the "half-year" rule which would otherwise apply in respect of the acquisition by the transferee.

As might be expected, Regulation 1102(20) contains an anti-avoidance rule which is operative for the purposes of Regulations 1100(2.2), 1100(19), 1101(1)(ad) and 1102(14). It provides that where a taxpayer is considered to be in a non-arm's length relationship as a result of a transaction or series of transactions, the principal purpose of which may reasonably be considered to cause the above provisions to apply in respect of the acquisition of a property, the taxpayer shall be considered to be in an arm's length relationship.

Effect on CCA Claims

This should be reviewed carefully. For example, the transferor cannot claim capital cost allowance if the assets are transferred prior to year end. If the transferee's taxation year is less than 12 months, CCA claims would have to be pro-rated.

According to paragraph 3 of Interpretation Bulletin IT-179R, the CRA has indicated that, where the transferee is precluded from claiming capital cost allowance because of a "mid-year" transfer, this would be acceptable as grounds for the transferor to change its fiscal period to end on the day immediately before the transfer. However, this acceptance is limited to situations where the transferor and transferee are not entitled to claim CCA on a particular property for a common time period. In any event, taxpayers must still request a change of fiscal period in the normal manner, prior to the transfer.

Loss of Reserves

Where the receivables give rise to reserves under paragraph 20(1)(*n*) or subparagraph 40(1)(*a*)(iii), a section 85 election will negate the right to take a reserve.

Trapped Losses

An unincorporated business, if unsuccessful, may provide relief to the individual given the ability to apply the losses against other sources of income. If, on the other hand, the business has been incorporated, losses might become trapped in the corporation and not be available to shelter personal income.

Subsections 20(24) and (25) — Payment to Transferee to Continue Services

Subsections 20(24) and 20(25) provide rules to deal with the situation where a taxpayer (e.g., the transferor) makes a payment to another person (e.g., the transferee corporation) in consideration for that other person undertaking to provide goods or services that the taxpayer had originally agreed to provide. The taxpayer would normally include in income the full sale price of the goods or services under paragraph 12(1)(*a*) and claim a reserve for the goods or services to be provided after the year end under paragraph 20(1)(*m*). Paragraph 20(24) permits the taxpayer to make payment to another party (i.e., the transferee corporation) which undertakes to provide the goods or services in the future and, if the two parties jointly elect, the taxpayer making the payment may deduct that payment in computing income.

Double Tax Exposure

When assets are transferred into a corporation, there is potential for double tax, particularly when they are transferred on a tax-deferred basis pursuant to section 85 or otherwise, since the original tax cost of the transferred asset will generally apply to both the transferred asset and the cost base of the shares received in consideration thereof.

Very generally, the disposition of assets at the corporate level is designed to generate corporate surplus accounts, such as capital dividend and refundable-dividend-tax-on-hand accounts, which are designed to "tax pay" distributions to a corporation's shareholders, resulting in so-called "integration" of tax at the corporate and personal level. However, this result does not always occur. For example, a disposition of eligible capital property or depreciable business property that generates recaptured depreciation does not generate refundable tax balances.

Conversely, where shares are disposed of, rather than the corporate assets, there is only limited ability for the transferee to use the cost base to increase the tax cost of underlying assets or decrease taxes on the distribution of such property to shareholders. Accordingly, when the underlying assets are subsequently disposed of, there may be a second incidence of tax. In particular, double tax exposure can arise as a result of the general tax rule that there is a deemed disposition of shares of a corporation (and other assets) at fair market value on death (unless the assets pass to a spouse or a qualifying spouse trust).

For further discussion of double tax issues see Michael Goldberg and Samantha Prasad's article in Appendix C at the end of this volume.

Receivables Election — Section 22

If the incorporation of business assets involves the transfer of receivables, the transferor and transferee corporation may frequently file a section 22 election (Form T2022).

If a section 22 election is not filed, the sale of receivables in the course of a business transfer would normally be considered to be a capital transaction. As a result, any loss on the sale will usually be treated as a capital loss. The vendor will not be entitled to deduct a reserve for doubtful debts since he or she no longer retains the receivables at the end of the taxation year in which the sale takes place.

However, the previous year's reserve will be included in his income, as well as amounts received in respect of bad debts previously written off for tax purposes. However, the CRA allows the vendor to claim bad debt deductions under paragraph 20(1)(*p*) as of the date of sale.[51]

Similarly, the receivables normally become a capital asset to the purchaser, and losses on the realization of these accounts will normally be treated as capital items. Accordingly, the bad debt provisions of the capital gains rules (subsection 50(1), etc.) will usually apply, whereas the bad debt and doubtful accounts reserves will not be available.

The purpose of section 22 is to alleviate the harshness of this result. It allows the vendor to obtain a deduction reflecting the discount on the sale, and the purchaser to claim reserves for doubtful accounts and bad debt expenses as if he had previously carried on the business generating the debts.

In order to take advantage of section 22, the following prerequisites must be met:

- The vendor must have been carrying on a business (as defined in section 248(1) of the Act) in Canada.

- The vendor must have sold all or substantially all of the property used in carrying on the business.[52] Note that this may not necessarily apply to the assets of the corporation as a whole — the only the assets involved in carrying on a particular business within the corporation.[53]

- It appears that the transfer must include all "accounts receivable" (defined as debts that have been or will be included in computing the vendor's income for the year of sale or the previous year that are still outstanding, and debts arising from loans made in the ordinary course of business, if part of the vendor's ordinary business was the lending of money, provided that those debts are still outstanding).

- The purchaser must "propose" to continue the business which the vendor has been carrying on.

- The vendor and purchaser must have jointly executed an election in Form T2022 that the section will be applicable.

If these prerequisites are fulfilled, paragraphs 22(1)(*a*) to (*d*) provide a set of rules applicable to both the vendor and purchaser.

Rules applicable to vendor

As stated above, the rules essentially allow a vendor to receive a final deduction in recognition of the discount from the face value of the receivables whether or not a previous reserve has been allowed. Pursuant to paragraphs 12(1)(*d*) and (*i*), the

---

[51] See paragraph 7 of IT-188RSR.

[52] For the CRA's views on "all or substantially all", see paragraph 1 of IT-188RSR.

[53] For the department's views on separate businesses, see Interpretation Bulletin IT-206R.

vendor will have to include the previous taxation year's reserves as well as bad debts recovered (if any). However, paragraph 22(1)(*a*) allows an offsetting deduction equal to the difference between:

- the face value of debts sold (except those previously deducted as bad debts under paragraph 20(1)(*p*)); and
- the amount paid by the purchaser.

Rules applicable to purchaser

Under paragraph 22(1)(*d*), the final deduction received by the vendor must be included in computing the purchaser's income for the taxation year of sale. The provisions then allow the purchaser to claim reserves for doubtful accounts and bad debt expenses in respect of the receivables. Paragraph 22(1)(*c*) provides that the accounts receivable are deemed to have been included in the purchaser's income for the taxation year or a previous year. Technically, this allows the doubtful accounts and bad debt deductions to be taken, but no deductions may be taken by the purchaser under paragraph 20(1)(*p*) in respect of a debt on which the vendor has previously claimed a deduction.

Paragraph 22(1)(*d*) provides that any debt that was deducted by the vendor under paragraph 20(1)(*p*) as a bad debt but which is subsequently recovered by the purchaser will be included in the purchaser's income.

It should be noted that the fact that receivables are sold at their full face value (so that there is no terminal deduction claimed by the vendor) does not necessarily mean that a receivables election should not be filed. If, for example, unforeseen events result in a bad debt or doubtful allowance claim by the purchaser, the section 22 election will enable the purchaser to take a deduction.[54]

Manner of election

For the election to apply, it is necessary for the vendor and purchaser to jointly complete and execute an election in prescribed Form T2022.

It should be noted that section 22 does not specify a time limit for filing. However, in Interpretation Bulletin IT-188R, the CRA states that the election should be filed with the tax return in the year of sale.[55] At the 1991 conference for L'Association de Planification Fiscale et Financiére,[56] the CRA indicated that the election would be accepted before a notice of assessment for the year is issued or before the expiry of the time the taxpayer can object to the assessment for the year. However, the time for filing an election will not be extended to cover a subsequent reassessment.[57]

---

[54] See paragraph 22(1)(*c*) of the Act.

[55] See paragraph 4 of IT-188R.

[56] See *Tax Window Files*, Document 3M05110, Q.30.

[57] Technical Interpretation, Business and Publications Division, October 8, 1996 — see *Window on Canadian Tax*, CCH Canadian Limited, at ¶4394.

The amount stated in the election to be the consideration for the accounts receivable is final for tax purposes as far as the vendor and purchaser are concerned, and cannot later be altered.[58] However, this is not necessarily binding on the CRA and may be questioned on an assessment if it is considered not to reflect the facts of the sale, for example, when the face value of the debts sold is incorrectly stated, or when the consideration actually paid is different from that set out in the election as paid. If the vendor and purchaser are not dealing at arm's length and the fair market value of the accounts receivable sold was more or less than the consideration paid for them, paragraphs 69(1)(*a*) or (*b*) may be applied to the transaction.[59]

If the agreement of purchase and sale does not specify what part of the total consideration is allocated to accounts receivable, the CRA requires a reasonable allocation to be made between accounts receivable and other assets. It should be noted that the consideration received may include an assumption of the vendor's liabilities, which should also be allocated in a reasonable manner.

Other Consequences to Transferor and Transferee

It should be remembered that, irrespective of whether the business assets are transferred pursuant to section 85 of the Act, a purchase and sale of business assets is nevertheless involved, and may give rise to a host of tax and other considerations.

Tax consequences that may arise on the purchase and sale of business assets include, among others, the following.

Federal and Provincial Capital Tax

A number of provinces levy taxes on a corporation's capital (this usually includes paid-up capital, retained earnings and contributed surplus, shareholder and bank loans, and mortgages). The rates of capital tax are modest, especially in view of the fact that a reduction in the capital tax base is available in respect of various eligible investments (potentially including bonds, debentures, mortgages, and corporate equities). However, capital intensive businesses, real estate holding companies, etc., may find capital tax a more significant burden, especially since the tax is exigible irrespective of the profitability of the corporation.

 In the 2004 budget, Ontario announced the abolition of capital tax. The capital tax exemption is to increase from the former threshold of $5M, to increase to $15M in 2008. Starting in 2009, the rate will decrease from the current rate of .3% to .075% in 2011, with the elimination of the tax the following year.

---

[58] See subsection 22(2) of the Act.

[59] See IT-188R, paragraph 5.

In addition to this, in the 2003 federal Budget, the government announced the phase-out of capital tax as follows:

	2003	2004	2005	2006	2007
Rate	0.225%	0.200%	0.175%	0.125%	0.0625%
Capital deduction threshold ($ millions)	10	50	50	50	50

Further, the November 13, 2005 *Economic and Fiscal Update* proposed moving the repeal of federal capital tax forward to 2006.

Principal Business or Chief Source of Income Requirements

The transferee's eligibility to claim an unrestricted farm loss per section 31, or the "principal business corporation" exemption for the purposes of rental and leasing property restrictions, may differ from that of the transferor.

Clearance Certificates — Section 116

Where a non-resident disposes of taxable Canadian property pursuant to a section 85 election, it will still be necessary to comply with section 116 of the Act, particularly, subsections 116(5) and (5.3), under which the transferee is liable to remit 33 or 50 per cent of the "cost"/"amount payable" for the property (less the "certificate limit" where the transferor has obtained a "clearance certificate").

According to paragraphs 31 and 32 of Information Circular 72-17R5, the CRA's position is that it will not issue a clearance certificate unless the section 85 election form has been submitted along with the request. Because these forms are normally not prepared until well after the transaction is completed, this is obviously an onerous requirement. Apparently, however, the CRA has often been flexible and has accepted an agreement of purchase and sale that stipulates the parties' intention to elect under section 85 so as to effect the transfer on a fully tax-deferred basis.

The CRA has indicated that, where taxable Canadian property is transferred to a corporation under section 85, the "certificate limit" would be the elected amount for the purposes of section 85 (the shares received as consideration for such property transferred would be taxable Canadian property).[60]

Of course, the section 116 procedure comes into play only with respect to the types of property specified therein (notably, "taxable Canadian property" as defined in subsection 115(1) of the Act). Included, however, are such items as real property situated in Canada, the shares of a Canadian resident corporation (other than a public corporation as defined in the Act), and so on.[61]

---

[60] See CCH Canadian Limited's *Window on Canadian Tax*, ¶3416.

[61] For further discussion, see Andrew W. Dunn and Kimberley A. Nielsen, "Exchanges of Property for Shares: Section 85 — Part II", *Canadian Tax Journal*, Vol. 43, No. 1, at p. 502.

Non-Income Tax Considerations

The following are some other areas that should be addressed in respect of the transfer of assets to a corporation:

- Federal and provincial sales taxes.[62]

- Where there is a sale "in bulk" out of the usual course of business, bulk sales legislation may apply; unless the transferor makes adequate provision for the payment of its creditors, a creditor can have the transaction set aside.

- Shareholders' rights. Most corporate statutes provide shareholder protection in respect of asset sales.

  For example, subsection 184(3) of the *Ontario Business Corporations Act* provides that a sale, lease or exchange of substantially all of the property of a corporation other than in the ordinary course of the business requires shareholder approval by special resolution (two-thirds majority). Subsection 184(6) provides for special voting rights (i.e., if not ordinarily present) where a sale would affect a particular class or series of shares in a manner different from others. Shareholders who dissent on such a resolution may be entitled to relief under section 185 of the *Ontario Business Corporations Act*.

- Where accounts receivable that have been pledged as security are assigned pursuant to personal property securities legislation, a creditor may require a financing statement to be filed.

- Consideration should be given to restrictive covenants or consent clauses, e.g., in respect of the indebtedness of the transferor, leases, and so on.

- Where the result of the transaction could delay, hinder or defeat creditors, fraudulent conveyance and bankruptcy legislation should be reviewed.

- Does the purchase of assets gives rise to Investment Canada implications?

- Is there any impact in respect of government assistance?

- Can the transferee corporation carry on with the same name/business name?

- What is the impact on pension and other deferred income plans? Consider also the transfer of insurance and fringe benefits.

- Insurers (e.g., fire insurance) should be notified. Where appropriate, municipalities should be notified.

- Are there regulatory constraints in respect of the transfer of assets? This may include municipal licensing requirements, etc.

- Employment law considerations should be addressed.[63]

---

[62] See the following sections on the GST and Provincial Sales Tax.

[63] For discussion of some of these consequences, see "Transferring Assets to a Private Corporation", in *Taxation of Private Corporations and their Shareholders*, Canadian Tax Foundation, 3rd Edition, 1999.

Goods and Services Tax

As there is no overall symmetry between GST legislation and "rollovers" under the Act, the transfer of assets to a corporation often may give rise to Goods and Services Tax issues. Initially, therefore, it must be determined whether a particular transaction may be problematic in respect of GST. Accordingly, it is necessary to examine whether the transfer involves a taxable supply — that is, a supply made in the course of a "commercial activity" other than an "exempt supply".

An "exempt supply" may include the supply of "financial services" which, according to the definition contained in subsection 123(1) of Part IX of the *Excise Tax Act* (the "ETA"),[64] includes the "transfer of ownership of a financial instrument". A financial instrument, in turn, is defined to mean a debt security, an equity security, an interest in a partnership, and a number of other items, again as contained in the definition section. Accordingly, the transfer of shares, partnership interests, accounts receivable or cash (which is not a "supply") should not normally attract GST. However, the transfer of many other assets is potentially subject to GST. For example, intangibles (e.g., patents, trademarks, goodwill), inventory, real estate (which is subject to GST unless specific exemption applies), and so on.

If GST is potentially exigible, there are a number of exemptions that may apply. Notably, subsection 167(1) of Part IX of the ETA provides for an election to exempt the transaction from GST. It is potentially available where "all or substantially all of the property used in a commercial activity that forms all or part of a business carried on" by the transferor is involved.

The section 167 election is available where both the transferor and transferee are either registered or non-registered, or where the transferee is registered but the transferor is not. However, the election will not be available where the transferee is not registered and the transferor is. The scope of section 167 of the ETA has been broadened to include property used in non-commercial activities.[65]

The election (using Form GST 44, *Election Concerning the Acquisition of a Business or Part of a Business*) must normally be filed by the recipient, if a registrant, not later than the day on which a return is required to be filed for the recipient's reporting period in which the supply is made. Subsection 156(2) of the ETA provides for an exemption in respect of the supply of goods and services between members of a "qualifying group" of corporations or partnerships (using Form GST 25, *Closely Related Corporations and Canadian Partnerships*). The election eliminates GST on supplies of goods and services, other than on the sale of real property or on the supply of a property or a service not used "exclusively" in the commercial activities of the recipient. The election will be available where a "specified member" of a "qualifying group" files an election made jointly with the corporation that is also a specified member of the group. If the election is filed, every taxable supply between the two parties to the election (other than those mentioned above) shall be deemed to have been made for no consideration, while the election is in effect.

---

[64] R.S. 1985, c. E-15.

[65] For further discussion of GST in relation to a section 85 transfer, see Andrew W. Dunn and Kimberley A. Nielsen, "Exchanges of Property for Shares: Section 85 — Part II", *Canadian Tax Journal*, Vol. 43, No. 1, at pp. 512-513.

For the meaning of "specified member" of a "qualifying group", reference should be made to subsections 156(1) and 156(1.1) of the ETA, in respect of partnerships, and section 128 of the ETA, in respect of corporations. The form and filing of the election are provided for in subsection 156(3) of the ETA. The election may be revoked but may also cease to be effective if either party ceases to be a member of a "qualifying group" or ceases to be a "specified member" of such a group. The latter requirement may be problematic since the concept of a "specified member" requires that all or substantially all of its supplies be taxable supplies. It is possible that a large dividend or interest payment, being exempt supplies, may result in the "all or substantially all" requirement not being met.

A third election, contained in subsection 150(1), can be made jointly by any two corporations that are members of a "closely related group" of which a "listed financial institution" is a member. The election applies to deem every supply of services and property by way of lease, licence or similar arrangement between the two electing companies to be a financial service, as long as the election remains in force. As a result, all such supplies are classified as exempt supplies. However, the subsection 150(1) election does not generally apply to supplies of property transfers, nor to property held or services rendered by a member of a closely related group as a participant in a joint venture with another person where an election for joint reporting under section 273 of the ETA is in effect between the member and the other person. For the meaning of "listed financial institution", refer to section 123 of the ETA and paragraph 149(1)(*a*).[66]

Provincial Sales Taxes

Provincial sales taxes may also apply in respect of a transfer of property to a corporation. Obviously, the exigibility of such taxes requires a detailed review of the relevant provincial legislation. For example, section 2 of the *Retail Sales Tax Act of Ontario* (the "RSTA")[67] generally provides that every purchaser of tangible personal property ("TPP") shall pay the tax at the relevant rate (8% at time of writing) in respect of the consumption or use thereof. The tax may apply, for example, to machinery or office equipment. There are, however, exemptions for particular properties, including:

- inventory acquired for resale;
- real estate;
- fixtures;
- qualifying production machinery; and
- intangibles.

Other provinces have fairly similar rules; however, each transaction should be reviewed with respect to the appreciable provincial legislation.

---

[66] For further details on asset transfers and GST, reference should be made to Israel H. Mida, C.A., "The Goods and Services Tax and Corporate Matters", *1990 Canadian Tax Foundation Conference Reports*, at page 14:1 *et seq.*

[67] R.S.O. 1990, Chapter R.31.

Tax relief for transfers of assets between related persons is available under certain specific circumstances. Under the old Regulation 1013 of the RSTA, the exemption between related persons was somewhat limited and available only where tax-paid assets were not previously transferred on a tax-exempt basis under this Regulation. However, new legislation was proposed in the 2004 Ontario Budget and brought into force on December 13, 2004 to make the exemption somewhat more user-friendly. The modernized Regulation 1013 of the RSTA includes the following provisions:

Beneficial ownership — The definition of "wholly owned" ownership has been expanded to allow the exemption to be used within a corporate group. This is achieved by including direct and indirect beneficial ownership of shares of at least 95% of the stated share capital of all classes of shares of the corporation.

Transfers between related corporations — The restriction of transferring tax-paid assets only once among related corporations has been eliminated. Assets to be transferred would be considered eligible property (i.e., property on which tax has been paid under the Act) and thus no tax would be payable on any transfer of eligible property:

- from a person to a corporation wholly owned by that person;
- from a corporation to a person who wholly owns that corporation; or
- from a corporation to another corporation, provided both are wholly-owned by the same person.

To ensure the asset transfer is between *bona fide* related persons, the wholly owned relationship must continue for at least 180 days following the date of the transfer.

In order to be considered eligible property, and thus eligible for the tax-free transfer, the property must not have been originally acquired using an exemption under the Act or acquired tax-free as goods for resale. This will ensure that tax is paid once by the corporate group. However, if the corporation purchasing the assets is entitled to an exemption, such as for manufacturing or resale, that exemption will still be available.

Transfers between unrelated corporations — The new rules also address situations where the corporations are not wholly-owned by another corporation or individual. In these instances, tax may be pro-rated in the same manner as allowed for partners and partnerships. The new rules permit a tax-free transfer on the portion of assets transferred that relates to the proportion of the share capital owned on the transfer between:

- unrelated corporations, where the transferor owns shares of the purchaser either directly or indirectly;
- unrelated corporations, where the purchaser owns shares of the transferor either directly or indirectly; or
- an eligible shareholder to a corporation (or vice versa), where the eligible shareholder owns shares of the corporation either directly or indirectly. An

eligible shareholder is defined to be individual or partnership that directly or indirectly owns shares of the corporation, but does not wholly own the corporation.

Any shares used to calculate the portion of exemption must be held for at least 180 days after the asset transfer.

Upon the formation of a partnership, TPP transferred into the partnership by the partners is not taxable provided that it was tax-paid by the partner when acquired. During the life of the partnership, goods sold by a partner to the partnership are taxable, though the tax payable may be reduced based on the proportionate partnership interest of the seller if the partner paid tax when acquiring the goods. If a partner repurchases goods sold by her to the partnership, no tax is payable on the repurchase provided that the partner paid tax on the goods originally. TPP purchased by the partnership from a third party that is subsequently sold to one of the partners is taxable, though tax may be reduced based on the proportionate partnership interest of the purchasing partner, provided that the goods were tax-paid by the partnership.

Upon dissolution of a partnership:

- no tax is payable on goods transferred to the partners where the goods were originally supplied by the same partners and tax was paid on their acquisition;

- tax is payable on goods transferred to a partner where the goods were originally supplied to the partnership by a different partner; and

- tax is payable on tax-paid goods acquired by the partnership from a third party, though reduced based on the proportion of the acquiring partner's share of the partnership.

Exemption from retail sales tax is granted to transfers by bequest or for no consideration between family members or same-sex partners.[68]

Full exemption from retail sales tax is available for property transferred for consideration between a person and the person's spouse or same-sex partner upon the dissolution of their conjugal relationship.[69]

Land Transfer Taxes

Ontario land transfer tax also generally applies to transfers of land where deeds are registered. Regulation 563, section 1 of the *Land Transfer Tax Act (Ontario)* (the "LTTA"),[70] potentially provides for an exemption in respect of qualifying conveyances to "family farm corporations" or "family business corporations" as defined in the Regulation. This latter exemption, however, is more restrictive than it appears.

---

[68] Subsections 8(1) and 8(4) of the Act.

[69] Subsections 8(3) and 8(4) of the Act.

[70] R.S.O. 1990, Chapter L.6.

Section 3 of the LTTA provides for land transfer tax in respect of most disposi- tions of beneficial interest in land, that is, transfers of interests that are not regis- tered. Subsection 3(9) provides for transfers of beneficial interests in land between corporations which are "affiliates" as described in subsection 1(2) of the *Securities Act (Ontario)*.[71] To apply for the deferral, the transferee must furnish security for the tax (usually in the form of a letter of credit), and must give an undertaking that the property will be held within the "group" for at least three years after the disposition. If the deferral is granted, then upon satisfaction of the undertaking, the security will be returned with the result that the deferral effectively becomes an exemption from the tax.

Regulation 70/91 of the LTTA would also exempt so-called "butterfly" reorga- nizations — that is, those which are effected in accordance with paragraph 55(3)(*b*) — upon approval by the Ministry of Revenue.

Canada Pension Plan

A section 85 transfer will often involve the assignment of employees to the transferee corporation. Historically, if the transfer was made midway through a calendar year, both the employees and the employer must recommence CPP contri- butions as if the transferee were a new employer. Although the employees are entitled to a refund of over-contributions upon the filing of their T1 income tax return, there was no analogous relief for the employer. However, new legislation to correct this discrepancy has recently come into force, effective for years after 2003. Essentially the "successor employer" may take into account amounts paid, deducted, remitted, or contributed by the former employer in the year for an employee as if the amounts had been paid, deducted, remitted, or contributed by the successor employer.

Issues may also arise in respect of Workers' Compensation. Reorganization guidelines are contained in certain "Operational Policy Guidelines" released by the Workers' Compensation Board. Generally, a sale of shares, change of name, or mergers will not be problematic. Where a section 85 type transaction is involved, it appears that the WCB will look to certain tests, as outlined in the Guidelines, including whether:

- there is an arm's length transaction;
- the "new company" continues to employ the "old company's" workers;
- the same business continues to be carried on;
- the new company reports the wages of the old company; and
- the new company has the payroll records of the old company.

If the answer to the first question is no, and the answers to the remaining questions are yes, the WCB normally requires that the same file be retained by the new company.[72]

---

[71] R.S.O. 1990, Chapter S.5.

[72] See Document No. 08-03-07, July 25, 1997.

Accounting Consequences

There appear to be several options with respect to the accounting treatment where a section 85 rollover is involved. One option would be to ignore current values completely. Conversely, the transfer could involve a full recognition of fair market value (in which case alternatives pertaining to deferred taxes should be considered).

However, within the private-corporation context, at least, most section 85 rollovers involve "related-party transactions" under section 3480 of the *CICA Handbook*. According to paragraph 3840.04, a related party could include, for example:

(a) an enterprise that directly or indirectly, through one or more intermediaries, controls or is controlled by, or is under common control with the reporting enterprise;

(b) an individual who directly, or indirectly through one or more intermediaries, controls the reporting enterprise;

(c) the other party, when an investment is accounted by the equity or the proportionate consolidation method and the reporting enterprise is either the investor or the investee;

(d) with regards to management, any person(s) having authority and responsibility for planning, directing and controlling the activities of the reporting enterprise (usually including directors, officers and others fulfilling senior management functions);

(e) an individual having an ownership interest in the reporting enterprise that results in "significant influence" or "joint control"; or

(f) members of the immediate family of individuals described in paragraphs (*b*), (*d*) and (*e*) (including a spouse and dependants).

In most cases, section 3840 of the *CICA Handbook* will restrict the measurement of the transaction to the "carrying amount", that is to say, the amount of the item transferred as reported on the accounts of the transferor after adjustment (if any) for amortization or impairment in value.[73]

In some cases, however, the transaction could be measured at the "exchange amount", that is to say the amount of the consideration paid or received as established and agreed to by related parties.[74]

In determining whether a transfer between related parties is measured at the exchange amount, one first determines whether the transaction is in the "normal course of operations". However, in the context of a section 85 transaction, this would be very unusual. Pursuant to paragraph 3840.24 of the *CICA Handbook*, examples of transactions in the normal course of business include the sale or purchase of an inventory item, a sale or purchase of real estate by an enterprise that is in the business of selling real estate as part of its ongoing activities (such real estate would probably not be eligible for a rollover), and investing activities by an investment

---

[73] *CICA Handbook*, paragraph 3840.03(*a*).

[74] *CICA Handbook*, paragraph 3840.03(*b*).

company. According to the *CICA Handbook* paragraph 3840.27, examples of transactions not in the normal course of operations include the purchase and sale of capital assets, settlement of debts, and the issue or redemption of an enterprise's capital.

Accordingly, it would seem that a section 85 rollover would not typically be in the normal course of operations. Under these circumstances, a (non-monetary) related party transaction that has commercial substance which is not in the normal course of operations should be measured at the exchange amount when:

- the change in the ownership interests in the item transferred or the benefit of a service provided is substantive; and

- the exchange amount is supported by independent evidence.

For further discussion, reference should be made to paragraphs 3840.29 *et seq.* of the *CICA Handbook*.

Retractable Preferred Shares — Disclosure Rules

Section 3860 of the *CICA Handbook* requires the reclassification of retractable preferred shares as financial liabilities. However, Section 1300 of the *CICA Handbook*, relating to "differential reporting", has been finalized, allowing for partial differentiation in the application of GAAR by making available to qualifying enterprises specified exemptions and alternative accounting treatment tailored to financial reporting needs of the users of those enterprises' financial statements. For further discussion, reference should be made to Chapter 6.

Precedent — "Rollover Agreement" and Corporate Ratifying Document

The following is a precedent Asset Sale Indenture (also known as a "rollover agreement") along with resolutions authorizing the purchaser corporation to enter into the asset transfer as part of an estate freeze, as well as to issue special shares pursuant thereto.

The asset sale indenture (commonly known as a "rollover agreement") assumes that an individual is selling business assets to a corporation and freezing the value thereof. In this example, the assets being transferred include real property and other chattels, having an assumed aggregate value of $1,386,000. The transferee corporation will satisfy the purchase price by assuming liabilities (i.e. a mortgage on the real property) relating to the transferred asset in the amount of $153,875; as to the remainder of the purchase price, the corporation will issue 1,232.125 special shares redeemable and retractable in the amount of $1,000 per share, having one vote per share and a 1% per month non-cumulative dividend. The issuance of these shares will have the effect of "freezing" the value of the various assets transferred to the corporation, which will be locked into the special shares. A family trust will then subscribe for common shares of the transferee corporation.

The rollover agreement contains a covenant by the purchaser and vendor to execute a subsection 85(1) election. A price adjustment clause is also contained therein.

It will be noted that, in the event of a discrepancy between the fair market value of the transferred assets and that of the consideration receivable by the transferor, the price adjustment agreement will operate primarily to vary the redemption and retraction amount.

It should also be noted that the resolution to issue shares by the purchaser corporation contains a resolution establishing the amount of money the corporation would have received had these special shares been issued for money rather than property. This is in compliance with subsection 23(4) of the *Ontario Business Corporations Act.*

While the rollover agreement operates as an actual conveyance, depending on the property which is transferred, it may be advisable to prepare additional transfer documentation, such as a deed (in the case of the transfer of real property), or a bill of sale (in the case of chattels), along with other documents which are normally inherent in a transfer of a particular asset (e.g., third-party notices, etc.).

The documentation reproduced assumes that there is a "non-arm's length" transfer involved, and that there are minimal economic conflicts between the parties. If this is not the case, other matters will have to be addressed in the rollover agreement and accompanying documentation.

Because the transferee is not at arm's length with the transferor it is possible for the stated capital of the issued shares to be an amount less than the total market value of the transferred net assets.[75] Accordingly, the director's resolution relating to the issuance of special shares pursuant to the rollover agreement contains a paragraph which provides for an addition to the stated capital of less than the full amount that would otherwise occur.[76]

Precedent — Asset Sale Indenture

Prepared by David Louis, B.Com., J.D., C.A., Minden, Gross, Grafstein & Greenstein LLP.

Precedent ───

ASSET SALE INDENTURE

THIS INDENTURE made this _____ day of _____, 20____.

BETWEEN:

D. LOUIS, of the Municipality of Metropolitan Toronto,

(the "Vendor")

OF THE FIRST PART

— and —

LOUCO LIMITED, a corporation incorporated under the laws of the

---

[75] See subsection 24(3) of the *Ontario Business Corporations Act.*

[76] For considerations relating to the stated capital that should be attributed to shares received as consideration for the transfer of assets, see "Restrictions on Paid-Up Capital", p. 55 *et seq.*

Province of Ontario,

(the "Purchaser")

OF THE SECOND PART

— and —

_____, _____, and
_____, all of the Municipality of Metropolitan Toronto,
Trustees of the _____ Family Trust,

(the "Shareholders")

OF THE THIRD PART.

WHEREAS:

(a) the Vendor is the registered and beneficial owner of certain lands and premises in the Municipality of *, in the Province of Ontario, as delineated in Schedule "A" annexed hereto (the "Lands" and the "Buildings");

(b) the Vendor is the Lessor under leases of the units in the Buildings delineated in Schedule "A" (the "Leases");

(c) the Vendor is the beneficial owner of certain chattels located on the lands and premises delineated in Schedule "A" (the "Chattels");

NOW THEREFORE IN CONSIDERATION of the premises and the mutual covenants and agreements contained herein, and other good and valuable consideration, the receipt and sufficiency of which is hereby acknowledged, the parties hereto covenant and agree as follows:

1. The Vendor hereby sells, transfers and assigns unto the Purchaser and the Purchaser hereby purchases, on and subject to the terms and conditions hereinafter contained, all of the Vendor's right, title and interest in and to the Lands, Buildings, Leases and Chattels (all of the foregoing properties being herein collectively referred to as the "Purchased Assets").

2. The Vendor shall take or cause to be taken all proper steps, actions and proceedings on the Vendor's part to enable the Vendor to fully assure to the Purchaser a good and marketable title to the Purchased Assets free from all mortgages, charges, security interests, liens, pledges, adverse claims or other encumbrances and shall deliver to the Purchaser such transfers, assignments and consents as may be required to transfer the Purchased Assets from the name of the Vendor to the name of the Purchaser.

3. The purchase price payable for the Purchased Assets shall be $1,386,000, being an amount equal to the fair market value of the Purchased Assets as at the date hereof (the "Purchase Price") as determined jointly by the parties hereto on the basis of generally accepted accounting and valuation principles, which amount shall be confirmed in writing by a resolution of the board of directors of the Purchaser.

4. The Purchase Price shall be paid and satisfied in the following manner:

(a) as to $153,875, or thereabouts, by the assumption by the Purchaser of the Vendor's liability for the outstanding principal balance owing by the Vendor as at the date hereof under charges granted by the Vendor on the properties located in the premises municipally known as *, as delineated in Schedule B hereto;

(b) as to the balance of the Purchase Price, being $1,232,125, or thereabouts, by the allotment and issuance by the Purchaser to the Vendor of 1,000 Special Class A Shares as fully paid and non-assessable shares of the Purchaser.

For the purposes of this Indenture, the "Class A Redemption Amount" and the "Aggregate Class A Redemption Amount" shall have the same meaning as in the Articles of Incorporation of the Purchaser.

5.

(a) The Vendor and the Purchaser hereby covenant and agree to execute jointly an election pursuant to subsection 85(1) of the *Income Tax Act* (Canada) R.S.C. 1985 (5th Supp.), c. 1, as amended (the "Act") in connection with the purchase and sale of the Purchased Assets.

(b) For purposes of the joint election referred to in subsection 4(*a*), the agreed amount for the transfer of the Purchased Assets (the "Elected Amount") shall be the cost amount (as that term is defined in the Act) of the Purchased Assets to the Vendor.

(c) The Vendor and the Purchaser hereby covenant and agree to execute any other elections under the Act, the *Corporations Tax Act*, R.S.O. 1990, c. C.40 (the "CTA"), or either of them which may be necessary or desirable in connection with the transaction of purchase and sale provided for herein (including any amended elections that may be desirable pursuant to subsection 85(7.1) of the Act).

(d) The Vendor and the Purchaser further covenant and agree to file each of the elections referred to in this section 4 as required by the Act and the CTA in the time and form required by the Act and the CTA.

(e) It is the intention of the parties that the Elected Amount as recorded on any elections or other forms under the Act or the CTA (the "Recorded Elected Amount") shall be the cost amount of the Purchased Assets to the Vendor. Should the Minister of National Revenue, the Minister of Finance for Ontario or any duly authorized officer of the Canada Customs and Revenue Agency or the Ministry of Finance for Ontario or any other taxation authority having jurisdiction assert by assessment, reassessment or otherwise that the cost amount of the Purchased Assets is not equal to the Recorded Elected Amount, or if it shall otherwise subsequently be determined that there was an error or omission with respect to any of the calculations with respect thereto, the agreed amount for purposes of the election pursuant to subsection 85(1) of the Act contemplated herein shall be adjusted as to equal the cost amount of the Purchased Assets and the Recorded Elected Amount shall be deemed always to have been such amount. The Vendor and Purchaser further agree to file a revised election under the provisions of subsection 85(1) of the Act, the CTA or other legislation to give effect to the foregoing.

6. The parties hereto have used their best efforts when determining and agreeing upon the Purchase Price as determined and agreed upon by the parties (the "Class A Initial Determined Amount") and the aggregate fair market value of the Purchased Assets. It is the intention of the parties that the Class A Initial Determined Amount equal the fair market value of the Purchased Assets. Consequently, the parties agree that if the Minister of National Revenue, the Minister of Finance for Ontario or any duly authorized officer of the Canada Customs and Revenue Agency or the Ministry of Finance for Ontario or any other taxation authority having jurisdiction:

(a) Refuses to accept the fair market value of the Purchased Assets as determined and agreed upon by the parties, or

(b) Makes or proposes to make an assessment or reassessment on or in respect of any person on the basis that any advantage or benefit was conferred, either directly or indirectly, by reason of the fair market value of the Purchased Assets not being equal to the Initial Class A Determined Amount, or by virtue of or as a direct or indirect result of any transaction or event or series of transactions or events which include the issuance of Class A shares, or

(c) Should any such taxation authority make a determination of the fair market value of the Purchased Assets or the fair market value of the 1,000 Class A shares issued pursuant to this Indenture to be an amount other than that relied upon by the parties hereto, and suggest some alternative amount or value to that determined and agreed upon by the parties,

then the following shall apply:

(d) Either of the parties hereto may challenge such assessment or proposed assessment or alternative amount or value and negotiate with such taxing authority or object to and appeal from any such assessment or reassessment issued by such taxing authority. In the event of such negotiation, objection or appeal by either of the parties hereto, the other party (or its respective successors and assigns) covenants to co-operate with the party negotiating, objecting or appealing.

(e) For the purposes of the adjustments contemplated in subsection 6(*f*) herein, the fair market value of the Purchased Assets shall be considered redetermined as a result of such negotiation, objection or appeal, upon agreement with such taxing authority as to the fair market value of the Purchased Assets or upon a determination by or arising from a decision of the Tax Court of Canada, or any successor or higher tribunal (after all appeal rights have been exercised or have expired).

(f) In the event that the fair market value of the Purchased Assets so redetermined (the "Substituted Value") is greater or less than the Initial Class A Determined Amount, then the Purchase Price shall be automatically adjusted with effect on and as of the date hereof, so that the Purchase Price is equal to the Substituted Value and the Aggregate Class A Redemption Amount shall be adjusted to equal the Substituted Value, provided that, should the foregoing not eliminate any such benefit or advantage conferred, then the Aggregate Class A Redemption Amount shall be adjusted to such amount which, insofar as possible, eliminates any benefit or advantage conferred, all with effect on and as of the date hereof, and the Class A Redemption Amount shall be deemed to have always been equal to the Aggregate Class A Redemption Amount as so adjusted divided by 1,000; if articles of amendment are necessary to effect such adjustment, then the Purchaser shall forthwith file such articles of amendment as are so necessary.

(g) In the event that the Class A Redemption Amount is increased pursuant to subsection 6(*f*) hereof following a redemption or purchase for cancellation or otherwise of a Class A share or following the payment of a dividend on the Class A shares, the Purchaser shall pay to the Vendor to reflect an increase in the Class A Redemption Amount or additional dividend per such share an amount equal to the aggregate of:

(i) such additional amount as is required to ensure that the Vendor will have received the amount which the Vendor would have been entitled to receive if the said increase had been made prior to such redemption, retraction, purchase for cancellation or otherwise, or payment of a dividend, as the case may be; and

(ii) an additional amount equivalent to interest computed at the prescribed rate in effect from time to time as defined in Regulation 4301(*c*) to the Act on the amount described in paragraph 6(*g*)(i), calculated from the date of the redemption or purchase for cancellation or otherwise or the date of payment of such previous dividend, as the case may be, up to and including the date of such payment by the Purchaser.

(h) In the event that the Class A Redemption Amount is decreased pursuant to subsection 6(*f*) hereof following a redemption or purchase for cancellation or otherwise of a Class A share or following the payment of a dividend on the Class A shares, the Vendor shall pay to the Purchaser, to reflect a reduction of the Class A Redemption Amount or a reduction of the dividend per such share, as the case may be, an amount equal to the aggregate of:

   (i) such amount as is necessary to reduce the amount which the Vendor has so received to the amount which the Vendor would have been entitled to receive if the said reduction had been made prior to such redemption, retraction, purchase for cancellation or otherwise, or such payment of a dividend, as the case may be; and

   (ii) an additional amount equivalent to interest at the prescribed rate in effect from time to time as defined in Regulation 4301(*c*) to the Act on the amount described in paragraph 6(*h*)(i) hereof, computed from the date of the redemption or purchase for cancellation or otherwise or the date of payment of such previous dividend, as the case may be, up to and including the date of such payment by the Vendor.

7. The Vendor and the Purchaser agree that the board of directors of the Purchaser shall elect pursuant to subsection 24(3) of the *Business Corporations Act*, R.S.O. 1990, c. B.16, as amended, to add to the stated capital account maintained in respect of the Class A shares of the Purchaser an amount equal to the agreed amount referred to in subsection 4(*b*) above as a result of the issue of the 1,000 Class A shares provided for in section 3 of this Indenture.

8. The parties hereto agree to execute such further and other papers and documents, and do and perform and cause to be done or performed such further and other acts or things, including, without limitation, all corporate actions as may be necessary or desirable to give full force and effect to this Indenture and every part thereof.

9. The Vendor warrants and represents to the Purchaser that it is the absolute and beneficial owner of the Purchased Assets with good, valid and marketable title thereto, free and clear of any and all mortgages, liens, charges, pledges, security interests, encumbrances, adverse claims and rights of others whatsoever.

10. The Purchaser warrants and represents to the Vendor that:

   (a) The Purchaser has the power and authority to purchase the Purchased Assets from the Vendor;

   (b) The Purchaser has the power and authority to issue to the Vendor the 1,000 Class A shares referred to in section 3 hereof;

   (c) The Purchaser is registered under Part IX of the *Excise Tax Act* (Canada), R.S.C. 1985, c. E-15, as amended.

11. The covenants, agreements, representations and warranties of the Vendor and Purchaser contained in this Indenture shall survive the closing of the transaction of purchase and sale provided for herein and continue thereafter in full force and effect for the benefit of the Purchaser or the Vendor, as the case may be.

12. This Indenture shall operate as an actual conveyance, transfer, assignment and setting over of the Purchased Assets by the Vendor to the Purchaser.

13. The Vendor hereby declares that, as to any of the Purchased Assets and any rights or interests therein or claim thereto intended to be hereby sold, assigned, transferred and set over unto the Purchaser and the title to which may not have passed to the Purchaser by virtue of this Indenture or any deeds, transfers or conveyances which may from time to time be executed and delivered in pursuance of the covenants herein contained, the Vendor holds the same in trust for the Purchaser to assign, transfer and set over the same as the Purchaser may from time to time direct.

14. Each of the parties hereto agrees, upon the request and at the expense of the other of them, to do, perform, execute or cause to be done, performed, executed and delivered, all such deeds, transfers, documents, assurances, acts and things as may be necessary or desirable to carry out and give full force and effect to this Indenture and every part thereof.

15. The Purchaser hereby waives compliance by the Vendor with the *Bulk Sales Act* (Ontario).

16. The Vendor hereby indemnifies and shall forever save the Purchaser harmless from and against all debts, liabilities, expenses, accounts, actions, causes of action, suits, damages, costs, claims, demands and losses to which the Purchaser has or may become subject arising as a result of the Vendor's non-compliance with the *Bulk Sales Act* (Ontario).

17. This Indenture shall be governed by and construed in accordance with the laws of the Province of Ontario, and, to the extent applicable, the laws of Canada.

18. This Indenture shall enure to the benefit of and be binding upon the parties hereto and their respective heirs, executors and other legal representatives, successors and assigns.

19. This Indenture may be executed in one or more counterparts, each of which when so executed and delivered shall be deemed to be an original and such counterparts together shall constitute one and the same Indenture.

IN WITNESS WHEREOF this Indenture has been duly executed by the Vendor and the Purchaser and the Shareholders and each agree to be bound hereby as of the day, month and year first above written.

SIGNED, SEALED
AND DELIVERED

D. Louis

LOUCO LIMITED

Per: _____

TRUSTEES OF THE
* FAMILY TRUST

_____
(Trustee)

_____
(Trustee)

_____
(Trustee)

Precedent — Resolution of the Director of Louco Limited

Precedent ————————————————————————————

[Authorization Of Asset Sale Indenture]

WHEREAS:

    (a) The Corporation is desirous of entering into an Asset Sale Indenture with D. Louis to be substantially in the form of the draft Asset Sale Indenture annexed hereto as Schedule "A";

    (b) D. Louis is interested in the aforesaid Asset Sale Indenture and the transactions provided for therein and that he is a director, officer and one of the Trustees of the D. Louis Family Trust, the sole shareholder of the Corporation;

NOW THEREFORE BE IT RESOLVED THAT:

    1. The entering into by the Corporation of an Asset Sale Indenture in the terms of the draft Asset Sale Indenture, a copy of which is annexed hereto as Schedule "A", providing for the transfer of certain assets as more particularly described in the Asset Sale Indenture in exchange for the issuance by the Corporation of 1,232,125 special shares in the capital of the Corporation to D. Louis, be and the same is hereby authorized and approved;

    2. The President of the Corporation be and he is hereby authorized and directed to execute under the corporate seal and to deliver the Asset Sale Indenture in the terms of the said draft Asset Sale Indenture with such modifications, alterations and additions as the President may approve, the execution of the said Asset Sale Indenture by the President to be conclusive proof of his approval of any such modifications, alterations or additions contained in the said Asset Sale Indenture; and

    3. The President of the Corporation be and he is hereby authorized and directed to do all acts and things and to execute or cause to be executed whether under the corporate seal or otherwise all such deeds, transfers, assignments, instruments and documents as in his opinion may be necessary to complete the transaction provided for in the said Asset Sale Indenture and without limitation to issue the said 1,232,125 special shares in the capital of the Corporation to D. Louis.

The undersigned, being the sole director of the Corporation, hereby consents to the foregoing resolution.

DATED the _____ day of _____, 20____ .

Precedent — Resolution of the Shareholder of Louco Limited

Precedent ————————————————————————————

[Confirmation And Approval Of Asset Sale Indenture]

Be It Resolved as a special resolution that:

    1. The execution and delivery by the Corporation of the Asset Sale Indenture, be and the same are hereby confirmed and approved.

2. All actions taken and documents executed by the Corporation in connection with the Asset Sale Indenture and for fulfilling the Corporation's obligations under the Asset Sale Indenture, be and the same are hereby confirmed and approved. The undersigned, being the sole shareholder of the Corporation, hereby acknowledges that the nature and extent of the interest of * in the aforesaid transaction was declared and disclosed to it in reasonable detail in the above recital to the director's resolution and hereby consents to the foregoing as a special resolution

DATED the _____ day of _____, 20____.

_____

_____

_____

TRUSTEES OF THE _____ FAMILY TRUST

Precedent — Resolutions of the Directors of Louco Limited

Precedent

[Issuance Of Special Shares Pursuant To Asset Sale Indenture]

WHEREAS by an Asset Sale Indenture (the "Asset Sale Indenture") dated as of _____ the Corporation agreed for valuable consideration to issue to D. Louis 1,232,125 special shares in the capital of the Corporation as fully paid and non-assessable shares;

AND WHEREAS the Corporation has now received the consideration provided for in the Asset Sale Indenture, namely, D. Louis's interest in certain lands and premises more particularly described in the Asset Sale Indenture (hereinafter referred to as the "Purchased Assets");

NOW THEREFORE BE IT RESOLVED THAT:

1. 1,232,125 special shares in the capital of the Corporation be and the same are hereby allotted and issued to D. Louis as fully paid and non-assessable, the Purchased Assets having been transferred to the Corporation pursuant to the Asset Sale Indenture as consideration for the issuance of such shares;

2. The amount of money the Corporation would have received if the said special shares had been issued for money is $1,232,125.00;

3. The Purchased Assets in consideration of which the 1,232,125 special shares have been issued have a fair value that is not less than $1,232,125,00;

4. The Corporation having issued the said 1,232,125 special shares in exchange for the Purchased Assets which were the property of D. Louis, who immediately before the exchange thereof pursuant to the Asset Sale Indenture did not deal with the Corporation at arm's length within the meaning of that term in the *Income Tax Act* (Canada), hereby adds to the stated capital account maintained by the Corporation in respect of the special shares the sum of $_____, being a portion of the consideration the Corporation has received for the said 1,232,125 special shares as determined by the directors in paragraph 2 above; and

5. The Purchased Assets having been transferred to the Corporation and the Corporation accordingly having received the consideration for the allotment and issue of the said 1,232,125 special shares, it is hereby directed that a certificate representing the said 1,232,125 special shares be issued to D. Louis.

The undersigned, being the sole director of the Corporation, hereby consents to the foregoing resolution.

DATED the _____ day of _____, 20____ .

Chapter 3

Internal and Holding Company Freezes

TOPICS DISCUSSED

As noted at the beginning of the previous chapter, while the freeze of previously unincorporated assets may sometimes occur, it is more usual to freeze a pre-existing corporation. In this case, there are two basic alternatives:

- Reorganizing the pre-existing corporation so that its shares are in a freeze configuration — this is referred to as an "internal freeze" (the most common method of doing this is by means of section 86; however, there are other alternatives); and

- Rolling the shares of the pre-existing corporation into a holding company and taking back freeze shares[1] — a so-called "holding company freeze".

Internal Freezes

The diagram at the beginning of Chapter 4 illustrates a typical internal freeze. As usual, the freezor ("Freezor") holds shares of the corporation having the following attributes:

- redeemable/retractable at the value of the pre-existing shares at the time of the freeze;

- voting (either as an attribute of the redeemable/retractable shares or with the voting shares sequestered in a separate class, which has virtually no rights apart from the votes themselves);

- non-cumulative dividends — either fixed or to a ceiling, usually based on the redemption/retraction amount (e.g., up to .75% per month); plus

- the usual preferences on dissolution.

The growth shares are held either directly by one or more children, or as is more commonly the case, through a family trust, which will have the usual discretionary features, with the issue of the Freezor as beneficiaries.

There are a variety of ways to arrive at this configuration. Typically, an internal freeze is effected by means of section 86 of the *Income Tax Act*. However, it is also possible to utilize section 85, e.g., by effecting a standard section 86 reorganization, but also filing a section 85 election form. (This is also known as an "offside section 86" reorganization or, even more simply, an "offside 86".) In more unusual circumstances, an estate freeze could be effected through an amalgamation pursuant to section 87, e.g., where two corporations are involved in the freeze. It is also possible to effect an estate freeze via a stock dividend. Conceptually, at least, section 51 (share and debt conversions) could also be used.

---

[1] Or freeze shares and nominal value common shares, which are gifted or otherwise transferred or gifted to children/family trusts.

Use of a Holdco vs. an Internal Freeze — Some Considerations

The most notable advantage of internal freezes is that they do not require the formation of a second corporation; accordingly, legal and accounting fees may be decreased. However, the following should also be considered:

- The use of a Holdco affords a degree of creditor protection, e.g, by allowing the payment of dividends to Holdco; the proceeds can then be lent back to Opco if necessary, on a secured basis.

- As mentioned later in the chapter, a Holdco structure may facilitate continuation of Opco's status as a small business corporation on a tax-efficient basis. The basic test of small business corporation status is that substantially all of the corporation's assets must be devoted to Canadian active business activities. Accordingly, it is possible to implement freeze structures utilizing a Holdco to hold the freeze shares, whereby excess cash or other assets can be jettisoned to the holding corporation as a tax-free inter-corporate dividend, leaving OPCO "pure". (For further discussion, reference should be made to the section on the "Corporate Attribution Rules" in Chapter 4 at p. 132.)

Of course, if a Holdco is already in place, and a freeze of Holdco is desired, it is probably preferable to effect an internal freeze in respect of Holdco itself.

In general, implementing an internal freeze does not avoid any of the basic issues in respect of estate freezes commented on elsewhere in this book. The valuation issues are similar; freeze shares received in exchange for common shares must have virtually the same attributes, and the implications of redeeming such shares do not change.

Section 86 Freezes

Being the most common method of effecting an estate freeze, many rulings, technical interpretations, and articles have been written on section 86 freezes. Consequently, the technical issues pertaining to section 86 freezes are, by and large, well settled.

The following is an example of a section 86 freeze:

Example 1

Assume that Mr. Louis, an Ontario resident, is the sole shareholder of Louisco Enterprises Inc. ("Louisco"), holding one issued common share, with a cost and stated capital of $1. Assume also that the shares of Louisco have a value of $2,000,000.

By Articles of Amendment, the one common share of Louisco could be changed into freeze shares redeemable and retractable at the fair market value of the one issued common share, less $1 (i.e., $1,999,999), as well as one common share. (As will be discussed shortly, a new class of common shares having slightly different attributes to the pre-existing commons should be authorized.) Mr. Louis could then gift the common share to a family trust (e.g., if Mr. Louis had married children, this should provide family law protection in Ontario).

In this example, all of the conditions necessary for the application of section 86 have been met, namely:

- there has been a reorganization of capital;

- in all likelihood the shares are capital property, and Mr. Louis has disposed of all of the shares of the class;

- property consisting of shares has been received.

The following are prerequisites to the application of subsection 86(1), which provides for the rollover.

Reorganization of Capital

There must be a "reorganization" of the capital of a corporation. The meaning of this term is not specifically defined in the Act, but pertains to corporate law principles. Accordingly, most practitioners follow relevant corporate law procedures, e.g., pertaining to "fundamental changes" (for example, provisions analogous to section 168 of the *Ontario Business Corporations Act*). Although it might be possible to have a reorganization of capital through other means (discussed later in this chapter), practitioners typically effect a section 86 reorganization by means of Articles of Amendment, the wording of which follows the corporate provisions relating to reorganizations. (For this reason, it is common to effect the "conversion" as a "change" of the common shares to freeze shares — that is, following the wording of relevant corporate provisions.)

☞ **Amendments to section 51 have rendered the reorganization of capital requirement less significant. Section 51 allows a rollover for share conversions without the necessity of a pre-existing convertibility feature in respect of the shares that are exchanged. Accordingly, provided that no non-share consideration is received, an exchange that does not qualify under section 86 may qualify under section 51.**

Capital Property and Disposition of All Shares of a Class

In the course of the reorganization of capital, the taxpayer must dispose of capital property constituting all of the shares of a particular class of the capital stock owned by the taxpayer. Usually, status as capital property should not be problematic, i.e., since the Freezor is not in the business of trading these shares.

Potentially more problematic is the requirement that all of the shares of the particular class owned by the taxpayer be disposed of. Section 86 will not be available if the taxpayer disposes of only some of the shares of a class. However, it will be available if the taxpayer holds other classes of shares which are not included in the reorganization of capital. In this respect, a potential pitfall might arise if the Freezor receives shares of the same class as a result of the reorganization. It could then be arguable that the taxpayer has not disposed of all of the shares of a particular class.

For example, this problem could occur in respect of a partial freeze. Because of this, many practitioners will create a similar, but new class of share if this is a problem. This could be done, for example, by a variation of voting or dividend rights.

Shares Receivable

Property must be receivable from the corporation which includes other shares of the capital stock of the corporation.

Effect of Section 86

Pro-Rated cost base

Most section 86 estate freezes involve changing the pre-existing shares to freeze shares, without the receipt of non-share consideration. Where no property other than shares is receivable, the adjusted cost base of the old shares immediately before the disposition carries over (subject to subsection 86(2)) as the adjusted cost base of the new shares. However, if more than one class of new shares is received by the taxpayer, the adjusted cost base of the old shares is apportioned between the classes of new shares on the basis of their relative fair market values. In some types of estate freeze reorganizations, this could be a suboptimal result. For example, if the cost base is allocated to a class of shares, and this is followed by a spin-off reorganization, the reorganization could involve the cancellation of such shares (e.g., through an inter-corporate redemption), and the consequent "disappearance" of such cost base.

Example 2 ————————————————————

Mr. Louis has previously crystallized the enhanced ($500,000) capital gains exemption by transferring his common shares of OPCO into Holdco in consideration for Holdco common shares, so that Mr. Louis wholly owns Holdco which in turn wholly owns OPCO, and the cost base of the shares of each corporation is $500,000. Mr. Louis now wishes to effect a spin-out reorganization whereby Holdco cash of $200,000 is to be spun out to Sisterco, which would also be wholly owned by Mr. Louis.

To effect this result, the common shares held by Mr. Louis are changed (i.e., pursuant to section 86) to freeze-type shares redeemable and retractable at $200,000 and common shares. The former are to be rolled into Sisterco in consideration for common shares of Sisterco and then redeemed, funded by the $200,000 cash. Two problems with this reorganization are:

- Part of Mr. Louis's cost base in respect of the pre-existing common shares will be allocated to the freeze-type shares, based on the relative fair market values of the two classes of shares. The cost base allocated to the freeze-type shares will be lost when these shares are redeemed. Furthermore, it may not be clear how much of the cost base is lost, i.e., if the fair market value of the new common shares is not clear.

- Arguably, section 86 may not apply if the common shares of Holdco received by virtue of the section 86 reorganization are the same class as the old common shares, on the basis that Mr. Louis has not disposed of all of the shares of a class. Hopefully at least section 51 would apply (which has a similar cost base pro-rating formula).

Where property other than shares is received by the taxpayer as consideration (or part-consideration) for the old disposed-of shares, the cost to the taxpayer of such property is deemed to be the fair market value, according to paragraph 86(1)(a). According to paragraph 86(1)(c), the taxpayer is deemed to have disposed of the old shares for proceeds equal to the cost of all new shares, and other property receivable by the taxpayer for the old shares — i.e., the fair market value of the non-share consideration, according to paragraph 86(1)(a). Accordingly, if non-share consideration is received, this will trigger a gain to the extent of the excess over the pre-existing cost base. Although, in most cases, a section 86 reorganization involves a "straight exchange" of shares, it might be argued that non-share consideration could be received as part of the reorganization. An example of this could be intangible rights, e.g., from a shareholders' agreement implemented in connection with the freeze. Obviously, however, the valuation of such rights would be debatable.

Other Effects of Section 86

The following are other effects of a section 86 reorganization, as compared with other internal freeze mechanisms:

- The CRA has taken the position that, pursuant to subsection 84(9), the corporate attribution rules will potentially apply in a section 86 reorganization — see, for example, Q.42 of the 1986 Revenue Canada Round Table. (For a detailed discussion of the consequences of the corporate attribution rules in the context of an estate freeze, see Chapter 4.)

- Where a section 86 reorganization is effected, it is not necessary to file a tax election form with the CRA. The effects of section 86 are automatic.

Subsection 86(2) — Benefit to Related Persons

Subsection 86(2) limits the rollover provisions under subsection 86(1) where a taxpayer has effectively gifted (loosely speaking) a portion of the value of his or her shares to a related person. The effect of subsection 86(2) may be to force a recognition of the capital gain on the old shares and to alter the adjusted cost base of the new shares received on the reorganization. Subsection 86(2) may apply if the fair market value of the old shares before the reorganization is greater than the fair market value of share and non-share consideration received and the difference can reasonably be considered to be a benefit that the taxpayer desired to have conferred upon a person related to him or her.[2] In regard to minimizing the risk of the application of subsection 86(2) and other benefit provisions, see the discussion under "Benefits" in Chapter 4, p. 130.

Subsection 86(2.1)

Subsection 86(2.1) limits the paid-up capital in respect of a freeze. Essentially, the paid-up capital of the new shares issued on the exchange is limited to the paid-up

---

[2] Not surprisingly, the CRA has indicated that the fact that the benefit is in favour of a trust for the freezor's children does not vitiate the application of subsection 86(2). See Q.11 of the 2000 APFF Round Table.

capital of the old shares, less any non-share consideration. The provision contains a pro-ration formula in respect of paid-up capital where more than one class of share is received. (Unlike the cost base pro-rating formula in paragraph 86(1)(*a*), the formula subtracts the increase in paid-up capital, based on relative increases in paid-up capital, rather than fair market value.)

This provision applies only where the paid-up capital is increased over the pre-existing paid-up capital, i.e., where the stated capital is increased pursuant to corporate law. (But for specific provisions such as subsection 86(2.1), paid-up capital for tax purposes is dependent on stated capital under corporate law.) More often than not, the stated capital — and therefore the paid-up capital for tax purposes — will be limited under corporate law as part of the reorganization, thus pre-empting the application of subsection 86(2.1).

If the stated capital is limited, most corporate statutes appear to be silent as to the allocation of stated capital between classes. It appears that the CRA will usually accept an allocation by the taxpayer. However, the CRA has indicated that the GAAR could apply to a shift in paid-up capital, i.e., if the purpose of this shift was "abusive". In any event, for most estate freezes, the amount of paid-up capital will be relatively nominal, so that the tax risks inherent in the shift will be modest.

> ☞ **The CRA has stated that it is its general view that a shift of paid-up capital to restore each shareholder to the amount of paid-up capital that the shareholder would have had, had he originally purchased a separate class of shares, is not abusive.**

Section 85 Freezes ("Offside 86")

Subsection 86(3) provides that section 86 of the Act does not apply where subsection 85(1) applies. In other words, the results of filing a section 85 election in conjunction with the freeze can override the results of the rollover under subsection 86(1), as described previously.

The application of section 85 in the context of a freeze involves the disposition of shares of the corporation to the corporation in return for other shares of the corporation. The CRA has indicated that if an estate freeze is effected directly through Articles of Amendment (i.e., the usual section 86 mechanism), subsection 86(3) applies, such that subsection 85(1) election can be filed in connection with the reorganization. (See Q.20 of the 1992 Revenue Canada Round Table.)

It also appears to be possible to effect an Offside 86 outside of the Articles by means of a "share exchange agreement". Some years ago, a large accounting firm expressed some concern that the issue and allotment by a corporation of shares of one class in exchange for the surrender to the corporation by a shareholder of shares of another class might not be in compliance with the provisions of the *Ontario Business Corporations Act*. Many lawyers appear to be of the view that these concerns are not well founded and this issue seems to have been discounted. Of course, shares having the proper freeze attributes must be in place.

☞ One possible method of avoiding the necessity of filing Articles of Amendment is to create one or more classes of freeze shares in advance, redeemable and retractable based on the value of the consideration received by the corporation in respect of the "first issuance" of the shares. Obviously, care must be taken not to reuse these shares. It is suggested that the authorized capital be restricted. Several different classes of first issuance shares could be created to facilitate future section 85 rollovers.

Section 86 vs. "Offside 86" Considerations

The following are instances in which Offside 86 methodology is most commonly used and may be preferred over section 86.

Capital gains crystallizations

The section 85 methodology will, of course, allow a taxpayer to elect into a gain, thus bumping the cost base of the shares received. Pursuant to subsection 85(1), where the taxpayer receives both common and preferred shares, the cost base would be allocated to the preferred shares as defined in the Act to the extent of their value (see paragraph 85(1)(g) and (h); for further discussion, see Chapter 2).

Availability

An internal section 85 reorganization may be available in cases where section 86 does not apply. For example, section 86 requires the transferor to dispose of all of the transferor's shares of a particular class and will not be applicable unless such shares are capital property.

Cost base sequestering

The effect of the application of section 86 is to average the pre-existing adjusted cost base among all classes of shares received, based on their relative fair market values. In many cases, this may not be a desirable result. (In fact, the allocation may be uncertain unless the value of all of the shares is known.) The section 85 election mechanism sequesters the cost base in preferred shares in priority to common shares, to the extent of the value of the preferred shares received.

☞ In the past, the CRA has indicated that the use of subsection 86(3) to sequester cost base in a class of shares such that the cost base is not proportional to the fair market value could trigger the GAAR. However, since subsection 86(3) specifically envisions the utilization of subsection 85(1), the correctness of this interpretation is debatable.

Example 3

Assume that Mr. Louis, an Ontario resident, is the sole shareholder of Louisco Enterprises Inc. ("Louisco"), holding one issued common share. Assume also that Louisco is determined to qualify for the $500,000 capital gains exemption[3], which Mr. Louis has never utilized previously, and that the shares of Louisco have a value in excess of this amount, say $2,000,000.

1. *Internal Freeze and crystallization.* By Articles of Amendment, the one common share of Louisco could be changed into freeze shares redeemable and retractable at the fair market value of the one issued common share, less $1 (i.e., $1,999,999), as well as one common share[4]. Mr. Louis would then gift the common share to a family trust (e.g., if Mr. Louis had married children, this should provide family law protection in Ontario). Mr. Louis would file a section 85 election, electing into a $500,000 capital gain. Pursuant to paragraph 85(1)(g) and (h), the elected amount would be allocated to the freeze shares.

2. *Crystallization.* If Mr. Louis did not want to effect a freeze, Mr. Louis could do a similar reorganization, changing the common shares into freeze shares redeemable and retractable at $500,000 as well as one common share, in this case worth $1,500,000. Mr. Louis would file a section 85 election, electing into a $500,000 capital gain. Pursuant to paragraph 85(1)(g) and (h), the elected amount would still be allocated to the freeze shares, i.e., to the extent of their value, so that they would have a cost base and value of $500,000.

Section 87 (Amalgamation) Freezes

In some circumstances, an internal freeze could be implemented by amalgamating two corporations. For example, this technique might be used where the Freezor owns shares in two sister corporations which are to be frozen. By issuing freeze shares to the previous common shareholders, the value of the amalgamated corporation is frozen, allowing beneficiaries of the freeze to acquire common shares at a nominal amount.

It should be noted that the amalgamation methodology may give shareholders rights under corporate law which differ from other internal freeze methods.

For an amalgamation to qualify under section 87, all of the property of each predecessor corporation, excluding inter-company receivables and shares, must become property of the "new corporation"; all the liabilities of the predecessor corporations, excluding inter-company balances, must become liabilities of the new corporation; and all of the shareholders of the predecessor corporations, except any predecessor corporations, must receive shares of the new corporation. Another of the limitations of section 87 is that the shareholders of the predecessor corporation

---

[3] If it does not, because of non-qualifying assets, the reorganization could be preceded by a spin-out purification. (Such spinouts are discussed in Chapter 10 of *Tax and Family Business Succession Planning*, by David Louis and Samantha Prasad Weiss, particularly at ¶1005.) If such a reorganization is effected and combined with a freeze, it is critical that subsection 55(3)(a) applies to the reorganization. This will probably not be the case if a third-party sale is anticipated. Otherwise, it is necessary that the family trust is related to the parties to the reorganization. According to paragraph 55(5)(e), a person who is related to every beneficiary of a trust (other than a registered charity) who is or may (otherwise than by reason of the death of another beneficiary of the trust) be entitled to share in the income or capital of the trust is deemed to be related to the trust.

[4] For the reasons indicated previously, a new class of common shares, having slightly different attributes to the pre-existing commons, should be authorized.

cannot receive consideration other than shares of the new corporation. This is a strict requirement for the rollover to occur (for further discussion, see "Section 51 Freezes", below). However, it may be possible to distribute corporate assets after the amalgamation, e.g., through a reduction in paid-up capital of the amalgamated corporation.

Section 87 deems a corporation formed as a result of an amalgamation to be a new corporation, so that the amalgamation will trigger a year-end. Though the consequences of this should be considered, section 87 provides that most of the tax attributes of the predecessor corporation will flow through to the new corporation. However, there may occasionally be difficulties. For example, post-amalgamation losses cannot generally be carried back to a predecessor corporation. For further discussion of the implications of amalgamation, reference should be made to Interpretation Bulletin IT-474R.

Section 51 Freezes

It may be possible for an estate freeze to be effected pursuant to section 51 of the Act. Although section 51 formerly allowed rollovers only in respect of convertible shares and debt, the convertibility of shares requirement was dropped some years ago. Accordingly, section 51 allows shares of a corporation to be exchanged for other shares of the corporation on a tax-deferred basis. Of course, the "other" shares could be freeze shares — hence, the possibility of a freeze being effected under section 51.

It is doubtful that many practitioners take advantage of these provisions, because it is usually necessary to create freeze shares via Articles of Amendment in any event. If this is the case, it is not much more difficult to change the pre-existing shares into freeze shares pursuant to the Articles themselves so that section 86 will presumably apply. (Per subsection 51(4), section 51 does not apply where subsections 85(1),(2) or section 86 apply.) Since this is the traditional method of effecting an internal freeze, most practitioners tend to rely on this procedure.

The requirement in section 51 that no consideration other than the shares can be received on the conversion may prove to be problematic. It is possible that, depending on the particulars of the freeze, non-share consideration might be received, e.g., if the common shareholder would enjoy certain contractual rights, or pursuant to a shareholders' agreement. In the case of section 86, the rollover would remain intact except to the extent that the value of these rights exceeded the cost base of the old shares. However, the receipt of any non-share consideration would undermine the rollover in section 51, regardless of its value, thus forcing reliance on the prerequisites of section 86 to obtain the rollover.

For both section 51 and 87 freezes, the acb of pre-existing of pre-existing shares is apportioned between the classes of shares acquired based on relative fair market values — i.e., the fair market value of shares of a particular class acquired relative to the fair market value of all shares acquired (paragraphs 51(1)(*d*) and 87(4)(*b*)), so that the effect is similar to section 86 except that, since no non-share consideration can be received, the provisions do not contemplate this.

Stock Dividend Freezes

It may also be possible to effect an internal freeze via a stock dividend mechanism. For example, the Freezor may start out with all of the issued (common) shares of a corporation. The Articles of the corporation would be amended to provide for freeze shares. The corporation would then pay a stock dividend on the common shares consisting of the freeze shares in an amount sufficient to reduce the value of the corporation's common shares to a nominal amount. The shares would have a low stated capital — if possible under corporate law — in order to minimize the deemed dividend for tax purposes which, in turn, is based on the increase in stated capital. New common shares would then be acquired by the children or family trust (having due regard to the personal attribution rules).

☞ **One possible advantage of a stock dividend freeze is that, technically, it may not run afoul of the corporate attribution rules.**

One interesting result of a stock dividend freeze is that, since the cost of the stock dividend is nominal, this methodology can shift value to the freeze shares without adding to the acb, thus leaving the acb in the common shares. It should be noted that this result is obverse to an "offside 86", whereby, per section 85, the acb is sequestered in the preferred shares, to the extent of their value. Thus the various methodologies can offer differing results in respect of sequestering acb: pro-rated as to fair market value, in the case of sections 86, 87 and 51; skewed to the preferred shares, in the case of an "offside 86", and skewed to the growth shares, in the case of a stock dividend freeze.

For further discussion of stock dividend freezes, see Chapter 4.

Holding Company Freezes

The third method of freezing the value of a pre-existing corporation is to transfer the shares thereof to a holding company in return for freeze shares with the nominal value common shares held by children/family trusts.[5] Thus, the shares of the holding company replace the assets which are subject to subsection 85(1).

However, in the vast majority of cases, the shares transferred are those of a connected corporation. As a result, in addition to section 85, section 84.1 will become relevant (and will override subsection 85(2.1)).

Section 84.1 is one of the most dangerous tax traps in the Act. It can be triggered by seemingly simple transactions. Accordingly, practitioners who wish to implement holding company freezes should be familiar with the intricacies of section 84.1.

---

[5] Or taking back freeze shares and nominal value common shares, with a transfer or gift of the common shares to the children/family trust.

Section 84.1 — Non-Arm's Length Holding Company Strips

Section 84.1 may operate in circumstances where an individual (or other non-corporate transferor) transfers shares of a corporation to a second corporation with whom the transferor does not deal at arm's length. Were it not for this provision, such a transfer may enable the transferor to extract surplus of the transferred corporation reflecting his cost base thereof. This type of manoeuvre is considered abusive where a surplus is removed, in circumstances where the cost base in the transferred shares results from:

- a tax-exempt gain (i.e., due to the capital-gains exemption); or

- V-day value increment (that is, the increase in value of the shares from the original cost to V-day)

by the transferor or a non-arm's length person.

Under these circumstances, section 84.1, if applicable, can result in an immediate deemed taxable dividend to the transferor, or a reduction of the transferor's paid-up capital in the shares of the transferee corporation so as to increase subsequent exposure to taxable dividends on future distributions.

The section may apply where a transfer of shares of any class of a Canadian resident corporation ("subject corporation") which are capital property of a (non-corporate) transferor is made to a purchaser corporation with whom the transferor does not deal at arm's length, and immediately after the transfer, the purchaser corporation is "connected" with the subject corporation within the meaning of subsection 186(4) (see Figure 1 below).

☞ **Section 84.1 will be operative whether or not a section 85 election is filed.**

If these pre-conditions are met, the basic rule under section 84.1 is that the maximum amount that can be received by the transferor from the transferee corporation as proceeds in the form of any non-share consideration and/or paid-up capital is restricted to the greater of the paid-up capital of the transferred shares and what we will refer to as the transferor's "84.1 cost base" of the transferred shares, which essentially excludes V-day value increments and exempt capital gains from dispositions of the taxpayer or non-arm's length persons. If these constraints are violated, there will be a paid-up capital reduction of the shares received by the transferee corporation, and/or the immediate recognition of a taxable dividend. This depends on whether shares or other property are received as consideration for the transfer. The former tends to result in a paid-up capital reduction; the latter results in a deemed dividend.

Figure 1 — When Section 84.1 Applies

Figure 1 illustrates the prerequisites for the application of section 84.1.

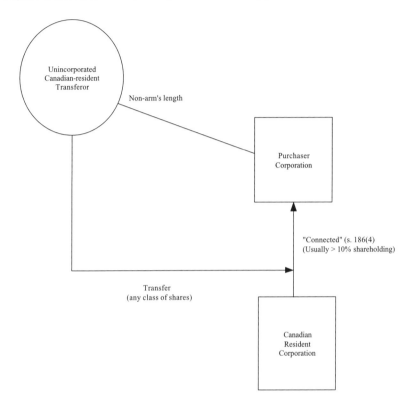

"Unincorporated"/"Canadian Resident Corporation"

For example, assume that Mr. A holds the shares of Opco (Canadian Resident Corporation). Mr. A has previously crystallized the capital gains exemption (e.g., in an Offside 86 described previously in this chapter), so that Mr. A has a $500,000 cost base in respect of preferred shares of Opco. Mr. A transfers all of his shares into Holdco (Purchaser Corporation), taking back a promissory note for $500,000, in view of the cost base. In this simple example, section 84.1 would be triggered, resulting in a deemed dividend of $500,000. Note that the deemed dividend results from the issuance rather than payment of the promissory note. Thus, a taxpayer who unwittingly stumbles into section 84.1 may suffer immediate adverse tax consequences prior to the receipt of cash or other assets from the corporation.

Details of Section 84.1

Prerequisites for section 84.1

Section 84.1 will apply if the following prerequisites are met:

- There is a disposition of shares of any class ("subject shares") of a Canadian-resident corporation.

- The disposition is made by a Canadian resident taxpayer, other than a corporation.

- The "subject shares" constitute capital property to the transferor.

- The transfer is made to a corporation ("purchaser corporation") with which the transferor does not deal at arm's length. Related persons are deemed not to deal at arm's length. In addition, a non-arm's length relationship could arise as a result of a given fact situation. Furthermore, the non-arm's length concept is broadened in the context of section 84.1.[6]

- Immediately after the disposition, the purchaser corporation was "connected" with the subject corporation. This involves ownership of more than 10% of the issued share capital having full voting rights under all circumstances, as well as having a value of more than 10% of the fair market value of all issued shares of the subject corporation. A purchaser corporation will also be connected if the subject corporation is controlled, within the meaning ascribed by subsection 186(4), by the purchaser corporation. This would occur where there is *de jure* control by the purchaser corporation and/or non-arm's length persons.[7]

"84.1 Cost base" — paragraphs 84.1(2)(a) and (a.1)

Paragraphs 84.1(2)(a) and (a.1) provide rules for determining the "84.1 cost base" of the transferor's shares. These rules will "modify" the usual adjusted cost base and have the effect of eliminating the possibility of the taxpayer taking advantage of V-Day protection or capital gains deductions so as to extract assets from the corporation as a distribution without adverse tax consequences. If the adjusted cost base of the shares includes an amount claimed as a capital gains exemption, then the 84.1 cost base will be determined by ignoring the capital gains exemption claimed. Similarly, if the shares were owned before 1972, then the 84.1 cost base will be determined by ignoring the V-Day value.

More precisely, the "84.1 cost base" of a share acquired by the transferor after 1971 from a person with whom the transferor was not dealing at arm's length (as well as a share substituted for such a share, or a share substituted for a share owned

---

[6] See note 1 at "Notes to Section 84.1" at p. 117.

[7] For further details, see p. 117.

by the taxpayer at the end of 1981),[8] is the adjusted cost base as reduced by the following two amounts:

1.   The aggregate of any previous post-1984 capital gains of the taxpayer or any non-arm's length individual who owned the share as is established to be deductible pursuant to the capital gains exemption (per section 110.6). As stated previously, this step removes any previous share gains which were eligible for the capital gains exemption. However, as can be seen, this adjustment may do more than this as it initially refers to the entire post-1984 capital gains, rather than the exempt gains. Accordingly, where a taxpayer can establish that the capital gains exemption was actually claimed in respect of an amount that is less than the aggregate of all previous post-1984 non-arm's length gains, then such lesser amount would be deducted in computing the taxpayer's adjusted cost base under paragraph 84.1(2)(a.1). As in the case with paragraph 84.1(2)(a) (see below), this rule extends to substituted shares.

2.   The excess of the share's fair market value on Valuation Day over its "actual cost" on January 1, 1972, where the share (or a substituted share) was owned at the end of 1971 by a non-arm's length person — that is, V-day increments.[9]

Paragraph 84.1(2)(a) provides that where the share was acquired by the taxpayer before 1972, the taxpayer's "84.1 cost base" will essentially be calculated by taking the original arm's length cost, and ignoring the upward adjustment occasioned by the V-day rules.[10]

It should be emphasized that these rules do not prevent taxpayers from obtaining from a corporation assets equal to their actual arm's length cost ("84.1 cost base") of the share, plus or minus any cost base adjustments under the Act. The cost base modifications will not occur where the increased cost base is attributable to an arm's length purchase of shares, even where the vendor claimed the capital gains exemption (or V-day increment). Accordingly, a "holding company strip" could be used to extract corporate assets equal to the cost base of the purchased shares without regard to section 84.1.

---

[8] While this provision appears at first to have limited application, paragraph 84.1(2.01)(a) provides that where a share is acquired as an unissued treasury share, it is treated as having been acquired in a non-arm's length transaction. Therefore, paragraph 84.1(2)(a.1) would apply to determine the adjusted cost base of the share for the purposes of section 84.1. Paragraphs 84.1(2.01)(b) and (c) contain rules clarifying non-arm's length circumstances for the purpose of paragraph 84.1(2)(a.1).

Also, in *Estate of Karma May v. M.N.R.*, 88 DTC 1189, the Tax Court of Canada found that the transfer of shares from a deceased to the estate of the deceased was not an arm's length transaction.

[9] Also subtracted from the V-day value will be dividends subject to a subsection 83(1) election received by the taxpayer or a non-arm's length person, in order to compensate for the fact that the V-day value would have been reduced by such dividends.

[10] More precisely, the cost base of the shares is determined under the provisions of the Act as if the ITAR rules were read without reference to subsections 26(3) and (7). Also, dividends in respect of which an election under subsection 83(1) of the Act has been made will be added to the cost base.

Effects of Section 84.1

Reduction of Paid-Up Capital

Paragraph 84.1(1)(*a*) provides for a reduction of paid-up capital for each class of shares of the purchaser corporation that are issued as consideration for the purchaser corporation's acquisition of shares of the subject corporation.

The reduction will be required in circumstances where the increase in legal paid-up capital of the purchaser corporation's shares, arising as a result of the share transfer, exceeds the greater of the paid-up capital of the transferred shares and the "84.1 cost base" to the transferor of the transferred shares. Where non-share consideration is also paid by the purchaser corporation as part of the transaction, this would be subtracted from the greater of the two amounts in calculating the paid-up capital reduction. This is because the non-share consideration can trigger an immediate deemed dividend in itself.

Conceptually, paragraph 84.1(1)(*a*) causes a reduction in paid-up capital so that the paid-up capital of the shares after the reduction will be equal to the "actual cost" (the greater of paid-up capital and the "84.1 cost base") that has not been recovered by the non-share consideration received in the transfer.

As a formula, the reduction in the paid-up capital of shares of the purchaser corporation paid as consideration for the transfer equals:

$$(A - D) \times (E/F)$$

where:

A   is the paid-up capital increase in all classes of shares of the purchaser

B   is the greater of:

— the paid-up capital of the subject shares; and

— the "84.1 cost base" of the subject shares (see below) less the fair market value of non-share consideration received by the purchaser for the subject shares; and

C   is the paid-up capital increase of the shares of the particular class of the purchaser.

The paid-up capital reduction is allocated among the different classes of shares of the purchaser corporation based on the legal paid-up capital increases occurring as a result of the share transfer.

Immediate Deemed Dividend

Essentially, a deemed dividend results to the extent that non-share consideration exceeds the greater of the 84.1 cost base or the paid-up capital of the shares in the subject corporation that are transferred to the purchaser company.

More precisely, paragraph 84.1(1)(*b*) deems the purchaser corporation as having paid a dividend to the transferor where the aggregate of the amount of the increase in the legal paid-up capital of its shares as a result of the transfer and the fair market value of the non-share consideration given by it for the transferred shares exceeds the total of:

— the greater of the "84.1 cost base" and the paid- up capital of the transferred shares; and

— the total paid-up capital reductions as required in paragraph 84.1(1)(*a*) (see above).

Conceptually, the deemed dividend is essentially equal to the non-share consideration that is in excess of the "actual cost" (i.e., the greater of paid-up capital and the 84.1 cost base).

As a formula, this can be expressed as follows: There will be an immediate deemed dividend to the taxpayer equal to

$$(A + D) - (E + F)$$

where:

A   is the paid-up capital increase in all classes of shares of the purchaser

D   is the fair market value of any non-share consideration received by the transferor

E   is the greater of:

— the paid-up capital of the subject shares; or

— the "84.1 cost base" of the subject shares; and

F   is the paid-up capital reduction as calculated under paragraph 84.1(1)(*a*) — see above.

Notes to Section 84.1

1. As noted below, section 84.1 includes provisions which expand the arm's length concept. Nevertheless, in addition to related persons being deemed to be not at arm's length, it is also possible to be factually not at arm's length, such as where there is a directing mind, *de facto* control, or parties who act in concert. As is quite apparent in a number of recent technical interpretations, the CRA has made it abundantly clear that it has not lost sight of this.[11] For example, in Technical Interpretation No. 2002-0166655, dated March 28, 2003, the shares of Opco are held as follows: Mr. A 26%, Mrs. A 12%, Mr. B 26%, Mrs. B 12%, Mr. X 12%, Mr. Y 12% (only the spouses are related to one another). Essentially, X and Y would form Xyco to hold the Opco shares; Messrs As and Bs would sell their shares to Xyco, claiming the capital gains exemption. The CRA indicated:

> In this particular situation, Mr. A, Mrs. A, Mr. B, Mrs. B, Mr. X and Mr. Y appear to be acting in concert to direct Xyco in connection with the sale of the shares of Opco. While there may be arm's length bargaining concerning the price to be paid for the shares of Opco, the shareholders appear to be acting in a highly interdependent manner to avoid tax on the transactions. In our view, Xyco may be viewed as merely accommodating the shareholders by structuring the transactions in this manner, since it does not appear to have any independent interest in acquiring the shares of Opco. Consequently, section 84.1 may apply to the above-described situation.

---

[11] See, for example, Doc. No. 2002-0159525, September 13, 2002; Doc. No. 2003-0006675, November 07, 2003; Doc. No. 2004-0106161E5, January 12, 2005; Doc. No. 2004-0103061E5, December 07, 2004; Doc. No. 2004-0104321E5, December 07, 2004; Doc. No. 2003-0049105, December 30, 2003; Doc. No. 2003-0008645, March 26, 2003; Doc. No. 2002-0166655, March 28, 2003.

However, in *Brouillette*, 2005 DTC 1004 (T.C.C.), there was a fairly similar fact situation. The taxpayer and F each owned 50% of the shares of "Brouillette Inc.". To facilitate the acquisition by B and C, two numbered corporations, 9016 and 9017, were used. The taxpayer controlled 9016, and C and B controlled 9017. 9016 purchased the shares of Brouillette Inc. owned by F; on the same day, the taxpayer exchanged his shares of Brouillette Inc. for Class E non-voting preferred shares of 9016, which he later sold to 9017 for a promissory note. Relying on section 84.1 of the Act, the Minister assessed the taxpayer on the basis that the proceeds of disposition of his Class E non-voting preferred shares of 9016 constituted a deemed dividend in his hands, because he was not dealing at arm's length with 9017 (in the alternative, relying on GAAR). The taxpayer's appeal was allowed. The evidence showed that the interests of C and B were totally distinct from those of the taxpayer (notwithstanding the CRA's assertion that the appellant dictated the terms of the agreement to the other party, or both parties acted in concert when they accepted the terms proposed by accounting consultants who acted for both parties, or the appellant had *de facto* control over 9017).

2. As mentioned previously, one of the prerequisites for the operation of section 84.1 is that a purchaser corporation does not deal at arm's length with the transferor. For the purposes of section 84.1, the non-arm's length concept is expanded in paragraphs 84.1(2)(*b*), which provides that a non-arm's length situation will be deemed to arise with respect to a particular taxpayer when he is one of a group of five or fewer persons who control the subject corporation immediately before the transfer, as well as the purchaser corporation immediately after the transfer.[12]

Pursuant to paragraph 84.1(2.2)(*a*), the "five or fewer" concept described above is expanded further by including in a taxpayer's holdings shares held by a taxpayer's spouse, child (per subsection 70(10)) who is under 18 years of age, as well as certain trusts and controlled persons.

In addition, paragraph 84.1(2)(*d*) provides that in determining (for the purposes of section 84.1) whether a taxpayer has disposed of shares of the corporation with which he does not deal at arm's length, a trust and a beneficiary of the trust or a person related to a beneficiary will be treated as not dealing with each other at arm's length. As a result, a disposition by a trust to a corporation that is controlled by beneficiaries of the trust or persons related to such beneficiaries will be treated as a disposition to a corporation with which the trust does not deal at arm's length.[13]

---

[12] For further comment, see paragraph 2 of IT-489R.

[13] Paragraph 84.1(2.2) provides that, for the purpose of this concept (i.e., paragraph 84.1(2)(b)):

(i) a group of persons means any two or more persons each of whom owns shares of the corporation in question (paragraph 84.1(2.2)(*b*));

(ii) a corporation controlled by one or more members of a particular group shall be considered to be controlled by that group (paragraph 84.1(2.2)(*c*)); and

(iii) a corporation may be controlled by a person or particular group of persons notwithstanding the fact that the corporation is also controlled by another person or group of persons (paragraph 84.1(2.2)(*d*)).

(continued on next page)

These provisions can be quite problematic in circumstances where an individual "swaps shares" of a corporation, notably in a minority buy-out situation. For example, a minority shareholder of Targetco ("Mr. Vendor") in which the controller of Acquireco ("Mr. Controller") is also a shareholder may sell his or her shares in return for cash and shares of Acquireco (i.e., so that the vendor becomes a minority shareholder of Acquireco), along with Mr. Controller, who might continue to control Acquireco.

Given the Ministerial powers outlined above, it appears that section 84.1 could apply to defeat what might otherwise appear to be a "tax-free" gain, pursuant to the capital-gains exemption.

Even though Mr. Vendor is a minority shareholder — perhaps one of many — and is also a minority shareholder of Acquireco, the Minister may designate Mr. Vendor and Mr. Controller as a group, pursuant to subsection 84.1(2.2), such that, per paragraph 84.1(2)(*b*), Mr. Vendor and Mr. Controller are a group of five or fewer persons who control Targetco immediately before the acquisition, and Acquireco, immediately after the acquisition.[14]

3. It should be noted that the reduction of paid-up capital provided for in paragraph 84.1(1)(*a*) works "automatically", notwithstanding the existence of a higher paid-up capital for corporate-law purposes ("stated capital"). In other words, it is not necessary to limit the paid-up capital for corporate purposes. However, in order to avoid confusion between the tax and corporate paid-up capital, it may be prudent to limit the paid-up capital for corporate purposes, if this can be done pursuant to the corporations law of the relevant jurisdiction.[15]

Notwithstanding the automatic nature of the paid-up capital reduction, taxpayers usually want to ensure that the deemed dividend provided for in paragraph 84.1(1)(*b*) does not take place. Essentially, this can be avoided by ensuring that the non-share consideration received from the purchaser corporation does not exceed the greater of the paid-up capital or "84.1 cost base" of the subject corporation's shares.

4. As stated previously, in the situation where the share of a subject corporation was acquired after 1971 from a person with whom the transferor did not deal at arm's length, the "84.1 cost base" will be diminished to the extent of capital gains by the non-arm's length person. However, a lesser reduction will be allowed as is established by the taxpayer to be the capital gains exemption previously claimed. This raises two points:

(a) In an acquisition from a non-arm's length person, it would be prudent for the taxpayer to retain records to establish the capital gains exemption previously claimed. Presumably, this would include a copy of the tax return of the non-arm's length transferor.

(continued from previous page)
As will be evident, these provisions are largely reminiscent of paragraph 256(1.2)(*b*), relating to the association rules.

[14] See also CRA Document number 9405015.

[15] For further discussion, see the commentary on subsection 85(2.1) in Chapter 2.

(b) A technical problem may arise if no capital gains exemption was claimed by the transferor in the first place, since under these circumstances, no lesser amount can be established. In other words, if the transferor claims only a small capital gains exemption, this will limit the "modified cost base" reduction, whereas not claiming the capital gains exemption at all may increase the reduction substantially. The Department of Finance has apparently indicated that this was a drafting oversight. Even so, until the situation is clarified, it will be prudent to ensure that the transferor claims at least some capital gains exemption in order to diminish the reduction of cost base under paragraph 84.1(2)(*a*.1).

5.   Subsection 84.1(2.1) is designed to deal with an anomaly relating to the "84.1 cost base" calculation whereby the amount subject to the capital gains exemption could be decreased by claiming a reserve. Very basically, where the taxpayer or a non-arm's length person has claimed the capital gains reserve for the year in which the previous disposition occurred, subsection 84.1(2.1) is designed to treat the transferor as if the maximum capital gains exemption had been claimed and no reserve had been taken.

6.   Until recently, there was some uncertainty as to whether Opco would be connected under subsection 186(4), by virtue of subsection 186(2), for the purposes of section 84.1. In *Olsen v. The Queen*, 2000 DTC 2121 (T.C.C.),[16] the Tax Court of Canada held that this was not the case, especially since section 84.1, which is an anti-avoidance provision, must be strictly interpreted.

After this, subsection 186(7) was introduced and provides that, for greater certainty, where a provision of the Act or the regulations indicate that the term "connected" has the meaning assigned by subsection 186(4), that meaning is to be determined by taking into account the application of subsection 186(2), unless the provision expressly provides otherwise.

As it turns out, this amendment was not necessary, as Olsen was overturned by the Federal Court of Appeal, 2002 DTC 6770.

7.   Subsection 84.1(3) provides for an addition to the paid-up capital of any class of shares of the purchaser where dividends are subsequently deemed to be paid. The addition is equal to the amount of a dividend deemed to be paid on the redemption or reduction of paid-up capital, minus the amount of the dividend that would have been paid had there been no paid-up capital reduction pursuant to paragraph 84.1(1)(*a*).

The effect is to provide that the paid-up capital reduction will be reversed to the extent of any dividends that are subsequently deemed to be paid on the affected class of shares.

The addition is restricted to the amount of the previous paid-up capital reduction pursuant to paragraph 84.1(1)(*a*).

8.   The CRA's views on section 84.1 (prior to recent amendments) are expressed in IT-489R.

---

[16] Overturned by 2002 DTC 6770 (F.C.A.).

Capital Gains Exemption

The capital gains exemption in respect of qualified small business corporation shares can have a fundamental impact on estate planning methodology. This, of course, potentially allows for up to $500,000 in tax-free capital gains and can be claimed against capital gains arising on death, as well as during one's lifetime.

In some cases, the capital gains exemption will be adequate to cover death tax exposure, especially if shares are held by both spouses, with each being able to utilize the exemption. Note that technically speaking, at least, the ability to "double up" on the exemption in this manner may depend on whether the initial subscription was subject to the personal attribution rules. For example, if one spouse funded both spouses' acquisitions, both gains will be attributable to the funding spouse, with only the funding spouse's exemption being available. Query, however, whether as a practical matter, the CRA would be inclined to vigorously pursue this technical issue, e.g., if the subscription was nominal and occurred many years earlier, with dividends reported by both spouses. It may even be the case that the original organization of the corporation was "sloppy", e.g., the subscription price was never actually paid, but was accounted for as a receivable.

Crystallizations

There are fairly stringent tests that must be passed before the exemption is available. The "small business corporation" requirement, for example, may be breached where the corporation invests in "non-qualified" assets. In addition, if the individual has a positive "cumulative net investment loss" account, access to the capital gains exemption may be restricted. While the capital gains exemption has turned out to be one of the more enduring tax benefits, it is also possible that the exemption might be restricted by future legislation. Finally, it is possible that only $400,000 of the exemption will be available, since the small business corporation capital gains exemption is the calculated net of amounts claimed under the regular capital gains exemption, which was repealed in 1994.

Because of the risk that access to the capital gains exemption might be restricted in the future (due to the considerations outlined in the previous paragraph), it is often advisable to crystallize the exemption as part of the estate freeze reorganization, i.e., by electing into a (tax-exempt) capital gain in respect of the freeze shares. This can be done with both a holding company and an internal freeze. In the latter case, a section 85 election could be filed in connection with a share reorganization, as was discussed earlier in the chapter. If the shares of the frozen corporation qualify for the exemption, e.g., there are no problematic non-qualifying assets, this should be a simple procedure. Otherwise, it may be necessary to undertake a more complex reorganization involving the purification of the corporation, i.e., the removal of non-qualifying assets.

Crystallizations and Holding Company Freezes

The previous example (Example 3) illustrates a crystallization in the context of an internal freeze. The following is an example of a crystallization in the context of a holding company freeze:

Example 4 ——————————————————————————

Mr. & Mrs. Louis each own one common share of Opco, the shares of which qualify for the capital gains exemption[17]. Mr. Louis has previously used his capital gains exemption, but Mrs. Louis has not (it is assumed that the attribution rules do not apply to attribute the capital gain to Mr. Louis). Mr. and Mrs. Louis could each roll their common shares of Opco into Holdco, in exchange for, say, 1,000 freeze shares, redeemable and retractable based on the value of the consideration received on the first issuance thereof, with nominal value common shares held by a family trust. Mrs. Louis could elect into a capital gain of $500,000 while Mr. Louis would roll at cost. Assuming further that the pre-existing cost base of the shares of Opco was nominal (nil), the following results would occur:

• Holdco would have a $500,000 cost base in respect of Opco.

• Mrs. Louis would have a $500,000 cost base in respect of her 1,000 freeze shares of Holdco.

• Mr. Louis would have a nominal cost base in respect of his 1,000 freeze shares of Holdco.

☞ **This structure would allow a degree of creditor protection, since dividends could be paid to Holdco, and either lent back, preferably on a secured basis, or invested by Holdco.**

Were Mrs. Louis to sell the shares of Holdco, the benefits of the cost base resulting from the capital gains crystallization would be straightforward. It should be noted, however, that if Holdco were to sell the Opco shares for an exempt gain, the proceeds would effectively be locked into Holdco. The reason is that, for the purposes of section 84.1 of the Act, Mrs. Louis would be considered to have a nominal paid-up capital in respect of the Holdco shares, even though she otherwise has a $500,000 cost base. In this example, even if shares with a higher stated capital were issued by Holdco, the effect of section 84.1 would be to reduce the paid-up capital of Holdco to a nominal amount. Therefore, an attempt to extract the proceeds from Holdco would give rise to a deemed dividend.

As stated previously, however, the individual shareholders could instead sell the shares of Holdco to obtain the benefit of the increased cost base, without the section 84.1 "lock in" effect. If a freeze had also been undertaken, additional capital gains exemptions would potentially be available in respect of growth shares held

---

[17] If it does not because of non-qualifying assets, the reorganization could be preceded by a spin-out purification. This is discussed in greater detail in a footnote 3 to the previous example (Example 3) on p. 109.

either by a family trust or the children/grandchildren.[18] However, the holding company may have accumulated investment and other assets. If so, it may be possible to spin out the assets to a newly formed holding company prior to a third party sale. Essentially, the shareholders of Holdco would transfer a portion of their shares to a newly-formed holding company with the investment assets distributed to "Newco".[19] Potentially, the distribution could be in the form of a tax-free intercorporate dividend; however, if a third party sale is anticipated, the tax-free dividend to Newco would probably be limited to the "safe income" attaching to the shares held by the Newco.[20]

Besides a crystallization, another possibility is not to crystallize but to put a structure in place whereby small business corporation status can be maintained. This can be done by utilizing holding companies in favour of the parents — i.e., to hold the freeze shares. This structure might be used where it is desired to gain continuing income splitting advantages. The reason is that the maintenance of the frozen corporation as a small business corporation will mean that the corporate attribution rules do not apply.

Multiplying the Exemption

In cases where the exemption is not sufficient to provide adequate death tax coverage, an estate freeze might also be beneficial in that the entitlement to the exemption might be multiplied as a result of family members holding growth shares. However, there are two potential roadblocks to the multiplication of the capital gains exemption — the personal and corporate attribution rules. The former do not generally impose a significant problem: in the case of children, the personal attribution rules do not apply to capital gains, irrespective of the age of the child. Accordingly, each child is potentially eligible for separate capital gains exemption. In the case of a spouse, the personal attribution rules apply to both income and capital gains. However, since the funding of the growth shares is typically nominal, it is possible to structure the freeze such that the personal attribution rules would not apply (e.g., by the use of independent capital or the prescribed interest rate loan exemption).

---

[18] If the shares were held by a family trust, in order to multiply the exemption it would be necessary for the capital gains realized by the trust to be paid or payable to the children, e.g., in the form of a promissory note, as a trust itself does not qualify for the exemption (see subsection 110.6(2.1)). However, as discussed elsewhere in this book, it may be desirable to insert a "subsection 74.4(4) clause" in the trust, prohibiting any distributions to minors, in order to avoid the application of the "corporate attribution rules". This would preclude multiplication of the exemption in respect of minors.

[19] For example, assuming that the shareholder of Holdco owns only common shares, Holdco could be restructured so that the individual would retain preferred shares with a value equal to the unused exemption, with the remaining value reflected in common shares which are rolled into Newco, to maximize the safe income attaching to these shares. After the investment assets are distributed to Newco, the individual would sell the preferred shares and Newco would sell the common shares of Holdco. If a freeze had been effected, e.g., in favour of a family trust, a similar reorganization might be effected, e.g., the family trust would retain the preferred shares and roll the common shares into a Holdco.

[20] There would be a disposition of the investments by Holdco when distributed to Newco. A full scale spin-out reorganization of the assets would not be possible if the spin-out is part of a series of transactions involving a third-party sale, because subsection 55(2) would apply to deemed dividends in respect of the spin-out, thereby triggering capital gains tax.

The corporate attribution rules can be more problematic, however, since they potentially apply in respect of benefits conferred on a "designated person", including a minor child or grandchild, or a spouse. The corporate attribution rules will not apply where the corporation maintains small business corporation status. However, since it may be difficult to maintain this status, reliance thereon can be a dangerous course of action, unless special structures/procedures are in place to continually maintain this status.

As discussed in more detail in "Corporate Attribution Rules" in Chapter 4, there is a further exception to the corporate attribution rules in respect of estate freezes, contained in subsection 74.4(4). However, this exemption (which requires the use of the family trust) is designed to preclude benefits to a "designated person" (see in particular paragraphs 74.4(4)(*b*) and (*c*)). In the case of a child or grandchild, for example, this restriction would be problematic in terms of multiplying the exemption if the child is a minor. In order to access the exemption, where shares are held by a trust, the capital gain must normally be "paid or payable" to the individual beneficiary; however, a "subsection 74.4(4) clause" would preclude this. This would no longer be a problem once the child or grandchild reaches the age of majority since "designated person" status will no longer apply. However, as long as a person is a spouse of the transferor, he or she will not be entitled to receive benefits from a subsection 74.4(4) trust. Accordingly, if capital gains splitting with a spouse is desired, it would seem to be necessary to rely on the small business corporation exemption, or attempt to escape the corporate attribution rules through the various means of technical escape as outlined in Chapter 4.

In addition to the above, careful consideration should be given to the structure of the estate freeze and how it impacts on the availability of the capital gains exemption. For example, the use of a holding company may give rise to more severe requirements in respect of the two-year holding period requirement contained in paragraph (*c*) of the definition of "qualified small business share" contained in subsection 110.6(1). (In this respect, the provisions of subsection 110.6(14) should be considered carefully, especially paragraph (*f*).)

Note that if preserving the ability to obtain the capital gains exemption is an objective, it should be borne in mind that subsection 110.6(8) can potentially deny the exemption, especially where non-cumulative dividends are an attribute of the freeze shares, as is usually the case. Subsection 110.6(8) denies, in entirety, the capital gains exemption where it may reasonably be considered that a significant portion of the capital gain is attributable to the fact that dividends were not paid on a share (other than a prescribed share) of a corporation, or that dividends on such a share were less than 90% of the "average annual rate of return" for the year or any preceding year. Subsection 110.6(9) specifies rules with respect to the "average annual rate of return", by reference to the annual return that a "knowledgeable and prudent investor" would expect to receive in the particular year under the circumstances (reference should be made to the exact wording of this subsection).

As will be apparent from an examination of these anti-avoidance provisions, the rules in this respect are somewhat vague and ill-defined. Further, the CRA has been of little assistance in providing certainty in respect of the non-application of these provisions.

Fortunately, Regulation 6205 exempts certain shares from the application of subsection 110.6(8). Besides ordinary common shares (i.e., having no fixed dividend rate or redemption amount and no minimum entitlement on liquidation), Regulation 6205(2), in essence, exempts preference shares issued in the course of an estate freeze for the main purpose of permitting any increase in value of the issuing corporation's property to accrue to newly issued common shares (growth shares) that will be held by persons that do not deal at arm's length with the holder of such preference shares.

☞   **Regulation 6205(2) is very specific and it is possible that certain technical anomalies may arise. Accordingly, it should be reviewed carefully in respect of an estate freeze involving the capital gains exemption, especially if there is something unusual about the freeze structure.**

Capital Gains Exemption — Basic Requirement

The following points should be noted in respect of the $500,000 capital gains exemption.

Eligibility

For a share to fit within the definition of a "qualified small business corporation share" under the Act and therefore be eligible for the $500,000 exemption, the shares must be those of a small business corporation, as defined in the Act at the time they are disposed of. There are also two additional conditions which must be met: a holding period requirement; and a requirement that the shares must be shares of a corporation that meets an active business test during the required period.

Small business corporation

A small business corporation is defined in the Act (section 248(1)) as a Canadian-controlled private corporation "all or substantially all" of the fair market value of the assets of which were, at the time, attributable to assets that were:

(a) used principally in an active business carried on primarily in Canada by the particular corporation or a corporation related to it;

(b) shares or indebtedness of one or more small business corporation "connected" (as defined in the Act) with the particular corporation; and

(c) a combination of the assets described in (a) and (b) above.

Basically, a corporation is "connected" with another corporation if it controls that other corporation or owns more than 10% of the shares in respect of both votes and value — see subsections 186(2) and (4).

The CRA's administrative policy is that "all or substantially all" means "at least 90% of the fair market value of the assets".

☞ **The CRA has developed very detailed guidelines as to whether or not particular assets will qualify as being used in an active business. Such items as significant cash or investment balances (not necessary for current operations), assets used outside of Canada, shareholder loans, land held for future expansion, real estate with mixed use (e.g., partly rental and partly business) and so on, may result in the 90% test not being met.**

Holding period requirement and active business test

The holding period requirement provides that, throughout a period of 24 months immediately before the time of disposition, the shares must not have been owned by any person other than the individual or a person or partnership that was "related" to him (special rules are contained in the Act for this purpose).

The active business test requires that throughout the holding period (see above) more than 50% of the fair market value of the corporation's assets must have been used in an active business. For this purpose, assets considered to be used in an active business consist of:

(a) assets used principally in an active business carried on primarily in Canada by the particular corporation or a corporation related to it;

(b) shares or indebtedness of a connected corporation; and

(c) a combination of the assets in (a) and (b).

Where a corporation does not hold assets used by related corporations, or shares or debt in connected corporations, it must use more than 50% of the fair market value of its assets in an active business carried on primarily in Canada throughout the required two-year holding period.

Where, however, a corporation holds shares or debt of a connected corporation, those shares or debt will qualify as active business of the corporation if certain conditions are met. These conditions are technical in nature. Generally, the analysis of whether a multiple corporation structure qualifies for the $500,000 capital gains exemption can become quite complicated, and very often, these stringent tests will knock a business off-side. (One common example of this is where a corporation has a U.S. subsidiary or otherwise carries on business outside of Canada, since the $500,000 exemption is based on Canadian business activities.)

Restrictions on exemption

In addition to the shares themselves qualifying for the exemption, it should be noted that recourse to the exemption could be restricted in a number of instances. If an individual has a Cumulative Net Investment Loss ("CNIL") account, capital gains will be non-exempt except to the extent that the taxable amount of the qualifying capital gain exceeds the amount of the CNIL account. Furthermore, a taxpayer's allowable business investment losses for the year or a previous year (after 1984) will reduce the extent to which capital gains for the year may qualify for the exemption.

Conversely, previous years' capital gains exemption claims will reduce the ability to claim allowable business investment losses.

☞ **Other factors that could have a negative impact on capital gains exemption tax planning include "low-dividend preferred shares" (subsection 110.6(8) of the Act), minimum tax, failure to report the capital gain or file the exemption on a timely basis, etc.**

For a more detailed discussion of the capital gains exemption, crystallizations, purification spin outs, and other topics discussed above, reference should be made to *Tax and Family Business Succession Planning*, by David Louis and Samantha Prasad Weiss (2003, CCH Canadian Limited).

Chapter 4

Corporate Estate Freezes — Technical Issues

TOPICS DISCUSSED

By and large, the technical issues that may arise in a corporate estate freeze are generic — they may apply to estate freezes where personally held assets are rolled into a corporation, internal freezes (notably, section 86 reorganizations) and so on. Apart from these considerations, additional issues arise by virtue of the specific methodology used — issues relating, for example, to transfers to corporations pursuant to section 85 In order to appreciate the technical issues, it may be helpful to envision a basic corporate freeze structure (illustrated in the diagram below). The basic freeze configuration is that the freezor ("Freezor") holds freeze shares of the corporation — that is to say:

- redeemable/retractable at the value of the pre-existing shares at the time of the freeze;

- voting (either as an attribute of the redeemable/retractable shares or with the voting shares sequestered in a separate class which has virtually no rights apart from the votes themselves);

- non-cumulative dividends — either fixed or to a ceiling, usually based on the redemption/retraction amount (e.g., up to .75% per month);

with the usual preferences on dissolution, and so on.

The growth shares are assumed to be held either directly by one or more children, or as is more commonly the case, through a family trust, which will be assumed to have the usual discretionary features, with the issue of the Freezor (i.e., lineal descendants) as beneficiaries.

Benefits

It must be ensured that the estate freeze reorganization is effected so as not to confer a benefit on any of the parties to the reorganization. Otherwise, a number of provisions may potentially come into play, including:

- subsections 15(1), 56(2) and 246(2);

- paragraph 85(1)(e.2) where the freeze involves a section 85 transfer of assets to a corporation;

- subsection 86(2) where the freeze involves a section 86 reorganization; and

- subsection 51(2), were section 51 (the convertible property rollover) to apply to a freeze.

Figure — Basic Freeze

BASIC FREEZE

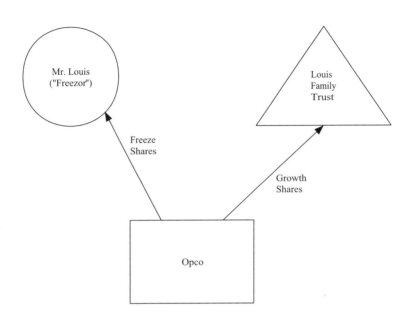

As can be seen, several provisions — notably sections 85 and 86 — contain anti-benefit provisions which are specific to each section (and therefore the particular estate freeze methodology). These anti-benefit provisions pertain to benefits conferred on related persons and may result in a deemed capital gain to the person conferring the benefit. Other provisions of the Act do not depend on related status and may tax the person receiving the benefit (or conferring the benefit, as is the case with subsection 56(2)).

Do not assume that the CRA will not seek to assess on the basis of a generic section, if a specific section is not applicable in the circumstances.

Of course, in an estate freeze, the primary benefit issue pertains to whether the holding of growth shares — usually acquired for nominal consideration by family members or a family trust — will constitute a benefit. By convention, practitioners and the CRA have accepted the premise that, in general, provided that the freeze shares reflect the full fair market value of the property "exchanged" for them (e.g., common shares in an internal freeze), there will be no benefit. However, various provisions are typically included in an estate freeze in order to minimize the possibility of the benefit provisions applying, notably the following.

Retraction Rights

The share should be retractable (i.e., redeemable at the option of the holder) based on the fair market value of property transferred or "exchanged". A formal written valuation should be obtained to support the fair market value. In addition to retraction rights, most practitioners include a redemption right, i.e., at the option of the corporation, based on the same value. However, the purpose of this feature does not pertain to the benefit issue; the redemption feature is included to "hold down" the value of the shares. If the shares are redeemable at the specified amount, it would be argued that a "willing buyer" would not pay any more than this amount.

Liquidation Rights

On the liquidation, dissolution or winding up of the corporation, the holders of the freeze shares should be entitled to receive the redemption price of the freeze shares and any dividends which have been declared in respect of the frozen shares but not paid, prior to the distribution of assets of the corporation to other shareholders.[1]

Dividend Rights

To buttress the foregoing, most practitioners consider it prudent to include a dividend feature (not in excess of a reasonable amount). In Q.13 of the 1980 Revenue Canada Round Table it was stated that: "The preferred shares should be entitled to a dividend. In any case, the dividend must not exceed a reasonable amount." In Q.45 of the 1981 Revenue Canada Round Table, it was stated that:

> In an estate freeze, the Department prefers that the preferred shares bear a reasonable dividend rate but the absence of one would not, in and by itself, be viewed as reducing the value of the preferred shares to cause paragraph 85(1)(e.2) to be applied.

Most commonly, a non-cumulative dividend is used. Another advantage of this, of course, is that it provides a source of income to the Freezor, if necessary.

☞ **Flexibility is often increased by inserting a monthly non-cumulative dividend feature and, where advisable, making even the non-cumulative dividends discretionary in the sense that dividends can be declared "up to" the ceiling amount.**

Price Adjustment Clause

Of course, the purpose of a price adjustment clause is to attempt to eliminate taxable benefits in the event that the CRA takes issue with the freeze value. Typically, the clause will be operative only in the event of a dispute with the CRA which is unsuccessful. The clause usually seeks to restore the equilibrium between the value of the "exchanged" property and the value of the consideration received. The primary mechanism for achieving this result is usually an adjustment to the

[1] See Q.13, 1980 Revenue Canada Round Table.

retraction/redemption amount of the freeze shares. This purports to be effective retroactively to the time of the freeze.

For further discussion of price adjustment clauses, see Chapter 6, p. 202.

Non-Impairment Clause

This refers to a provision in the Articles to the effect that dividends or reacquisitions of subordinate classes of shares cannot be effected if the result would be to impair the ability to redeem or retract freeze shares. Examples of share provisions with the foregoing attributes, and further discussion thereon, is contained in Chapter 6. In addition to the rights specified above, in the CRA's view, at least, the following rights should also be included.

Freeze shares may or may not have voting rights, but should at least have voting rights on any matter involving a change to the rights, conditions, or limitations attaching to them sufficient to protect those rights. These voting rights can be provided by corporate law or in the articles of incorporation (see Q.47, 1993 Revenue Canada Round Table).

There should be no restriction on the transferability of the shares other than restrictions required by corporate law to qualify the corporation as a "private" corporation. See Q.13, 1980 Revenue Canada Round Table.

In addition to the foregoing, the CRA has suggested that there be a clause in the share attributes indicating that if the corporation at any time acquires any of the freeze shares, the acquisition must take place at a price equal to the lesser of the aggregate redemption value of the freeze shares and the realizable value of assets less liabilities of the corporation immediately before the acquisition of the freeze shares by the corporation.

Besides the above provisions pertaining to a conferral of benefit, practitioners should also be aware of the possibility that, where shares having material value are simply issued for less than full fair market value consideration such that a person's "equity" in the corporation increases relative to other shareholders, the CRA could attack the transaction as a "transfer" or taxable disposition to such persons.[2] In addition, where a spouse or minor family member obtains such shares, the personal attribution rules might be imposed, i.e., as a consequence of the "transfer".

Valuation Issues

A fundamental issue in respect of estate freezes is the value of the frozen property. Valuation is, of course, a topic unto itself; the following is only a cursory discussion.

"Fair market value" involves the willing buyer/willing seller standard; it necessarily contemplates uncompelled, arm's-length, reasonably informed parties, acting in their respective self-interests.

---

[2] In particular, see *The Queen v. Kieboom*, 96 DTC 6382 (F.C.A.).

There are many issues in respect of the valuation of shares in an estate freeze. These include the following:

- Where an earning approach is used, the selection of the price earnings multiple that applies to maintainable earnings.

- Adjustments to "normalize" earnings.

- The identification and valuation of redundant assets.

- The effect of cycles or seasonality on earnings.

- The effect of maintainability of earnings where there is a dependency upon a key person.

- Off-balance sheet items.

The valuation in respect of a freeze might take into account various discounts, including the following:

- Discounts in respect of larger real estate portfolios.

- Minority discounts.

- Discounts for lack of marketability or liquidity.

- Discounts for fractional interests in real estate (e.g., co-ownership interests). This may be a particular issue in respect of real estate companies which were started by the older generation in which subsequent generations are now involved. Experience has shown that after a generation or two, there may be little cohesion/common interests. Worse still, the value of the real estate itself may lead to an atmosphere of distrust and conflict. Query the fair market value of properties held in co-tenancy under such circumstances, particularly where the structure of the holdings themselves precludes butterfly or other divisive reorganizations.

One other discount issue that often arises is whether the value should take into account deferred tax exposure in respect of the frozen assets.[3]

The CRA's long-standing policy has been that this should not be the case in respect of a rollover of properties to a corporation under section 85 of the Act, in view of the fact that an arm's length buyer would not "inherit" this tax liability. The value of property relates to the attributes of the property itself and is unaffected by the tax position of the owner. Although this means that, on an immediate redemption, the freeze shares might not realize their redemption price, the CRA's view is that the intent of a freeze contemplates a long-term hold rather than quick redemption and the preferred shares could be redeemed at their full amount after some period.[4]

However, a different result would appear to occur in respect of the freeze of corporate shares in which there is an underlying tax exposure in respect of the

---

[3] For further discussion of these issues, reference should be made to *Valuations and Price Adjustment Clauses*, Richard M. Wise, 98 CR, p. 33:1, *et seq.*

[4] This policy was expressed in Q.53 of the 1981 Revenue Canada Round Table.

corporation's assets, including a section 86 reorganization or a connected company freeze (i.e., a roll into Holdco in consideration for freeze shares). In such cases, it is likely that a willing buyer would seek a discount in respect of the deferred tax exposure in respect of the corporate-held property itself, as well as the possibility of a further discount in respect of the cost of distribution from the corporation, where applicable.

Where shares of a corporation are valued using an earnings multiple, the level of corporate tax is, of course, relevant in determining the value. Where a net asset value approach is used, a discount would appear to be appropriate under the fair market value test, since a knowledgeable buyer would presumably factor in the tax costs of liquidation. However, a further issue becomes whether the deferred tax liability should be discounted — i.e., because a liquidation of corporate assets would be deferred — and if so, by how much. This might depend to some extent upon the facts of the situation. Practically speaking, it may also depend upon the aggressiveness of the valuator.

Business Valuations

The CRA delineates a substantial number of valuation policies in Information Circular 89-3, Policy Statement on Business Equity Valuations, including the following:

- The earnings and asset value methods are the two most generally accepted bases for determining value. The earnings method is of primary concern when valuing shares of operating companies that manufacture or market products or services. (See paragraph 8 of IC 89-3.)

- Asset value methods are useful where:

  (a) A reasonable and viable alternative to buying an existing business is to start one from scratch, such as small construction subcontractors operating on competitive bids, auto body repair shops, machine shops, or some retail outlets.

  (b) A business sells largely on an asset basis, that is, it derives its income largely from the assets, either tangible or intangible, rather than from the personal efforts of the owners and personnel, e.g., real estate holding companies, equipment leasing or investment companies, or franchise or dealership operations. (See paragraph 9 of IC 89-3.)

- Options and buy-sell agreements affect fair market value determination as required by several sections of the Act, notably section 69 and subsection 70(5). (See paragraph 17 of IC 89-3.)

- In a closely held corporation, fair market value must be determined by referring to share rights and restrictions, whether found in the company's articles, by-laws or valid contracts between shareholders. These rights or restrictions can have an appreciatory or a depreciatory effect on the price a willing purchaser would pay for the shares in the notional market. (See paragraph 18 of IC 89-3.)

- The Department recognizes that in certain situations either a related group or an unrelated group of shareholders may control a corporation if they owned amongst themselves at least 50% plus one of the issued and outstanding voting shares of the corporation at the same time and if they have historically acted in concert as a group. It is a rebuttable presumption that a family group has acted in concert to control a corporation.

An assertion by a minority shareholder that he/she is part of a family-controlled group must be considered in light of all relevant factors, including the rights and restrictions attributable to his/her particular shares.

In a situation where the existence of family control is recognized, the CRA will employ a rateable valuation for each family group member's shares. (See paragraph 32 of IC 89-3.)

Non-Arm's Length Buy-Sells

A continuing issue has been the relevance of a buy-sell between non-arm's length persons in the valuation of shares of a corporation. The CRA's policy as expressed in IC 89-3 is as follows:

If a buy-sell agreement, normally determinative of value, is executed between parties not acting at arm's length, its provisions should be determinative of value, as long as it meets the following criteria:

(a) It is a *bona fide* business arrangement.

(b) The stipulated price or formula price in the agreement provides full and adequate consideration, and represents the fair market value of shares determined without reference to the agreement at the time it is executed.

(c) It is a legal and binding contract. (See paragraph 29 of IC 89-3.)

This policy, simply stated, is that the CRA will generally accept buy-sell agreements as being determinative of fair market value when they are prepared on an arm's length basis. This has been the subject of considerable criticism by practitioners. For example, the following statement is made in *Taxation of Private Corporations and Their Shareholders:* "In the final analysis, it appears that the Canadian courts are prepared to follow the buy-sell price in arriving at fair market value, or at least to give significant weight to that price".[5]

Discretionary Dividends/Waivers

Issues arise in respect of estate freezes and income splitting reorganizations which rely on "discretionary dividend shares", "waivers", etc. — namely, whether such structures could be viewed as conferring a benefit on the shareholder receiving the dividends. For example, one might wish to make both parents' and children's shares discretionary as to dividends, so that they may be sprinkled as between parents and children. Subsection 56(2) of the Act, if applicable, taxes the person who confers the benefit.

---

[5] Third edition, chapter 11:19.

In *McClurg v. The Queen*, 91 DTC 5001 (S.C.C.), the taxpayer successfully survived an attack in respect of a discretionary dividend scheme. However, in this case, the Supreme Court left the door open in respect of situations in which the shareholder does not make a "legitimate contribution" to the corporation. *Neuman v. The Queen*, 98 DTC 6297 (S.C.C.), appears to settle this issue, indicating that subsection 56(2) would generally not apply to discretionary dividends, and more specifically, that there is no distinction in respect of the application of subsection 56(2) in cases where the shareholder does not make a legitimate contribution to the corporation.

However, the *Neuman* case was prior to the enactment of the corporate attribution rules in section 74.4 of the Act, as well as prior to the enactment of the GAAR (subsection 245(2)). Specifically, a freeze reorganization involving a discretionary dividend scheme in favour of "designated persons" (per the section, including a spouse or minor child or grandchild) may well trigger the corporate attribution rules, thus resulting in a significant tax exposure. Accordingly, caution continues to be advised in respect of discretionary dividend arrangements.

It should also be noted that the above-mentioned cases may have only a peripheral effect where dividends are waived, as opposed to situations where a discretionary structure is in place. In plain words, the CRA could continue to attack waivers, notwithstanding the above-mentioned cases.

Finally, where a discretionary family trust is used to hold the growth shares in an estate freeze, discretionary-dividend structures are probably not necessary, as the trust itself may allow dividends to be sprinkled between children, while the parent(s) can receive non-cumulative dividends on the freeze shares. This flexibility can be increased by inserting a monthly non-cumulative dividend feature and, where advisable, making the non-cumulative dividends discretionary in the sense that dividends can be declared up to the ceiling amount.

Personal Attribution Rules

The personal attribution rules may come into play in an estate freeze, particularly where growth shares of the incorporated business are subscribed to or otherwise acquired by children under 18 years of age or a spouse (or indirectly for such individuals through a trust).

More precisely, if property is transferred (or loaned) for the benefit of a child or other non-arm's length person, or a niece or a nephew, who has not reached the age of 18 in the year, the income therefrom or substituted property will be deemed to be the income of the transferor until the year in which the individual reaches the age of 18 (see subsection 74.1(1)). Thus, in an estate freeze, where growth shares are transferred from a parent to a child, or money is given or lent (on an "interest-subsidized" basis) to a child in order to fund the purchase or subscription to such shares, income from the shares — that is to say, dividends paid on the shares — will be attributable to the parent. In the case of property transferred (or loaned) to or for the benefit of a spouse, both income (i.e., dividends) and capital gains will be taxed in the transferor's hands (see subsections 74.1(2) and 74.2(1)).

The attribution rules refer to a transfer (or loan) "directly or indirectly, by means of a trust or by any other means whatever" to a spouse, minor child, etc. This means that a transfer to a trust of which a spouse or minor child is a beneficiary will also be subject to the personal attribution rules.

The following are methods by which the personal attribution rules are most commonly circumvented in a freeze situation:

Loans for Value

Subsections 74.5(1) and (2) provide for exceptions to the personal attribution rules in the case of "loans for value". The personal attribution rules will not apply if interest is charged at a rate at least equal to the lesser of:

(a) the prescribed rate in effect at the time the indebtedness occurred (this refers to the rate prescribed pursuant to regulation 4301(c), and does not include the surcharge which is applied to unpaid taxes, etc.); and

(b) a rate that, having regard to all the circumstances, would have been agreed upon at the time the indebtedness was incurred between parties dealing at arm's length with one another.

For this exemption to apply, under both circumstances, interest that is payable in respect to the particular year must be paid no later than thirty days after the end of the particular year.

Most practitioners use the prescribed rate option (i.e., (a) above) for the loan, rather than relying on the "reasonable rate" exception, especially in view of the fact that, in an estate freeze situation, it is usually for a relatively small amount. Although prescribed rates may change quarterly, the interest rate can be based on the prescribed rate in effect at the time of the loan.

Thus, it is most common for the acquisition of growth shares to be funded by a prescribed interest rate loan, e.g., from a parent. Because of the thirty-day requirement, a dividend may be paid in the first year, which is used to retire the loan, plus the interest, so that timely interest payments are no longer required. (If a trust is used, this may result in taxable income in the trust return, since part of the dividend must remain at the trust level in order to retire the loan; however, since the amount of the loan is usually small, the tax in the trust is usually modest.)

Fair Market Value Swaps

A second exemption from the personal attribution rules is contained in subsection 74.5(1). It provides for an exception to the attribution rules for transfers based on "fair market value consideration". For example, the personal attribution rules do not apply if, at the time of the transfer, the fair market value of the transferred shares does not exceed the fair market value received by the transferor in consideration for the shares. (In the case of property transferred to a spouse, the parties cannot take advantage of the spousal rollover provided for in subsection 73(1); otherwise the exception will not apply.) Although this exception might be occasionally relied on in respect of the acquisition of growth shares in an estate freeze situation, it is much more common for the loans for value exception to be relied on.

Independent Capital

Of course, the personal attribution rules do not apply if the growth shares are acquired using independent capital to fund the acquisition. Sources may include income from employment, an inheritance, etc. If this exception is relied on, care should be taken to be in a position to substantiate the fact that independent capital is used. For example, the source should be from a bank account which is not tainted with offside transfers/loans.

One potential source of independent capital is a gift from a non-relative. Note, however, that the personal attribution rules may be triggered when the transferor does not deal at arm's length with the transferee. In an estate freeze situation, it might be asserted that, although the transferor is not related (and thus not deemed to be in a non-arm's length relationship for tax purposes), the transferor is in a factual non-arm's length position, e.g., if the transferee does not exercise independent judgment, or the transferor and transferee are acting in concert. This might be a consideration for a person who is asked to fund a share subscription in an estate freeze, e.g., in order to avoid the somewhat more cumbersome prescribed interest loan route described previously. There may be a possibility that the person could be faced with a substantial tax liability were the CRA to take an adverse position in this respect.

☞ **The personal attribution rules do not apply to family members (other than a spouse) who are adults. Subsection 56(4.1) is an exception; it applies to interest-subsidized loans or indebtedness to non-arm's length individuals, where one of the main reasons for the loan is tax reduction. In addition, for children, the attribution rules apply only to income from property, rather than capital gains. Thus, the personal attribution rules will threaten only the income-splitting aspects of an estate freeze — usually, dividends on growth shares. However, for the reasons discussed below, this threat may be academic.**

The "Kiddie Tax"

The advantages of income splitting in respect of a corporate estate freeze have been adversely affected by the so-called "kiddie tax", which clamps down on certain aspects of income splitting with minors. This refers to a special tax, levied at the highest marginal tax rate, which applies to individuals 17 or under. Included are dividends on shares of private corporations (and other shareholder benefits).

Trust Attribution Rules

Section 74.3 applies where an individual has loaned or transferred property to a trust in which a "designated person" is beneficially interested at any time. A "designated person" in respect of an individual is defined to be the individual's spouse, or a child or other non-arm's length person or a niece or nephew, who has not reached the age of 18 (see subsections 74.3(2) and 74.5(5)).

The trust attribution rules determine the amount of income to be attributed pursuant to the basic attribution rules contained in sections 74.1 and 74.2. Thus, if these provisions do not apply in the first place, e.g., because of the exemptions discussed previously, section 74.3 will be not be applicable. In addition, if no income or capital gains are recognized in the hands of a "designated person", there will be no attribution pursuant to section 74.3. For example, if income from a trust is distributed and taxed in the hands of a child who has reached the age of 18, the trust attribution rules will not apply.

Corporate Attribution Rules

A Significant tax trap

The corporate attribution rules, per section 74.4, present an obstacle to a successful estate freeze. In general, the rules — which can impose a substantial and continuing taxable benefit — apply where an individual has (directly or indirectly) transferred (or loaned) property to a corporation, and one of the main purposes of the transfer or loan may reasonably be considered to have been to reduce the individual's income and benefit (directly or indirectly) a "designated person" in respect of the individual. A "designated person" in respect of an individual is defined to be the individual's spouse, or a child or other non-arm's length person or a niece or nephew who has not reached the age of eighteen (see subsection 74.5(5)).

The corporate attribution rules may apply to any period (i.e., at any time) throughout which all of the following conditions apply:

- the designated person is, in broad terms, a "specified shareholder", whether or not resident in Canada (according to subsection 248(1), this refers to a person having 10% or more of the shares of any class of the transferee corporation; however, in this case, non-arm's length shareholders are not counted in the determination);

- the transferor was resident in Canada; and

- the transferee corporation was not a small business corporation.

The corporate attribution rules will cease to apply if any of these conditions ceases to apply. For example, if a spouse/shareholder ceases to be a spouse, the corporate attribution rules may cease to apply. If the conditions commence, once again, to apply, the corporate attribution rules would become operative, once again.

If an exception is not applicable, the corporate attribution rules will probably have an extremely negative impact on a corporate estate freeze. Where an estate freeze involves the transfer of assets from an individual to a corporation, arguably at least, one of the main purposes for the transfer (or loan if applicable) is the reduction of income of the transferor and a benefit to other family members. It is understood that the CRA is of the view that, in addition to the more immediate reduction of a parent's ongoing income resulting from the transfer of income-earning assets to a corporation, the reduction of capital gains tax on death may also constitute a reduction of income for the purposes of the corporate attribution rules. In addition, it could be argued that the basic effect of the accumulating growth characteristic of an estate freeze is to benefit children. Finally, it appears that the corporate attribution rules can apply both to estate freezes which involve transfers to holding companies, as well as those involving internal freezes, notably a section 86 reorganization (see subsection 84(9)).

Accordingly, most practitioners agree that, for "standard" corporate estate freezes (notably, involving a section 85 transfer of assets to a corporation by an individual, or a section 86 reorganization where an individual's common shares are changed to freeze shares), the corporate attribution rules must be complied with, in order to avoid a material tax penalty. Very basically, the corporate attribution rules may impose a taxable benefit based on prescribed interest rates from time to time, applicable to the value of property transferred or loaned to the corporation. In an internal estate freeze (for example, under section 86), this would normally be the value of the shares to be frozen.

The following are methods by which the application of the corporate attribution rules can be circumvented.

Small business corporation exemption

The corporate attribution rules apply for any taxation year that includes a period (after the transfer or loan in question) throughout which the corporation was not a small business corporation. Therefore, once a corporation loses its status as a small business corporation — even temporarily — the corporate attribution rules may apply for that period, despite the fact that, at the time of the original reorganization, the corporation may have qualified for small business corporation status. Essentially, a small business corporation is a Canadian-controlled private corporation all or substantially all of the assets of which are used in active business activities carried on primarily in Canada by the particular corporation or a related corporation, and/or shares and indebtedness of other small business corporations which are "connected" within the meaning of subsection 186(4) with the corporation.

Given the continuing status requirement, it can be dangerous to rely on this exemption. There are a variety of circumstances in which a corporation might lose its exempt status. For example, a successful business corporation which does not require its retained earnings in the active business itself may reinvest the earnings in non-qualifying activities at the corporate level, rather than distribute the excess funds to the shareholders and quite possibly attract additional tax by doing so.

☞ **It may be possible to maintain the corporation's exempt status by forming a second corporation to hold the shares of the parent/freezor. If so, and the business generates earnings which are not needed for business operations, they could then be passed out on an ongoing basis to the holding company as an inter-corporate dividend, so that the operating company may maintain its status as a small business corporation. But, it is still necessary to be diligent in ensuring that non-qualifying assets are systematically distributed to the holding company.**

Subsection 74.4(4) Clause

If small business corporation status cannot be ensured, a subsection 74.4(4) clause is normally inserted in an estate freeze trust. This exception to the corporate attribution rules is conditional on the only interest of the designated person being an interest in a trust with a subsection 74.4 clause. In plain words, for this exemption to apply, a trust must be used to hold the growth shares.

This exemption is designed to preclude income splitting in respect of "designated persons". Basically, such a clause prohibits benefits from the trust being enjoyed by anyone who is a designated person at the time, e.g., the spouse of the Freezor or a child while still a minor.

However, the prerequisites are quite onerous. The exemption will potentially be available only where:

- the only interest that the designated person has in the corporation is a beneficial interest in the shares of the corporation, which are held through a trust;

- the terms of the trust provide that the person may not receive or otherwise obtain the use of any income or capital of the trust while the person is a minor or spouse of the individual; and

- the designated person has not received or otherwise obtained the use of any of the income or capital of the trust and no deduction has been made under subsection 104(6) or (12) in respect of income paid or payable to, or included in, the person of that income while a "designated person".

It should be noted, for example, that the insertion of a subsection 74.4(4) clause would rule out a spouse being a beneficiary of a trust.

For the reasons indicated above, where other methods of dealing with the corporate attribution rules are not available, it is advisable to ensure that this provision is adhered to, i.e., an estate freeze should use a trust to receive growth shares, with a suitable subsection 74.4(4) clause included in the trust indenture itself.

It should be noted that, for the clause to be completely effective, there must be a blanket prohibition on the receipt of use of income or capital while a designated person, as stipulated above. Some practitioners attempt to limit the scope of such a clause to situations where the corporate attribution rules would otherwise apply; for example, the clause would not be operative where the corporation was qualified as a small business corporation or the transferor is not resident. While it might be argued that such a clause demonstrates that one of the main purposes of the transfer was not to benefit a designated person (this, of course, would depend on the circumstances), strictly speaking, such an approach would not be in compliance with subsection 74.4(4), which requires a blanket prohibition.[6]

Technical Escape

Subject to the application of anti-avoidance rules, it may be possible to escape the corporate attribution rules by undertaking procedures which do not involve an individual transferring or lending assets to a corporation.

Reverse freeze

Depending on the circumstances, it may be arguable that the corporate attribution rules may not apply for a so-called inter-corporate or reverse freeze. This involves a situation whereby an existing corporation ("Oldco") rather than an individual lends or transfers assets — usually under section 85 — to a new corporation ("Newco") in return for indebtedness and/or "freeze shares". The children or a family trust would subscribe for growth shares of Newco. Procedures described above relating to avoiding the personal attribution rules would be used; for example, a prescribed interest rate loan could be used to subscribe to the common shares of Newco. (For further discussion of reverse freezes, see Chapter 5.)

Stock dividend freeze

It may be possible to effect an estate freeze without running afoul of the corporate attribution rules through a stock dividend mechanism. For example, the Freezor may start out with all of the issued (common) shares of a corporation. The Articles of the corporation would be amended to provide for freeze shares. The corporation would then pay a stock dividend on the common shares consisting of the freeze shares in an amount sufficient to reduce the value of the corporation's common shares to a nominal amount. The applicable corporate law would have to permit the suppression of stated capital, in order to minimize the deemed dividend (which is based on the increased stated capital rather than the redemption/retraction amount of the freeze shares). "New common shares" would then be acquired by the children or family trust (again, having due regard to the personal attribution rules).

Section 74.4 may not apply to a stock dividend freeze since no loan or transfer has been made to the corporation under such circumstances. However, an issue arises as to the application of subsection 15(1.1). Subsection 15(1.1) was originally enacted as an anti-avoidance rule to counter certain manoeuvres that would increase

---

[6] See, for example, Doc. No. 2005-0126381E5, where the CRA indicated that where the terms of the trust agreement would allow for income or capital of the trust to be distributed to a person who is a designated person but only when the corporation is a small business corporation throughout the particular period in question, the requirements of paragraph 74.4(4)(*b*) would not be met.

recourse to the capital gains exemption. The provision indicates that, where in a taxation year, a corporation has paid a stock dividend to a person and it may be reasonably considered that one of the purposes of the payment was to "significantly alter the value of the interest of any 'specified Shareholder' of the corporation", the value of the stock dividend is included in the person's income. "Specified shareholder" is defined in subsection 248(1), relating basically to 10% or more equity positions, counting non-arm's length shareholders.

Proceeding from the premise that subsection 15(1.1) is limited to cases where the stock dividend results in a significant increase in the value of a shareholder's interest, it could be argued that none of the purposes of the stock dividend is to "significantly alter the value" (as required under subsection 15(1.1)) of the interest of any specified shareholder of the corporation. Therefore, one would conclude, it is not applicable to an estate freeze situation. However, it might possibly be counter-argued (for example) that, although the overall value has not significantly changed, "interest" refers to specific shares, such that the value of the common shares has been significantly altered.

☞ **In several technical interpretations the CRA has indicated that subsection 15(1.1) would not apply if the stock dividends are paid to all shareholders of the payor, pro rata in proportion to their shareholdings (see, for example, Document. No. FE91-213.214 and ACC9277).**

Such a manoeuvre would have to be considered in the light of the application, if any, of the GAAR.

For further discussion of stock dividend freezes, see Chapter 3.

"Step-down" Share Arrangements

In many instances, share conditions will be drafted in such a manner that, on the triggering of various events, the rights attaching to shares will be altered. For example, it is common to provide for a cessation of voting rights of freeze shares on the death of a Freezor in an estate freeze situation. In addition, reorganizations may be undertaken which provide for "first holder" rights whereby the redemption and/or voting and other rights attaching to the shares would be stepped-down in the event of a person other than the "first holder" (as defined) owning the shares. For example, such an arrangement might be used in an attempt to creditor-proof the shares, and so on. ("First holder" could be defined as encompassing a number of persons, e.g., the original subscriber and related persons.)

In *Bowater Canadian Ltd. v. R.L. Crane Inc.*,[7] the Ontario Court of Appeal struck down a step-down provision in which the voting rights would be restricted in the event that the shares passed to someone other than the person to whom the shares were originally issued. The holding appears to be based on corporate law principles which require an equality of rights within a class of shares. In *Bowater*, it was possible

---

[7] (1987), 62 OR (2d) 752; (1987), 46 D.L.R. (4th) 161 (C.A.).

for shares within the class to have differing voting rights under the step-down arrangement.

In an estate freeze or other situation in which step-down provisions are desired, it might be argued that the impact of Bowater could be avoided if the share provisions were drafted in a way such that all of the shares of the class were to be affected by the event which triggers the step-down, rather than only some of the shares.

 Shares containing identical provisions could be considered to be of the same class.

Reversionary Trust Rules

"Reversionary Trust" Rules — Subsections 75(2) and 107(4.1)

Where an individual transfers property to a trust, but continues to control the property or have a veto over it, the income or capital gains from the property may continue to be taxed in the hands of the transferor. More specifically, subsection 75(2) imposes attribution of income and capital gains where property is transferred to a trust and the property (or substituted property) is held on condition that it:

- may revert to the person from whom the property was (directly or indirectly) received (subparagraph 75(2)(a)(i));

- may pass to a person determined by the transferor after the creation of the trust (subparagraph 75(2)(a)(ii)); or

- may not be disposed of during the transferor's existence without the consent of the transferor or in accordance with the transferor's direction (subparagraph 75(2)(b)), i.e., the transferor has a veto power over the transferred property.

Where any of the foregoing conditions exist, both the income and the capital gains from the property are included in the transferor's income, while the transferor is resident in Canada.

The following are some situations in which subsection 75(2) may apply to transferred property:

- The trust is revocable by the transferor (i.e., the trust should be irrevocable).

- The transferor is a beneficiary of the trust, including a discretionary beneficiary.

- The trust requires a majority of trustees, but stipulates that the transferor must be part of the majority. In this case there is a veto power — the transferred property may not be disposed of during the transferor's lifetime without the consent of the transferor.

- The transferor is one of two trustees (and thus has a similar veto over the disposition of the property), or is the sole trustee. This could come about because other trustees pass away or resign.

Regarding the application of this provision, the CRA has indicated that where the settlor retains a general power of appointment or any other power — such as a power of encroachment on capital which he might exercise in his own favour so as to regain the capital of the trust — subsection 75(2) will apply. In at least one technical interpretation, the CRA has gone so far as to suggest that if the transferor had the power to replace trustees, this might trigger subsection 75(2), depending on the facts (although this statement is viewed by many practitioners to be questionable in most situations).

The CRA has also indicated that a genuine loan to a trust would not, in and of itself, be considered to result in the application of subsection 75(2), provided that the loan is outside and independent of the terms of the trust (see Interpretation Bulletin IT-369R, paragraph 1; see also Document No. 9811115, for example). The CRA has also indicated that a non-interest bearing loan may qualify as a genuine loan.

Relation of Subsection 75(2) to Freeze Mechanisms

Very often, growth shares will be acquired by the trust using a *bona fide* loan to fund the acquisition, thereby pre-empting the application of subsection 75(2) (at least under the CRA's administrative policies). For example, a loan at prescribed interest rates may provide the funding for the acquisition of treasury shares, in order to avoid the personal attribution rules. However, in many cases this will not occur. In Ontario, for example, the shares may be gifted to a trust, in order to provide protection from marital claims (i.e., to attempt to take advantage of the exemption for gifts acquired after marriage). In these cases, subsection 75(2) might apply, depending on the composition of the trustees, etc. To avoid problems such as those noted above, many practitioners avoid (where possible) having the transferor as a trustee.

Effect of Subsection 75(2) on Freeze

Where a conventional freeze is used, the application of subsection 75(2), in itself, means that dividends on growth shares, as well as capital from the sale of the shares themselves, would be attributed to the transferor. In many cases, this may not be perceived to be a major problem. It may not be envisioned that dividends would be paid on the shares, e.g., if the freeze is in favour of older children with high income, or there is a subsection 74.4(4) clause precluding such income splitting, e.g., in favour of minor children (this may be advisable because an estate freeze potentially triggers the corporate attribution rules).

Subsection 107(4.1)

However, in 1988, subsection 107(4.1) was added to the Act. This provision, which is dependent on the application of subsection 75(2), could result in fundamental problems in respect of a freeze. Subsection 107(4.1) precludes a rollout of trust property — that is, on a tax-deferred basis — to anyone other than the person from whom the property was received or a spouse, if subsection 75(2) was applicable at any time in respect of any property of the trust, and the transferor is alive at the time the property is distributed. It should be emphasized that, technically, the application of subsection 107(4.1) will occur if subsection 75(2) is applicable to any property transferred to the trust, not just the settlement itself.[8] Furthermore, the rectification of the situation such that subsection 75(2) no longer applies will not pre-empt the application of subsection 107(4.1).

The effect of the application of subsection 107(4.1) may well be to undermine the effects of the freeze, since, if the transferor is still alive, the property can be distributed only to the transferor, or his or her spouse (etc.). In this respect, it should be remembered that, in order to avoid a deemed disposition, the growth shares (and other trust property) must be distributed before the 21st anniversary of the creation of the trust. It is, of course, quite possible that the transferor would still be alive at this date, thus eliminating the possibility of a rollout to another beneficiary.

If the provision is applicable, a threshold issue is whether it is possible to distribute the shares to the transferor (or spouse) to begin with, i.e., pursuant to the terms of the trust. Depending on the structure of the freeze, the transferor (or his or her spouse) may be a bail out beneficiary; but in other cases, the transferor (or a spouse) may not be a beneficiary. In such a case, it would presumably be necessary to attempt to obtain a variation of the trust in order to add the transferor as a beneficiary.

☞ **A variation of trust may raise other tax issues, notably whether the changes are of such magnitude that there is a disposition of beneficiaries' interest in the trust or even the trust assets themselves; a Ruling in this respect may be advisable.**

Although subsection 107(4.1) was enacted in 1988, there are no grandfathering rules. This can be very problematic since, as stated previously, some estate freezes may have been purposely formulated with the knowledge that subsection 75(2) would apply, e.g., because dividend splitting was not desired and the Freezor wanted a high degree of control of the trust assets.

There have been a number of technical interpretations in respect of the application of subsection 107(4.1). For example, if there are identical properties in the trust, some of which were transferred into the trust by the settlor and some of which were

---

[8] The CRA has indicated that the provisions of subsection 107(4.1) could apply if subsection 75(2) could apply to an asset of the trust, even if the asset did not generate income. See Doc. No. 2005-0118181E5, November 17, 2005, *Window on Canadian Tax* ¶8506.

not, the CRA will apparently allow the trust to identify the properties that are to be distributed so as to avoid the application of subsection 107(4.1).[9]

Recent administrative developments

The CRA seems to have recently softened its position in respect of the application of subsections 75(2) and 107(4.1). Technical Interpretations 2000-0042505 (April 30, 2001) and 2001-0067955 (January 3, 2002) involve transfers to trusts where the transferor was one of the trustees, and unanimity was required. Accordingly, most practitioners would be concerned that such a trust would violate paragraph 75(2)(b)[10] (because the transferor has a veto), and, arguably, subparagraph 75(2)(a)(ii) (i.e., the property may pass to a person determined by the transferor after the creation of the trust).

While both Technical Interpretations indicate that it is a question of fact as to whether subsection 75(2) applies to a particular situation, standard trust terms (particularly the inability to change beneficiaries) and fiduciary duties inherent in trusts may combine to overcome the application of these troublesome provisions.

In respect of the condition set out in subparagraph 75(2)(a)(ii) — that the transferred property may pass to a person determined by the transferor after the creation of the trust — the CRA indicates:

> Where the beneficiaries under a trust are named in the trust indenture and cannot be modified (i.e., the person from whom the property was received by the trust cannot select additional beneficiaries after the creation of the trust), subparagraph 75(2)(a)(ii) is generally not considered applicable. This is true even though the person from whom the property was transferred to the trust may be able to determine the amount of the trust property that is to be distributed to beneficiaries already identified in the trust documents.

However, both Technical Interpretations go on to indicate that subparagraph 75(2)(a)(ii) is broadly worded and there could be exceptions to the general position, depending on the situation.

Perhaps even more remarkable is the view expressed in respect of the so-called veto power in subsection 75(2)(b). The Technical Interpretations suggest a distinction between powers exercised as trustee in a fiduciary capacity versus powers reserved in some other capacity. In plain words, fiduciary duties in respect of a trust could effectively override subsection 75(2)(b). Note, however, that the two Technical Interpretations indicate that the policies in question do not apply where the contributor to the trust is the sole trustee.

Technical Interpretation 2000-0042505 indicates that:

> Our current position is that where a person contributes property to a trust and is one of two or more co-trustees acting in a fiduciary capacity in administering the trust property and there are no specific terms outlining how the trust property is to be dealt with, but rather the property is subject to the standard terms of the trust, paragraph 75(2)(b) may not

---

[9] See Guy Fortin, "Economic Reality versus Legal Realty; Planning for Trusts: Deemed Disposition on January 1, 1999; Subsection 107(4.1) of the *Income Tax Act*", 1996 C.R. p. 5:31, which contains a detailed discussion of subsections 75(2) and 107(4.1).

[10] Paragraph 75(2)(b) provides that subsection 75(2) will apply where a property is held on the condition that it may not be disposed of during the transferor's existence without the consent or in accordance with the transferor's direction.

be considered applicable. However, such determinations will only be made on a case by case basis following a review of all the facts and circumstances surrounding a particular situation.

The second Technical Interpretation (2001-0067955) contains similar views.

For a summary of subsections 75(2) and 107(4.1) see "Reversionary Trust Review", by Robert Spenceley, in Appendix C. The article includes discussion of two new technical interpretations, Doc. No. 2004-0086921C6, October 8, 2005 and Doc. No. 2003-0050671E5, which affirm the recent administrative developments discussed above.

The Association Rules

An Overlooked problem

Estate freezes and other structures in which family trusts hold shares in closely held corporations can give rise to unintended and unforeseen tax penalties because of the interaction of family trusts with the association rules. These penalties can arise on both new and previously established family trusts — including those that were established years ago. The problem concerns the impact of certain deeming rules relating to associated corporations, which came into effect in the late 1980s. The following are among the problematic provisions:

(a) for the purposes of the association rules, it appears that each discretionary beneficiary of a trust is normally deemed to own all of the shares in the trust (paragraph 256(1.2)(*f*));

(b) where a child under the age of 18 is deemed to own shares, e.g., under (a) above, the CRA's position is that those shares, in turn, are deemed to be owned by the parents, in the absence of certain (unusual) circumstances (subsection 256(1.3)).

Although these rules are fairly well known, there seems to have been relatively little thought given to the interaction of these rules and commonplace estate planning structures. These tax rules can result in unforeseen and unintended association problems. The most common result of the association rules is that it is necessary to share the small business deduction. Loss of this benefit could mean an increase in corporate tax rates, plus exposure to double tax effects.

Consider the following examples where a discretionary trust can have unexpected tax consequences:

Example ————————————————————————————

Father implements an estate freeze in which all of the common shares are sequestered in a discretionary trust for the benefit of his children, some of whom are under the age of 18. Several years later, Mother decides to set up her own incorporated business.

Result: The shares, deemed to be held by the minors, will in turn be deemed to be held by both Father and Mother (in most cases). Therefore Father's and Mother's companies will be associated, and will have to share the $300,000 base.

Note that by virtue of subparagraph 256(1.2)(*c*)(ii), a majority of common shares are deemed to be a control block, even though they may originally have a nominal value.

The above example shows that the associated corporation trap can arise after a trust is set up.

Example

An individual undergoes a freeze whereby the common shares of Fatherco are placed in trust for children (adult or minor). Years after the family trust is set up, one or more of the children establish wholly owned corporations. Each child is deemed to own all of the common shares of Fatherco while the shares continue to be held by the family trust.

Result: Each Childco and Fatherco are associated. (Also, all Childcos are, *prima facie*, associated; because they are all associated with Fatherco, they are considered to be associated with one another, unless a special election under subsection 256(2) — relevant in respect of the small business deduction only — is filed.)

Other Tax Consequences

Apart from the small business deduction, associated corporation status is used for other tax incentives (and disincentives). In Ontario, in particular, these include:

- low rates of Ontario capital tax;
- the Ontario small business deduction clawback surtax which applies to associated corporations with income in excess of $400,000 per year;
- research and development (SR&ED) tax incentives;
- the threshold for Ontario's corporate minimum tax.

As a result, it may often be advisable to insert a special term in a discretionary trust in order to cope with this problem. For example, the trust could contain a provision to allow trustees to distribute property of the trust in full satisfaction of the discretionary beneficiary's entitlement to shares in the trust. However, because of the advisability of the distribution of growth shares prior to the 21st anniversary of the trust, by the time a beneficiary has established a successful business, the shares may no longer be held by a family trust.

Other Association Issues

Although the discretionary trust problems may be the most pervasive in respect of estate freezes, a number of other provisions may give rise to unintended adverse tax consequences. For example, it may be prudent to ensure that freeze shares adhere to the "specified class" definition in subsection 256(1.1), since such shares will generally be ignored for the purpose of the "25% cross ownership rules" (paragraphs 256(1)(*c*) to (*e*)), as well as the expanded concepts of control contained in subsection 256(1.2) (subsection 256(1.6)). In addition, where retractable shares are taken back, the "*de facto* control" provisions (subsection 256(5.1)) may have to be considered on the basis that the retraction right may give the holder an inordinate degree of influence, so as to possibly trigger these provisions (consideration might be given to agreements not to retract and so on, to mitigate this possibility).

Taxable and Short-Term Preferred Shares

Typically, a corporate estate freeze will involve the issuance of so-called high-low preferred shares — that is, shares with a low paid-up capital and a high redemption/retraction amount. Besides section 86, which normally requires paid-up capital suppression due to deemed dividend considerations, where low cost base assets are rolled into a corporation in exchange for freeze shares, subsection 85(2.1) will restrict the paid-up capital of such shares; where a holding company freeze is used, section 84.1 will probably be applicable.

When high-low shares are to be redeemed, a significant deemed dividend will be triggered. In fact, it may often be advisable to trigger the redemption in the first year of an estate, in order to take advantage of the subsection 164(6) loss carryback mechanism to alleviate certain double-tax effects that would otherwise occur.

Under the taxable and short-term preferred share regime, the redemption of such shares may potentially give rise to significant tax exposure pursuant to Part VI.1 of the Act. For a larger freeze, the deemed dividend resultant on a preferred share redemption may often exceed the dividend allowance safe harbour contained in subsection 191.1(2) (normally $500,000 of dividends per year, per associated group of corporations).

Besides the dividend allowance, there is an exemption for dividends paid to a shareholder that has a "substantial interest" in the payor corporation (according to subsection 191(2)). Basically, a substantial interest will arise either where the shareholder is "related" to the corporation (otherwise than by reason of a right referred to in paragraph 251(5)(*b*)), or where the shareholder owns (in terms of both votes and value) 25% or more of the issued shares, as well as either common shares (i.e., non-taxable preferred shares) representing at least 25% of the fair market value of all common shares, or 25% or more (in terms of value) of each class of shares (for particulars, see paragraph 191(2)(*b*)). Related shareholders count in this determination.

In most estate freezes, where freeze shares are held, the latter branch of the definition would not ordinarily be met unless a partial freeze is involved (unless shares which meet the latter branch of the definition are held by related shareholders — as will be seen, this may soon be problematic).

If during the freezor's lifetime, or after, the shares are distributed to beneficiaries, there may not be a problem. The substantial interest exemption may be available (e.g., if the freezor retains control of the corporation, as is typically the case). Moreover, a large scale redemption of the shares may be a relatively infrequent occurrence. However, it appears that a different result might arise when the shares are held by the estate — the very time in which it may be advisable to effect a redemption. By virtue of the "related persons" definition contained in subsection 251(2), an estate would not be related to the redeeming corporation unless the executors were related to the corporation. This may not be the case where control of the corporation does not pass to the executors. If, for example, after death, control of the corporation was in the hands of the common shareholders, typically children, there would appear to be a problem if the children were not related to the executors.[11]

Examples of where the foregoing could be problematic include where the decedent has selected a corporate trustee as executor, or a majority of executors are unrelated, e.g., professional advisors.

In cases where the "substantial interest" exemption does not apply and deemed and/or actual dividends exceed the annual dividend allowance, it would appear to be necessary to rely on subsections 191(4) and (5) — the "specified amount" exemption. Essentially, subsection 191(4) may apply to exempt a deemed dividend from Parts IV.1 and VI.1 of the Act where the terms and conditions of the shares (or an agreement in respect of the shares) specify an amount for which the shares are to be redeemed, acquired or cancelled, which amount does not exceed the fair market value of the consideration for which the shares were issued. (In the case where either the terms or the conditions of the shares are changed or an agreement in respect of the shares is changed or entered into, the specified amount cannot exceed the fair market value of the shares immediately before the particular time.)

In the CRA's view, the "specified amount" must be a dollar amount and cannot be subject to a price adjustment clause or be described by way of formula (see 1989 Revenue Canada Round Table Q.20, Document No. AC59342, for example). However, in the past at least, the CRA has accepted (in a private ruling) a redemption amount that was subject to a price adjustment clause but where a separate specified dollar amount was also provided for, i.e., for the purposes of satisfying subsection 191(4). If the redemption amount turned out to be greater than the specified amount, the excess would be subject to Part VI.1 tax. If the redemption amount turned out to be lower than the specified amount, Part VI.1 would apply to the entire dividend (because subsection 191(4) does not allow the specified amount to exceed the fair market value of the consideration for which the share was issued, which presumably is what the adjusted redemption amount equalled).

However, practically speaking, it is unlikely that a price adjustment clause would result in a downward adjustment.

---

[11] See paragraph 251(2)(b), section 104; see also *M.N.R. v. Consolidated Holding Company Ltd.*, 72 DTC 6007; *Lusita Holdings v. M.N.R.*, 82 DTC 6297 — the look-through rules in the association provisions would not apply for these purposes, nor is paragraph 251(5)(b) applicable.

☞   **Where the related exemption is relied upon, the estate may control the corporation. Until recently, this could result in the application of subsection 40(3.6) to deny the loss inherent in the subsection 164(6) procedure. However, the December 6, 2004 Notice of Ways and Means Motion in respect of the 2004 federal Budget included proposed subsection 40(3.61), which would essentially pre-empt the application of subsection 40(3.6), to the extent of a subsection 164(6) election. But, at time of writing, this amendment has not been extended to loss carrybacks in spouse trusts.**

Other Rules Relating to Preferred Shares

In addition to so-called taxable preferred and short-term preferred shares (although usually not applicable in the normal private corporation context) practitioners should also be aware that other stringent rules may apply in respect of preferred shares, including the so-called "term preferred", "collateralized preferred", "guaranteed preferred" and similar provisions.[12]

Accounting Considerations

CICA Handbook section 3860 requires the reclassification of retractable preferred shares as financial liabilities. As this normally includes freeze shares, reclassification as a financial liability could be problematic, for example, where covenants limit debt equity ratios, and so on.

However, section 1300 of the *CICA Handbook*, relating to "differential reporting", allows for partial differentiation in the application of GAAR by making available to qualifying enterprises (see below) specified exemptions and alternative accounting treatment tailored to financial reporting needs of the users of those enterprises' financial statements.

More specifically, "non-publicly accountable enterprises" are now eligible for a number of differential reporting options, including for retractable preferred shares. It appears that non-publicly accountable enterprises would include most private corporations, since "public enterprises" are enterprises that have issued debt or equity securities that are traded in a public market (including over the counter), that are required to file financial statements with a securities commission, or provide financial statements for the purpose of issuing any class of securities in the public market. (See paragraph .02(*b*) of section 1300 of the *CICA Handbook*.)

Paragraph .96 of section 3860 of the *CICA Handbook* now indicates that "an enterprise that qualifies under differential reporting may elect to present as equity

---

[12] See section 112 and subsection 248(1) in these respects.

preferred shares issued in tax planning arrangements under sections 51, 85, 85.1, 86, 87 or 88 of the *Income Tax Act*".[13]

It should be noted that the differential reporting appears to apply only in tax planning arrangements under the sections mentioned above. While these provisions would apply to most estate freezes, there may be situations where this is not the case. For example, if there is a cash injection in consideration for "high-high" retractable shares, or a stock dividend freeze, it does not appear that differential reporting would apply.

Paragraph .21 of section 1300 of the *CICA Handbook* provides that when a qualifying enterprise applied one or more differential reporting options, it should:

(a) disclose in its summary of accounting policies the fact that, with the unanimous consent of its owners, its financial statements have been prepared in accordance with differential reporting requirements available to non-publicly accountable enterprises; and

(b) identify in the financial statements the differential reporting options it has applied.

Appendix "B" to section 1300 of the *CICA Handbook* shows a sample note to the financial statements disclosing that the corporation has opted to apply differential reporting options.

General Anti-Avoidance Rule ("GAAR")

The CRA has stated that estate freezes would not ordinarily result in "misuse or abuse" given the scheme of the Act, such that the GAAR would not ordinarily apply to a freeze. It is, however, possible that GAAR could apply to certain mechanics of a freeze. In Q.22 of the 1990 Revenue Canada Round Table, the CRA was asked whether it would apply the GAAR to an estate freeze in favour of a discretionary family trust, if the Freezor were a discretionary beneficiary, i.e., owing to the reversionary nature of the freeze. It was indicated that whether the department would apply subsection 245(2) to a particular situation could be determined only following a thorough review of all the facts of the situation. However, the fact that a discretionary trust of which the Freezor is a beneficiary has been used to accomplish the

---

[13] Pursuant to paragraph .97 of the *CICA Handbook*, when an enterprise adopts the alternative presentation, it should:

(a) present those shares at par, stated or assigned value as a separate line item in the equity section of the balance sheet, with a suitable description indicating that they are redeemable at the option of the holder;

(b) disclose on the face of the balance sheet the total of the redemption amount for all classes of such shares of standing; and

(c) disclose:

• the aggregate redemption amount for each class of shares;

• the aggregate amount of any scheduled redemptions required in the next five years; and

• the method of accounting for the redemption of these shares and any dividends paid thereon.

estate freeze would not generally, in and of itself, result in the application of the general anti-avoidance rule to the transactions.

Family Law Considerations

Family law considerations in respect of estate planning and estate freezes in particular involve the extrapolation of general family law principles. Family law principles and strategies may vary from province to province. In this section, it is assumed that Ontario laws apply. In particular, certain other provinces exclude business assets from family property. Family law and succession planning builds on the following general family law principles:

- It is possible to exempt gifts acquired after marriage, as well as income derived therefrom, from a division of property.

- Spouses can override division of property rules through a domestic contract.

- If a spouse passes away, and the surviving spouse has less net family property than he or she would be entitled to on an equalization, then the equalization right is available, notwithstanding the terms of a will.

Obviously, family law issues may arise in respect of estate freezes and the transfer of shares between generations. In particular, there is no restriction on shares of a family business being provided to a spouse who is entitled to an equalization. Accordingly, such an equalization may have a fundamental effect on other family members as well.

 The most effective way to protect shares from spousal claims is to exempt them from the asset division rules through a properly drafted domestic contract.

As a practical matter, it is not always possible to persuade a spouse (or spouse-to-be) to execute a domestic contract. The following are considerations and strategies that should be considered where a domestic contract is not possible.

Where an estate freeze is in favour of a child who is married, it is possible to gift the growth shares to the child and include a family law clause in the Deed of Gift that would exempt the shares from the division of property rules. The clause should be drafted so as to include income from the shares.

Where a freeze is in favour of an unmarried child, although the value of assets immediately prior to marriage may be exempt from the division of property rules, the growth and value of the shares after marriage will not be exempt.

If a marriage contract cannot be obtained, one possibility is to freeze the child's shares immediately prior to the marriage, e.g., by changing the growth (common) shares to freeze (redeemable/retractable) shares. These shares should be protected from division of property, since they were acquired before marriage, and should not increase in value. New growth shares could be subscribed to by the parents who could then gift the growth shares to the child after marriage, in a Deed of Gift that contains a suitable family law clause. It could then be argued that the gift is exempt from the division of property rules. (However, it is not clear whether such an arrangement could, nevertheless be successfully challenged, especially if the process was transparent.)

Complications arise in respect of a discretionary family trust. It appears that, based on the reasoning in *Black v. Black*,[14] where there is a freeze or other structure in which shares are lodged in a discretionary family trust prior to marriage and subsequently distributed, they may well be regarded as an asset acquired before marriage with a value at marriage equal to the value of the discretionary interest. The value of such an interest is extremely debatable; arguably, it could be nominal.

If a freeze in favour of a married child is effected through a discretionary trust, it is common practice for the discretionary trust to have a family law clause. In addition, the shares would be transferred to the family trust by means of a gift with a similar family law clause.

☞   **Care should be taken in the structuring of a freeze, especially where married children are involved. In such cases, it may make a material difference as to whether the shares are gifted to the child/family trust or purchased by the child/family trust, even though the shares may have a nominal value. Presumably, the former would be a gift acquired after marriage, whereas this would probably not be the case for the latter. Although some family law practitioners are of the view that a distribution from a trust after marriage may, in itself, constitute a gift after marriage.**

A shareholders' agreement can also have a certain amount of efficacy in a family law situation. For example, the agreement might require a shareholder to advise the other shareholders of an equalization claim and may generate buy-out rights at pre-determined amounts. The effect of this may be to freeze the value of the shares for equalization purposes. This could possibly avoid the need for a valuation of the shares and limit the need for financial disclosure. However, there is no guarantee that this approach would be accepted. Thus, a shareholders' agreement is not designed to protect the shareholder from family law obligations, but could be successful at protecting the business from extensive disclosure requirements in the valuation process and the potential problems that can be created by the control on the business exercised by the court.

As stated previously, the most prudent course of action is to execute a domestic contract.

Note on Capitalization

As can be seen, in Ontario at least, the methodology for family law protection may differ from other methodology, particularly in respect of dividend splitting considerations. Notably, if the Freezor makes a gift of the growth shares (e.g., to a

---

[14] (1988) 18 R.F.L. (3d) 303 (Ont. H.C.).

discretionary family trust), this could trigger the personal attribution rules. Further, depending on the terms of the trust, it is possible that subsection 75(2) and, accordingly, subsection 107(4.1) might apply (e.g., if the transferor maintained an effective veto power over the transferred property, according to the terms of the trust). The results of this, particularly the latter section, could be quite unsatisfactory.

Having said this, the use of an interest-bearing note or other methods which "trump" the personal attribution rules to fund the acquisition of growth shares has become less important in recent years. For children who reach the age of 18 in the year, this is not necessary. For younger children, the kiddie tax (applicable to individuals 17 or under) greatly restricts the advantages of dividend splitting, so that there is little or no point in using methods which avoid the personal attribution rules. In respect of a spouse, as explained earlier, unless the small business corporation exemption can be relied upon indefinitely, it is advisable to include a "74.4(4) clause" in a family trust, which thus precludes dividend splitting with a spouse.

For further discussion of family considerations, see Chapter 7, Estate Freeze from Hell: A Case Study.

Emerging Issues for Estate Freezes

Many practitioners think of estate freezes as tried-and-true strategies. However, it is often surprising how basic issues can emerge.

Crossing the Border

One of the most important of the emerging issues is the spectre of a beneficiary of a family trust with growth shares, or even more simply, a direct shareholder of a Canadian corporation crossing the border. The Internal Revenue Code is rife with punitive provisions relating to foreign corporations, especially of an investment nature. Even where a freeze of a business is involved, it is quite possible that complications could arise. For example, if a holding company freeze has been effected, it is quite possible that after a number of years, the holding company would have considerable investments, e.g., funded by dividends paid by Opco. For an in-depth discussion of the basic U.S. tax considerations that might arise from a freeze structure, refer to Allan Tiller's article in Appendix C.

Change of Trustees

A new issue pertaining to replacement of trustees has emerged by virtue of a recent CRA technical interpretation. The author summarizes the problem in his article, which can be found in Appendix C.

Chapter 5

Alternative Methods and Variations

While the basic estate freeze is perhaps the single most important estate planning structure — at least for incorporated businesses, real estate holdings, etc. — there are a number of variations or alterations to freezes which should be considered. Some of these involve alternative methods of effecting a freeze; others involve changes to the freeze itself. In order to illustrate what is distinctive in these configurations, it is useful to compare them to a basic corporate freeze structure (illustrated below). Accordingly, for the purposes of discussion, it is assumed that the basic freeze configuration is that the freezor ("Freezor") holds freeze shares of the corporation — that is to say:

- redeemable/retractable at the value of the pre-existing shares at the time of the freeze;

- voting (either as an attribute of the redeemable/retractable shares or with the voting shares sequestered in a separate class which has virtually no rights apart from the votes themselves);

- non-cumulative dividends — either fixed or to a ceiling, usually based on the redemption/retraction amount (e.g., "up to" .75% per month);

with the usual preferences on dissolution, and so on.

The growth shares are assumed to be held either directly by one or more children, or as is more commonly the case, through a family trust, which will be assumed to have the usual discretionary features, with the issue of the Freezor (i.e., lineal descendants) as beneficiaries.

Of course, one very common alternative structure is a "partial freeze", pursuant to which the Freezor holds some of the growth shares. While this would provide a certain amount of "economic protection" by retaining rights to some of the future growth, it would also be suboptimal from a tax standpoint since "death tax" exposure would also be increased. The alterations and variations on the basic freeze attempt to achieve similar economic protection, often without the tax "downside".

Melts

A "melt" normally refers to a transaction whereby part of the appreciation of the corporation is diverted back to the Freezor, but without modifying the corporate structure. This could be done through the payment of salary/bonus/management fees, dividends, the redemption of shares, charging interest on amounts owing by the corporation to the Freezor, and so on.

With respect to salary-type distributions, it should be remembered that in many smaller business situations, in the past, at least, it has been common to "bonus down" to the small business limit ($300,000 per associated group of corporations) in any event. The reason, of course, is to avoid the double-tax effect that eventually occurs by virtue of income being retained at the corporate level in excess of the small business limit. (Either the owner/manager will wish to receive the corporation's earnings at a later date, most likely forcing a distribution as a taxable dividend, or if the earnings are not distributed from the corporation, the value of the shares of the corporation will continue to increase, ultimately increasing the "death tax" exposure — assuming in the latter case that the share values are determined based on the value of net assets as opposed to a times-earnings basis only.) Accordingly, for many corporations, so-called "melts" are, in a sense, a standard procedure. (Note, however, that this may change if proposed reductions in tax on dividends are enacted; see page 18 for further discussion.)

A melt may diminish the need for a freeze. To begin with, since the purpose of a freeze is to avoid capital gains tax on death when the shares pass to a subsequent generation, the payment of bonuses usually reduces the value of the corporation, and therefore the resulting death tax exposure. (If bonuses are lent back to the corporation, there would be full cost base in the loan, so that there would be a commensurate amount of "death tax coverage".)

Looking at the matter another way, where the corporation "bonuses down" to the small business limit, the typical effect of the freeze is to defer tax on the build-up in value of the corporation's shares to the extent of (i) the remaining accumulating retained earnings (i.e., net of the bonus) and (ii) untaxed accrued gains in the corporation, notably attributable to goodwill and real estate values.

 Taxed gains may generate special tax accounts, such as refundable dividend tax on hand and capital dividends, which will enable tax-efficient distribution or permit death tax reduction pursuant to post-mortem procedures.

An issue arises as to the deductibility of bonuses to the corporation. The CRA's long-standing policy is that bonuses paid to owner/managers will normally be accepted, even if the purpose is to bring the corporation's income down to the small business limit. The traditional policy was articulated in Q.42 of the 1981 Revenue Canada Round Table.

> In general, the CRA will not challenge the reasonableness of salaries and bonuses paid to the principal shareholders-managers of a corporation when:
>
> (a) the general practice of the corporation is to distribute the profits of the company to its shareholders-managers in the form of bonuses or additional salaries; or
>
> (b) the company has adopted a policy of declaring bonuses to the shareholders to remunerate them for the profits the company has earned that are, in fact, attributable to the special know-how, connections, or entrepreneurial skills of the shareholders.
>
> Bonuses paid to shareholders other than the principal shareholders-managers will be subject to the normal test of reasonableness that is set out in (a) above.

However, while the CRA's policies with respect to bonuses from ongoing business operations is largely unchanged, more recently, the CRA has been somewhat more restrictive in some situations, such as when bonuses are paid out of the proceeds of a sale of assets. A more recent general statement on the deductibility of bonuses was articulated in Technical News No. 22 (January 11th, 2002), wherein the CRA indicated it would not challenge the reasonableness of remuneration if the following conditions were met:

1. The salaries and/or bonuses are paid to managers who are shareholders (either directly or indirectly) of a CCPC;

2. The shareholders-managers are Canadian residents; and

3. The shareholders-managers are actively involved in the day-to-day operations of the business and contribute to the income-producing activities from which the remuneration is paid.

Further, the CRA indicated that the ownership structure of a corporation is irrelevant with respect to this administrative policy as long as the above-mentioned criteria are met. However, it was also indicated that the CRA would continue to challenge the reasonableness of inter-corporate management fees.

The CRA has also adopted a surprisingly benign policy in respect of bonuses out of investment income, stating that it would not challenge the reasonableness of salaries and bonuses paid out of non-active business income as long as the foregoing criteria are met. Generally, non-active business income could include income incidental to an active business, as well as the income of a "specified investment business".[1] The CRA stated in the Technical Interpretation that if a corporation's only source of income is from stocks and interest-bearing investments, the income would be considered to be "non-active business income". However, the CRA has stated that if the corporation's only business activity is investments, which are managed through a third party, the shareholder is not considered to be active in the day-to-day operations of the business.

☞ **Questions may arise where remuneration is paid to family members who enjoy low marginal tax rates if that remuneration is unreasonably large relative to the value of services performed, or where it is paid to a non-resident.**

In addition to bonuses, it might be possible to charge rent, if the Freezor owns real estate or other assets used in the business, or interest, if the corporation is indebted to the Freezor. Of course, deductions are allowed only to the extent that these amounts are reasonable.

Another alternative is to pay dividends to the Freezor. Typically, a freeze structure will involve freeze shares having a non-cumulative dividend feature that is either fixed or discretionary but subject to a monthly/annual ceiling, usually based on a percentage of the redemption/retraction amount. Although this may be sufficient to address the day-to-day needs of the Freezor, such dividends would not generally be sufficient to bring about a substantial reduction in the value of the corporation itself. Accordingly, in a melt situation, it may be desired to increase the dividend rate. This can be done in a number of ways, for example, by reorganizing the share capital of the corporation, e.g., under section 86 of the Act. However, this

---

[1] See Technical Interpretation No. 2002-0128875, April 8, 2002.

may be contentious if it results in the application of one of the benefit provisions (subsections 15(1), 86(2), etc.).

Another possibility is the redemption of shares held by the Freezor (although the redemption may not, in itself, fully achieve the objective of a melt, since the return to the Freezor on the redemption would be limited to the value at the time of the freeze). If shares are redeemed, these redemptions tend to give rise to "deemed dividends" — generally to the extent of the excess of the redemption amount over the paid-up capital of the redeemed shares.

If dividends (deemed or actual) are received by an individual, there would, of course, be significant tax exposure. (In addition, if it is necessary to borrow to effect a redemption, certain interest deductibility issues arise.) It may, however, be possible to shelter this tax exposure by transferring the shares to be redeemed to a holding company, since inter-corporate dividends are potentially tax free. However, this does not ultimately reduce death tax exposure to the Freezor, in that the proceeds of the redemption would potentially be taxable to the Freezor as a dividend, if the Freezor were to extract the proceeds from the corporation, e.g., for personal use. If the proceeds remain at the corporate level, this does not decrease the value of shares held by the Freezor (and could increase the value to the extent that the proceeds are re-invested), thereby preserving the capital gains exposure when the shares of the holding company pass to another generation.

Tax-free inter-corporate dividend status may not apply if the result is to alter the respective interests in a corporation between siblings and/or non-related persons (e.g., if shares are held by the next generation and one sibling wishes to "cash out"). Under such circumstances, subsection 55(2) generally deems such redemption to be a capital gain. However, a reduction of this deemed capital gain will potentially be available to the extent of a shareholder's entitlement to "safe income" with respect to a corporation. Although this is determined by a complex set of tax rules, it is usually approximated by post-1971 retained earnings which have been subject to tax during the period of share ownership. However, an untaxed amount — e.g., the goodwill of a business — is not included and is, therefore, subject to capital gains tax on an inter-corporate redemption under these circumstances.

> ☞ **Melts may give rise to legal battles. For example, large bonuses might be challenged under oppression remedies. Material transactions between the Freezor and the corporation could be voidable unless "reasonable and fair".**

"Thaws"

A thaw refers to the process of unwinding an estate freeze. Of course, undoing an estate freeze entails potential tax exposure. If, for example, common shares are re-acquired by the corporation, there would be tax to the children/family trust, since the re-acquisition would normally constitute a deemed dividend, i.e., to the extent of proceeds in excess of the paid-up capital of the common shares, which is normally nominal. (As noted below, if the re-acquisition occurs at less than fair market value, section 69 would likely apply to deem the re-acquisition to occur at fair market value.)

It may be possible for the family trust/children to transfer the shares back to the parents. This would normally give rise to a capital gain based on the fair market value of the shares (see section 69). It is possible, however, that the capital gain could be "covered" by the lifetime of capital gains exemption — up to $500,000 per individual — provided that the shares of the corporation qualified for the exemption. If there are several children who hold the shares and/or are beneficiaries of the trust, this could multiply entitlement to the capital gains exemption. (In the case of ownership by a trust, it would be necessary to ensure that the capital gain is designated, as well as paid or payable, to the beneficiaries who have the exemption available.) To the extent that proceeds are received — i.e., the shares are not gifted back to the parents — this, of course, would not unwind the economic effects, although it would terminate the children's involvement in the corporation including rights to future growth. Of course, such procedures require the co-operation of the beneficiaries, which may or may not be forthcoming. Moreover, where shares are transferred from a trust back to the Freezor, issues may also arise as to whether the trustees are in breach of their fiduciary duties to the beneficiaries.

☞ **To the extent that a transferor not at arm's length with the transferee receives any proceeds, if the proceeds are below the fair market value of the property disposed of, there will be a deemed disposition of the shares at their full market value (see paragraph 69(1)(*b*)).**

"Gels"

"Gels" may well be the most common type of estate thaw. This is a variation on the freeze structure that allows the growth shares to revert (or "bail-out") to the parents. A common method of effecting a gel is to include the Freezor as a discretionary beneficiary of the family trust. In the 1990 Revenue Canada Round Table (Question 22), the CRA was asked whether it would apply subsection 245(2) (i.e., the GAAR) to an estate freeze, owing to the reversionary nature of the freeze. It was indicated that whether the CRA would apply subsection 245(2) to a particular situation can be determined only following a thorough review of all the facts of the situation. However, the fact that a discretionary trust of which the Freezor is a beneficiary has been used to accomplish the estate freeze would not generally, in and by itself, result in the application of the general anti-avoidance rule to the transactions.

That being said, other provisions could apply to a gel if it is not carefully structured. For example, if the Freezor is a beneficiary of the trust and has also transferred the shares to the trust, subsection 75(2) would apply. The normal effect of this subsection would be to attribute all income and capital gains from the transferred property to the Freezor. However, a more serious consequence of the applicability of subsection 75(2) could be the application of subsection 107(4.1), which is premised on the application of subsection 75(2) to a trust. Basically, this provision would normally vitiate the tax-deferred roll-out of shares to other beneficiaries, if the Freezor is still alive at the timeof the roll-out. This problem can become extremely serious if the 21st anniversary of the trust is approaching, and Freezor has not passed away. This could force a distribution back to the Freezor, thus vitiating the effects of the freeze.

It might be possible to avoid subsection 75(2) by having someone other than the Freezor subscribe to the growth shares; such person must act independently of the Freezor so that he or she is not an agent or nominee of the Freezor. (Another issue may arise as to whether the arrangement could be characterized as an indirect transfer by the Freezor.) Alternatively, relying on the CRA's policies, the acquisition could be funded through a ("genuine") loan.

Notwithstanding the subsection 75(2) issue, it appears that gels have become common practice. However, many practitioners are reluctant to effect gels unless there is a compelling reason to do so.

A gel may also be effected by having the Freezor's spouse as a "bail-out" beneficiary of the family trust. However, this may result in a technical complication. A freeze normally involves the application of the "corporate attribution rules" where the freeze is in favour of a "designated person" (e.g., the spouse or minor child of the Freezor — see subsection 74.4(5)). This can result in significant tax penalties, unless the corporation qualifies for an exception to the corporate attribution rules by retaining its status as a "small business corporation" (basically the corporation's asset base must continually remain devoted to qualifying Canadian active business activities). Otherwise, in order to counter the application of the corporate attribution rules (e.g., if continued "small business corporation" status cannot be ensured), a trust with a "subsection 74.4(4) clause" — a specific exception to the corporate attribution rules — is normally used to hold the growth shares.

Basically, such a clause must prohibit benefits from the trust being enjoyed by anyone who is a "designated person" at the time, e.g., the spouse of the Freezor or a child while still a minor. Accordingly, the insertion of such a clause would normally preclude a bail-out to the spouse of the Freezor. (However, such a clause should not be a problem with respect to a bail-out to the Freezor him- or herself, since the Freezor would not be a designated person.) Therefore, unless the "small business corporation" exemption can be relied on — on a continual basis — a bail-out to the spouse (i.e., by the spouse's inclusion as a discretionary beneficiary) would preclude the application of subsection 74.4(4), and put the freeze at risk in respect of the corporate attribution rules, unless other methods are used in an attempt to avoid the rules.

☞   **Subsection 74.4(4) requires that, by the terms of the trust, the designated person must be prohibited from receiving or otherwise obtaining the use of any of the income or capital of the trust while being a designated person in respect of the individual.**

Where the Freezor is the beneficiary, the question arises as to whether the Freezor might be taxable on death by virtue of the value of his or her interest in the discretionary trust itself. It appears that the prevailing view of most practitioners is that the value of a discretionary interest should be nominal, since a "willing buyer" would be unlikely to pay a material amount to acquire a discretionary interest in a trust. In a Memorandum from the Rulings Directorate, Legislative and Intergovernmental Affairs Branch,[2] the CRA expressed the view that the fair market value of an income or capital interest in a fully discretionary trust is, generally, "indeterminable" because of the discretionary power of the trustee. To this suggestion, it might be replied that the interest has a positive value if the individual is also a trustee. Even so, given that the interest in the trust is separate from the trusteeship, it remains doubtful that a third party would pay a material amount for the interest in the trust.

☞   **If the "bail-out" feature is to be used, so that the shares are distributed to the Freezor, issues will arise as to the fiduciary duties of trustees. It may, therefore, be prudent for "outside trustees" (e.g., other than parents) to resign.**

Thaws — Other Methods

Other methods of effecting a "thaw" have been suggested. One possibility is to provide a conversion right in respect of the freeze shares, so that they can be converted into shares with growth features. One problem with this structure, of course, is that it may vitiate tax benefits of the freeze itself; assuming there is post-freeze appreciation, it could be asserted by the CRA that the value of the shares — that is, with the conversion right — exceeds the freeze value. Arguably, "compensating" structures could be employed. One possibility that has been suggested is that the right to convert would cease "immediately before death"; however, this could also raise technical issues in terms of effectiveness.[3] Another method that has been suggested is the imposition of a notice period, e.g., the shares cannot be converted until one year after giving notice. However, issues may also arise if the Freezor, having the conversion right, fails to exercise it. For example, the question may arise as to whether somewhere along the line there is a conferral of benefit by failing to exercise.

---

[2] September 2, 1992, File Number 9213470.

[3] See *The Queen v. Mastronardi Estate*, 77 DTC 5217 (F.C.A.).

"Refreezes"

A refreeze refers to a reorganization where the estate freeze is modified, but not reversed. Perhaps the most common way to do this is to reorganize the capital of the corporation such that the common (growth) shares held by the children/family trust are changed into freeze shares, i.e., with redemption/retraction rights equal to the fair market value of the common shares at the time of the refreeze (see the diagram below). This process will normally allow the creation of new common "growth" shares having nominal initial value. These shares can be held by the parents, or perhaps a combination of the parents and the children/family trust, thus giving rise to a partial freeze in respect of future growth. This process will obviously give rise to fiduciary duty issues in respect of trustees.

There are other ways to effect a refreeze which may have a differing effect on fiduciary duty-type issues. It might be possible to effect a refreeze as a "downstream" freeze. In the diagram that follows, had a Holdco been interposed between Opco and the Louis family trust, it would be possible to freeze the Opco shares, with new growth shares issued to a new family trust. Although the effect would be similar to a conventional refreeze, the role of the trustees would be less active, thus making actions in respect of breach of fiduciary duty somewhat more remote. If a Holdco had not previously been in place, but were put in place as part of the downstream freeze, this may well impact on the fiduciary duties of the trustees under the circumstances, since the trustees would have a more direct and active participation in the refreeze. (Downstream freezes are discussed later in this chapter.)

Alternatively, a refreeze could be effected by declaring a stock dividend on the common shares consisting of freeze shares. The freeze shares would have a redemption value equal to the value of the common shares at the time of the refreeze. Although this potentially gives rise to a taxable dividend, the amount would be limited to the paid-up capital for tax purposes, which, in turn, is based on the stated capital of the dividend, which would be suppressed to a nominal amount. The effect of this would be to reduce the value of the common shares to a nominal amount. This would enable the subscription to new common shares by other shareholders at a nominal amount, i.e., the beneficiaries of the new freeze.

☞ **The question arises as to whether subsection 15(1.1) would apply in such circumstances; as well, the ability to limit the paid-up capital under relevant corporate law should be reviewed. It might also be possible to effect an estate freeze/refreeze through convertible shares.**

REFREEZE

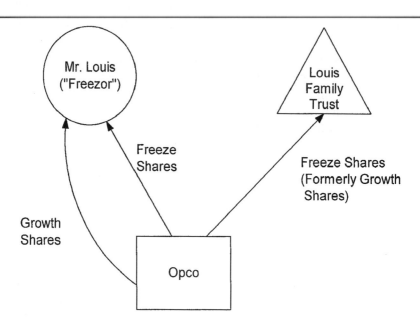

Refreeze at Lower Value

In some cases, an estate freeze might be implemented, only to find that the value of the frozen corporation has depreciated. Under these circumstances, it would obviously be beneficial to undertake a new freeze at a lower value. In the standard freeze configuration, the Freezor's freeze shares would be changed into shares with a lower redemption/retraction value.

Until fairly recently, however, the CRA's position was that, if this was done, a benefit would arise. Although this position was debatable (and some practitioners had devised schemes designed to reduce the possibility of a reassessment on this basis), the spectre of reassessment was enough to scare off many taxpayers from undertaking a refreeze. In 1997, the CRA reconsidered this position (as confirmed by Technical Interpretations No. 9229905, dated June 3, 1997, and No. 9607635, dated May 28, 1997). It is now the CRA's view that a benefit would generally not be considered to have occurred unless the decrease in value is the result of stripping of corporate assets.[4] In most instances, therefore, the ability to refreeze at a lower value is now open.

It is not completely clear what the CRA has in mind in respect of the stripping of corporate assets. If this were done by distributions on the freeze shares

---

[4] See, for example, Technical Interpretation No. 2003-0046823, January 28, 2003.

themselves, this would either trigger tax on dividends, if received by the individual himself, or, if received by a holding company (i.e., so that the dividend is tax-free), an increase in the corporation's obvious value, and therefore a corresponding increase in death tax exposure to the Freezor. One would think that either result would not be offensive. Perhaps the CRA may be more concerned with the strip relating to distributions in respect of the growth shares. However, it is often standard practice to insert a specific prohibition on such distributions, if they would impair the value of the freeze shares (i.e., in addition to prohibitions that may exist in corporate statutes) in view of the CRA's standard ruling requirement that the corporation should not be permitted to pay dividends on other shares in an amount that would result in net assets less than the redemption amount of the outstanding freeze shares.

Reverse Freeze

Another type of estate freeze that is often undertaken is a so-called "reverse freeze". This does not involve the transfer or reorganization of shares of an existing corporation, but instead involves the transfer of assets from the existing corporation to a new corporation. In return, the transferee corporation issues freeze-type shares to the transferor corporation having attributes similar to those used in a basic estate freeze, e.g., retractable at the fair market value of the assets transferred, redeemable by the transferee corporation at the same amount, and so on (see diagram below).

A reverse freeze transaction could be undertaken to achieve a "refreeze". In this case, the assets could be transferred to the new corporation in return for the freeze shares described previously, but with common shares being issued to the parents.

If a reverse freeze is an alternative to a normal freeze, common shares of the new corporation would be held by the children, or a family trust, thus giving rise to similar benefits in respect of future growth.

In comparison to an ordinary freeze, a reverse freeze has a number of potential advantages.

Disassociation

If the freeze shares taken back by the transferor corporation meet certain requirements (i.e., they are shares of a "specified class" as defined in subsection 256(1.1)), one might be tempted to file on the basis that the transferor or transferee corporations are not subject to the association rules, which would otherwise force the two corporations to share their entitlements to the low rate of tax for qualifying small businesses, as well as certain other tax benefits. Subsection 256(1.1) provides for a number of requirements to meet specified class status; however, these are quite similar to the normal attributes of freeze shares.

According to subsection 256(1.1), "specified class" means a class of shares of the capital stock of a corporation where, under the terms or conditions of the shares or any agreement in respect thereof:

(a) the shares are not convertible or exchangeable;

(b) the shares are non-voting;

(c) the amount of each dividend payable on the shares is calculated as a fixed amount or by reference to a fixed percentage of an amount equal to the fair market value of the consideration for which the shares were issued;

(d) the annual rate of the dividend on the shares, expressed as a percentage of an amount equal to the fair market value of the consideration for which the shares were issued, cannot in any event exceed the prescribed rate of interest at the time the shares were issued; and

(e) the amount that any holder of the shares is entitled to receive on the redemption (etc.) cannot exceed the fair market value of the consideration for which the shares were issued and any unpaid dividends.

However, there are certain anti-avoidance rules which (depending on the particular circumstances) may result in "deemed" association. Notably, if the freeze shares received by the transferor corporation included the usual retraction rights, subsection 256(5.1) could result in association on the premise that the retraction rights give the transferor corporation "*de facto* control" of the transferee corporation (see, for example Technical Interpretation No. 9201655; Interpretation Bulletin IT-64R3, paragraph 19(*b*)). It might be possible to lessen this risk, e.g., by placing restrictions on the ability to retract sometime after the freeze; however, this course of action might run the risk of conferring a benefit on other shareholders.

Corporate Attribution Rules

The "corporate attribution rules" may apply if a freeze is in favour of a "designated person" — including a spouse or a minor child. Therefore, a freeze by an individual may result in a taxable benefit to the Freezor unless the corporation maintains its status as a "small business corporation", or a "subsection 74.4(4) clause" is inserted in the trust. However, the corporate attribution rules are premised on a transfer by an individual to a corporation whereas a reverse freeze involves a corporate transferor. Accordingly, the corporate attribution rules may not apply to a reverse freeze ("in isolation" at least). If this is the case, however, care should still be taken that the corporate attribution rules do not otherwise apply. For example, a corporation may follow the practice of bonusing down to the small business limit, with the owner/manager lending part or all of the bonus back to the corporation, if not needed for personal use. This could possibly trigger the corporate attribution rules; however, query whether the loan is made for the purposes of benefiting a designated person, as required pursuant to subsection 74.4(2).

Of course, the corporate attribution rules may apply if the reverse freeze is done "in conjunction" with a transfer by an individual. Historically, the source of the corporate assets which are later the subject of the reverse freeze may ultimately stem from a transfer by a Canadian resident individual who is still alive at the time of the reverse freeze. Although the corporate attribution rules may apply to this transfer — i.e., if a reverse freeze is undertaken at a later time — the rules will not apply unless one of the main purposes of the (original) transfer (i.e., from the individual) was to reduce income of the individual and benefit a designated person. If the original funding was done many years ago, query whether the latter requirement would be applicable.

A reverse freeze may have other benefits. First, not all of the assets of Holdco need be subject to the freeze. Accordingly, if assets such as real estate are left in Holdco, they may not be subject to claims of creditors of New Opco should New Opco incur financial difficulty in the future. And, where Holdco carries on a business and the Freezor has children who are active in Holdco's business and other children who are not active in Holdco's business, Holdco may transfer its business assets to New Opco and retain its non-business assets. The "active children" acquire common shares in New Opco; the "inactive children" acquire common shares of Holdco through a section 86 freeze in respect of Holdco.

> ☞ **A reverse freeze may give rise to corporate and trust law considerations differing from those that arise in the context of a conventional freeze. These may be similar to those that arise in respect of a "downstream freeze"; the latter is discussed below.**

REVERSE FREEZE

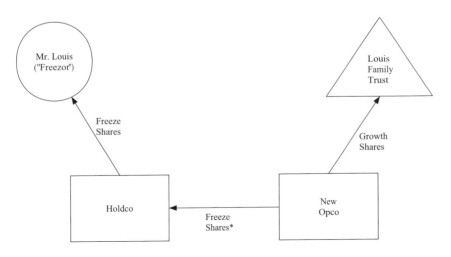

*Possibly "shares of a specified class" -- subsection 256(1.1)

"Downstream Freeze"

A "downstream freeze" refers to a freeze that is effected by a reorganization of a subsidiary or other downstream corporation — i.e., "below" the top corporation where a conventional freeze occurs. A downstream freeze may be considered in certain circumstances in which there has been an initial freeze, notably;

- when growth shares are to be distributed out of a family trust, e.g., because of the 21-year deemed disposition deadline, but a new freeze is desired, or

- where a "refreeze" is to be implemented.

The diagrams below illustrate a downstream freeze which might occur in the former situation. The scenario (see the first of the following diagrams) is that Opco was frozen using a holding company at the inception of the Louis Family Trust No. 1, i.e., "nearly" 21 years ago. (If a holding company freeze was not used, the growth shares could be rolled into a holding corporation prior to the downstream freeze procedures.) Because of the "twenty-one year rule", which would result in a deemed disposition of assets remaining in the trust, the shares of Holdco are to be distributed to the Louis children, the beneficiaries of the Louis Family Trust No. 1. (This is assumed to be a fully-discretionary trust, the beneficiaries of which are the issue of Mr. Louis.) However, it is desired that a new freeze be implemented in favour of the Louis Family Trust No. 2, so that the new growth shares — which will carry the rights to future growth after the second freeze — will be held in the new trust. In a downstream freeze, this is done by "converting" the common shares of Opco into freeze shares (see the second and third diagrams below).

☞   **Compare a downstream freeze with a conventional freeze. In a conventional freeze, the growth shares of Holdco would be "converted" into freeze shares, with new growth shares of Holdco held by a new family trust (i.e., the Louis Family Trust No. 2). In a downstream freeze, the common shares of Opco (held by Holdco) are "converted" to freeze shares, with the new growth shares of Opco being held by the new family trust.**

The advantages of a downstream freeze include the following:

Retraction Rights

In a conventional freeze, the children would receive retractable freeze shares, i.e., for the usual reasons of avoiding the conferral of a benefit on other shareholders (and other valuation considerations). The retraction rights could obviously be prejudicial, if exercised. Although it might be possible to impose restrictions under a shareholders' agreement, it is also possible that the CRA could take the position that such restrictions might affect the determination of market value or result in a conferral of benefit. In a downstream freeze the retraction rights are held in a corporation (Holdco), so that unilateral action to retract cannot be taken.

Trustee's and Director's Liability

 All comments pertaining to corporate law are premised on the *Ontario Business Corporations Act*; provisions may vary in other jurisdictions.

In comparison with a conventional freeze, the liability of directors and trustees — particularly the latter — may differ materially when a downstream freeze is effected. Generally, a conventional freeze requires a much more active participation of the trustees, if the shares to be frozen are held by a trust. This results in obvious issues pertaining to fiduciary duties, since the rights of the trust to future growth are to cease. A downstream freeze might — depending on the structure and timing of the reorganization — lessen this problem. If a Holdco had not previously been in place, but were put in place as part of the downstream freeze, this may well negatively impact on the fiduciary duties of the trustees under the circumstances, since the trustees would have a more direct and active participation in the new freeze.

As stated previously, the downstream freeze shown in the first diagram illustrates a situation in which the 21st anniversary of a trust (Louis Family Trust No. 1) is approaching, forcing a distribution of growth shares, with a new freeze to be implemented.

Consider the trustees' role in a new freeze, if effected in a conventional manner — for example, changing the growth shares of Holdco to freeze shares, with growth shares of Holdco to be held by a new family trust (the Louis Family Trust No 2). Of course, the new freeze could be implemented after the shares are distributed to the children, thus obviating the fiduciary duty issues in respect of the trustees. However, this, of course, would require the co-operation of the children. Needless to say, if the beneficiaries of Louis Family Trust No. 2 differ from those of Louis Family Trust No. 1, there are obvious fiduciary-duty issues. Even if the beneficiaries of the new family trust were ostensibly the same as the old family trust — e.g., the beneficiaries of both trusts are the issue of Mr. Louis — there could still be fiduciary issues. Without the freeze, the children of Mr. Louis would obtain the growth shares when distributed from the Louis Family Trust No. 1, which could continue to grow in value in the hands of the children. With the new freeze, future growth would be sequestered in the new trust, which would presumably be in force for the next 21 years. This may well enable the shares to be distributed to grandchildren of Mr. Louis, rather than the children.

The conventional freeze would generally require a special resolution of the shareholders of Holdco, and therefore the involvement of the trustees of the existing family trust. Even if Mr. Louis could pass a special resolution, it is possible that the growth shareholders may be entitled to vote separately as a class because their shares are adversely affected, to have dissent rights which would allow their shares to be acquired at fair value, or to launch an oppression action. These types of remedies are intended for this type of scenario — where the rights of the growth shares are to be limited. If such reorganization were completed and shares continued to be held in the trust, the trust would hold retractable shares; accordingly the beneficiaries might assert that the trustees should have demanded the redemption of the shares, especially if little or no dividends were paid thereon. Consequently, the beneficiaries of the Louis Family Trust No. 1 may well be in a position to assert that the trustees are in breach of their fiduciary duties by failing to take appropriate remedial action.

Compare this to a downstream freeze: although the trustees of Louis Family Trust No. 1 may still have rights as the holders of the growth shares of Holdco, they are less direct. If Holdco wholly owns Opco prior to the downstream freeze, the special resolution to change the common shares of Opco into freeze shares would be passed by Holdco through its directors. If the Freezor had voting control of Holdco, the Freezor could effectively control the special resolution process. Since the Articles of Amendment are those of Opco, there might not be dissent rights of minority shareholders of Holdco (although it might be asserted that Holdco is exchanging substantially all of its property.[5]) It is, however, possible that other actions could be brought, for example, against the directors of Holdco; alternatively, an oppression remedy could be sought.

A downstream freeze might also open the possibility of taking a more aggressive position in respect of the eventual valuation of the common shares held by the children. If a conventional freeze is undertaken, the shares of Holdco held by the children would be redeemable/retractable based on the market value of the Holdco shares at the time of the freeze. Although it might be open to assert that, ultimately, the shares may be worth less than this amount (i.e., if the value of the underlying corporations had decreased), this might be an uphill battle, even if the underlying value of Holdco were less than the retraction amount; the retraction amount would be specified in the corporation's minute book and financial statements and a downward deviation may well be treated with skepticism by the CRA. With a downstream freeze, the children hold common shares with no stated retraction value. Although the value of the common shares is, of course, defined by the downstream freeze shares, the valuation of the common shares may be more open-ended.

For further discussion of downstream freezes, and a case study of when one might be employed, see Chapter 7, Estate Freeze from Hell: A Case Study.

---

[5] This is discussed in more detail in Chapter 7, Estate Freeze from Hell: A Case Study.

Downstream Freeze

DOWNSTREAM FREEZE

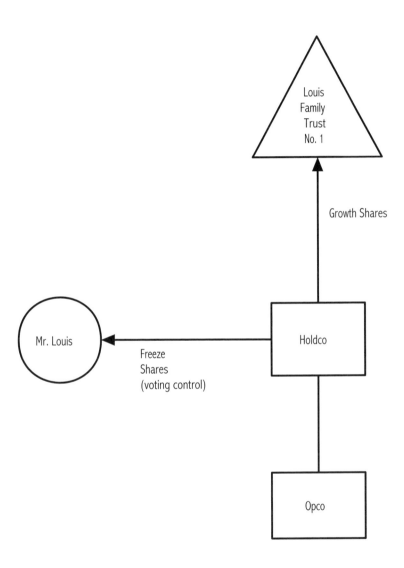

DOWNSTREAM FREEZE

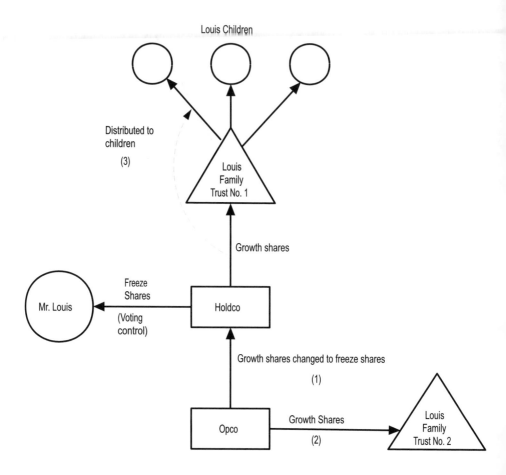

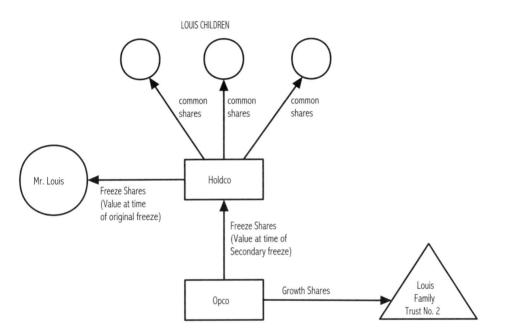

DOWNSTREAM FREEZE

Distributions from a Family Trust

The protection afforded by a family trust normally has a life of 21 years, there being a deemed disposition of trust assets at fair market value on the 21st anniversary of the trust. Accordingly, in order to avoid the deemed disposition, it is advisable to distribute growth shares held by the family trust in advance of the 21st anniversary. Particularly if beneficiaries were young at the time of the freeze, the 21st anniversary of the trust may come at a time when events are still unsettled for at least some of the beneficiaries: the strength of marriages may be unresolved or beneficiaries may not have yet married; it may be uncertain whether particular beneficiaries intend to enter the family business. Other beneficiaries may have had a falling out with parents, perhaps due to immaturity, with the prospect of reconciliation (which might occur at a later age) perceived to be uncertain or unlikely.

Estate Freeze from Hell: A Case Study (Chapter 7) presents a case study in respect of the impending 21st anniversary of a family trust which details these and other considerations. However, it is germane to summarize some of the issues that may arise as a result of the pending termination of the trust.

Who Gets What?

A threshold issue is whether children should be treated equally or unequally. Factors may include involvement in the business, personal difficulties (including marital considerations), whether the beneficiaries have sufficient business acumen, and so on.

Secondary Freeze

It may well be advisable to undertake a second estate freeze at this time. This may, of course, afford the opportunity to defer capital gains tax on future growth — i.e., after the 21st anniversary of the original trust — to a subsequent generation. However, another important feature is that, if it is advisable to distribute shares asymmetrically from the original trust, a secondary freeze may allow the family to equalize beneficiaries' interests at a later time (of course, another way to do this is through a bequest). One method of effecting another freeze is via the "downstream freeze" mechanism discussed above.

Shareholders' Agreement — A Replacement for a Family Trust?

When a family trust is no longer in place, a shareholders' agreement may become critical. The agreement can provide a degree of protection in respect of the distributed shares. In addition, in many instances, once the 21st anniversary arrives, the Freezor will be getting on in years and may well be interested in planning for the succession of the business, especially if at least some family members will continue to be involved in it. In this respect, a shareholders' agreement can become a constating document for the family business, which can potentially govern the affairs of the business after the Freezor passes away or is no longer involved in the business.

Special Elements of a Shareholders' Agreement

The following is a brief summary of some material items to be dealt with in a shareholders' agreement as part of the family's succession plan.[6]

Rights of the elder generation

One of the most difficult situations may arise when incapacity restricts the ability of the founder to effectively run the business (the "Transitional Period"): should these rights be curtailed/terminated as a result of a specific event, such as physical or mental incapacity (e.g., due to old age)? A properly drafted shareholders' agreement should specify what will happen in a variety of defined triggering events.

[6] For a more detailed discussion of family shareholders' agreements see Chapter 11 of *Tax and Family Business Succession Planning*, by David Louis and Samantha Prasad Weiss, CCH Canadian Limited, 2003.

Rights of other shareholders during the Transitional Period

Who will manage the business after the Transitional Period? In this respect there are several alternatives; specific functions could be determined in the shareholders' agreement itself. Alternatively, the agreement could provide for a designation by will, or a similar procedure.

Safeguards for succeeding generations

What limitations are to be placed on the functions of the succeeding generation? For example, there should be a specific provision to allow for the termination of functions by other shareholders. The procedures in this respect involve a balance between shareholders' rights and protection of one or more siblings who may be devoting significant time and attention to the business, at the sacrifice of other career opportunities.

Special majorities

In addition, consideration should be given to requiring a special majority of directors/shareholders (e.g., 66 $\frac{2}{3}$% or 75%) to approve certain actions, such as the sale of assets outside of the ordinary course of business, the issue of shares, expenditures/loans over a certain amount, etc.

Participation/Remuneration of family members

One of the biggest sources of acrimony in succeeding generations after the founder is no longer in the picture is the right to work in the family business. If some family members are shut out of a family enterprise, this could be a particularly bitter situation for them. The members that continue to be involved may defend their position by maintaining that the other relatives are not qualified or competent to work in the business, thus exacerbating the situation. If the shareholders' agreement clearly spells out the manner in which family members are chosen to participate in the business, it may be possible to at least reduce the ill feelings engendered by the situation, if not resolve it.

In addition, the agreement should speak to the manner/principles of remuneration of participating family members. One approach is to provide that remuneration is to be commensurate with the actual functions performed, on a comparative basis, to an arm's length business where the executive is not a significant shareholder. This approach involves the theoretical demarcation between shareholder return and owner/managerial remuneration.

Distributions to shareholders

Should there be a policy in respect of minimum distributions to family members? One important issue in this respect is the liquidity of shareholdings. Members of the succeeding generation may have shares that have significant value. However, if their rights to obtain distributions or to liquidate the shares are limited, as will typically be the case in a family-owned business, this value may exist only on paper. If so, this could lead to altercations between family members who actually control the business on a day-to-day basis, and those who are involved in the business essentially as passive investors. Providing for minimum distributions may ease frictions arising from these issues.

Liquidation rights

Many of these will be similar to rights in respect of normal shareholders' agreements. However, it may also be advisable to build in a "put right" in order to give a family member the ability to liquidate the shares on a systematic basis (e.g., if he or she wishes to pursue other business interests). As this will often put strains on the corporation, restrictions on these "put rights" based on profits or cash flow could be built into the agreement.

Creditor protection

It may be advisable to limit the rights attaching to shares or to give the corporation/other shareholders the right to acquire shares based on certain events of default, such as bankruptcy, and so on. For obvious reasons, it may be perceived to be desirable to build in a significant discount under such a scenario. However, whether or not this approach would be effective, for example, in the face of a hostile creditor, is often not clear.

Pledges

It is usually desired that restrictions will be placed on the ability of a family member to pledge the shares as security or otherwise encumber them.

Transferability provisions

Specific rights as to transferability should be built into the agreement. In many cases, these will be quite similar to those included in a normal shareholders' agreement. For example, if one shareholder receives an offer to purchase, another shareholder will want "piggyback" rights — that is, similar terms and conditions.

Dispute resolution mechanisms

A shareholders' agreement might specify major transactions or events which trigger objection rights by minority shareholders, as well as specifying a specific dispute resolution mechanism, usually through an arbitration clause.

The liquidation/distribution rights mentioned above will have a variety of tax consequences. It is usually possible to shelter ongoing dividend payments by interposing holding companies to receive such distributions. When shares are redeemed, there will typically be a "deemed dividend" created. However, where the redemption alters the proportion of shares as between siblings (for example), otherwise tax-free dividends occasioned by the redemption of shares may trigger deemed capital gains, pursuant to subsection 55(2).

General Elements of Shareholders' Agreements

The foregoing discussion focuses on special shareholders' agreement provisions which address succession issues. Standard shareholders' agreement provisions should also be considered. These provisions may address questions such as the following:

- What will happen if a shareholder decides to leave the company?

- To whom can he sell his shares and at what price?

- Will the remaining shareholders be able to obtain a non-competition clause from the departing shareholder to prevent him from starting a similar business in the same region?

- What will happen when one of the shareholders dies?

- Would the surviving shareholders be willing to have the deceased's spouse or another member of his family become a shareholder of the company?

- Is a shareholder willing to take the risk that his or her estate will have trouble obtaining a reasonable price for the shares after death?

- Where will the survivors find the necessary cash to pay for the deceased's shares?

- What will happen if one of the shareholders becomes disabled for a prolonged period?

- Will shareholders agree to work and share income with a shareholder who no longer participates in the company's operations?

One aspect of the implementation of a shareholders' agreement is whether this can/should be put in place prior to the distribution of shares out of the trust.

It is possible to enter into a unanimous shareholders' agreement prior to distribution, which, by virtue of the provisions of subsection 108(4) of the OBCA, could bind a transferee. Although there is a possibility of an attack by the new shareholders, it may be possible to obtain the consent of adult beneficiaries or have them join in the agreement after distribution. Another possibility is that the trust agreement could state that the beneficiaries' right to receive shares is contingent on their entering into a shareholders' agreement.

Although the more conservative course of action could be to enter into the shareholders' agreement after distribution, it is possible that there could be delays in the finalization of the agreement. It is usually a prudent course of action for the beneficiaries to obtain independent legal advice; where a number of children are involved, there could be significant delays. Also, care should be taken in respect of the choice of the lawyer providing the advice. Although the lawyer, of course, should carry out his or her functions conscientiously in respect of providing advice to the particular family member, in some cases, an overzealous lawyer could significantly delay the finalization of the shareholders' agreement.

☞ **Once the shares are distributed from the trust, the impetus to finalize what could become a complicated agreement may diminish. As can be seen, a shareholders' agreement among family members may actually be a more complex document than a normal shareholders' agreement, especially given its "constitutional nature".**

For further discussion, see Chapter 7, Estate Freeze from Hell: A Case Study.

Other Documents on Distributions from a Family Trust

Besides a shareholders' agreement, other documentation should be considered when shares are distributed from a family, including the following:

- release and indemnity of trustees;
- resolution of trustees in respect of the distribution (this, of course, should take into account the provisions of the trust itself in this respect);
- tax clearance certificates;
- resignation of trustees (where applicable); and
- corporate documentation of the distribution (including share transfer forms, consents, and amendments to shareholders' ledger).

In addition, the trust itself may be terminated. However, the 21st anniversary of the trust is not necessarily the termination date of the trust. This depends on the terms of the trust itself. Although growth shares may be distributed, there still may be other trust property, notably the "settlement instrument" (i.e., which creates the trust). Typically, this is an asset other than the growth shares themselves, e.g., a gold coin.

Legal Considerations Regarding Alterations of Freezes

Many of the transactions discussed in this chapter raise legal issues, particularly actions which restrict the effects of a freeze. Shareholders/beneficiaries of trusts may seek remedies available under corporate or trust law. Particularly if significant restrictions are involved and alterations are occasioned by family difficulties, the scenario of legal proceedings may be very real. It is also possible that a shareholder/beneficiary might use the possibility of proceedings as a basis for extracting a favourable result, i.e., so as to avoid embarrassing legal proceedings involving significant costs and disclosure of confidential business matters.

Corporate Considerations

The following is a summary of corporate considerations which may be relevant in respect of transactions which alter a freeze. It is premised on the OBCA, however, provisions may vary in other jurisdictions.

Freezor as Director

In the majority of cases, the Freezor will be a director or officer of a frozen corporation. Generally, directors and officers are required to act honestly and in good faith, with a view to the best interests of the corporation, as well as to exercise the care, diligence and skill that a reasonably prudent person would exercise in comparable circumstances.

In many cases, an alteration to a freeze might have the effect (or perceived effect) of furthering the interests of the corporation, e.g., by limiting the role of children as shareholders and increasing the role of the Freezor. However, jurisprudence seems to suggest that directors are obliged to act in the best interest of shareholders as a whole. In addition, where the Freezor is a director, it is possible that he or she might be regarded as promoting his or her own personal interest.

As noted previously, a director's fiduciary duties include a duty to avoid conflicts of interest and not to take advantage of corporate opportunities. The duty to the corporation has been interpreted to mean the interests of the shareholders of the corporation as a whole, rather than a controlling shareholder or particular class of shareholder.

 To lessen the risk of various directors' liability provisions (for example, for unremitted source deductions), there has been a trend in recent years to appoint directors who have a restricted asset base.

Dissent Rights

Pursuant to section 185 of the OBCA, where a corporation undergoes a reorganization or other fundamental change, it may trigger the right of dissent and buy-out. This might be used to prevent a delay of corporate reorganization or to cause shares of the dissenting shareholder to be purchased by the corporation at fair value when the reorganization or fundamental change is critical. The dissent right arises in a number of situations, including:

- the amendment of articles (under section 168 of the OBCA) to add, remove or change restrictions on the issue, transfer or ownership of shares of any class or series of the shares of the corporation;
- amalgamation with another corporation;
- "continuation" to another jurisdiction, i.e., under the corporate laws of another jurisdiction;
- selling, leasing or exchanging all or substantially all of its property.

As can be seen, the right of dissent can arise on at least some alterations to estate freezes, for example, a reverse freeze, since this would normally involve the sale of substantially all assets of the corporation. As indicated earlier, a downstream freeze may be asserted to involve an "exchange" and, depending on the circumstances, involve of "all or substantially all" of a corporation's property; this is discussed in more detail in Chapter 7's Estate Freeze from Hell: A Case Study.

Oppression Remedies

Section 248 of the OBCA provides for applications in respect of acts that are "oppressive or unfairly prejudicial to or that unfairly disregard the interest of any shareholder, or creditor, director or officer of the corporation". Pursuant to subsection 248(3) of the OBCA, a court is given virtually unlimited powers to remedy the oppression, including restraining orders, the appointment of a receiver, an order compensating an aggrieved person, or even the winding-up of the corporation.

This is the most pervasive corporate remedy. The oppression remedy is discussed at some length in Chapter 7, Estate Freeze from Hell: A Case Study. In addition to being used to enforce compliance with specific statutory protections, the oppression remedy has been used to protect "reasonable expectations" that may have arisen as a result of dealings between the shareholders. Oppression has become particularly important in respect of intergenerational disputes. Such cases involve issues relating to the Freezor's obligations to the corporation, specific statutory rights of shareholders, and protection of "reasonable expectations". The cases are largely based on specific factual situations and therefore may be of restricted precedential value. In the context of an estate freeze, an oppression remedy may (for example) impose buy-out remedies; however, there may also be a risk that a court may order the winding-up of a corporation. It should also be noted that at least one case has focused on an "estate melt" situation, whereby large bonuses were paid to the Freezor, in a situation where there had been a falling out with a child, who had been excluded from involvement from the corporation after he married an employee whom the parents considered to be undesirable.

Audit/Investigation/Shareholders' Meeting

It is possible that a shareholder could insist on an audit of the corporation, an investigation under section 161 of the OBCA, or requisition a shareholders' meeting. In most cases, these will be "nuisance" actions.

Shares Become Voting

Subsection 184(6) of the OBCA provides that if a sale, lease or exchange of all or substantially all of the property of a corporation outside the ordinary course of business would affect a particular class (or series) of shares of a corporation in a manner different from the shares of another class (or series) of the corporation which are entitled to vote on the transaction, the holders of the affected class or series are entitled to vote separately as a class on the transaction, whether or not they are otherwise entitled to vote.

Also, section 170 of the OBCA allows shareholders who are adversely affected by proposed Articles of Amendment to vote as a class requiring ratification by special resolution by the affected class. This would presumably occur where there is a refreeze, i.e., growth shares are to be changed to freeze shares.

Voidable Transactions

The Freezor will typically be a director or officer of the frozen corporation. If so, according to section 132 of the OBCA, transactions between the Freezor and the corporation which are material will be presumptively voidable unless they are "reasonable and fair". This may be a problem with many "melt" transactions. Examples include where interest on loans or rent on real estate held by the Freezor is unreasonably high, in an effort to drain the value of the corporation.

Trustee's Duties

Where a freeze has been implemented utilizing a trust, a subsequent alteration of the freeze structure could result in issues pertaining to the duties of trustees, who have a fiduciary duty (i.e., a duty of utmost good faith) to beneficiaries.

In the majority of cases, a discretionary trust mechanism will be used, which, of course, gives trustees the discretion to allocate trust capital and/or income therefrom to any beneficiaries the trustees choose. Most discretionary trusts purport to create the widest possible discretionary powers in this respect. Of course, an issue arises in respect of the actual distribution of income/capital, especially in an "asymmetrical manner". Although some advisors feel that a broadly worded discretionary trust allows the trustees to deal with the trust property with impunity, it is more likely that, under current Canadian law, a broadly worded discretionary family trust does not have the effect of completely overriding fiduciary duties.

In *Hunter Estate v. Holton* (1992), 7 O.R. (3d) 372, Steele J. stated:

> Trustees must act in good faith and be fair as between beneficiaries in the exercise of their powers. There is no allegation of bad faith in the present case. A court should be reluctant to interfere with the exercise of the power of discretion by a trustee. I adopt the following criteria in Re: Hastings-Bass as being applicable to the court's review of the exercise of such power:
>
> > "To sum up the preceding observations, in our judgment, whereby the terms of a trust . . . a trustee is given a discretion as to some matter under which he acts in good faith, the court should not interfere with his action, notwithstanding that it does not have the full effect which he intended, unless (1) what he has achieved is unauthorized by the power conferred upon him, or (2) it is clear that he would not have acted as he did (a) had he not taken into account considerations which he should not have taken into account, or (b) had he not failed to take into account considerations which he ought to have taken into account."

In addition to the distribution of property itself, an alteration to the freeze structure can be problematic to the trustees of a family trust. If an alteration to a freeze seeks to limit future growth opportunities of the beneficiaries of the trust, the trustees are obviously in a situation where the interests of the beneficiaries as a whole may be prejudiced.

Practically speaking, there may well be an element of protection from actions against the alteration of an estate freeze, stemming from the discretionary nature of a trust. Although this does not affect the issue of fiduciary duties in respect of reorganizations that limit benefits to the trust, a disgruntled beneficiary may be deterred from taking action against the trustees by the fact that, notwithstanding an alteration to the freeze, the trust would remain discretionary with respect to assets which remain in the trust, thus facing the beneficiary with the prospect of later being excluded under the discretionary terms of the trust, leaving the beneficiary with the much more difficult prospect of attempting to challenge the exercise of the discretion itself. If the alteration to the estate freeze involves the change of common-type shares to freeze-type shares, it might be argued that the rights of the shares, including retraction rights, mean that the beneficiaries have not been prejudiced; however, one would not hold out much optimism in respect of such an argument succeeding.

In order to decrease the risk of adverse proceedings, consideration might be given to the following:

- the preparation of a suitably worded letter of wishes by the settlor which supports the contemplated distribution;

- minutes or memoranda of the trustees evidencing the fact that they had turned their minds to relevant considerations relating to the contemplated distribution.

In general, the trustees should obtain releases and indemnities from beneficiaries.

☞   **In such situations, consider the resignation of "outside" trustees. If the parents are left as trustees, a disgruntled child faces the situation of being "cut out of the will", as well as a very unseemly action against his or her parents. However, the consequences of a resignation should be considered carefully, including the possible application of subsection 75(2) of the *Income Tax Act*. (See also "Change of Trustees" in Chapter 4.)**

It has been suggested that, at least to some extent, the terms of the trust itself may afford a degree of protection against actions against the trustees, whereas corporate remedies can be inherently more difficult to deal with, because of severe restrictions on the ability to contract them out. For example, another way to lessen the risks of these possibilities may be to build in mechanisms at the inception of the freeze which allow future actions to take place. For example, the subsequent actions could be implemented pursuant to the terms of the trust itself, a letter of wishes by the settlor, or in accordance with a unanimous shareholders' agreement. In addition, a trust may contain a clause for beneficiaries regarding beneficiaries who take actions against the trust/trustees. Finally, when making a distribution, trustees would be well advised to prepare minutes or memoranda evidencing the fact that they had turned their minds to relevant considerations relating to the contemplated distribution.

Chapter 6

Capitalization Considerations and Share Provisions for Estate Freezes

TOPICS DISCUSSED

Basic Issues

The capitalization of a corporation (i.e., consideration received from the corporation for cash and other assets transferred thereto) can be important in several respects. For example, basic tax issues may come into play, such as continuing interest deductibility where the source of the assets is financing, the ability to extract assets from the corporation on both a systematic and simple basis, income splitting and estate freezing considerations, and so on. Obviously, the attributes of the consideration may have economic and legal consequences, e.g., pertaining to return on the consideration, or control of the corporation.

Although we deal with attributes of freeze shares later, we will begin with a discussion of general issues pertaining to the capitalization of a corporation, which may apply to freezes and other corporate structures. The following discussion focuses largely on the practical aspects of capitalization of a corporation.

When capitalizing a corporation by means of the transfer of either cash or assets, the consideration received by the transferor is usually in the form of either indebtedness from the corporation or shares. Where assets are transferred to the corporation, various rules impose restrictions on the amount of indebtedness and paid-up capital (at least for tax purposes) that can be received in consideration for the transfer. For example, as discussed previously, pursuant to subsection 85(1) the amount of indebtedness received cannot exceed the cost amount of the assets transferred into the corporation otherwise there would be an immediate gain, according to paragraph 85(1)(*b*).

Where shares of a closely held corporation are transferred, section 84.1 may apply. If so, adverse tax consequences may result, particularly if the indebtedness received as consideration exceeds the "84.1 cost base" or paid-up capital (if greater) of the shares being transferred; the provision also suppresses paid-up capital for tax purposes.

Before dealing with rules that have specific reference to a transfer of assets to the corporation, a number of basic issues should be addressed. These include the following:

- When cash and other assets are injected into a corporation, will there be restrictions on the ability to withdraw equivalent amounts from the corporation on a tax-effective basis?

- Is it possible to be in a secured position *vis-à-vis* other creditors of the corporation?

- If the shareholder has borrowed in order to acquire cash or other assets which are then injected into the corporation, will the continuing ability to deduct interest be restricted?

Other factors include, for example, income splitting considerations (i.e., can the corporation be capitalized in a manner so as to facilitate income splitting with lower-bracket family members?); issues around control of the corporation; and the elimination of taxable benefits resulting from the transfer.

The Ability To Extract Assets

 For a discussion of cost base allocation and the ability to extract assets within the specific context of section 85 transfers, see Chapter 2.

When funds or other assets are injected into a corporation, it is usually considered desirable to take back indebtedness in order to facilitate the extraction of assets.

Of course, the reason is that where the indebtedness has a cost base equal to the principal amount, the corporate funds can be returned to the creditor in a very simple manner; for most shareholder advances, this is typically done by simply cutting a cheque in reduction of the corporation's credit balance.

For most owner/manager transactions, indebtedness of the corporation will usually have a cost base equal to the principal amount, unless it was purchased at a discount. (Exceptions arise where the debt limit provisions in section 84.2 apply, or paragraph 53(1)(*l*) applies.)

Extraction of Corporate Assets — Shares

The ability to extract funds from the corporation in consideration for the reduction of equity capital is a function of two factors:

- the paid-up capital for tax purposes relative to the value of assets extracted;

- the adjusted cost base of the shares in question.

Generally, capital can be returned to a shareholder in one of two ways:

(a) *Return as a redemption, reacquisition or cancellation of shares.*

In this case, the following rules apply:

(i) to the extent that the amount paid by the corporation exceeds the paid-up capital in respect of the shares redeemed, acquired or cancelled, there will be a deemed dividend;[1]

(ii) the amount of the deemed dividend will reduce the proceeds of disposition of the share to the shareholder.[2]

Thus, where either the adjusted cost base or the paid-up capital is deficient relative to the amount to be received in respect of the share to be reacquired, there will be either a capital gain or a deemed dividend. Due to various restrictions on the paid-up capital for tax purposes where assets other than cash are transferred to a corporation, a deemed dividend will more typically result.

It will often be advisable to structure the consideration received so that the cost base is crystallized in consideration that will not sustain any future increases in value

---

[1] See subsection 84(3).

[2] See the definition of "proceeds of disposition" in section 54.

(for example a demand note, or preferred shares redeemable at an amount equal to the cost allocated thereto). The reason, of course, is that any subsequent reacquisition by the corporation will not result in an accompanying capital gain. Similarly, if the cost base is to be crystallized in preferred shares, it may be desirable to ensure that the paid-up capital is not less than the redemption amount; otherwise, a deemed dividend will result, with a commensurate capital loss, the utilization of which may be restricted.

Although this approach has been the traditional method of ensuring that the cost base can be returned to the transferor without adverse tax consequences, practitioners should not overlook the possibility of a simple transfer for common shares with a possible reduction of paid-up capital in the future. This may avoid problems such as continued deductibility of interest where levered assets are transferred to the corporation but the transferor continues to bear the financing costs.

Although the foregoing delineates the basic tax effects of a redemption, reacquisition or cancellation of shares, other effects could occur, depending on the particular circumstances. These may include the following:

- Where the payor corporation has refundable tax balances and there is a deemed dividend, Part IV tax may apply to the recipient corporation, if it is connected with the payor corporation, and the payor receives a dividend refund.

- Pursuant to subsection 55(2), there could be a deemed capital gain where the shareholder is a corporation. To be very brief, the deemed capital gain occurs if one of the results of the deemed dividend on a redemption is to effect a significant reduction of a capital gain that would otherwise be realized on a disposition of any share. The problem may occur if the deemed dividend in question exceeds the safe income attributable to the particular share and the dividend may reasonably be considered to be received as part of a series of transactions or events resulting in either a sale or other disposition of assets to an unrelated person that increases such a person's percentage or value of a corporation (more precisely, if paragraph 55(3)(a) does not apply to the transaction; the deemed capital gain will not occur if there is a "proportional butterfly" reorganization to which paragraph 55(3) applies).

- The shares constitute "term preferred shares", "short-term preferred shares", "taxable preferred shares", or "distress preferred shares". With the possible exception of the taxable and short-term preferred share rules, these provisions are unlikely to apply where shares are issued to an owner/manager.[3]

The ability to redeem or reacquire shares under the relevant corporate law must also be considered.[4]

For example, pursuant to subsection 32(2) of the *Ontario Business Corporations Act*, a corporation is restricted from making any payment to purchase or redeem any redeemable shares if there are reasonable grounds for believing that:

---

[3] For a discussion of the interaction of the taxable preferred and short-term preferred share rules with an estate freeze, see the "Redemption Rights" section in this chapter on p. 198 and also see Chapter 4.

[4] All discussion contained here assumes that Ontario corporate law is applicable.

(a) the corporation is or, after the payment, would be unable to pay its liabilities as they become due; or

(b) after the payment, the realizable value of the corporation's assets would be less than the aggregate of

  (i) its liabilities; and

  (ii) the amount that would be required to pay the holders of shares who have a right to be paid, on a redemption or in a liquidation, rateably with or prior to the holders of the shares to be purchased or redeemed.

Of course, it will be necessary to enact suitable resolutions in order to effectuate the redemption of shares.

(b) Return as a reduction of stated capital

A corporation may also return capital by reduction of stated capital in respect of a share. For example, pursuant to paragraph 34(1)(*b*) of the *Ontario Business Corporations Act* (the "OBCA") a corporation may reduce its stated capital for any purpose, including for the purpose of distributing to holders of issued shares of any class or series of shares an amount not exceeding the stated capital of the class or series.

When stated capital is reduced by a distribution of assets, the adjusted cost base of the share will be reduced, to the extent of the distribution.[5]

It should be noted that a reduction of stated capital may result in a decrease of the adjusted cost base of the share, without an actual disposition thereof. Thus, in respect of a CCPC at least, there may be no adverse tax consequences until such time as the adjusted cost base of the share becomes negative, at which time there would be a deemed capital gain pursuant to subsection 40(3) of the Act (provided that there is equivalent paid-up capital as calculated for tax purposes — subsection 84(4) provides for a deemed dividend to the extent that the amount distributed exceeds the tax paid-up capital, which is reduced).

In fact, even a *negative* cost base may not be problematic if the capital-gains exemption is available to shelter the resultant capital gain. In fact, there does not appear to be any reason why the enhanced capital gains exemption, if available, may not be used to shelter a gain in this instance. Of course, there must be sufficient paid-up capital available to effect this type of transaction.[6]

To emphasize, it is possible to reduce the paid-up capital of a share without there being a deemed dividend; accordingly, to the extent that there is sufficient paid-up capital for tax purposes as well as positive adjusted cost base, this will allow for a distribution to shareholders without immediate adverse tax consequences.

---

[5] See subparagraph 53(2)(*a*)(ii).

[6] Paragraph 13 of IT-448 formerly provided that, where there was a reduction in paid-up capital in respect of a preferred share, the CRA's view was that there was a change in the holders' economic interest that is usually considered to give rise to a disposition, while this would not be the case in respect of a common share. However, by a Special Release dated June 21, 1982, the CRA indicated that, generally, a reduction in the paid-up capital in respect of a share, where not accompanied by a redemption or cancellation of that share, will not constitute a disposition of that share.

It should be noted that, like a redemption, there are corporate restrictions in respect of the reduction of stated capital. Pursuant to subsection 34(4) of the OBCA, for example, a corporation shall not reduce stated capital (other than for specified purposes) if there are reasonable grounds for believing that:

- the corporation is, or after the taking of such action, would be unable to pay its liabilities as they become due; or

- after the taking of such action, the realizable value of the corporation's assets would be less than the aggregate of its liabilities.

Whether a distribution is effected via a reduction of paid-up capital or a reacquisition of shares, it is necessary to ensure that the procedure is valid under the relevant corporate law, e.g., the requisite resolutions have been effected and duly executed; otherwise the CRA could take the position that the procedure did not validly take place and assess on the basis that there was a shareholder loan (e.g., pursuant to subsection 15(2) or section 80.4) or a fully taxable benefit (i.e., under subsection 15(1)).[7]

The following simplified example contrasts a redemption and paid-up capital reduction:

Example:

Assume that an individual holds two shares of a corporation. The aggregate cost base and paid-up capital in respect of the shares is $100. The shares have a fair market value of $200.

Assume that one of the shares is redeemed for its fair market value ($100).

The following results would obtain:

Deemed Dividend (Subsection 84(3)):

Amount received	$100
Paid-up capital (one share)	(50)
Deemed Dividend	$ 50
Capital Gain:	
Amount received	$100
Less deemed dividend (par. 54(j) — "proceeds of disposition")	(50)
Proceeds of disposition	50
Adjusted cost base (one share)	(50)
Capital Gain	NIL

Assume that, instead of a redemption of one share, the paid-up capital in respect of both shares is reduced by $100.

Under these circumstances, it appears that there would be no disposition solely as a result of the paid-up capital reduction. Pursuant to subparagraph 53(2)(ii), the adjusted cost base of the shares would be reduced by $100 — to nil. If a further reduction of paid-up capital were available, there would be an immediate capital gain, to the extent of the negative cost base that would result.

---

[7] See, for example, *Fingold et al. v. MNR*, 93 DTC 2011.

Security

Where an owner/manager advances funds or transfers other assets to a corporation, he or she will often be concerned with his or her security position in respect of the assets.

Where indebtedness is received, it is, of course, possible to take a security position in respect of the indebtedness. In Ontario, for example, a General Security Agreement can be registered under the *Personal Property Security Act (Ontario)*[8] in order to provide security in respect of underlying personal property held by the corporation. A "mortgage/charge" can be registered in respect of underlying real estate.

Of course, the effect of this security may be limited. For example, in Ontario, a creditor could attempt to attack the security under the *Assignments and Preferences Act*. Where institutional financing is involved at the corporate level, the creditor will usually ask for a subordination in respect of the owner/manager's security. Where such financing is involved at the personal level, the indebtedness owing to the shareholder, and related security, will typically be pledged to the financial institution. Where, on the other hand, shares are taken back as consideration for the transfer, the owner/manager will rank behind judgment and other creditors, as well as shareholders with preferences, e.g., where common shares are received.

Interest Deductibility

An asset transfer situation could result in issues pertaining to interest deductibility. Suppose that an individual has carried on an unincorporated business which has associated financing costs and now wishes to freeze the business, e.g., by transferring the assets to a corporation in consideration for freeze and common shares, with the latter subsequently gifted to a family trust.

More often than not, the indebtedness will be assumed by the frozen corporation, which should be able to continue to deduct the interest, to the extent it was previously deductible. However, there might be situations in which this is not advisable. For example, indebtedness can only be assumed to the extent of the cost amount of assets transferred to the corporation. Although the excess might be a promissory note to the corporation, this could result in adverse tax consequences, pursuant to the shareholder loan rules. In addition, continuing to deduct interest at the personal level would result in increased tax benefits, since personal tax rates would exceed corporate rates. To the extent that funds must be distributed as taxable salary or dividends to defray such costs, this would unwind the advantages. However, the individual may be able to fund the interest payments if he or she can access cash outside of the corporation or can receive the proceeds from the corporation in a tax-efficient manner, as described earlier in the chapter. In these cases, would the interest continue to be deductible, given that freeze shares have replaced the business assets and given, further, that these freeze shares would typically carry a non-cumulative dividend rate, perhaps without any realistic prospect of dividends?

---

[8] R.S.O. 1990, Chapter P.10.

Paragraph 20(1)(*c*) addresses the deductibility of interest (according to tax cases, interest is generally a capital expenditure unless it fits within this provision).[9] Specifically, subparagraph 20(1)(*c*)(i) allows a deduction for borrowed money used for the purpose of earning income from a business or property.

If the transferor has previously incurred deductible financing costs that are related to the cash or other assets which are subsequently transferred to the corporation, care should be taken that the consideration received on the transfer is not in a form that may jeopardize the continued ability to claim these deductions. For example, to the extent that non-interest-bearing debt is received as consideration for transferred cash or business assets, in some circumstances, the CRA might take the position that the financing charges previously incurred are no longer deductible, on the grounds that the business assets were replaced by property (e.g., interest-free debt) which no longer produces investment or business income to the transferor.

Generally, though, within the owner/manager context, the government has historically shown an enlightened attitude in respect of this sort of situation. In the majority of situations, interest incurred at the shareholder level will continue to be deductible (except under somewhat unusual circumstances) at least where the funds are to be used in Canadian business or investment operations which are subject to regular (Part I) tax.

The CRA's current policy in respect of interest deductibility is delineated in Interpretation Bulletin IT-533, which replaces a number of older bulletins. The bulletin was largely the result of the *Ludco*[10] and *Singleton*[11] cases which, generally, greatly strengthened the case for interest deductibility. The bulletin does not express views on investments in preferred shares in a closely-held corporation, presumably since, as long as the shares carry a material dividend rate, the *Ludco* case should apply. *Ludco* itself indicates that "... the requisite test to determine the purpose for interest deductibility under s. 20(1)(*c*)(i) is whether, considering all the circumstances, the taxpayer has a reasonable expectation of income at the time the investment is made". With regard to purpose, the court also stated:

> Absent a sham or window dressing or other vitiating circumstances, a taxpayer's *ancillary purpose* may be nonetheless a *bona fide*, actual, real and true objective of his or her investment, equally capable of providing the requisite purpose for interest deductibility in comparison with any more important or significant primary purpose.

Subparagraph 20(1)(*c*)(i) requires that the interest sought to be deducted be on "borrowed money used for the purpose of earning income from a business or property". The interpretation of the term income was addressed in *Ludco* as follows: "... it is clear that 'income' in s. 20(1)(*c*)(i) refers to income generally, that is an amount that would come into income for taxation purposes, not just net income". The court also said,

> The plain meaning of s. 20(1)(*c*)(i) does not support an interpretation of 'income' as the equivalent of 'profit' or 'net income' .... Therefore, absent a sham or window dressing or

---

[9] Generally, but not always — see *Gilford v. The Queen*, 2004 DTC 6120 (S.C.C.).

[10] *Ludco Enterprises et al. v. The Queen*, 2001 DTC 5505 (S.C.C.).

[11] *The Queen v. Singleton*, [2002] 1 CTC 121 (S.C.C.).

similar vitiating circumstances, courts should not be concerned with the sufficiency of the income expected or received.

Paragraph 31 of the bulletin states the general policies in respect of interest on funds borrowed to acquire shares and other investments:

> Where an investment (e.g., interest-bearing instrument or preferred shares) carries a stated interest or dividend rate, the purpose of earning income test will be met "absent a sham or window dressing or similar vitiating circumstances" (*Ludco*). Further, assuming all of the other requisite tests are met, interest will neither be denied in full nor restricted to the amount of income from the investment where the income does not exceed the interest expense, given the meaning of the term income . . ..

> Where an investment does not carry a stated interest or dividend rate such as some common shares, the determination of the reasonable expectation of income at the time the investment is made is less clear. Normally, however, the CCRA considers interest costs in respect of funds borrowed to purchase common shares to be deductible on the basis that there is a reasonable expectation, at the time the shares are acquired, that the common shareholder will receive dividends. Nonetheless, each situation must be dealt with on the basis of the particular facts involved.

Paragraph 25 of Interpretation Bulletin IT-533 relates to interest-free loans to corporations, and states the following:

> Generally, a deduction for interest would be allowed where borrowed money is used to make an interest-free loan to a wholly-owned corporation (or in cases of multiple share-holders, where shareholders make an interest-free loan in proportion to their shareholdings) and the proceeds have an effect on the corporation's income-earning capacity, thereby increasing the potential dividends to be received.

While continuing interest deductibility would usually not be a problem when previously financed assets are transferred to a corporation, there could be circumstances where this could be problematic, for example where the transfer takes back non-interest bearing debt to the cost base of assets transferred into the corporation or perhaps preferred shares carrying no rights to dividends and such debt/equity is not proportional to shareholdings.

Returning to the example above in respect of a freeze, it would appear that an individual wishing to continue to incur interest expenses should be in a fairly strong position, i.e., if he or she adheres to the provisions of Interpretation Bulletin IT-533. To be safe, it may be prudent to pay dividends from time to time, to be in keeping with the *Ludco* case.

Future Developments

The government has proposed section 3.1, which is essentially a legislative reasonable expectation of profit test. At the time of writing, however, it is understood that, in the face of widespread criticism of this proposal, the government intends instead to legislate a net income test which, prior to *Ludco*, many practitioners had generally thought to apply. If this is done, one would expect pressure on the CRA by practitioners to restate previous policies respecting investments in freeze and other preferred shares of closely held corporations.

Prior to *Singleton* and *Ludco*, the CRA's general policy had been that, where money is borrowed to invest in preferred shares, it will permit interest expense to the extent of the grossed-up dividend.[12]

However, the CRA had extended policies (analogous to interest-free loans by shareholders) in respect of investments in preferred shares.

The CRA had indicated that it would normally permit a deduction for the full interest expense incurred when a taxpayer borrows money at interest to acquire preferred shares of the corporation where the following four conditions are satisfied:

(a) The purchaser of the preferred shares may reasonably be considered to enjoy all rights and privileges attached to the ownership of a majority of all classes of shares of the issuing corporation through direct or indirect ownership of such shares.

(b) The proceeds of the share issue are used by the corporation in its own operations to produce income from business or property that will be subject to Part I tax in Canada, or are used by the corporation to loan to its Canadian subsidiary at less than a reasonable rate of interest (or at no interest) to be used in its operations to produce income from business or property that will be subject to Part I tax in Canada.

(c) The corporation has made every effort to obtain the necessary funds through the usual commercial money markets but cannot obtain financing, without the guarantee of the shareholder, at competitive interest rates at which the shareholder could borrow.

(d) The arrangement does not result in any undue tax advantages. Examples of situations in which an undue tax advantage will be found are listed in paragraph 8 of IT-445.[13]

Other Factors

The following are some other factors relevant in selecting an appropriate capital structure.

(a) Control

Individuals who want to maintain control of a corporation to which assets have been transferred can use a variety of mechanisms, irrespective of whether indebtedness or shares are issued.

For example, if it is otherwise desirable to receive indebtedness, there can be a conversion feature. Alternatively, it is possible to maintain control by the issuance of so-called "thin voting shares" — that is, shares that have minimal economic rights.

---

[12] See, for example, Q.3 of the 1979 Revenue Canada Round Table, and Q.8 of the 1993 Revenue Canada Round Table.

[13] Cancelled October 31, 2003; see 1990 Revenue Canada Round Table Q.11, and 1980 Revenue Canada Round Table Q.14.

These shares are typically retractable and/or redeemable at a nominal amount, do not participate in a liquidation, and so on.[14]

Preferred shares may contain whatever voting rights are desired.

It is generally considered that the attachment of voting rights does not, in itself, result in a premium being added to the value of shares.[15]

(b) Income Splitting

In selecting the appropriate capital structure, consideration should also be given to the ability and desirability to split income, e.g., with lower bracket family members. The ability to do this is significantly restricted by the "attribution rules", particularly the so-called "corporate attribution rules" which are potentially operative when assets are transferred to a corporation. More recently, the advantages of income splitting in respect of an estate freeze were restricted by the introduction of the so-called "kiddie tax".

(c) Elimination of Taxable Benefits

Where assets are transferred to a corporation, care must be taken that "full" consideration be received, especially where an estate freeze is involved; otherwise, a number of benefit provisions may come into play. For example, in a section 85 "rollover", where there is more than one shareholder of a transferee corporation, paragraph 85(1)(e.2) may impose harsh tax consequences if the value of the assets transferred to the corporations exceeds the value of consideration received as a result of the transfer, and such excess may reasonably be regarded as a benefit that the transferor desired to have conferred on a related person.

Other problematic benefit provisions may include subsection 15(1), subsection 56(2), and section 246, as well as the GAAR contained in subsection 245(2). Various reorganization sections also contain specific benefit provisions, including sections 51, 86 and 87.

(d) Association

The decision to issue shares, and their characteristics, may also have a bearing on whether the particular corporation is associated with another corporation, thereby forcing the two corporations to share their entitlement to the small business deduction as well as limit access to certain other tax benefits, e.g., the enriched investment tax credit in respect of Scientific Research and Experimental Development and the "dividend allowance" in respect of taxable preferred shares. Where freeze shares are to be issued, consideration should be given to ensuring that these are shares of a specified class, according to subsection 256(1.1), since these shares generally "don't count" in respect of association issues. (For further discussion, reference should be made to the section on reverse freezes in Chapter 5 at p. 169.)

---

[14] See the "Share Characteristics Relevant to Estate Freezes" section below for further discussion.

[15] See *Re Mann Estate*, [1974] 2 WWR 574 (S.C.C.); see however, discussion at the end of this Chapter under the heading "Voting Rights".

Share Characteristics Relevant to Estate Freezes

When issuing shares, careful consideration should be given to the attributes thereof. Where there is only one shareholder, common shares will usually suffice; however, where there is more than one shareholder, issues such as the conferral of a benefit, income splitting and earnings participation will come into play. Where an estate freeze is effected, a number of attributes have traditionally been used in order to ensure the effectiveness of the freeze and minimize benefit and other problems.

In respect of estate freezes, the most important rights and restrictions applicable to share capital include retraction and redemption rights, participation on dissolution, priorities or preferences (in respect of both income and capital participation) and profit participation. Other share attributes may include voting rights, pre-emptive rights, conversion rights, as well as "non-impairment" and "step-down provisions".

The following is a summary of some attributes that often come into play, with particular emphasis on estate freezes. All comments are subject to corporate law provisions for the relevant jurisdiction.

Redemption Rights

In an estate freeze, shares will typically be redeemable at the fair market value of the assets exchanged for the freeze shares. Because the corporation is entitled to redeem the shares at this value, it can be argued that the value of the shares is tied to the redemption amount, so that future growth may accrue to other shareholders (usually the common shareholders).

It is common for the redemption amount to be fixed at a specific dollar amount per share (typically $100 or $1,000). Alternatively, the redemption amount can be established with specific or general reference to the fair market value of the assets transferred or exchanged, which may be determined when the relevant financial data is analyzed. This is often done by establishing the redemption amount for the entire class (the mechanism is usually to provide for a confirming resolution by the directors of the corporation where the fair market value is determined after the reorganization, as is typically the case) and then dividing the amount by the number of issued and outstanding shares of that class.

In this respect, a particularly flexible approach is to base the redemption amount on the value of assets transferred to the corporation on the first issuance of the shares. This, of course, could allow assets to be transferred on short notice, without having to obtain Articles of Amendment. In fact, several first issuance classes (or series) could be created. (As stated previously, it may also be desirable to limit the authorized capital to the number of shares that are issued pursuant to the specific transaction. This may simplify drafting as well as prevent the "accidental misuse" of the shares in a later transaction.)

It has been suggested that there are several advantages to using a specific redemption amount, including certainty where there is an early redemption, and the actual amount of dividends, since these are typically based on the redemption value. Also, the greater the period of time between the transaction and the determination of the value, the more difficult this determination may be. (Where a section 85 election is filed, practically speaking, the delay will hopefully be limited to the time between the actual transaction and the filing deadline for Form T2057.) Finally, if an excessive period of time passes, it has been suggested that doubt may be cast on the ability to effect a price adjustment mechanism, on the grounds that the CRA could take the position that a reasonable attempt has not been made to determine fair market value.[16]

On the other hand, pragmatic factors may militate in favour of a formula approach. Where there may be some delay in obtaining the valuation, more of the corporate implementation of the freeze can be effected where a formula approach is used, since the aggregate redemption amount can be established in a directors' resolution. Practically speaking, this will enable the practitioner to save time (by not having to revisit the file) and even get the bill out sooner!

☞ **The interaction with the taxable preferred share rules should be considered: it appears that a formula redemption amount would jeopardize the subsection 191(4) exemption, perhaps forcing a reliance on the "substantial interest" exemption (subsection 191(2)).**

In CRA Document No. AC59342 (May 15, 1990), it is stated that a formula redemption whereby the redemption price would be determined by a subsequent directors' resolution would not qualify for the subsection 191(4) exemption. The redemption of preferred shares (and a consequent deemed dividend) may often be advisable, particularly in the first year after death. (For further discussion, see Chapter 4.)

The following is an example of a redemption provision:

Precedent — Redemption Provision

Precedent ——————————————————————————————————

Redemption Amount

7.A(iii)   The Aggregate Class A Redemption Amount shall equal the fair market value (at the time of the transfer) of the _____ common shares of _____ transferred to the Corporation, minus any liabilities assumed by the Corporation and any other non-share consideration issued by the Corporation in the course of such transfer, which fair market value shall be _____ as appraised by _____ in consultation with the accountants for and fixed by the board of directors of the Corporation and evidenced by a resolution of the board. The Class A Redemption Amount shall equal the Aggregate Class A Redemption Amount divided by _____ ;

---

[16] See *Taxation of Private Corporation and Their Shareholders*, 3rd edition, page 3:28.

Redemption at Option of Corporation

7.A(iv)   The Corporation shall have the right at its option at any time and from time to time to redeem all or any portion of the Class A shares at a price per share equal to the Class A Redemption Amount together with any declared and unpaid dividends thereon (the whole constituting and herein referred to as the "Class A Redemption Price").

In all cases of redemption, save and except when a holder of Class A shares has waived notice of redemption either before or after redemption, seven (7) days' notice (the "Class A Notice of Redemption") shall be given by letter directed to the respective shareholders whose shares are to be redeemed at their respective addresses appearing on the books of the Corporation. The Class A Notice of Redemption shall set out:

(i) the number of shares to be redeemed, if only part of the shares held by the shareholder to whom such notice is addressed are to be redeemed;

(ii) the Class A Redemption Price;

(iii) the date on which the redemption is to take place (the "Class A Redemption Date");

(iv) the place where such shares will be redeemed; and

(v) the name and address of the chartered bank, if any, in which unclaimed redemption monies will be deposited. On or after the Class A Redemption Date, the Corporation shall pay the Class A Redemption Price to the respective holders of the Class A shares to be redeemed, on presentation and surrender of the certificate or certificates for such shares, duly endorsed, at the place specified in the Class A Notice of Redemption. The Corporation shall have the right on or after the Class A Redemption Date to deposit any unclaimed redemption monies to a special account in the chartered bank named in the Class A Notice of Redemption, to be paid upon presentation and surrender of the share certificate or certificates as have not at the date of such deposit been surrendered by the holders thereof, to or to the order of such holders. Upon the later of the Class A Redemption Date and the date upon which payment of the Class A Redemption Price of a Class A share being redeemed or deposit of any unclaimed redemption monies as specified above is made in respect of a Class A share being redeemed, that share shall cease to be entitled to dividends and the holder thereof shall not be entitled to exercise any of the rights of holders of Class A shares in respect thereof which rights shall thereupon cease. If a holder has surrendered a certificate or certificates representing a greater number of shares than the shares to be redeemed, the Corporation shall at its own expense issue to such holder a new certificate representing the shares which have not been redeemed.

Retraction Rights

A right to retract refers to the ability of the shareholder to cause the corporation to reacquire the shares in question. The inclusion of this provision in a corporation's articles is critical to a successful estate freeze.

In an estate freeze, the basic purpose of a retraction right is to counter any arguments that the transferring or exchanging shareholder is conferring a benefit on other shareholders: if the shareholder can cause the reacquisition of shares based on the fair market value of the transferred or exchanged assets, it can then be readily argued that there is no conferral of a benefit on any other shareholder, due to this equivalence. In most estate freezes, retractability is typically buttressed by further rights, including a price adjustment clause, non-cumulative or other dividend features, preference on dissolution and a "non-impairment clause". These are discussed below.

The formulae for retraction prices are similar to those pertaining to redemption. In fact, the retraction clause typically is often cross-referenced to the redemption formula.

The following is an example of a retraction clause:

Precedent — Retraction Clause

Precedent

Redemption at Option of Holder

7.A(v)   Each holder of Class A shares shall have the right at its option and from time to time to require the Corporation to redeem at any time or times all or any portion of the Class A shares registered in the name of such holder on the books of the Corporation by tendering to the Corporation at its registered office a share certificate or certificates representing the Class A shares which the registered holder desires to have the Corporation redeem together with a request in writing specifying:

(i) the number of Class A shares the registered holder desires to have redeemed by the Corporation; and

(ii) the business day (the "Class A Retraction Date") on which the holder desires to have the Corporation redeem such Class A shares.

The Class A Retraction Date so specified in the request in writing shall be not less than thirty (30) days after the day on which the request in writing is given to the Corporation, save and except where the Corporation has in writing waived the requirement for such thirty- (30) day period and agreed to an earlier Class A Retraction Date. Upon receipt of a share certificate or certificates representing the Class A shares which the registered holder desires to have the Corporation redeem together with such a request, the Corporation shall on the Class A Retraction Date redeem such Class A shares by paying to such registered holder in respect of each Class A share to be so redeemed an amount equal to the Class A Redemption Price.

Such payment shall be made by cheque payable at par at any branch of the Corporation's bankers for the time being in Canada or in such other manner as may be mutually agreed upon by the Corporation and the holder of the Class A shares being so redeemed. The said Class A shares shall be redeemed on the Class A Retraction Date and from and after the Class A Retraction Date such shares shall cease to be entitled to any dividends and the holders thereof shall not be entitled to exercise any of the rights of holders of Class A shares in respect thereof unless payment of the Class A Redemption Price is not made on the Class A Retraction Date, in which event the rights of the holders of the said shares shall remain unaffected. If a holder has surrendered a certificate or certificates representing a greater number of shares than the shares such holder desires to have the Corporation redeem, the Corporation shall at its own expense issue to such holder a new certificate representing the shares which have not been redeemed.

It should be noted that, although a retraction right is considered to be essential to a freeze, the ability to retract shares may often create serious economic problems in the event that such rights are exercised (or even threatened). Where freeze shares are left in an estate or trust wherein the beneficiaries differ from those holding the common shares, trustees may find themselves in the position where the interests of the beneficiaries could favour retraction, especially where the dividend participation of these shares is limited.

Although the CRA has not been very helpful in terms of expressing positive views as to how this sort of problem can be coped with, probably the most common approach where retraction is a concern is to enter into a shareholders' agreement which would prevent the retraction of the shares except with the consent of other shareholders and/or directors sometime after the freeze is effected, notwithstanding the possibility that this might be considered to confer a benefit on other shareholders. (The CRA has indicated that, in a situation where a non-retraction agreement is ventured into immediately after a section 86-type freeze, a benefit under subsection 86(2) may apply, as the agreement would adversely offset the value of the shares.[17]) Another possibility is to have shares automatically convertible to non-retractable shares when certain events occur, e.g., the acquisition of shares by someone other than the first holder. Care must be taken to ensure that such provisions would be valid under corporate law (see below for further discussion).

Where assets with a low cost base relative to their fair market value or shares with a low paid-up capital are transferred to a corporation, there could be adverse tax consequences when shares received as consideration are reacquired by the corporation.[18]

☞ **As a result of various income tax provisions, the paid-up capital of the shares received as consideration will be restricted. The difference between the paid-up capital and the redemption amount is deemed to be a dividend; the proceeds of disposition are based on the paid-up capital.**

Price-Adjustment Clause

Where an estate freeze is effected, a price adjustment clause will typically be inserted in the Articles in order to "back stop" the retraction rights in terms of possible "conferral of benefit" problems.

In regard to the precedent below, the following should be noted:

- The clause will typically be operative only in the event of a dispute with the CRA which proves to be unsuccessful.

---

[17] See CRA Document No. 95005555, February 2, 1995; and CRA Document No. AU81-086.87, August 25, 1991.

[18] See "Extraction of Corporate Assets — Shares" on p. 189 for further details.

- The operation of the clause is conditional on the application of any of a number of factors, including the refusal to accept the value of the exchanged shares and most notably, a disparity between the value of the exchanged shares (the "Class A Initial Determined Amount") and the fair market value of the Class A shares such that a benefit has been conferred.

- The clause typically seeks to restore the equilibrium between the value of the exchanged shares and the value of the consideration received.

- The primary mechanism for achieving this result is usually by adjusting the retraction/redemption value of the freeze shares. This purports to be effective retroactive to the time of the freeze ("*nunc pro tunc*"). Another possibility is to effect an adjustment by issuing additional shares. In Q.14 of the 1980 Revenue Canada Round Table, however, the adjustment of the retraction amount was stated to be the preferred method: it was indicated that, in the CRA's opinion, the cancellation or issue of additional frozen shares carries with it a "host of technical difficulties that are best avoided from the point of view of both taxpayers and the Department". Presumably, the technical difficulties pertain to whether the adjustment to a change of the number of shares results in a disposition. Note: It is usually possible to adhere to the redemption/retraction adjustment mechanism; however, in some situations, the issuance/cancellation of shares cannot be avoided.

- In addition, in this particular precedent, subsequent clauses purport to create additional obligations (in this case, based on interest at prescribed rates), to compensate for dividends or redemptions based on values which prove to be "incorrect".

The price adjustment clause contained in the Articles will typically be "mirrored" by a similar price adjustment clause contained in the actual asset-transfer documentation. It has been observed that this is desirable since is possible that the articles only could not be relied upon if the clause was operative after all of the shares had been redeemed. If a similar clause is contained in the share transfer or exchange agreement, the shareholder in the corporation would still be contractually bound by the price adjustment clause under such agreement.

The following is an example of a price adjustment clause:

Precedent — Price-Adjustment Clause

Precedent ——————————————————————————————

Price Adjustment

In the event that at any time the Minister of National Revenue, the Minister of Revenue for Ontario, or any duly authorized official of the Canada Customs and Revenue Agency or the Ministry of Revenue for Ontario or any taxing authority having jurisdiction, refuses to accept the fair market value of the _____ common shares of _____ transferred to the Corporation in consideration of the allotment and issuance of _____ Class A shares which was relied upon by the Corporation and the transferor of such _____ common shares of _____ (the "Class A Initial Determined Amount") or makes or proposes to make an assessment or reassessment on the basis that any advantage or benefit was conferred by reason of the _____ Class A Initial Determined Amount not being equal to the fair market value of such _____ Class A shares or should such taxation authorities make a determination of the value of such _____ common shares of or the value of the _____ Class A shares of the Corporation issued in consideration of the transfer of such _____ common shares of _____ and suggest some alternative amount or value to that relied upon by the Corporation and the transferor of such _____ common shares of _____ , then:

(a) The Corporation may challenge such alternative amount or value and negotiate with such taxing authority or object to and appeal from any assessment or reassessment issued by such taxing authority which relies on such alternative amount or value;

(b) If as a result of such negotiation, objection or appeal it is finally determined, whether by agreement with such taxing authority or as a result of a hearing by the Tax Court of Canada or any successor or higher tribunal having jurisdiction (after all appeal rights have been exercised or have expired), that the fair market value of the _____ Class A shares is greater or lesser than the fair market value of the _____ common shares of _____ transferred to the Corporation as so finally determined (the "Class A Final Determined Amount") then the Aggregate Class A Redemption Amount shall be increased or decreased, *nunc pro tunc*, so that the value of such _____ Class A shares is equal to the Class A Final Determined Amount and the Class A Redemption Amount shall be equal to the Aggregate Class A Redemption Amount as adjusted divided by _____ ;

(c) In the event that the Class A Redemption Amount is increased pursuant to subparagraph 7.A(vii)(*b*) hereof following a redemption or purchase for cancellation or otherwise of a Class A share or following the payment of a dividend on a Class A share, the Corporation shall pay to the holder of such share that was so previously redeemed or purchased for cancellation or on which a dividend was so previously paid, to reflect an increase in the Class A Redemption Amount or to reflect an additional dividend, as the case may be, an amount equal to the aggregate of: (i) such additional amount as is required to ensure that such holder will have received the amount which such holder would have been entitled to receive if the said increase had been made prior to such redemption or purchase for cancellation or otherwise or such payment of dividend, as the case may be, and (ii) interest at the prescribed rate as defined in Regulation 4301(*c*) to the *Income Tax Act* (Canada) on the amount described in subparagraph 7.A.(vii)(*c*)(i) hereof computed from the date of the redemption or purchase for cancellation or otherwise or the date of payment of such previous dividend, as the case may be, up to and including the date of such payment by the Corporation;

(d) In the event that the Class A Redemption Amount is decreased pursuant to subparagraph 7.A(vii)(*b*) hereof following a redemption or purchase for cancellation or otherwise of a Class A share or following the payment of a dividend on a Class A share, the holder of such share that was so previously redeemed or purchased for cancellation or on which a dividend was so previously paid shall be liable to pay to the Corporation, to reflect a reduction of the Class A Redemption Amount or dividend previously paid per such Class A share, as the case may be, an amount equal to the aggregate of: (i) such amount as is necessary to reduce the amount which such holder has theretofore so received to the amount which he would have been entitled to receive if the said reduction had been made prior to such redemption or purchase for cancellation or otherwise or such payment of dividend, as the case may be, and (ii) interest at the prescribed rate as defined in Regulation 4301(*c*) to the *Income Tax Act* (Canada) on the amount described in subparagraph 7.A(vii)(*d*)(i) hereof, computed from the date of the redemption or purchase for cancellation or otherwise or the date of payment of such dividend, as the case may be, up to and including the date of such payment by such holder.

In respect of the above "sample price adjustment clause", as noted previously, the triggering of the adjustment mechanism is primarily based on a discrepancy between the fair market value of the assets transferred into the corporation (in this case, common shares) and the fair market value of the consideration received from the corporation (in this case, Class A shares). The primary adjustment mechanism, in this case, is an adjustment to the redemption and retraction amount of the Class A shares (the "Class A Redemption Amount").

Although a price adjustment mechanism will typically be used in a closely held situation, e.g., for an estate freeze among family members, it should be noted that the price adjustment mechanism (basically, resultant from a dispute with a taxation authority) effects real economic rights, namely, an adjustment of the redemption amount of the shares. In many instances, particularly in arm's length situations, the parties may not wish these economic rights to be altered, so a price adjustment clause should not be used in a "mechanistic" manner without considering this possibility.

In this respect, it should also be noted that the main purpose of a price adjustment clause is to prevent the CRA from attempting to apply one of the shareholder benefit provisions. Where parties do not wish their economic rights to be altered, it tends to be unlikely that any of the parties desire to confer a benefit on any of the other parties. Most of the benefit provisions are worded in a manner such that motivation is a factor in applying the particular benefit provision.[19] Obviously, however, the parties may not want to risk a dispute with the CRA, based on such amorphous issues.[20]

☞   **Consider the interaction of a price adjustment clause with the taxable preferred share rules. A price adjustment clause may jeopardize the subsection 191(4) exemption.**

Disclosure

In paragraph 1 of Interpretation Bulletin IT-169, the CRA indicates that the parties to a non-arm's length transaction must notify the CRA (by a letter attached by each party to the tax return) of the price adjustment clause and advise, further, that the parties are prepared to have the price in the agreement reviewed by the CRA, that they will take the necessary steps to settle any discrepancy, and that a copy of the agreement will be filed with the CRA if and when demanded.

[19] See, however, subsection 15(1).

[20] The interaction of a price adjustment clause with the taxable preferred share rules should be considered. It appears that a price adjustment clause would jeopardize the subsection 19(4) exemption. See Q.20 of the 1989 Revenue Canada Round Table.

Although the CRA has not withdrawn this Bulletin, it appears that these administrative policies are archaic. In Question 58 of the 1990 Revenue Canada Round Table, the CRA indicated that if the parties failed to notify it in the returns, this failure would not, in and of itself, preclude the application of the adjustment clause, if other conditions set out in the Interpretation Bulletin are met. The CRA has amended a number of relevant election forms to provide for a question pertaining to price adjustment clauses and has indicated that a yes answer is sufficient notification. Also, in circumstances where no form is required (e.g., section 86 or 51 of the Act), the CRA has stated that simply not notifying the CRA does not prevent the application of IT-169 if all other conditions are met. However, in order to give effect to a price adjustment clause, the parties would normally file an amended election under subsection 85(7.1) and pay the penalty under subsection 85(8).[21]

In any event, most practitioners do not follow the practice of notifying the CRA, presumably because price adjustment agreements are generally felt to be effective.

As stated above, the CRA has voiced concerns about adjustment mechanisms based on teh calculationor issue of shares. However, in an estate freeze situation, the CRA would be prepared to rule favourably where a clause varies the redemption amount and/or provides for a cash payment.[22]

The validity of a price adjustment clause was considered by the court in *Guilder News Co. (1963) Ltd. et al. v. M.N.R.*, 73 DTC 5048 (F.C.A.). The issue involved was whether a benefit had been received by a shareholder who acquired property from a corporation at less than fair market value. The agreement of purchase and sale contained the following price adjustment clause:

> 4. It being the intention of the Vendor and the Purchaser that the prices herein stipulated should represent the fair market value of the shares being purchased and sold herein, the parties hereto agree that in the event that the Minister of National Revenue should at any time hereafter make a final determination that the fair market value of the said shares as of the date of the Agreement is less than or greater than the prices herein stipulated, the prices herein stipulated shall be automatically adjusted *nunc pro tunc* to conform with such fair market value as finally determined and all necessary adjustments shall be made, including adjustment of the above mentioned promissory note.

The court rejected the price adjustment clause as a basis for adjusting the price and eliminating the benefit. In its decision, the court states (at page 5052):

> This agreement is radically different from a sale that is expressly made for a consideration equal to value. This is an agreement for a sale at a price obviously less than value, which price is to be the only amount payable until such time, if any, as the Minister of National Revenue determines the value of the shares that happen to be the subject matter of this sale. While it can be said, as a matter of law, that a simple sale for value, with no other provisions, cannot result in a benefit, it cannot be said, as a matter of law that the 1964 sale is such a sale merely because it is an agreement containing clause 4. That sale is at a substantial undervaluation and, except in a certain event, it will continue indefinitely to be so. Even if that event should arise at some subsequent time, the individual will have had the benefit of not having had to pay the amount in excess of the "price" until that subsequent time and this, in days of high interest, can be substantial benefit.

---

[21] See Document No. 2004-0081631E5, July 6, 2004.

[22] See 1980 *Canadian Tax Foundation Conference Report*, p. 603.

The court also considered the price adjustment clause to be a sham and went on to state (at page 5054):

> Clause 4 was a mere sham, and in any event has no application on the facts of the case, for the following reasons:
>
> 1. Fair value was not considered at the time the agreement was negotiated by the parties. Hence, there was never any intention to sell at the market value but only at par.
>
> 2. There was no finding by the Minister of the fair market value within the meaning of clause 4. There was at the most an assessment by the Minister under the power of the *Income Tax Act*, and not a valuation pursuant to clause 4.
>
> 3. Further, the agreement acknowledging the further indebtedness was a mere sham as it acknowledges that the balance of indebtedness is payable on demand of the selling company but without interest (AB p. 183) and as the company is wholly owned and controlled by the member acknowledging as a party there is no possibility that the company could collect.

Given the comments of the court, a formal valuation of the property being transferred to a corporation would support the intention of the parties to transact at fair market value. In *Miko Leung and Sit Wa Leung v. M.N.R.*, 92 DTC 1090 (T.C.C.), the court rejected the CRA's position that a price adjustment clause should not apply. The court was of the view that there had been a reasonable attempt to value the property, shares, which in fact had been over-valued.

Adjustment to Elected Amount

As discussed earlier, in addition to a price adjustment clause which deals with "benefit" issues, it may be prudent to include a clause which adjusts the elected amount of an asset transferred pursuant to section 85, where such amount is in doubt.

The following is an example of such a clause:

Precedent — Elected Amount Adjustment

Precedent

Adjustment to Elected Amount

It is the intention of the parties that the Elected Amount as recorded on any elections or other forms under the Act or the CTA (the "Recorded Elected Amount") shall be the cost amount of the Purchased Assets to the Vendor. Should the Minister of National Revenue, the Minister of Finance for Ontario or any duly authorized officer of the Canada Customs and Revenue Agency or the Ministry of Finance for Ontario or any other taxation authority having jurisdiction assert by assessment, reassessment or otherwise that the cost amount of the Purchased Assets is not equal to the Recorded Elected Amount, or if it shall otherwise subsequently be determined that there was an error or omission with respect to any of the calculations with respect thereto, the agreed amount for purposes of the election pursuant to subsection 85(1) of the Act contemplated herein shall be adjusted as to equal the cost amount of the Purchased Assets and the Recorded Elected Amount shall be deemed always to have been such amount. The Vendor and Purchaser further agree to file a revised election under the provisions of subsection 85(1) of the Act, the CTA or other legislation to give effect to the foregoing.

Dividend Rights

Generally, the CRA's position in respect of dividend rights relating to freeze shares is that the shares should generally be entitled to a dividend, but that the entitlement should not exceed a reasonable amount.[23] Within the context of an estate freeze, the dividend should support the retraction mechanism, i.e., so that, taken together, there will not be a conferral-of-benefit problem.

For the above and other reasons (particularly to assure a return to the freezor), "freeze shares" have traditionally featured a non-cumulative dividend rate (share rights attaching to freeze shares often provide for non-cumulative dividends which become cumulative if the company is unable to redeem shares when the retraction right is exercised).

A principle of corporate law is that, absent an express provision to the contrary, all shares participate rateably with each other. Accordingly, most knowledgeable corporate lawyers appear to be of the view that, in a period during which dividends are paid to common shareholders, the holders of shares which bear non-cumulative dividends have a right to receive the dividend in respect of the particular period, unless those shareholders waive their rights, even if the non-cumulative dividend is not expressly designated as a "preferred" dividend. For this reason, as well as to add further flexibility in terms of dividend payments, shares will often feature a monthly non-cumulative feature. In addition, shares may provide that dividends are discretionary, often to a ceiling amount per month or per year. The efficacy of discretionary-dividend clauses has been enhanced in light of *McClurg v. The Queen*, 91 DTC 5001 (S.C.C.) and *Neuman v. The Queen*, 78 DTC 6277, (S.C.C.).

Some practitioners also insert an "anti-waiver" clause, to the effect that dividends can be paid on one class of shares to the exclusion of another class of shares, which would otherwise have the right to receive a dividend in a particular period. The purpose of this clause is to abrogate the necessity of obtaining a waiver from the holders of the other class of shares. There are at least two reasons why this may be a prudent procedure: first, the obtaining of a waiver for a particular period may often be overlooked; second, notwithstanding the *McClurg* and *Neuman* cases, it is quite possible that the CRA could apply a benefit provision (particularly subsection 56(2)) in respect of a waiver, particularly in a closely held situation.

The following is an example of a non-cumulative dividend clause:

---

[23] See, for example, *Window on Canadian Tax*, ¶1369.

Precedent — Non-Cumulative Dividend Clause

Precedent ──

Dividends

7.A(i)   The holders of the Class A shares shall in each month in the discretion of the board of directors be entitled, as and when declared by the board directors, to non-cumulative dividends at the rate of _____ % of the Class A Redemption Amount (as defined herein); if in any month of any financial year, the board of directors of the Corporation in its discretion does not declare the said monthly dividend on the Class A shares, then the rights of the holders of the Class A shares for such month shall be forever extinguished. The holders of the Class A shares shall not be entitled to any dividend other than or in excess of the non-cumulative monthly dividends hereinbefore provided for.

The following is an example of an "anti-waiver clause":

Precedent — Anti-Waiver Clause

Precedent ──

Participation as to Dividends

7.C(i)   The Class A shares and common shares need not participate equally as to dividends, and for greater certainty, the directors may declare and pay dividends on the Class A shares or the common shares of the Corporation without declaring or paying a dividend on the other class of shares of the Corporation.

The CRA has expressed the view that preferred shares having terms which permit dividends to be paid on the common shares without payment of dividends on the preferred shares would be acceptable, provided that the CRA's normal requirements are met, namely:

- the preferred shares must be redeemable, retractable and have a reasonable dividend rate;

- the preferred shares should be voting (at least in matters affecting the shares);

- the preferred shares must have preference on any distribution of the assets of the corporation on any liquidation, dissolution or winding-up;

- there should be no restriction on the transferability of the preferred shares (other than as required by corporate law); and

- the issuing corporation must undertake that no dividends will be paid on the other classes of shares which would result in the corporation having insufficient assets to redeem the preferred shares at their redemption amount.

☞   **The payment of dividends on the common shares must not result
in the corporation having insufficient net assets to redeem the
freeze shares at their redemption amount.**

Besides supporting the efficacy of a freeze, dividend rights are often perceived
to be important by the individuals who are freezing the corporation. For this reason,
non-cumulative dividends may often be enhanced, e.g., by providing for a participation with common shares or perhaps a discretionary dividend feature, relying on the
McClurg and *Neuman* cases. Arguably, this could open up the possibility that the
shares are worth more than the freeze values, although the redemption feature
would, of course, provided a counter argument. It should be noted, however, that
practically speaking, income protection will often be available in the form of
owner/manager bonuses. However, individuals relying on such mechanisms should
be aware that, in the event of a serious family altercation, it might be open for
shareholders to challenge bonus arrangements, e.g., based on corporate law oppression remedies.

In most instances, it is preferable to base percentage dividends on the redemption or retraction amount, rather than the stated capital of the shares since, in many
instances, the latter amount will be much smaller, such as where corporate stated
capital is suppressed under corporate law, or where stated capital is otherwise
limited, such as where there has been a section 86 reorganization.

☞   **In Q.45 of the 1981 CRA Round Table, the CRA was asked its
position with respect to shareholder benefits resultant from
preferred shares given as consideration in a section 85 transfer,
specifically whether a retraction right was sufficient. The CRA's
response was that a retraction right would be sufficient. In
situations where the preferred shares are to be held as an
investment, the CRA would normally insist on a dividend rate. It
was stated that, in an estate freeze, the CRA prefers that
preferred shares pay a reasonable dividend rate, but the absence
of one would not, in and of itself, be viewed as reducing the value
of preferred shares so as to cause the benefit provisions in
paragraph 85(1)(e.2) to be applied. Note, however, that, at the
time of the question, the wording of paragraph 85(1)(e.2) was not
as stringent as it now is.**

Preference on Dissolution

In an estate freeze situation, preference on liquidation will invariably be given
to the freeze shares. Again, the purpose of this preference is to counter the argument
that a benefit has been conferred on another shareholder.

The following is an example of a clause relating to preference on dissolution:

Precedent — Preference on Dissolution Clause

Precedent ——————————————————————————————

Participation in Assets on Dissolution

7.A(ii)   Upon the liquidation, dissolution or winding-up of the Corporation or upon final distribution of its property and assets and after the payment of its debts, the holders of the Class A shares shall be entitled, in preference and priority to the holders of the common shares, to payment in respect of each Class A share of an amount equal to the Class A Redemption Amount (as defined herein) together with all dividends declared thereon and unpaid (the whole constituting and being referred to herein as the "Class A Dissolution Amount") but such holders shall not be entitled to share any further in the distribution of the property or assets of the Corporation; if the assets of the Corporation, including surplus, are not sufficient to pay in respect of each Class A share the Class A Dissolution Amount, in full, then all the said assets or their proceeds remaining after such payment shall be distributed rateably among the holders of the Class A shares.

Voting Rights

Tax practitioners have often speculated whether the concentration of voting rights would result in a "control premium", e.g., in respect of the valuation of freeze shares passing on death. The Tax Appeal Board's decision in *Barber Estate v. MNR*, 66 DTC 315, has been cited for the proposition that voting control could enhance the value of shares.

However, in 1972, the Supreme Court of Canada was of a different view, in light of the specific protection afforded to minority shareholders under the *British Columbia Corporations Act*. As indicated in Taxation of Private Corporations and Their Shareholders, 3rd ed., the line of reasoning pertaining to control premiums was "laid to rest by the Supreme Court of Canada's decision in *Re Mann Estate*".[24]

Or was it? More conservative tax practitioners have always been nagged by this issue (in fact, the above publication goes on to list various methods to protect against a control premium). Perhaps one reason for these doubts lies in the fact that, as a practical matter, legal proceedings by a disgruntled minority are expensive, and therefore rather unlikely to occur in most situations.[25]

---

[24] See page 3:30.

[25] Cases such as *Winram Estate v. MNR* [1972] 5 WWR 23 (B.C.S.C.), affirmed [1974] 2 WWR 574 (S.C.C.) illustrate the danger of attaching sprinkling dividend clauses to shares that have voting control. The deceased's shares carried sufficient votes to control the company, and the articles provided for "exclusionary dividends" — that is, dividends could be paid on one class of shares only. It was held that, for estate tax purposes, the deceased, holding 90% of the outstanding voting shares, could have caused the company to pay 90% of the surplus to themselves. Query whether such a result would occur in view of oppression remedies. However, it is possible that in some circumstances, the case for oppression remedies may not be good, i.e., because such results are "reasonably expected".

However, in the typical estate freeze situation, the client will usually insist on maintaining control of the corporation, notwithstanding the protection that can be built into a family trust, and in addition, will often want the ability to pass these voting rights on to his or her selected beneficiary. Accordingly, most practitioners will allow the freezor to retain the desired voting control, relying on the *Mann* case.

In fact, in an estate freeze and other situations, some practitioners will use so-called "thin voting shares", in order to isolate voting rights. These shares will be redeemable and/or retractable at a nominal amount, have very limited or nil dividend rights, but contain a "concentration" of voting rights. Thin voting shares are used in a variety of situations where an objective is to sequester control in the hands of certain shareholders. This approach is the "purest" way of separating voting and equity rights.

Non-Impairment Clause

In order to buttress the "conferral of benefit" problem, a prudent practitioner will often insert a provision in the Articles to the effect that dividends or reacquisitions of subordinate classes of shares cannot be effected if the result would be to impair the ability to redeem or retract freeze shares.

In Q.13 of the 1980 Revenue Canada Round Table, it was indicated that, in a freeze, the corporation must undertake that no dividends will be paid on other classes of shares which would result in the corporation having insufficient net assets to redeem its preference shares at their redemption amount. (A selection of Revenue Canada Round Table questions and answers are reproduced in Appendix B.)

It is the CRA's standard ruling requirement that a non-impairment clause must be in place, as described above. However, in the absence of a ruling, many practitioners are apparently reluctant to insert such a clause. One reason is that there is concern in respect of the obligations of directors, especially where the redemption price of the freeze shares has not been discounted in respect of the underlying tax liability.[26]

It is submitted, however, that the CRA have justification for imposing this requirement in order to avoid the conferral of benefit.

In Ontario, at least, the corporate law protection afforded to so-called "high-low" shareholders (i.e., where the corporate stated capital is suppressed but the redemption price is high) is surprisingly limited. The "solvency" restrictions in respect of both dividend payments and the reacquisition of shares (subsections 30(2) and 38(3) of the OBCA) are based on the difference between realizable value of assets and the aggregate of the corporation's liabilities and stated capital. Therefore, since the stated capital of the freeze shares is typically suppressed, a corporation could pay dividends or reacquire growth shares with little to fear in respect of the solvency requirements. (Per subsection 32(2), the restriction on redemption, on the other hand, is not based on stated capital, but "the amount that would be required to pay holders of shares" on a redemption or liquidation (this relates to shares which

---

[26] See H. Kellough and P. McQuillan's *Taxation of Private Corporations and Their Shareholders*, 3rd edition, pages 3:32-33.

have priorities or participate rateably on redemptions, etc.). However, it is rather unusual to have a redemption feature in respect of "growth" shares.) It may be possible for a preferred shareholder to proceed under the "oppression" remedy; however, the likelihood of being granted relief probably depends largely on the particular circumstances.

Finally, in many cases, the requirements on directors from a non-impairment clause (mentioned earlier in this section) may not be a practical problem. For example, where a family trust is used as a freeze vehicle, there will often be restrictions on income splitting in respect of "designated beneficiaries" (e.g., minors and the spouse of a freezor) pursuant to the requirements of subsection 74.4(4) of the Act.

The following is an example of a non-impairment clause:

Precedent — Non-Impairment Clause

Precedent ────────────────────────────────────

Non-Impairment

7.C(ii)   The Corporation shall not declare or pay any dividends on the common shares of the Corporation nor purchase, including by way of redemption, any of the common shares if such dividend or purchase would result in the Corporation having insufficient net assets to redeem any issued and outstanding Class A shares as provided for respectively in subparagraphs 7.A(iii) and 7.A(iv) above, or to pay the Class A Dissolution Amount in respect of any issued and outstanding Class A shares as provided for in subparagraph 7.A(ii) above.

Other Share Rights in Respect of an Estate Freeze

Besides the rights specified above, in the CRA's view, at least, the following rights should also be included:

1. Freeze shares may or may not have voting rights, but should at least have voting rights on any matter involving a change to the rights, conditions, or limitations attaching to them sufficient to protect those rights.

2. There should be no restriction on the transferability of the shares other than restrictions required by corporate law to qualify the corporation as a "private" corporation.

In many jurisdictions, the corporate statute will, in itself, build in significant protection in respect of changes to rights, conditions or limitations attaching to shares. For example, under the OBCA, otherwise non-voting shares may be given the right to vote under such situations[27] and may, in addition, allow dissenting shareholders of the affected class to be bought out at fair market value.[28] The CRA has

---

[27] See section 170.

[28] See section 185.

indicated that the requisite voting rights may arise as a matter of applicable corporate law or specific share conditions.[29]

"Step-Down" Provisions

The Articles of a corporation may contain provisions whereby certain rights pertaining to shares will cease as a result of specified events.

For example, it has been suggested that one way to avoid a control premium on death is to provide in the Articles that freeze shares lose their vote on the death of the freezor or on the transfer of any freeze preferred shares during his or her lifetime.

Another, perhaps even more common, rationale for a step-down provision is to reduce the rights and value of shares, should they "fall into the wrong hands", such as the shareholder's creditors. For example, the shares could cease to be voting and/or retractable.

The efficacy of step-down provisions under corporate law was called into question in the case of *Bowater Canadian Ltd. v. R.L. Crain Inc.* (1987), 62 O.R. (2d) 752, where the Ontario Court of Appeal struck down a "step-down" provision in which the voting rights would be restricted in the event that the shares passed to someone other than the original holder. The holding appears to be based on corporate law principles which require the equality of rights within a class of shares. In the *Bowater* case, it was possible for shares within a class to have different voting rights under the "step-down" arrangement; accordingly, the arrangement was struck down. Taken literally, it might be possible to abrogate the impact of this case if the share provisions are drafted in such a way that all of the shares of the class are affected by the "triggering event", rather than some of the shares.

Stated Capital Suppression

The directors' resolutions issuing the shares will often contain a stated capital suppression clause. The most common purpose of this clause is to restrict the corporate stated capital to correspond with the "tax capital" amount ("paid-up capital") e.g., as restricted by sections 84.1 or 212.1, subsection 85(2.1), etc.

It should be noted that, in most instances, the purpose and effect of a stated capital suppression clause is not to prevent immediate adverse tax consequences, i.e., a deemed dividend, but to guard against future adverse tax consequences resultant from the mistaken assumption as to the equivalence between tax and corporate capital: various provisions in the Act are automatically operative to suppress paid-up capital, without the necessity of further corporate action. (One instance in which an excess of paid-up capital results in an immediate deemed dividend is pursuant to subsection 84(1).)

The ability to suppress stated capital should be reviewed under relevant corporate law. For example, subsection 24(2) of the OBCA indicates that a corporation shall add to the appropriate stated capital account in respect of any shares it issues the full amount of consideration it receives as determined by the directors. However,

[29] See Q.47 of the 1993 CRA Round Table.

subsection 24(3) provides that, despite subsection 24(2) and the requirement for fully paid shares, a corporation may suppress the stated capital where it issues shares:

> (a) in exchange for,
>> (i) property of a person who immediately before the exchange does not deal with the corporation at arm's length within the meaning of that term in the Act, or
>> (ii) shares of a body corporate that immediately before the exchange or that, because of the exchange, does not deal with the corporation at arm's length within the meaning of that term in the Act; or
> (b) under an agreement referred to in section 175 or an arrangement referred to in clause 182(1)(c) or (d) or to shareholders of an amalgamating corporation who receive the shares in addition to or instead of securities of the amalgamated corporation.

☞ **If this provision does not apply, it may be possible to subsequently reduce stated capital under section 34 of the OBCA.**

Precedent — Asset Sale Indenture

The following is an example of a resolution authorizing the issuance of shares pursuant to an Asset Sale Indenture, with a "stated capital suppression" clause (paragraph 4):

Precedent ——————————————————————————————

Resolution of the Board of Directors of

A. Authorization of Asset Sale Indenture

Whereas:

> (a) The Corporation has entered into an Asset Sale Indenture with ("_____") (the "Asset Sale Indenture"), an executed copy of which is annexed as Schedule "A" hereto, providing for the sale by _____ to the Corporation of its interest in the land and building located at _____ , for the purchase price therein set out and the satisfaction of such purchase price by the issuance of _____ Class A shares in the capital of the Corporation to _____ ;
>
> (b) _____ and _____ are interested in the aforesaid Asset Sale Indenture and the transaction provided for therein in that they are directors and officers of the Corporation and directors and officers of _____ ;
>
> (c) There is no disinterested quorum of directors in relation to the said Asset Sale Indenture and the transaction provided for therein;

NOW THEREFORE BE IT RESOLVED that:

> 1. The entering into by the Corporation of the Asset Sale Indenture and the execution and delivery of the Asset Sale Indenture by the directors of the Corporation be and the same are hereby ratified, sanctioned and approved;

2. The directors and/or proper officers of the Corporation be and they are hereby authorized and directed to do all acts and things and to execute or cause to be executed whether under the corporate seal or otherwise all such deeds, transfers, assignments, instruments and documents as in their opinion may be necessary to complete the transaction provided for in the said Asset Sale Indenture.

B. Issuance of Class A Shares Pursuant to Asset Sale Indenture

WHEREAS by the aforesaid Asset Sale Indenture, the Corporation agreed to issue to _____ Class A shares in the capital of the Corporation as fully paid and non-assessable shares;

AND WHEREAS the Corporation has received the consideration provided for in the Asset Sale Indenture, namely, _____'s interest in the land and building located at _____ (hereinafter referred to as the "Purchased Asset");

NOW THEREFORE BE IT RESOLVED that:

1. _____ Class A shares in the capital of the Corporation be and the same are hereby allotted and issued to _____ as fully paid and non-assessable shares;

2. The amount of money the Corporation would have received if the said _____ Class A shares had been issued for money is $_____ ;

3. The Purchased Asset in consideration of which such _____ Class A shares are issued have a fair value that is not less than $_____ ;

4. The Corporation having issued the said _____ Class A shares in exchange for the transfer of the Purchased Asset which was the property of _____ which immediately before the transfer thereof pursuant to the Asset Sale Indenture did not deal with the Corporation at arm's length within the meaning of that term in the *Income Tax Act* (Canada), hereby adds to the stated capital account maintained by the Corporation in respect of the Class A shares the amount of $_____ , being an amount equal to the aggregate of the agreed amounts as referred to in subsection 4(*b*) of the Asset Sale Indenture;

5. The Purchased Asset having been transferred to the Corporation and the Corporation accordingly having received the consideration for the allotment and issue of the said _____ Class A shares, it is hereby directed that a certificate representing the said Class A shares be issued to _____ .

The undersigned, being all the directors of the Corporation, hereby acknowledge that the nature and extent of the interests of _____ and _____ in the aforesaid Asset Sale Indenture and the transaction provided for therein were declared and disclosed to them in reasonable detail in the foregoing recitals and hereby consent to the foregoing resolutions.

DATED the _____ day of _____ , 20_____ .

The undersigned, being the sole shareholder of the Corporation, hereby acknowledges that the nature and extent of the interests of _____ and _____ in the aforesaid Asset Sale Indenture and the transaction provided for therein were declared and disclosed to _____ in reasonable detail in the recitals to the directors' resolution dated the _____ day of _____ , 20_____ and hereby consents to the foregoing as a special resolution.

DATED the _____ day of _____ , 20_____ .

Capitalization — Specific Tax Considerations

In addition to the forgoing general comments, a number of more specific provisions may affect the nature and extent of the capital taken back in consideration for assets transferred to a corporation. In this respect, the following should be considered:

- the rules relating to taxable and short-term preferred shares (as noted elsewhere, it may be prudent to include a subsection 191(4) clause in respect of freeze shares);

- the capital gains anti-avoidance rules;

- the rules relating to cost-base allocation and the consequent ability to extract assets without adverse tax effects;

- the cost-base averaging rules; and

- the effect of the transfer on the continuing ability to deduct financing costs by the transferor.

For further discussion, see Chapter 2 and 6.

Chapter 7

Estate Freeze From Hell: A Case Study

TOPICS DISCUSSED

The following is a case study involving succession, tax and estate planning issues arising from the 21st anniversary of a freeze into a discretionary family trust.

Introduction[1]

The Meeting[2]

You've just met with Ben Lewis, a longstanding client and friend. About 30 years ago, Ben (now in his late 60s) started Les Trés Expensife Sports Equipment Limited ("Expensife"), a sports equipment manufacturing operation that distributes all over North America and is beginning to distribute globally.

While Ben runs a successful business, age is starting to catch up to him. Last year, Ben was diagnosed with a medical condition that may materially reduce his life expectancy. Although he is still firmly at the helm of Expensife, the news has hit him hard and he has shown increasing signs of unusual behaviour.

Ben has been married to Anne for about 25 years (his first wife passed away after their third child was born). Last Saturday, Ben invited his three children, Robin, Larry and Alan, to lunch. It was a bombshell — Ben intends to divorce Anne. About a year ago, Ben was introduced to Anne-Marie, a 40-something socialite who has been active in many Toronto-area charity events. It is obvious that a relationship has developed; Ben indicated that he may move in with Anne-Marie and possibly marry her. However, Ben told his children that he would "make sure" that the bulk of his estate goes to his children and grandchildren. He is therefore concerned about family law implications of his relationship with Anne-Marie. Anne-Marie is obviously used to an affluent lifestyle (this would be her third marriage, her first being to a prominent lawyer who passed away; her second to a businessman, was short-lived).

Ben is also upset over his son, Larry. Larry recently announced that he and his girlfriend were having a child and getting married. One thing led to another, and Larry is no longer speaking to the family.

Things got even worse when Ben learned that his family trust would have to be disbanded soon with everything going to his kids. This couldn't come at a worse time. Ben has always treated his children equally. But his distress over Larry's situation has most recently led him to say that he wants Larry's distribution from the Lewis Family Trust to be cut in half. And while Ben didn't actually say it, it was obvious that he wasn't too thrilled with your advice to get into the family trust, even though this occurred more than twenty years ago.

---

[1] This section was written by *David Louis* of *Minden Gross Grafstein & Greenstein LLP*. The author wishes to thank *Michael Atlas* for his comments on the case study materials.

[2] *Any resemblance to persons dead or alive is strictly coincidental.*

The Freeze

In 1985, Ben transferred his shares of Expensife into Hoots-Paw Holdings Limited[3] ("Hoots-Paw"), taking back 10,000 voting freeze shares, with a total redemption value of $10 million.[4] The 100 common shares are held by the Lewis Family Trust (the "Trust"), a discretionary family trust established for Ben's issue (children, grandchildren, etc.) at the time to effect the freeze. Ben and Anne, two of the original trustees persuaded you, an accountant, to be the third trustee. As Ben has the power to replace trustees, Ben now wants to dismiss Anne. Expensife is now worth at least $25 million (excluding investments).[5]

In the early '90s, an insurance specialist persuaded Ben and Anne to take out a universal life joint and last survivor insurance policy to ensure coverage of death tax exposure and provide a cash inheritance for his children. The amount of the death benefit is $5,000,000, and is held by Hoots-Paw. At the time, you and the insurance agent discussed the fact that there are ways in which corporate ownership would actually reduce exposure to death taxes, but no formal memos were put in place as Hoots-Paw is a family-owned corporation.

The Kids

Robin is 45 and has an MBA and an accounting designation. Robin worked with a large downtown accounting firm until just after she obtained her designation and then started in the family business. Robin has become increasingly skilled as a business person and more actively involved in the business as the years have passed.

She is married to John, a very successful neurosurgeon (who has no interest in the business) and has two children, ages 14 and 10. Ben has confided to you that, after 23 years of marriage, Robin and John have grown apart. Robin and John never signed a marriage contract. When Ben found out that the growth shares of Hoots-Paw should be distributed to the children in 2005, resulting in a possible family law claim by John in the event of marital breakdown, he hit the roof.

Larry is 40 and has an engineering degree from Pepperdine University in California. Larry worked in the family business for a few years but often fought Ben and Anne because he thought they were from "the old school". While he was there, he met Desiré Laflamme, a secretary. When Larry "took up" with Desiré, Ben did not approve of the relationship — for this and other reasons, his relationship with Larry started to deteriorate. Desiré is an American citizen.

Several years ago, Larry and Desiré moved to California, where Larry started his own internet company. He was positive that he would make several hundred million dollars by going public, but things didn't go well. He ended up getting an engineering job in San José, California (he has a Green Card). He lives there with Desiré.

---

[3] The intent was to dividend excess cash to Hoots-Paw so that investments outside the business could be made by that corporation.

[4] Including goodwill not reflected on the financial statements.

[5] Deferred taxes are ignored.

Although Larry and Desiré intend to get married in six months, Desiré refuses to sign a marriage contract.

Alan is 33 years old. He is considered by many to be brilliant, although somewhat disorganized. He has just started to work in the family business and seems hardworking. However, with his traditional background, Ben has always considered Alan to be somewhat of a puzzle. A few years ago, Alan dropped out of the University of Toronto law school to play bass in a band specializing in the works of "Tower of Power" — an obscure '70s rhythm and blues group. He has spent several summers windsurfing in Maui.

Other Facts

Although bonuses had periodically been paid to Ben and Anne, no dividends were ever declared from Hoots-Paw and the Trust has always filed nil returns. The children are only vaguely aware of the existence of the Trust.

Ben's current will leaves his estate to his children or family (if a child has passed away) in equal shares (i.e., *per stirpes*).

Ben's personally-held portfolio is well into seven figures. He anticipates further appreciation.

A variety of investments is held at the corporate level, including real estate and stocks (with a low cost base), cash and near-cash, the total value being in the $10 million range.

The freeze shares provide for a non-cumulative discretionary dividend of 12% per annum.[6]

The universal policy also has a cash value as payments have been made in excess of the required minimum. Ben is no longer insurable, due to his medical condition.

The following issues will be discussed (see the diagram below for a corporate chart illustrating the current corporate structure):

- the 21-year deemed disposition rule;

- a second estate freeze;

- associated corporation issues;

- "reversionary trust" rules/restrictions on "roll-outs";

- relevant trust law/fiduciary issues;

- distributions to U.S. resident and other cross-border issues;

- double tax issues;

- planning avenues in respect of the insurance policy;

---

[6] Assumed not to be unreasonably high for a 1985 freeze.

- shareholders' agreement and other corporate law matters; and
- family law considerations.

Current Structure

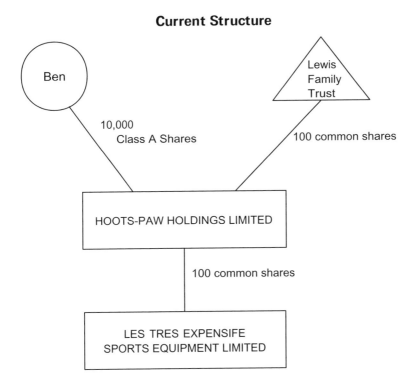

The Succession Plan — Income Tax Issues[7]

Introduction

In the case study, Ben Lewis is in his late 60s. Given his age and recently diagnosed medical condition, it seems likely that he intends to withdraw from the family business over the course of the next few years and perhaps sooner, depending on his health situation. The imminent 21st anniversary of the settlement of the Trust will force Ben to address the issue of succession and ultimate ownership of the business. The facts indicate that Ben Lewis has historically treated the children equally, but now he has openly voiced different views. In the case study, two of the children are involved in the business (one child, Robin, on a dedicated basis and one child, Alan, for the first time) while there is open dissension with the third child, Larry. Should final decisions about ownership of the business be made when the children's ambitions and potential are not yet settled and amidst the rift with Larry? Ben probably wishes that there was more time. With the benefit of time, the children's contributions to the business, their abilities and economic circumstances will mature and there may be a resolution of the rift with Larry.

---

[7] This section was written by *Joan Jung* of *Minden Gross Grafstein & Greenstein LLP.*

The suggestions set out below are intended to present the opportunity to postpone the ultimate ownership decision to a large degree. The children are given some ownership interest currently but Ben retains control and it may be possible to differentiate among the children at a later point in time.[8]

The Trust — 21-Year Deemed Disposition

In the fact situation, the 21st anniversary of the date of settlement of the Trust will occur in 2006. In the absence of any further steps being taken, the Trust shall be deemed to dispose of its capital property, being the 100 common shares of Hoots-Paw, at their fair market value at that time.[9] Such deemed disposition shall result in a capital gain of approximately $25,000,000, being equal to the increase in value of Hoots-Paw and Expensife since 1985 (i.e., the date of the estate freeze).

This $25,000,000 capital gain to the Trust may be avoided if the Trust distributes the common shares of Hoots-Paw to Canadian resident beneficiaries of the Trust. If Ben can be counselled to put aside the rift with Larry for immediate purposes and the trustees of the Trust determine in the exercise of their discretion to treat the children equally, such common shares could be distributed $1/3 — 1/3 — 1/3$ among the three children. Subject to the discussion below regarding subsection 75(2), such a distribution to the Canadian resident children, Robin and Alan, shall occur on a "roll-out" basis whereby each beneficiary shall inherit the adjusted cost base of the distributed assets to the Trust.[10] However, this does not apply in the case of a distribution to a non-resident beneficiary. Larry is a non-resident of Canada. Absent any planning, a distribution of common shares of Hoots-Paw by the Trust to Larry shall result in a deemed disposition by the Trust of such shares at fair market value.[11] Planning in respect of a distribution to Larry, the non-resident beneficiary of the Trust, is discussed in the materials written by Samantha Prasad, "Canadian Tax Issues Involving Non-Resident Beneficiaries of a Trust" on p. 260.

If the shares of Hoots-Paw constitute "qualified small business corporation shares" as that term is defined in subsection 110.6(1), then the deemed disposition on the 21st anniversary of the date of settlement of the Trust may provide a means of crystallizing the capital gains exemption, provided that the terms of the Trust enable

---

[8] Subject to appropriate fiduciary considerations.

[9] See paragraph 104(5)(*b*) of the *Income Tax Act* (Canada), R.S.C. 1985 (5th Supp.), c. 1 as amended (the "Act"). Unless otherwise indicated, all statutory references herein are to the Act. Technically, the Trust is deemed to dispose of its capital property at the end of the day that is the 21st anniversary of the date of settlement.

[10] See subsection 107(2).

[11] See subsections 107(5) and (2.1). Note that there are certain exclusions to this rule being the properties listed in subparagraphs 128.1(4)(*b*)(i) to (iii), e.g., real property situate in Canada. In the case of a distribution by a Canadian resident trust to a non-resident beneficiary, the CRA considers that the non-resident beneficiary has disposed of all or part of his capital interest in the trust with resultant section 116 compliance requirements. See CRA Document Number 2002-0131015, February 24, 2003.

the resultant deemed capital gain to be payable to beneficiaries.[12] Subject to the foregoing, consideration might be given to distributing some Hoots-Paw common shares out of the Trust prior to the 21st anniversary (subject to planning in respect of the distribution to Larry, a non-resident) but retaining a sufficient number of shares in the Trust to "suffer" the deemed disposition on the 21st anniversary to the extent of $1,000,000. (The foregoing figure assumes that each Canadian resident beneficiary has the full $500,000 capital gains exemption available.) The capital gain could thereafter be paid to each Canadian resident child to the extent of $500,000 by means of the distribution of shares which would have a stepped-up adjusted cost base.[13] In the fact situation, it is unclear whether the corporate level investments valued at approximately $10,000,000 (consisting of real estate, low cost base stocks, cash and near-cash) are owned by Hoots-Paw or Expensife. If these investments are held by Hoots-Paw, then the common shares of Hoots-Paw may not meet the qualification criteria for the enhanced capital gains exemption.[14] If the corporate level investments are held by Expensife, it is nonetheless possible that the common shares of Hoots-Paw may not constitute "qualified small business corporation shares", depending on the relative value and composition of Expensife's assets.

If the trustees of the Trust simply distributed the common shares of Hoots-Paw to the three children prior to the 21st anniversary (and subject to planning in respect of the distribution to Larry, a non-resident), that would address the 21-year deemed disposition rule and in the absence of any other steps, finalize the ultimate share ownership by the children. Ben would remain the holder of the 10,000 Class A shares of Hoots-Paw (being the 1985 "freeze" shares valued at $10,000,000) and would therefore retain voting control, but there would be no further ability to differentiate among the children *vis-à-vis* ownership of the family business. In other words, an outright distribution of the assets of the Trust in isolation would not provide an opportunity to postpone any portion of the ownership decision. Rather, that decision would be made at the time of and by virtue of the distribution of the common

---

[12] For trust law purposes, a deemed capital gain (such as that resulting from the operation of paragraph 104(4)(*b*)) may not be income to the trust and therefore may not be payable to a beneficiary as income but rather, as capital. Subsection 104(21) permits a trust to designate a portion of its net taxable capital gains to be a taxable capital gain of a particular beneficiary from the disposition of capital property where such portion of the trust's net taxable capital gains may "reasonably be considered (having regard to all the circumstances including the terms and conditions of the trust arrangement)" to be included in computing the income of the beneficiary by virtue of subsection 104(13). Subsection 104(13) refers to the trust's income for the year that became payable to the particular beneficiary. It is the interaction of these provisions that creates the issue. See CRA Document Number 9504985, March 30, 1995, in which the CRA held that "deemed gains and other such 'phantom income' could never be recognized as income for trust law purposes ... we would accept an amount as being payable for the purposes of 104(24), (13), (6), (21) and (21.2) if the terms of the trust specifically require or allow an amount equivalent to the 'phantom income' to be paid or payable, or alternatively, where the trustees have a discretionary power to pay to beneficiaries amounts that are defined as income ...". As an alternative, consideration might be given to distributing out of the Trust that number of shares with a value equal to the available capital gains exemption of the beneficiaries, electing pursuant to subsection 107(2.001) with respect to such transfer so as to trigger a fair market value distribution and allocating such resultant capital gain to beneficiaries.

[13] See subsections 104(21) and 104(21.2).

[14] A purification transaction may be possible subject to Expensife meeting the "all or substantially all" test in paragraph (*d*) of the definition of the term "qualified small business corporation share" in subsection 110.6(1).

shares of Hoots-Paw out of the Trust. Thus, each child would become an owner of the business, subject to Ben's "freeze" preferred shares and voting control during his lifetime.

A Second Estate Freeze

Consideration might be given to implementing another estate freeze to effectively postpone the ultimate ownership decision while the contributions of the children to the family business mature and the current family rift resolves itself. The facts indicate that Robin is very heavily involved in the business. Larry is no longer involved in the family business and indeed no longer on speaking terms with his father, while Alan is somewhat of an unknown factor at this point in time. Ben's desire may be that neither son be fully excluded or included until Alan's potential has been determined and Larry's situation is resolved. In addition, although Robin is very heavily involved in the business, Ben may not yet be ready to "anoint" her as the "heir apparent" and therefore, Ben may wish to preserve his ability for any one of the children to ultimately have a larger equity interest. He may, however, wish to recognize Robin's greater contribution to date in comparison to her siblings.

Ben may decide to not act rashly with respect to Larry. Assume that the common shares of Hoots-Paw are distributed[15] equally[16] so that each child will own shares effectively representing $1/3$ of the appreciation since the date of the 1985 estate freeze. However, future appreciation may be dealt with differently. Entitlement to the future appreciation need not currently be fixed among the three children and indeed, may ultimately accrue to the benefit of their children (i.e., a generation-skip to Ben's grandchildren). With respect to all of the above, it must be noted that the distribution of common shares of Hoots-Paw is a decision of the trustees of the Trust and Ben is only one of the trustees. Similarly, as described below, future appreciation shall be held by a new trust where Ben is also only one of the trustees and thus it is not Ben alone who may choose to later differentiate among the children. The trustees are fiduciaries, holding the property of the trust (whether the existing Trust or the new trust) for the benefit of others and must act accordingly.[17]

The proposed estate freeze could be implemented as:

- a "downstream" freeze of the common shares of Expensife held by Hoots-Paw;

   OR

- a freeze of the common shares of Hoots-Paw held by the Trust.

The latter would result in the Trust (and therefore the beneficiaries subsequent to distribution of the shares out of the Trust) directly holding redeemable and

---

[15] Consideration should be given to obtaining a clearance certificate pursuant to section 159.

[16] Reference should be made to the materials written by Howard Carr, "Trust and Fiduciary Issues" on p. 237 for discussion of the discretionary powers of the trustees being exercised to discriminate against Larry.

[17] Reference should be made to the materials written by Howard Carr, "Trust and Fiduciary Issues", p. 237 for discussion of the trustees' fiduciary obligations in this process.

retractable preferred shares of Hoots-Paw.[18] A retraction right means that the shares are redeemable at the option of the holder, subject to any notice provisions in the terms and conditions of the shares and the solvency requirements under the *Ontario Business Corporations Act*.[19] But it may not be desirable for the children (and, in particular, Larry given the current dissension) to hold retractable preferred shares. Furthermore, although restrictions on retraction might be imposed by a shareholders' agreement, the CRA has taken the position that such a restriction may adversely affect the determination of fair market value.[20] This may create tax benefit issues.[21] Both freeze methodologies will result in the equity interest of the Trust being frozen; either directly in the case of a freeze of the common shares of Hoots-Paw owned by the Trust; or indirectly in the case of a "downstream" freeze of the common shares of Expensife owned by Hoots-Paw. However, an estate freeze of the common shares of Hoots-Paw requires the "active" participation of the trustees of the Trust since the Trust (being the common shareholder) must consent to the transfer or exchange of those shares for redeemable and retractable "freeze" preferred shares. In other words, the trustees of the Trust must consent to a freeze of the very shares held by the Trust. This raises the question of whether the trustees would be disregarding their fiduciary obligations to the beneficiaries by consenting to such a "freeze".[22] Accordingly, it seems preferable to implement the estate freeze by means of a "downstream" freeze of the common shares of Expensife held by Hoots-Paw although this is not a complete answer to the fiduciary obligation issue.[23] Also, such a

---

[18] The foregoing assumes that an estate freeze of the common shares of Hoots-Paw would be implemented by means of a section 86 reorganization. In other words, the foregoing assumes that the "pre-existing" 100 common shares of Hoots-Paw presently held by the Trust shall be disposed of by the Trust in consideration of redeemable and retractable "freeze" shares of Hoots-Paw. An alternative means of implementing a freeze of the common shares of Hoots-Paw would involve the Trust transferring its 100 common shares of Hoots-Paw to a newly incorporated corporation pursuant to subsection 85(1) in consideration of the issuance of redeemable and retractable preferred shares by such new corporation. Such preferred shares would be held by the Trust. This alternate methodology appears to be an unnecessary complexity compared to a section 86 reorganization, but in any event, as discussed above, it is suggested that an estate freeze of the common shares of Hoots-Paw may be less defensible from a trustee fiduciary obligation perspective than an estate freeze of the common shares of Expensife.

[19] R.S.O. 1990, c. B.16, as amended (the "OBCA"). See subsection 32(2) of the OBCA.

[20] See CRA Document Number 9500555, February 2, 1995; and CRA Document Number AU81-086.087, August 25, 1991.

[21] Pursuant to paragraph 85(1)(*e*.2) or subsection 86(2), depending on the means by which the proposed freeze is implemented.

[22] In other words, are the trustees acting in the best interests of the beneficiaries by taking steps which effectively limit the value of the assets of the Trust?

[23] The fiduciary obligations and the potential liability of the trustees must be considered even if the freeze is implemented "downstream," i.e., in respect of the shares of a lower tier corporation rather that a direct freeze of the assets of the Trust. For example, query whether a beneficiary of the Trust could claim that the trustees of the Trust breached their fiduciary obligations by not exercising any shareholder remedies that might be available under the OBCA as a result of the proposed reorganization:

1. If there is a freeze of the common shares of Expensife held by Hoots-Paw, could the Trust as the common shareholder of Hoots-Paw have brought an oppression action pursuant to section 248 of the OBCA and if the trustees of the Trust fail to take such action, do the beneficiaries have a cause of action against the trustees?

(continued on next page)

freeze at the inter-corporate level may not be subject to the corporate attribution rule in subsection 74.4(2).[24]

As previously stated, it is unclear in the fact situation whether the corporate level investments valued at approximately $10,000,000 (consisting of real estate, low cost base stocks, cash and near-cash) are owned by Hoots-Paw or Expensife. Logically, it seems that these investments would be held by Hoots-Paw representing the investment of dividends from Expensife. If the investments are held by Hoots-Paw, then an estate freeze of the common shares of Expensife shall not freeze the value of these investments. It would, of course, be necessary to obtain instructions to clarify the intentions with respect to these investments. It may be that the accumulated passive investments should be dealt with differently than the ownership of the operating business. If it is appropriate that the children's entitlement to the value of the operating business only is frozen but that they will benefit both from the current value and the future appreciation of the accumulated passive investments (albeit in defined percentages, or specifically, $1/3$ each given the assumption that the common shares of Hoots-Paw shall be distributed equally out of the Trust), then the estate freeze of the common shares of Expensife can proceed as described below,[25] but if the accumulated passive investments are owned by Hoots-Paw and these assets are also to be frozen, then other alternative reorganization steps would have to be considered, such as implementing the freeze by means of freezing the common shares of Hoots-Paw or transferring such investments[26] to Expensife[27] pursuant to

---

(continued from previous page)

    2. Does the freeze of the common shares of Expensife held by Hoots-Paw give the Trust as the common shareholder of Hoots-Paw the right to dissent pursuant to paragraph 185(1)(e) of the OBCA? Is there a sale, lease or exchange of all or substantially all of the property of Hoots-Paw? Is the form of the freeze relevant, i.e., whether the freeze is implemented by Articles of Amendment which pursuant to paragraph 168(1)(h) of the OBCA changes the 100 common shares of Expensife into 10,000 redeemable and retractable Class A shares versus implementation by the Share Exchange and Cancellation Agreement whereby Hoots-Paw transfers the 100 common shares to Expensife in exchange for 10,000 redeemable and retractable Class A shares? If this gives rise to a right of dissent, do the beneficiaries of the Trust have a cause of action against the trustees if they fail to exercise such right?

For a more detailed discussion, reference should be made to the materials written by Howard Carr, "Trust and Fiduciary Issues" on p. 237.

[24] However, the "kiddie tax" rules in section 120.4 must be considered if dividends from Expensife are paid to a "specified individual" (such as a minor grandchild of Ben) directly or through a trust.

[25] Based on the given facts, and assuming that the corporate level investments remain in Hoots-Paw, the freeze value, i.e., the aggregate redemption and retraction value of the freeze preferred shares of Expensife, would be $25,000,000.

[26] Again, the fiduciary obligations of the trustees of the Trust must be considered.

[27] Or to another subsidiary corporation to facilitate a "downstream" freeze. For example, a new corporation could be incorporated to which the investments could be transferred pursuant to subsection 85(1) in consideration of redeemable and retractable preferred shares of such new corporation. Such new corporation and Expensife would be sister corporations. The use of another subsidiary corporation may be desirable to separate investment assets from the operating assets in Expensife for liability protection reasons. In theory, the growth or common shares of such new corporation and Expensife could be dealt with differently.

subsection 85(1)[28] prior to freezing the common shares of Expensife. For the same reasons as outlined above, the latter seems preferable.[29]

Assuming that the corporate level investments are either owned by Expensife or transferred to Expensife as a preliminary step, it is suggested that the estate freeze of the common shares of Expensife, including action to recognize Robin's contribution to the business, be implemented as follows:

- pursuant to section 86, Hoots-Paw will dispose of the issued and outstanding common shares of Expensife (all of which are held by Hoots- Paw) and receive in consideration therefor 10,000 redeemable and retractable non-voting preferred shares (designated as Class A shares)[30] with an aggregate redemption and retraction value equal to the current fair market value of the issued and outstanding common shares of Expensife;[31]

- consideration should be given to causing these "freeze" shares to have the attributes necessary to qualify as shares of a "specified class"[32] as this may assist in avoiding future associated corporations issues.[33] In the case study, note that even if the Class A shares of Expensife to be held by Hoots-Paw constitute shares of a "specified class," this will not prevent Hoots-Paw, Expensife and, for example, another company owned by Alan, from being associated at present or immediately following the distribution of the common shares of Hoots-Paw out of the Trust (see further discussion below);

- regardless of associated corporation planning, as it seems prudent to segregate the "freeze value" and voting control in separate classes of shares, the

---

[28] In consideration of the issuance of, say, 100 common shares of Expensife. Note that the transfer of real estate will attract land transfer tax, subject to the availability and use of the election to defer and often to extinguish such tax pursuant to subsection 3(9), *Land Transfer Tax Act*, R.S.O. 1990, c. L.6 as amended.

[29] Although as indicated above, it may be prudent to use a separate subsidiary corporation to hold the investment assets, for purposes of simplicity, the following discussion of the proposed freeze assumes that the investment assets are transferred to Expensife.

[30] Pursuant to paragraph 96 of section 3860 of the CICA Handbook, a "non-publicly accountable enterprise", such as Expensife, that qualifies for "differential reporting" under section 1300 of the CICA Handbook will not be required to comply with CICA Handbook section 3860 and reclassify preferred shares, such as the freeze shares, as financial liabilities for financial statement purposes so long as they were issued "in tax planning arrangements under Sections 51, 85, 85.1, 86, 87 or 88 of the [Act]".

[31] Based on the given facts, the freeze value would be $35,000,000 which includes the current value of the corporate level investments.

[32] See subsection 256(1.1). The required attributes of shares of a "specified class" are somewhat similar to those for typical "freeze" preferred shares but, shares of a "specified class" must be non-voting, and, in addition, the dividend rate cannot exceed the prescribed rate of interest at the date of issuance of the shares. Note that because paragraphs 256(1.1)(*c*), (*d*) and (*e*) refer to the "fair market value of the consideration for which the shares were *issued*" [emphasis added], if it is desirable that the Class A shares of Expensife constitute shares of a "specified class", then it may be preferable to implement the section 86 transaction by means of contract (i.e., a Share Exchange and Cancellation Agreement in conjunction with any necessary Articles of Amendment of Expensife to create preferred shares with the desired attributes) rather than simply changing the existing 100 common shares of Expensife into 10,000 Class A shares pursuant to Articles of Amendment.

[33] Subject to *de facto* control considerations (see subsection 256(5.1)).

"freeze" shares could be non-voting[34] and Ben should subscribe to a sufficient number of "thin" voting shares so that he will have direct voting control of Expensife; and

- immediately subsequent to the section 86 reorganization, an appropriate person will subscribe for 100 "new" common shares at a nominal subscription price. Twenty of such new common shares will be transferred to Robin by gift and the remaining 80 shares will be gifted to the Lewis Family Trust No. 2 ("Trust No. 2"), a discretionary family trust whose beneficiaries shall be the issue of Ben, being Robin, Larry, and Alan and their issue.[35]

The above results in less than 100% of the future appreciation accruing to the benefit of Trust No. 2. This clearly highlights the fiduciary obligations of the trustees in consenting, directly or indirectly, to the "downstream" freeze and their obligation to take action as discussed in the materials written by Howard Carr, "Trust and Fiduciary Issues."

See the diagram on "Proposed Reorganization" later in this section for a corporation chart illustrating the post-reorganization corporate structure.

From a succession planning perspective, the second estate freeze will achieve the following objectives:

- it has effectively frozen the value of the common shares of Hoots-Paw at the value of Expensife. Thus, after the distribution of the common shares of Hoots-Paw out of the Trust, each child will hold common shares whose value is effectively limited to 1/3 of $25,000,000;

- it has recognized Robin's past and ongoing involvement with the family business in that, unlike the other children, she shall become the direct owner of 20% of the issued and outstanding common shares of Expensife. This seems prudent from a motivation perspective;

- it results in 80% of the future appreciation in value of Expensife[36] accruing to the benefit of Trust No. 2 rather than to the children directly which will facilitate a generation skip, if considered appropriate, upon the eventual distribution of common shares of Expensife out of Trust No. 2;

- it will enable equalization of all three children at a later time or greater differentiation among them, if considered appropriate in the exercise of the discretion of the trustees of Trust No. 2, by means of distribution of an appropriate number of common shares of Expensife out of Trust No. 2; and

- it ensures that Ben will retain voting control of Expensife during his lifetime.

[34] If the Class A shares of Expensife are to be shares of a "specified class," they must be non-voting (see paragraph 256(1.1)(b)).

[35] With respect to the gift of the post-freeze common shares to Robin and Trust No. 2 and family law considerations, see the materials written by Daniel Sandler, "Family Law Considerations" on p. 297.

[36] Depending on the ownership of the corporate level investments and any other steps taken prior to implementing the second estate freeze, this will be the value in excess of $25,000,000 (if the corporate level investments remain in Hoots-Paw) or the value in excess of $35,000,000 (if the corporate level investments are owned by or transferred to Expensife).

Consideration might have been given to including Ben as a discretionary capital beneficiary of Trust No. 2. If so, this may enable the subsequent "unfreezing" of Expensife, if appropriate at a later time, at least to the extent of 80% of the common shares of Expensife. In other words, if Ben was included as a discretionary capital beneficiary, then the common shares of Expensife held by Trust No. 2 could subsequently be distributed out of trust to Ben, assuming that this would be a proper exercise of the trustees' discretion. Since Ben is in his late 60s, and as at least one child (Robin) has taken an active interest in the business — a sufficient interest shall be given a direct 20% common share ownership of Expensife — this fact situation does not seem appropriate for a so-called estate "gel". Subsection 75(2) is the major issue that must be considered in implementing an estate "gel" and this statutory provision is further discussed below.

Associated Corporations

The associated corporation rules should be noted in the event that any of the children subsequently incorporate their own businesses. Each beneficiary of a discretionary family trust is deemed to own all of the shares owned by such trust. Thus, for example, prior to any distribution of assets by the Trust, Alan is deemed to own all of the common shares of Hoot-Paw owned by the Trust.[37] If Alan incorporates his own business, his corporation and Hoots-Paw shall be associated as Alan is related to the person controlling Hoots-Paw (i.e., Ben) and in addition, he is deemed to own more than 25% of the common shares of Hoots-Paw and after the distribution by the Trust, Alan will own $\frac{1}{3}$ of the common shares of Hoots-Paw.[38] Hoots-Paw and Expensife are clearly associated as they are both controlled by Ben[39] and therefore prior to the distribution by the Trust, Alan's corporation would also be associated with Expensife.[40] After the distribution by the Trust and the second estate freeze discussed above, Alan would be deemed to own all of the common shares of Expensife owned by Trust No. 2. Since Ben shall control Expensife, Alan is related to the person who controls Expensife and since Alan is deemed to own more than 25% of the common shares of Expensife, Alan's corporation would also be associated with Expensife after the second estate freeze.

Associated corporations must share various tax preference items, including the "business limit" for purposes of the small business deduction,[41] the "expenditure limit" in respect of scientific research and experimental development for purposes of the enhanced investment tax credit[42] and the "capital deduction" for purposes of large corporations tax.[43]

---

[37] See paragraph 256(1.2)(*f*).

[38] See paragraph 256(1)(*d*).

[39] See paragraph 256(1)(*b*).

[40] By virtue of the commutative rule in subsection 256(2).

[41] See subsection 125(2).

[42] See subsections 127(10.1) and 127(10.2).

[43] See section 181.5.

The associated corporations problem may be unforeseen at the time that a discretionary trust is settled. This issue is highlighted merely to illustrate an unintended effect of an estate freeze involving a discretionary family trust.[44]

"Reversionary trust" rules / restrictions on "roll-outs"

To paraphrase subsection 75(2), where a person transfers property to a trust, but continues to control the property or have a veto over it, the income or capital gains from the property may continue to be taxed in his/her hands. More specifically, subsection 75(2) applies where by means of a trust, property is held on condition that it or substituted property:

- may revert to the person from whom the property was directly or indirectly received (the "75(2)(a)(i) Condition");

- may pass to a person determined by that person after the creation of the trust (the "75(2)(a)(ii) Condition") ; or

- may not be disposed of during the existence of a person without the consent of, or in accordance with that person's direction (the "75(2)(b) Condition").

Where any of the foregoing conditions exist, the income or loss and the taxable capital gains or allowable capital losses from the property and substituted property are included in that person's (sometimes referred to herein as the "transferor")[45] income, while he/she is resident in Canada.

Much of the commentary on subsection 75(2) refers to the above powers existing in respect of the settlor of the trust. However the provision could apply to any transfer of property to a trust. In other words, the transferor of the property may be a person other than the settlor.

In a typical estate freeze, it might seem that even if subsection 75(2) could be applicable, it would be a technical consideration only. Specifically, if the trust in question (i.e., the trust which received property directly or indirectly from a transferor) had no income or capital gains, then the attribution would be of no effect. It is not uncommon for a discretionary family trust holding common shares of a corporation to have no income or gains.[46] However, the adverse consequences may not be caused by the actual attribution of income or taxable capital gains pursuant to subsection 75(2) but rather by subsection 107(4.1) which is merely dependent on the application of subsection 75(2) and not on any previous actual attribution of income or taxable capital gains.

---

[44] For a reported case involving these issues, see *431543 B.C. Ltd. v. The Queen*, 2000 DTC 1512 (T.C.C.).

[45] Note that the CRA considers that the person referred to in subsection 75(2) is not restricted to individuals but may include a corporation — see Interpretation Bulletin IT-369R, paragraph 9 and also CRA Document Number 9610435, August 13, 1996.

[46] For example, the trust may contain a subsection 74.4(4) clause to preclude the operation of the corporate attribution rule in subsection 74.4(2). Thus no dividends would be declared on the common shares held by the trust as the subsection 74.4(4) clause would preclude allocation and distribution of such income to a "designated person".

Subsection 107(4.1) effectively precludes a "roll-out" of trust property — that is, on a tax-deferred basis — to anyone other than the transferor or his/her spouse, if subsection 75(2) was applicable *at a particular time in respect of any property of the particular trust*[47] and the transferor is alive at the time the property is distributed. It should be emphasized that, technically, subsection 107(4.1) will apply if subsection 75(2) is applicable to *any property* transferred to the trust, not just the settlement itself, and as stated above, does not require that any income or gains actually be attributed to the transferor pursuant to subsection 75(2). Rather, subsection 107(4.1) requires only that subsection 75(2) *was applicable* at a particular time in respect of any property of the trust. Furthermore, the rectification of the situation such that subsection 75(2) seems to no longer apply to the particular trust will not pre-empt the application of subsection 107(4.1) as that provision applies if subsection 75(2) was applicable *at a particular time* in respect of the trust.

If subsection 107(4.1) applies in respect of a trust which holds the "post-freeze" common shares of a corporation, the estate freeze may effectively be undermined since, if the transferor is still alive, the property of the trust can be distributed only to the transferor, or his/her spouse on a "roll-out" basis.[48] A distribution to any other beneficiary would not occur on a "roll-out" basis. In this respect, it should be remembered that in order to avoid the adverse tax consequences of the 21-year deemed disposition rule, the common shares must be distributed prior to the twenty-first anniversary of the creation of the trust. Thus, if subsection 75(2) was applicable and if the transferor is still alive at the time of the proposed distribution, subsection 107(4.1) may effectively preclude a "roll-out" to any other beneficiary.

In the case study, there are presently three trustees being Anne, Ben and you, the accountant. Ben wishes to remove Anne as a trustee. The following discussion assumes that Anne is removed as a trustee, and no replacement trustee is appointed with the result that there will be only two trustees.

A prerequisite to the application of subsection 75(2) is that there be a transferor as described above. The question is whether the Trust received property (e.g., the common shares of Hoots-Paw) either directly or indirectly from either Ben or the second trustee (i.e., do either Ben or the second trustee constitute the "person" referred to in subsection 75(2)?) The case study does not indicate how the common shares of Hoots-Paw were acquired by the Trust. If the common shares of Hoots-Paw were acquired by the Trust using a *bona fide* loan[49] to fund the acquisition, then

---

[47] Or a trust whose property was acquired pursuant to a subsection 107.4(3) "qualifying disposition". See subparagraph 107(4.1)(*b*)(ii), applicable to distributions made on or after March 16, 2001.

[48] If subsection 107(4.1) applies and it is desirable to distribute the shares to the transferor or his/her spouse, one must determine whether the terms of the particular trust will permit same. Other than in an estate "gel" situation, the transferor or his/her spouse may not be a beneficiary. A variation of trust may be necessary and the tax consequences of same would have to be considered.

[49] In the fact situation, the original estate freeze was implemented in 1985. At that time, typical estate planning practice would likely have involved the pledge of the gold coin or bond (i.e., the asset used to settle the Trust) to the bank to fund a nominal loan which in turn would be used to acquire the common shares of Hoots-Paw from treasury or alternatively, such shares might have been funded by means of a "genuine loan" from the freezor in accordance with the then administrative practice of the CRA as set out in Interpretation Bulletin IT-258R2 (since repealed as a result of the repeal of subsections 74(1) and 75(1) and related amendments which expanded the scope of the attribution rules to include a loan).

based on certain administrative statements by CRA,[50] such a *genuine* or *bona fide* loan, in and of itself, would not result in the application of subsection 75(2).

The balance of the following discussion regarding subsection 75(2) assumes that the above prerequisite was met, i.e., the Trust did receive property directly or indirectly from either Ben or the second trustee so that one of them was the "transferor" as described above for purposes of subsection 75(2). The question is then whether any one of the 75(2)(*a*)(i) Condition, the 75(2)(*a*)(ii) Condition or the 75(2)(*b*) Condition is met.

If there are only two trustees, this means that either trustee has a negative veto in respect of decisions of the Trust. Consideration of the parameters of the 75(2)(*b*) Condition is required. In other words, does this mean that property of the Trust may not be disposed of without the consent of each of Ben and you, the second trustee (to paraphrase paragraph 75(2)(*b*))? Depending on the means by which the Trust acquired the common shares of Hoots-Paw in 1985 in the course of the original estate freeze, the answer may be "yes". However, notwithstanding the negative veto to each of Ben and the second trustee, comfort may be taken from recent Technical Interpretations (discussed below) that paragraph 75(2)(*b*) may not be applicable. In a recent Technical Interpretation,[51] the CRA stated that paragraph 75(2)(*b*) will generally not apply where the person who transferred property to the trust exercises powers in a fiduciary capacity as one of two or more co-trustees:

> It is a question of fact as to whether property is held by a trust under either of the conditions described in paragraphs 75(2)(*a*) or (*b*). When the settlor is one of two or more co-trustees acting in a fiduciary capacity in administering the trust property and there are no specific terms outlining how the trust property is to be dealt with, but rather the property is subject to standard terms ordinarily found in trust indentures, we accept that paragraph 75(2)(*b*) will generally not be applicable.

This administrative position seems to have strengthened in recent years. A comparison may be made to Technical Interpretations of 2001 and 2002[52] where the language used was that the condition in paragraph 75(2)(*b*) "might not be met" rather than the "generally not be applicable" language reproduced above. The CRA

---

[50] See Interpretation Bulletin IT-369R, paragraph 1 and Q.7 of the 1991 Revenue Canada Round Table. See also CRA Document Numbers 9811115, July 6, 1998; 9225695, January 13, 1993; and 2000-0042505, April 30, 2001. Note that in CRA Document Number 2004-086941C6, October 8, 2004, a fair market value transfer of property did not prevent the potential application of subsection 75(2). In that particular Technical Interpretation, the freezor transferred the one post-freeze common share to a trust of which he was one of the beneficiaries for proceeds of disposition equal to $1.

[51] See CRA Document Number 2003-005067, April 5, 2004.

[52] See CRA Document Number 2000-0042505, April 30, 2001 and Document Number 2001-0067955, January 3, 2002. Both Technical Interpretations considered the application of subsection 75(2) to an irrevocable discretionary trust that originally had three trustees, one of whom was the settlor. In each case, the terms of the trust provided that, among other things, the settlor's children were to be the beneficiaries and decisions of the trustees were to be made unanimously.

> With respect to paragraph 75(2)(*b*), it is our view that the condition in paragraph 75(2)(*b*) might not be met in respect of property which is contributed to the trust by a person who is one of two or more co-trustees acting in a fiduciary capacity in administering the trust property where the property is subject to standard terms ordinarily found in trust indentures and there are no specific terms outlining how the trust property is to be dealt with. However, a determination of whether this condition is met in respect of any particular property can only be made on a case-by-case basis following a review of all the facts and circumstances surrounding a particular situation.

was specifically asked about the meaning of "standard terms ordinarily found in trust indentures" in a recent Technical Interpretation and responded as follows:[53]

> Generally speaking, when no specific provision is made in a trust indenture as to the way in which the trust's property must be administered, the administration of this property is subject to the standard terms in the trust indenture. In this case, the fact that an individual from whom the trust received property is a co-trustee of the trust with one or more individuals and the trustees' decisions must be made by a majority or unanimously does not in and of itself mean that paragraph 75(2)(*b*) I.T.A. applies. However, paragraph 75(2)(*b*) I.T.A. will apply when, among other things, under the terms and conditions of the trust indenture, specific provision is made that the consent of the settlor of the trust or any other person who contributed property to the trust is required in connection with any decision the trustees made concerning the disposition of the trust's property.

Thus even if the Trust received property directly or indirectly from Ben or the second trustee, subsections 75(2) and 107(4.1) may not be an issue in the case study. It should be noted that there are no grandfathering rules with respect to the application of subsection 107(4.1) and therefore, the above issues must be considered for all trusts, even those which were settled prior to the enactment of this provision in 1988.[54] What is particularly problematic about the lack of grandfathering is that, in some cases, it will amount to retroactive legislation by causing subsection 107(4.1) to apply to deny the distribution of assets from trusts that were in existence prior to the enactment of the provision, if subsection 75(2) was applicable to such a trust at any time.

In the discussion above under the sub-heading *A Second Estate Freeze*, there was reference to a possible estate "gel", (i.e., including Ben as a discretionary capital beneficiary of Trust No. 2). The CRA has indicated that although such a transaction would not generally result in the application of the general anti-avoidance rule, other provisions such as subsection 75(2) may have application.[55] The adverse consequences of the application of subsection 75(2) and in particular, subsection 107(4.1) have been described above. At first blush, it appears that one may plan around subsection 75(2) and thereby include the freezor as a beneficiary — for example, the freezor might be one of three trustees with majority decision making prevailing, and it would not be the freezor who subscribes for the "post-freeze" common shares but rather an appropriate third party who does so and then transfers such shares by means of gift to the trust. However, a gel may give rise to a number of potential subsection 75(2) issues. For example, a concern may be that such an appropriate third party constitutes an agent or nominee of the freezor. In this regard, it should be noted that subsection 75(2) refers to the person from whom the property was directly or *indirectly* received.[56] The question is whether the freezor may, depending on the particular facts, be the person from whom property is directly or indirectly received. If so, circumstances may arise (e.g., death or resignation of co-trustees) such that the freezor becomes the sole trustee with the result that any one of the 75(2)(*a*)(i) Condition, the 75(2)(*a*)(ii) Condition or the 75(2)(*b*) Condition may

---

[53] See CRA Document Number 2004-0086921C6, October 8, 2004.

[54] The lack of grandfathering has been confirmed by the CRA in Document Number 9514275, August 21, 1995.

[55] See Q.22 of the 1990 Revenue Canada Round Table.

[56] See also CRA Document Number 9832385, October 13, 1999 in which the CRA comments on the transfer of an "economic interest" (according to *The Queen v. Kieboom*, 92 DTC 6382 (F.C.A.)) and subsection 75(2).

apply.[57] Does the inclusion of the freezor as a discretionary beneficiary, in and of itself mean that the property may revert to the person from whom it was received (i.e., the 75(2)(a)(i) Condition) or that the property may pass to persons determined by the transferor (i.e., the 75(2)(a)(ii) Condition)? With respect to the question of "persons determined by" the transferor, in certain Technical Interpretations,[58] the CRA appears to have set out a restrictive view of circumstances where subsection 75(2)(a)(ii) may apply:

> Where the beneficiaries under a trust are named in the trust indenture and cannot be modified (i.e., the person from whom the property was received by the trust cannot select additional beneficiaries after the creation of the trust), subparagraph 75(2)(a)(ii) is generally not considered applicable. This is true even though the person from whom the property was transferred to the trust may be able to determine the amount of the trust property that is to be distributed to beneficiaries already identified in the trust documents. However, subparagraph 75(2)(a)(ii) is worded broadly and there could be exceptions to this general position depending on the situation.[59]

With respect to the possibility of property reverting to the person from whom it was the received (the 75(2)(a)(i) Condition), in a Technical Interpretation,[60] the CRA stressed the word "may" and the lack of need of certainty that such property would in fact revert:

> The word "may" implies that the subsection applies even though there is only a possibility that the property reverts to the transferor. We would like to stress that the condition found in subparagraph 75(2)(a)(i) of the Act does not refer to the notion of control or certainty in order to be met.

In the particular Technical Interpretation the trust indenture provided that the trust property would pass according to a power of appointment exercisable by the transferor's spouse in such spouse's will (although the property did not become property of the estate nor pass through the estate) and as there was no prohibition against the transferor being appointed as a capital beneficiary under such power of appointment, the mere possibility that the power of appointment could be so exercised was considered sufficient to satisfy the 75(2)(a)(i) Condition.

In the case study, there do not seem to be any compelling reasons to implement a "gel" given the ages and circumstances of Ben and the children. However, where the circumstances of the freezor warrant consideration of a "gel," the above issues should be considered.

---

[57] Note that the Technical Interpretations referred to in footnotes 45 and 46 above referred to the person (i.e., the transferor) being one of <u>two or more</u> co-trustees. See the extracts reproduced above. Notwithstanding that a transferor of property to a trust who is the sole trustee makes decisions with respect to the property in accordance with and pursuant to the trust deed and his/her fiduciary obligations, the CRA would continue to apply subsection 75(2). See CRA Document Numbers 1999-0013055, June 20, 2002; and 2001-0110425, June 20, 2002. Neither *Technical Interpretation* makes reference to the sole trustee dealing with the property as a fiduciary, but simply state that in the circumstances the property cannot be disposed of without his consent.

[58] See Technical Interpretations referred to in footnote 45.

[59] In an informal discussion with a Rulings Officer, the officer indicated that, even where a class of beneficiaries was named as opposed to the actual naming of beneficiaries, in most cases, the administrative position described in the two Technical Interpretations referred to in footnote 45 in respect of subparagraph 75(2)(a)(ii) would apply.

[60] See CRA Document Number 2002-0162855, April 25, 2003. See also CRA Document Number 2004-0086951C6, October 8, 2004, where the spouse of the settlor was given the power in the trust deed to determine in her will when the trust would become non-discretionary and each beneficiary's share of trust income and capital but could not add the settlor as a capital beneficiary.

PROPOSED REORGANIZATION

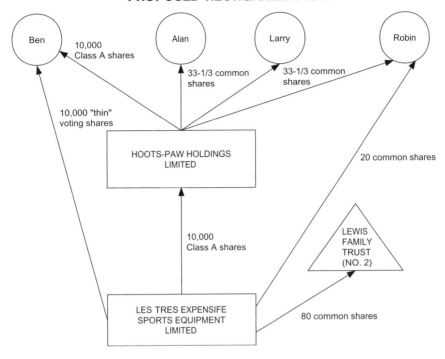

Trust and Fiduciary Issues[61]

Introduction

"Ben, the plan is great. We achieve wonderful tax savings. By capping the growth potential on your interest in Expensife, we'll reduce your estate's exposure to capital gains tax, save more money by multiplying the availability of the capital gains exemption to each of your children, ensure that the company ultimately passes to your children (every parent's dream), and accomplish all of these goals without your paying a cent in tax, and all the while preserving your control over all operations of your business. We'll shelter your children's shares in the company in a trust. A trust is great — and fully discretionary. It will enable you to discriminate among your kids if any of them get out of line. You'll control all income and capital distributions to them. Well, you can't be the sole trustee. We do need there to be three; strictly for tax reasons and decisions need to be made by majority, but don't worry. Why not name Anne — your marriage is great, and she is one of your closest professional advisers. Your lawyer is not a good idea — you know, with conflicts and all that, but your good friend, your accountant should be fine. But I know that you like flexibility, and you might change advisors in the future. You'll be able to remove and replace trustees whenever you want. And to secure your iron grip on the entire enterprise, the shares replacing your equity shares will be voting and effectively control Hoots-

---

[61] This section was written by *Howard Carr* of *Fasken Martineau DuMoulin LLP*.

Paw and through Hoots-Paw, Expensife. Ben, the plan is great. There is one minor thing, and it's probably academic. If the trust is still around in 21 years we may have to collapse it for tax purposes. But I wouldn't worry; 21 years is a long time and your kids will probably be well ensconced in the business by then, and heck I suspect that the tax rules will be amended several times in the interval."

In 1985, the Bens of our world were commonly given this type of advice. If only it were accurate. Ben was delighted of course to hear these words of wisdom. They fed directly into his view of his world and into his biases. His marriage was secure and his young children were his treasures. Of course his business would continue to thrive and his children would naturally succeed. In the event that anything went amiss, which was highly unlikely, he controlled the trust and he controlled the company. He didn't want to pay one more dollar than was absolutely necessary in taxes. The plan suited him ideally.

Legally our world is not that different today than it was 20 years ago. Trust law moves at a glacial pace and the current corporate regime is not significantly different either. What has changed and has changed dramatically is Ben's life. His business has succeeded as he had hoped, but that is perhaps the only matter that has proceeded according to plan. His family life is in the throes of upheaval. He is disenchanted with his wife, alienated from his son, Larry, and only one of his children, his daughter Robin, seems to have a flair for and interest in the family business. Ben's life is about to become more complicated because we are about to clarify the advice given to him in 1985, and he is unlikely to be pleased with what we are about to convey to him.

The Downstream Freeze — Trustees' Obligations to Take Action

If prior to the distribution of the Hoots-Paw shares to Alan, Larry and Robin, a corporate re-organization is transacted at the Expensife level, this will effectively crystallize the value of the trust's shares at their current fair market value and accrue all future share appreciation to the new trust. Ben prefers to provide Larry with a disproportionately smaller share than his siblings. Ben will test his advisors on the trustee's ability to discriminate among beneficiaries, but our trials are just beginning.

Ben could make all of our lives much easier and allow us to sleep peacefully at night by replicating the provisions of the Lewis Family Trust in the new trust. We could simply say: "no harm, no foul". No one is injured; no one is going to complain. Sure he may alter the trustees, but then he enjoyed that power under the existing trust. Anne won't be there and perhaps the accountant has also had enough. The power of removal and replacement granted to Ben is personal to him and most likely without fiduciary overtones. Anne may balk at her forced retirement and apply to court for relief, but she is unlikely to be successful. She will argue that she continues to be fit to act and should remain. The court will be hard pressed to impose a duty on Ben regarding his actions, but it will also be grudgingly sympathetic to his conundrum. Though trustees are obliged to always use their trust powers *bona fide* and in the best interests of the beneficiaries, estranged spouses rarely make for good co-trustees.

But Ben's plans may not make our life so pleasant, at least not without a good tussle and a profanity or two. So let's assume that the new trust is different, perhaps only slightly — neither Larry nor his children will be potential beneficiaries, or the children are completely bypassed in favour of the next generation. (To digress briefly, I continue to be amazed at the confidence grandparents have in the futures of young grandchildren that they barely know, if they are even born yet, and the complimentary distrust that they have in some of their own children. I do perhaps exaggerate, though not by much. There are many instances where second freezes naturally prefer grandchildren over children, where the family is close-knit and the children already enjoy more than sufficient assets to continue to make their way in the world and where the children fully concur with their parent's decision.)

Let me first be trite, because at times the difference between trite and profound is quite small. The hallmarks of the trustees' duties are "honesty, objectivity and care", a dedication to impartiality, maintaining an even hand among beneficiaries and demonstrating equity through equality. These fiduciary duties are often described as the duty of loyalty, the duty of care and the duty of impartiality. A brief description of each is as follows:

Duty of Loyalty

No trustee can profit from his own trust; a trustee cannot put himself in a position of conflict of interest.

Duty of Care

This is the duty described as being of "vigilance, prudence and sagacity". The trustee must reflect the standard of care of the reasonable man of business who is administering another person's assets; this duty also applies on an individual asset basis rather than viewing the portfolio as a whole.

Duty of Impartiality

This is the even-hand rule; where there are beneficiaries with competing interests they must be treated equitably by the trustees. The personal circumstances of each beneficiary are irrelevant to the duty of impartiality. This duty applies to all trusts, but is often in issue where there are competing interests in the income and capital of the trust, i.e., where A has a life income interest, and B is entitled to the capital on the death of A. The trustee is obliged to balance income return and capital maintenance. (As an aside — it is still not perfectly clear whether capital "maintenance" involves an allowance for capital growth, though there is a compelling argument that maintenance should involve capital growth to at least cover inflation.)

The duty of impartiality also applies to the exercise of trustees' discretionary powers. When exercising their discretion, trustees are obliged to comply first with the terms set out in the trust document, and second, with the intentions of the settlor of the trust, to the extent that such intentions can be determined. Sometimes these intentions are contained explicitly in the trust document and sometimes they are contained in a separate, contemporaneous document. However, the intentions of the settlor are the intentions of the settlor *at the time that the trust was settled*, and trustees cannot properly take intentions contained in "letters of wishes" or other documents made subsequently to the establishment of the trust into account when exercising their discretion.

The imposition of trustees' duties does not deny the trustees their right to exercise discretion where granted by the trust instrument, but rather provides a context for the execution of those powers. Trustees must adhere to the fundamental purpose of a trust, discerned through the trust document; often, this is not an easy task. If they wish to deviate from an equal treatment of all beneficiaries, trustees must do so based upon rational principles and must not exercise their judgement either arbitrarily or capriciously. We all know that these expressions are difficult to construe, and that 'arbitrary' to one judge is 'rational' to another. But in this example, the appropriate decision for the trustees, with regard to basic trust principles, is fairly simple. The proposal to disentitle one beneficiary is an action that they or, at least the innocent accountant, will find difficult if not impossible to accomplish.

If Larry is not treated equitably under the first trust or is not a beneficiary of the new trust or if there is no potential to distribute income or capital amounts to him in the future, then the trustees of the Lewis Family Trust should be concerned. There must be an excellent reason, well beyond making a bad choice on mate, to disenfranchise him from existing or future trust benefits. Where there is a downstream freeze, one might argue that Larry's shares fetched a fair market value exchange and so he should have no complaint — and perhaps this is so. But if the corporate reorganization was oppressive or required the consent of the Lewis Family Trust, but such consent was never sought, the trustees have obligations to consider initiating remedial actions.

The Case For Oppression

The trustees of the Lewis Family Trust need not and should not automatically accept all decisions of Hoots-Paw or Expensife notwithstanding the Trust's lack of voting shares in Hoots-Paw. The trustees must be cognizant of their rights as shareholders and consider appropriate action if those rights are being abused. Ben will be indignant at the prospect of his corporate actions being questioned by his co-trustees; his response will be that he created the Trust's interest by gift and that he deliberately provided the Trust with emasculated non-voting shares. Expensife is his to run without interference from the Trust. However, unfortunately, he is only partially correct.

The high water mark for Ben, albeit briefly enjoyed, came in *Re Giroday Sawmills Ltd. et al.*[62] Mr. de la Giroday reorganized his company to provide shares, for no consideration, to his wife and children. Later he exercised his voting control (together with others forming a 75% majority) to provide the directors with the ability to redeem shares on a disproportionate basis. Some of the children, being minority shareholders, sought to have the resolution set aside as being oppressive. Although the court agreed that such conduct would be oppressive in a typical commercial enterprise, under the circumstances and as long as the father was in

---

[62] 49 B.C.L.R. 378.

control of the company, and "so long as the company is his and continues to serve as an instrument for distribution of his estate, any changes he wishes to make in the rights attaching to the shares, and for which he obtains necessary shareholder consent, cannot thereafter be attacked on equitable grounds by one of the donee shareholders".[63]

More instructive of the current law are *820099 Ontario Inc. v. Harold Ballard Ltd.*[64] and *Naneff v. Con-Crete Holdings Limited.*[65]

In 1966, Harold Ballard engaged in an estate freeze with respect to his holdings of Maple Leaf Gardens. His shareholdings were then valued at about $3 million. The beneficiaries of this transaction were Mr. Ballard's three children. As is typically the case, voting control was maintained by the parent, Harold Ballard. By 1988, the value of this portion of the family's Maple Leaf Gardens shareholdings had grown to around $60 million, but relations between the father and the children had deteriorated, and Mr. Ballard engaged in a series of transactions designed to repatriate the shares he had given to his children. He bought his daughter's shares in 1989 for $15.5 million; in 1989 he bought his son, Harold Jr.'s shares for $21 million; but still outstanding were his son's, Bill Ballard's, shares which Harold also coveted. Bill rejected all offers from his father. Harold and his co-directors engaged in a number of corporate transactions, designed to assist Mr. Ballard in financing the purchase of his children's shares and in asserting control over Maple Leaf Gardens. The Maple Leaf Gardens shares were held in a holding company of which Bill Ballard was a minority shareholder. Following his father's incompetence in February, 1990, Bill brought an action to nullify the corporate manoeuvres as being oppressive to, unfairly disregarding of, and unfairly prejudicial to his interests in the company. His Honour, Judge Farley allowed the application. Judge Farley spoke not only to the issue of oppressive conduct, but also to the role of nominee directors and the confirmation that they must act in the best interests of the corporation and not as dupes for the controlling shareholder.

In *Ballard*, the divisional court neatly side-stepped *Giroday* on the basis that *Giroday* stood for the proposition that a statutory majority of shareholders may properly vote in favour of charter changes. In the court's view, the source of the shareholdings by way of parental gift was irrelevant. However, the court did not entirely ignore the "gift" issue; rather the court concentrated on the concept of expectations. It astutely concluded that expectations were dynamic, changing over time, regardless of whether the shares were originally acquired by way of gift or by purchase. Mr. Ballard was chided by the court for not better securing his position and control over the Maple Leaf Gardens shares in a more enduring trust. This last comment is perhaps most perplexing for estate planners, as our tax laws effectively mandate that trusts terminate prior to their 21st anniversary, or face potentially huge capital gains tax liabilities.

---

[63] *Supra* at p. 382.

[64] (1991) 3 B.L.R. (2d) 113 (Ont. G.D.).

[65] (1993) 11 B.L.R. (2d) 218 (Ont. G.D.), aff'd (1994) 19 O.R. (3d) 691 (Div. Ct.) rev'd in part 23 O.R. (3d) 48 (C.A.).

Giroday is perhaps an easier decision for estate planners to understand, though its reasoning calls for some caution. The Ballard case, notwithstanding Harold Ballard's outrageous conduct, alarmed most estate planners — perhaps not enough — notwithstanding its excellent and thorough reasoning. It has taken the Ontario Court of Appeal's decision in *Naneff v. Con-Crete Holdings Limited et al.*[66] to eliminate our naivety and to force us to embrace the new reality.

In *Naneff*, at trial, Blair J. analyzed the "reasonable expectations" of the share-holders in order to determine, first, whether there was oppression, and second, what remedy to grant. The dispute in *Naneff* involved a family-owned business founded by the applicant's father ("Mr. Naneff") in the 1950s. As part of an estate freeze, the applicant ("Alex") and his brother ("Boris") each acquired 50% of the common shares of the holding corporation and Mr. Naneff and his wife ("Mrs. Naneff") acquired all of the preference shares of the corporation.

Alex and Boris had worked in the family business since they were young. Blair J. found that up until the events giving rise to the dispute, both had contributed significantly to the operation and the management of the business. As a result of a falling out between Alex and his parents and brother, Alex was removed as an employee, manager and officer. Although Alex continued as a director, Blair J. found that he was excluded from the day-to-day management of the business, which pre-vented him from making any meaningful contribution at directors' meetings.

Blair J. considered the reasonable expectations of the parties as they evolved over the years, recognizing that such expectations may change over time. It was found that although the sons had worked in their father's business from a young age, the expectation that they would join in the business did not achieve the status of a "shareholders' reasonable expectation" until some later date when the corporate relationship between the sons and their father had matured. Having regard to the family background and, in particular, the sons' increased role in the family business over time, Blair J. held that Alex's expectation that he would one day take over the family business was "a reasonable one, and one which underlies the entire corporate relationship between the members of the Naneff family". Assessing the respondents' conduct against Alex's reasonable expectation that he would, together with his brother, take over the family business on his father's death, Blair J. made several findings of oppressive conduct. He found the conduct oppressive in that it did not conform with Alex's legitimate shareholder expectation, which he had been led to hold over the years, that control in the business would pass to him and his brother on their father's death.

Having determined that the respondents had breached Alex's reasonable expec-tation and hence acted in a manner that was oppressive to him, Blair J. discussed the appropriate remedy to be ordered having regard to the circumstances. Alex took the position that he should be reinstated to his former positions within the corporations, while the respondents argued that the appropriate remedy was a buy-out of Alex's shares. Applying a reasonable shareholders' expectation analysis to the question of remedy, Blair J. rejected both submissions.

---

[66] *Supra.*

Blair J. considered the possibility that Alex be reinstated and Alex and Boris be permitted to run the corporation — an option which would apparently entail removing Mr. Naneff from his position of voting control. Blair J. rejected this option which, in his view, would defeat Mr. Naneff's reasonable expectation that he would continue to exercise all final decision-making power. After balancing the reasonable expectations of the parties, Blair J. concluded that the appropriate remedy would be for the corporations to be placed on the open market for sale so that "[a]ny family member, singly or in combination, may bid for the companies, as may a third party". Such a remedy provided Alex with "an opportunity to continue in the business" and did not "arbitrarily expropriate" Mr. Naneff's control position. Blair J. held that to order otherwise would defeat the reasonable expectations of one or other of the shareholders.

Naneff demonstrates that where an employee/shareholder makes a claim for wrongful dismissal in such a way that it clearly demonstrates that his employment and his interest in the corporation are an indivisible package, an application may be properly brought as an oppression remedy.

Naneff made its way to the Ontario Court of Appeal, not on the issue of "oppression" but on the appropriateness of the remedy. Ultimately, even the remedy of the Court of Appeal was severe; although Blair's ordering the sale of the business was overturned, the court ordered that the son's shares were to be bought at fair market value without a minority discount. As an interesting aside, the son had built up a substantial shareholder's loan account. Typically, these accounts arise for tax reasons. To minimize corporate tax in active businesses, the earnings at the corporate level are reduced by large bonuses to the shareholders, which are in turn loaned back to the company for working capital. The transactions are largely artificial. The court equated these balances to profit sharing. Presumably, if the advances were not made and the funds left in the company, the value of the shares would have been greater.

The *Naneff* reasoning was not new but the classic structure of the fact situation and the imposed remedy emphasizes the nature and strength of the law in this area and its importance to estate planners.

Ben and his co-trustees ignore *Ballard* and *Naneff* at their peril. If the new trust is not similar to the existing trust, and beneficiaries such as Larry and his issue are not included, the contemplated freeze may be oppressive to the shareholder interests of the Trust.

The Fiduciary Duties of Directors

The question often arises as to the rationale for the oppression remedy when the directors of a corporation are already subject to statutory fiduciary obligations.

Both the federal and provincial *Business Corporations Acts* provide that directors must act honestly, in good faith, and with a view to the best interests of the corporation they serve. The problem for shareholders is that the primary responsibility of the directors is to act in the "best interests of the corporation" which is not necessarily equivalent to the "best interests of the shareholders". F.W. Wegenast in

The Law of Canadian Companies has described the powers of directors in the following terms:[67]

> This, then, is what is meant when the directors are spoken of as trustees. The various powers committed to them as directors are held by them in trust, to be used, not for the benefit or aggrandizement of the directors as individuals, but for the good faith for the company as a whole. Thus the property of the company, though in the control of the directors, cannot be appropriated by the directors, either directly or indirectly to their own use.

The use of the oppression remedy to provide redress where directors or senior officers have breached their fiduciary obligations has become more prevalent in oppression cases. While traditionally these obligations were owed by directors directly to their corporation and did not extend to individual shareholders, the courts have recently allowed the invocation of the oppression remedy even though the courts may not be prepared to recognize a fiduciary duty of directors owed directly to shareholders or creditors. As noted by Farley J. in *Ballard*:

> [the oppression remedy] does not have a life of its own; it must be interpreted in the light of the overall corporate legislation and case law. [Oppression] can be a help; it can't be the total law with everything else ignored or completely secondary. In other words, there must be some interplay between directors' fiduciary duties generally and [the oppression remedy].

However, that discussion is not for this paper. It is sufficient for our purposes to recognize the potential obligations of directors to shareholders and the possibility of a remedy. These comments will also be relevant in the discussion below on the requisite corporate process in approving the downstream freeze.

Trustees' Obligations

But what then are the trustees' obligations? If the shares held by the trust are voting shares, then if a corporate act is contrary to the best interests of the beneficiaries of the trust, the trustees should vote their shares against the proposal. Regardless of whether the shares are voting or not, if the act is contrary to the trust's interest, prudent trustees would obtain independent advice on their rights and then based upon the legal opinions received carefully weigh their options. Trustees, notwithstanding their independent management of the trust, are ultimately accountable to their beneficiaries. Ben may be unhappy to receive this advice, but he must fully understand the potential cost of discriminating among his children.

In the future, perhaps it would be appropriate for the Bens of our world to carefully express their intentions in the body of the trust, and to provide a blueprint to facilitate discriminatory treatment of potential beneficiaries. Lawyers have perhaps hesitated from being overly verbose for fear of compromising the ability of the trustees to exercise their discretion broadly because of the confines of the language of the document. In the past we have often felt that it was better to say nothing and provide a wide discretion than to be specific on motive and restrict the parameters of trustees' considerations. Well, the lessons learned from contemporary jurisprudence unfortunately is that the strategy is seriously flawed. The proper description of the settlor's intentions, as long as those intentions are not offensive in law

---

[67] *Supra*, at 366-367.

(e.g. restraint on marriage based on religion or race) are most likely to preserve the ability of the trustees to effectively exercise discretionary powers. Additionally, the trust document might be worded so as to dilute Ben's duty of loyalty by specifically enabling him to vote his shares as he wishes. We all should put more creative effort into tailoring and customizing trusts to the needs, inclusive of the future needs of our clients. One might even contemplate a downstream freeze with different beneficiaries in the original trust document itself.

An important question arises as to what extent these duties may be modified by the terms of the trust. Here, there is considerable scope for the trust's creator. Commonly, the duty of loyalty is intentionally diluted by specific or implied consent to conflicts of interest or to the trustee dealing with the trust on the purchase of sale of trust assets. Absent such consents, the authority to authorize such transactions resides with the court. It is probable that the standard of care imposed on trustees can be eroded by the provisions of the trust, though one might query why the settlor or testator would want to do so. Encouraging the engagement of professional advisers or the imposition of a portfolio perspective on performance rather than regard to each asset may make some sense, but otherwise reducing the degree of care or the inability to delegate should be carefully considered. The even-hand rule is constantly affected, usually deliberately, by the specific provisions of a trust; consider powers of encroachment or statements of bias in favour of the needs of particular beneficiaries over those of others.

Discretionary Powers

Ben may want the other trustees to exercise their discretion to discriminate against Larry and provide him with a smaller proportion of the Trust's Hoots-Paw shares than his two siblings. After all, the trustees enjoy absolute discretion in their decision making — what could be broader! Ask any client — certainly with that type of authority, the trustees' actions are beyond question, but unfortunately, ordinary English parlance, even if it appears clear, can take on a dramatically different perspective in a legal context. How then do the courts view "absolute discretion"? It is certainly not viewed as being beyond scrutiny. However, the courts will generally only intervene if the trustees have acted *mala fides*.

Where a court exercises its supervisory jurisdiction over trustees, the general rule is that the courts will not consider whether a decision was right or wrong. An exercise of discretion is not usually set aside on the grounds that the court would have reached a different decision.[68] A review of the cases reveals, however, that the courts have stepped in and exercised a trust's discretion in a different way, as a means of ensuring that the purpose of the trust is not defeated. It is important as practitioners that we provide guidance to trustees, either in the trust instrument itself or during the administration of the trust, as to the manner in which their discretion should be exercised.

The starting point on any discussion concerning the supervisory jurisdiction of the courts over discretionary powers given to trustees is the House of Lords decision

---

[68] This general rule was approved and applied in *Re Gulbenkian's* and *McPhail v. Doulton*.

in *Gisborne v. Gisborne*.[69] In that case, the trustees were given an "uncontrollable authority" to apply the whole or such part of the annual income of a trust as they should think expedient for the benefit of the testator's widow. The trustees proposed to apply only such income of the trust as would be required to pay for the widow's needs, after her other income had been exhausted. The court held that in the absence of *mala fides*, it would not interfere with the decision of the trustees. In reaching this conclusion, Lord Cairns commented on the effect of the grant of "uncontrollable authority" in the following statement:

> My lords, larger words than those, it appears to me, it would be impossible to introduce into a will. The trustees are not merely to have discretion, but they are to have 'uncontrollable', that is, uncontrolled, 'authority'. Their discretion and authority always supposing that there is no *mala fides* with regard to its exercise, is to be without any check or control from any superior tribunal.[70]

While the court articulated this rule in the context of a discretion described by the testator as "uncontrollable", it appears that it is equally applicable to discretions which are not absolute. This is evidenced by the fact that it has been applied in cases where the discretion at issue did not include such amplifying adjectives as "absolute" or "uncontrolled".[71] Accordingly, so long as there is no *mala fides* on the part of a trustee, the exercise of a discretionary power is to be without any check or control by the courts.

It is important to point out that in Canada the courts have essentially been more aggressive than their English counterparts in interfering with a trustee's exercise of discretion, even where it is "absolute".[72] The courts have generally accomplished this not by overruling *Gisborne v. Gisborne*, but by either broadening the meaning of *mala fides* or by establishing several possible means in which a court can intervene to strike down a trustee's exercise of discretion; these means could be said to fall within a broadened concept of *mala fides*.

What is meant by the term *mala fides*? The House of Lords in *Gisborne v. Gisborne* did not assist us in understanding this concept. While the doctrine of *mala fides* is a very elastic concept and has been described as "a concept which is sufficiently broad to make the use of the term undesirable",[73] it is clear that the

---

[69] (1877), 2 A.C. 300 (H.L.) In this decision the court dealt with the court's supervisory jurisdiction in the context of a power which is absolute or uncontrolled — which is at present virtually the standard type of discretionary power granted to trustees.

[70] *Supra*, at 305.

[71] See for example, *Re Rutherford*, [1933] O.R. 707 (C.A.); *Re Bell* (1923), 23 O.W.N. 698. See also D.M. Maclean, *Trusts and Powers* (London: Sweet & Maxwell, 1989) at 59-60 where the author states: "It should probably now be said that there is a serious question whether there is a distinction between absolute discretion in this or any other context". The context he was referring to was the examination and control by the courts of discretionary powers.

[72] In England, the concept of *mala fides* has not been widely interpreted. As a result there is little jurisprudence where the courts have interfered with a trustee's absolute discretion. See: Maurice C. Cullity, "Trustees' Duties, Powers and Discretions — Exercise of Discretionary Powers", *Estate Planning and Administration*, 13 at 18.

[73] Maurice Cullity, "Judicial Control of Trustees' Discretions" (1975), 25 *U. of T. Law Journal* 99 at 119.

doctrine is not limited to the traditional sense in which the notion of bad faith is used; fraud is not the basis upon which the concept of *mala fides* rests.[74]

An examination of the cases reveals that the grounds upon which the doctrine of mala fides has been used to justify intervention rest on an overriding concern to ensure that the fundamental purpose of the trust is not defeated. This follows logically from the trustee's duty to consider the purpose of the discretionary power when exercising it. Where a trustee attempts to exercise a discretion in a way which is outside or contrary to the fundamental purpose of the trust, the court will likely be inclined to strike down its use.

However, the improper purpose must form part of the trustee's decision in order for the trustee to be said to have acted for an improper purpose. A determination of the purpose of a discretionary power is dependent upon a construction of the power in the context of the entire instrument and any relevant extrinsic evidence. An example of the courts using this ground to strike down a trustee's exercise of discretion is the recent decision of the Ontario Court of Appeal in *Fox v. Fox Estate*.[75]

In *Fox*, the testator gave his wife (who was also the trustee) a life interest as to 75% of the income of the residue of his estate and his son a life interest as to the remaining 25%. The son also had the remainder interest. There was a power to encroach on capital for the benefit of the son during his mother's life. In addition, the testator provided that:

> Out of the capital thereof, to pay such amount or amounts as my Trustee may, in its absolute discretion, consider advisable from time to time to or for the benefit of my said son's issue or such one or more of them as my Trustee may select from time to time.[76]

Sometime after the death of the testator, the son decided to marry his secretary, who was a gentile; the Fox family was Jewish. The news of the impending marriage became a source of tension. The mother immediately disinherited the son from her own will and began making a series of encroachments of capital from the estate of her husband, in favour of the son's children. With these encroachments she transferred all the assets comprising the residue of the estate to the two children.

The first question considered by the court was the factual issue — namely, the reason of the executrix for exercising the power to encroach. A second question related to the legal issue of whether the exercise of the power was a proper one.

With respect to the factual issue, Galligan J.A. accepted the trial judge's finding that the executrix used her power to encroach in order to deprive her son of his interest in the bulk of the residue of his father's estate because he had married a gentile. The trial judge had also found that this motive was perhaps coupled with a concern for the welfare of her grandchildren, but that her dislike of her son's marriage was throughout her prime motivation in encroaching as she did.

---

[74] Bad faith as it is generally understood depends upon an intent or design to do wrong. In *Re Blow* (1978), 11 E.T.R. 209 (Ont.H.C.) at 217 Rutherford J. considered the meaning of *mala fides* and stated that in his opinion the doctrine of *mala fides* extended beyond cases of personal dishonesty.

[75] (7 February 1996), Toronto C20011 (Ont.C.A.).

[76] Ibid.

Galligan J.A. then proceeded to examine the legal issue in light of this finding of fact. The trial judge had determined that because there was no finding of *mala fides* on the part of the executrix, the exercise of her discretion had been a proper one. Galligan J.A. began his analysis by relying on the principle articulated in *Gisborne v. Gisborne* that so long as there is no *mala fides* on the part of a trustee, the exercise of an absolute discretion is to be without any check or control by the courts. He pointed out that the courts have not always equated *mala fides* with fraud, but concluded on a review of the authorities that some conduct which does not amount to fraud will be characterized as *mala fides* so as to bring it within the scope of judicial supervision. He supported the position that a court may interfere if a trustee's discretion is influenced by extraneous matters and referred to the case of *Hunter Estate v. Holton*.[77] He concluded that, in his view, the fact that the executrix's son intended to marry a gentile was completely extraneous to the duty which the will obviously imposed upon her, namely, to be concerned about the welfare of her grandchildren. He concluded that this extraneous consideration demonstrated sufficient *mala fides* to bring her conduct within any reasonable interpretation of that term. He further concluded that it was contrary to public policy to permit a trustee to effectively disinherit the residual beneficiary because he intended to marry outside the religious faith of the executrix.

McKinley J.A. reached the same conclusion as Galligan J.A., but her analysis focused more on determining the purpose of the will and whether the encroachments were made within that purpose. In her view, the testator intended that his son have a life income from the estate and a remainder interest following the death of his mother. The discretionary power to encroach in favour of the grandchildren had to be considered in that context. She concluded that given her conclusion as to the intention of the testator, it was not a proper exercise of such a discretionary power for the trustee to encroach entirely in favour of one beneficiary so as to wipe out the life interest in income and remainder interest in capital of another beneficiary.

A second ground upon which the courts will intervene to strike down the exercise of a discretion is if it can be said that the trustee has failed to consider whether he or she should exercise the discretion. An obvious corollary to the duty to consider is the requirement that when considering a decision, the trustee must take into account all relevant considerations — relevance being determined by a construction of the testator's or donor's purpose as well as the circumstances — and must not take into account irrelevant considerations. In *Re Manisty's Settlement*,[78] the court noted some of the difficulties in the determination of what is and is not relevant. For instance, not all powers necessarily inform the trustee how they are to consider the exercise. In such circumstances, the court concluded:

> The court cannot judge the adequacy of the consideration given by the trustees to the exercise of the power, and it cannot insist on the trustees applying a particular principle or any principle in reaching a decision.[79]

---

[77] (1992), 7 O.R. (3d) at 372.

[78] [1973] 2 All E.R. 1203.

[79] *Supra*, at 1209.

In other words, where a trust document does not articulate the criteria the trustees are to use when deciding to exercise their discretionary power, the issue of what to consider when exercising the power is the trustees' to decide.

Finally, a trustee cannot make a decision that is unreasoned or unreasonable. In other words, if the trustee makes a decision that is arbitrary or capricious the court will likely interfere on the basis that the trustee acted for an improper purpose or was motivated by extraneous factors.

Regarding the constraints imposed upon the use of discretionary powers, while the law has articulated principles that are simple to state in the abstract, in practice it is difficult to determine with certainty how these principles will apply to a given set of facts. One cannot advise trustees and settlors that the use of the words "absolute" and "uncontrolled" will give the trustee total freedom to act. Similarly, given the elastic nature of the concept of *mala fides*, a trustee should not take total comfort in a decision simply because it was reached honestly. In drafting trusts, we should strive for explicitness when attempting to articulate the level of freedom a trustee should have, while not compromising the flexibility with which these powers are utilized. If the trustees do determine to treat Larry differently, they would be well advised to minute their considerations and their reasoning. This process might convince Ben to provide an equal share to Larry, but if the trustees remain adamant, their reasons for the unequal division should focus more so on family relations and harmony and the best interests of Expensife and its future operations, and conversely less so or not at all on Larry's choice of a mate.

Corporate Procedure To Approve the Downstream Freeze

Section 184 of the OBCA[80] sets out the following provisions:

> (3) A sale, lease or exchange of all or substantially all the property of a corporation other than in the ordinary course of business of the corporation requires the approval of the shareholders in accordance with subsections (4) to (8) ...

> (6) If a sale, lease or exchange by a corporation referred to in subsection (3) would affect a particular class or series of shares of the corporation in a manner different from the shares of another class or series of the corporation entitled to vote on the sale, lease or exchange at the meeting referred to in subsection (4), the holders of such first mentioned class or series of shares, *whether or not they are otherwise entitled to vote, are entitled to vote separately as a class or series in respect to such sale, lease or exchange.*

The downstream freeze proposed in this case would result in the conversion of a key asset of Hoots-Paw, namely it's equity shares in Expensife, for non-voting preference shares of Expensife. By effectively removing the possibility of any further appreciation in the equity of Hoots-Paw, clearly this would affect the common shareholders "in a manner different from" the preference shareholders of Hoots-Paw. If the conversion represents an "exchange", as contemplated by section 184, then the approval of the Trust is required to effect the reorganization.

There are two technical requirements to the imposition of section 184 in this instance; the transaction must be a "sale, lease or exchange", and the sale, lease or

---

[80] See also the virtually identical section 189 of the *Canada Business Corporations Act*, R.S.C. 1985, c. C-44, as amended (the "CBCA").

exchange must involve "all or substantially all" of the property of Hoots-Paw.[81] However, conversions of shares are often, albeit not always, determined to be equivalent to "exchanges", and 71% of the assets of a corporation[82] appears to be a substantial proportion of its assets.

Assuming that section 184 of the OBCA is applicable, it is difficult to imagine a rationale by which the trustees of the Lewis Family Trust could justify approving of such a transaction, if the beneficiaries of the new trust were to be different from the beneficiaries of the original trust. Given the overriding obligation of the trustees to act in the best interests of the beneficiaries and to preserve the value of the trust property vested in them,[83] the trustees would be hard-pressed to approve such an exchange.

Dissent Rights[84]

As noted above, the 21st anniversary of the Trust is soon approaching, and with it, a deemed disposition by the Trust of all its assets. The discussion has centred on distributing the trust property to Larry, Robin and Alan prior to the 21st anniversary, and implementing a second estate freeze at the level of Expensife. It is possible, however, that such a downstream freeze may not be welcomed by Larry, Robin and Alan (especially Larry, who presently is not on good terms with the family) since their entitlement to future growth of Expensife will essentially be capped (subject of course to any entitlement under the second trust at the level of Expensife). Accordingly, the Trustees must be aware of the possible risks associated with going along with a freeze of Expensife in the event that the beneficiaries of the Trust are unhappy with the new reorganization. Notably, the Trustees should be aware of possible corporate issues that could be triggered by virtue of the second freeze.

A reorganization or other fundamental change in respect of a corporation may trigger rights of dissent and buy-out under subsections 184(3) and 185(1)(e) of the OBCA. These rights can be a successful way to prevent or delay a corporate reorganization or cause shares of a dissenting shareholder to be purchased by the corporation at fair market value. These rights, therefore, can have a devastating effect on a corporate reorganization. Shareholder's dissent rights arise upon the occurrence of any of the following fundamental changes:

(i) amendment of articles;

(ii) amalgamation;

(iii) continuance of a corporation to another jurisdiction; or

(iv) sale, lease or exchange of all or substantially all of a corporation's assets.

---

[81] This issue is discussed further below under the sub-heading "Dissent Rights".

[82] In this fact scenario, the Expensife shares account for about 71% of the assets of Hoots-Paw.

[83] Underhill and Hayton, *Law Relating to Trusts and Trustees*, 15th Edition, (London: Butterworths, 1995) at pg. 678. Also, although this transaction does not involve a necessary diminution in value, all upside potential is removed.

[84] This section was written by *Samantha Prasad* and *Glen Lewis* of *Minden Gross Grafstein & Greenstein LLP.*

In this case the Trustees would have to consider whether the second freeze will constitute a "sale, lease or exchange of all or substantially all" of the assets of Hoots-Paw, which could trigger dissent rights under the OBCA. A review of the jurisprudence indicates that this determination is difficult, particularly because it turns on the interpretation of two different phrases in paragraph 185(1)(*e*) of the OBCA, specifically, the meaning of "exchange" and the meaning of "all or substantially all" of the assets of the corporation.

The interpretation of the term "exchange" is to be accorded its generally accepted meaning at common law.[85] Canadian cases have defined an "exchange" as "a situation where one thing (other than money) has been taken for another thing (other than money)".[86]

A second estate freeze could arguably involve the "exchange" of Hoots-Paw's 100 common shares in Expensife for freeze shares even though the language in subsection 168 of the OBCA relating to an internal freeze refers to a "change". Based on the aforementioned definition of exchange, it would appear that this type of transaction could possibly constitute an "exchange" as that term is used in subsection 185(1)(*e*) of the OBCA.

Therefore, the issue of whether the "exchange" of Hoots-Paw's 100 common shares in Expensife into freeze shares constitutes "all or substantially all" of the assets of Hoots-Paw is germane to a determination of whether the shareholders' dissent rights will be triggered. In addition, if at the time of the second estate freeze the trust property has not yet been distributed to Larry, Robin and Alan, the Trustees would have to be wary of the fact that they may have an obligation to dissent on behalf of the beneficiaries of the Trust.

Consider also how the investment assets valued at approximately $10,000,000 (consisting of real estate, low cost base stocks, cash and near-cash) owned by Hoots-Paw would factor into the determination of whether the common shares of Expensife would constitute, on their own, "all or substantially all" of the assets of Hoots-Paw.

The meaning of the words "all or substantially all" has been considered by the courts in a variety of contexts involving the interpretation of contracts, taxation legislation, and statutes which provide for shareholders' rights upon disposition by a corporation of material assets. In the context of shareholders' rights, it is important to note that dissent rights were created to protect shareholders from fundamental changes in the corporation that would effectively destroy or significantly alter the corporate business.

The phrase "substantially all" is not defined in the OBCA, and has received limited judicial consideration in Canada. In *Canadian Broadcasting Corp. Pension Plan (Trustee of) v. BF Realty Holdings Ltd.*[87] Cronk J.A. on behalf of a unanimous Court of Appeal held that an inquiry into whether a given transaction constitutes the sale of "all or substantially all" of the assets of a corporation is both qualitative and

---

[85] Dennis Peterson, *Shareholder Remedies in Canada* (Butterworths, Toronto, 1989).

[86] See generally *Mason & Risch Ltd. v. Christner* 44 O.L.R. 146, *Deyell v. Deyell* [1991] S.J. No. 49, *Radomski v. Radomski* [1981] A.J. No. 19.

[87] [2002] O.J. No. 2125.

quantitative. Quantitatively the assets transferred cannot represent a significant proportion of the total value of the assets of the company. Qualitatively an asset transfer represents all or substantially all the assets if the disposition or transfer strikes at the heart of the transferor's existence and primary corporate purpose.

In *Benson v. Third Canadian General Investment Trust Ltd.*,[88] Farley J. held that a proposed sale of a transferor's 35 per cent interest in a corporation would require a special resolution because it constituted a sale of "substantially all of the property" of the transferor. Farley J. stated:

> the percentages set out earlier in these reasons take one well over the 50 per cent level. However, the 50 per cent level is not the test. But if one views the contribution to revenue and profit one sees that there is not much else left for the calculation of the other assets of Third (the transferor) — a rather curious event especially when one looks at the non-income contribution of these remaining assets.

In light of the doctrine and the jurisprudence, a strong argument may be made that a freeze of the shares of Expensife by Hoots-Paw (which in effect "exchanges" approximately 71% of the value of Hoots-Paw) would both quantitatively and qualitatively fundamentally change the primary corporate purpose of Hoots-Paw, that being to hold the assets of Expensife for the benefit of Robin, Larry, Alan or Ben, and thereby trigger the shareholders' dissent rights.[89] In light of the fact that the dissent right could be used by Larry (assuming the Trust has distributed out the common shares), Ben and the Trustees may be persuaded to treat Larry equally on such a distribution. Otherwise, Larry could dissent and force a buy-out of his shares at their fair market value.

Distributions to U.S. Residents and other Cross-Border Issues[90]

Introduction

Larry's U.S. tax status introduces extraordinary complications and compliance requirements that should be taken into account in the design and implementation of the estate freeze. Assume, for purposes of this section, that there is a desire to minimize the potential tax liabilities and compliance requirements from Larry's point of view. That approach requires an understanding of the ramifications under two U.S. tax regimes — the transfer tax system (gift and estate taxes) and the income tax system. It also must be understood that certain transactions involved in the implementation of the estate freeze may be tax-free for Canadian purposes but are taxable events for U.S. purposes, which events may well be "carried out" to Larry. A primary objective of cross-border planning, as implicated in this case study, is to

---

[88] 14 O.R. (3d) 493.

[89] It is arguable, however, that a dissent right could be avoided at the level of the Trust and/or children if Expensife were to roll down its operating assets into a wholly-owned subsidiary and take back freeze shares in consideration. Therefore, it would be a disposition of all or substantially all of the assets at the level of Expensife, rather than Hoots-Paw. Accordingly, the dissent right would be available only to the shareholder of Expensife, that being Hoots-Paw. Since the Trust and/or children are one level above, the dissent right would not extend to them. However, the transfer of an operating business can be a complex matter, and may cause more issues therein.

[90] This section was written by *Edward Northwood* of *Hodgson Russ LLP*.

co-ordinate and synchronize the occurrence and timing of the tax events in both jurisdictions and enable Larry, in this case, to take maximum advantage of foreign tax credit opportunities.

1. Larry's U.S. Transfer Tax Issues

U.S. estate taxes are imposed on the worldwide assets of a non-citizen if he or she dies domiciled in the U.S. Gift taxes are imposed on lifetime asset transfers of a person domiciled in the U.S. for no (or less than adequate) consideration. "A person acquires a domicile in a place by living there, for even a brief period of time, with no definite present intention of later removing therefrom. A residence without the requisite intention to remain indefinitely will not suffice to constitute domicile, nor will intention to change domicile effect such a change unless accompanied by actual removal."[91] Larry is a long-term green card holder. In order to obtain the permanent resident visa, Larry had to swear under oath that he intended to remain in the U.S. permanently. Given his impending marriage and parenthood, Larry no doubt will be considered to be domiciled in the U.S.

Because Larry's assets will be subject to U.S. estate tax, it would be preferable for him to receive any gifts or inheritances from his parents in a trust that has terms that would not make the value of the trust inclusive in his U.S. estate. This is relatively easy to accomplish through the use of encroachment powers that are limited by so-called ascertainable standards. Any plan that involves an outright distribution of shares or other assets to Larry from the trust does potentially expose such assets to U.S. estate taxes upon Larry's death.

The downstream freeze proposal does involve the distribution of one-third of the common shares of Hoots-Paw from the trust to Larry. The shares have an estimated value in excess of $8,000,000 (without regard to valuation discounts). Thus, $8,000,000 plus of assets that had been sheltered from U.S. estate tax will now become part of Larry's estate tax base, potentially subject to an approximate 50% federal and state estate tax rate.

Under the proposal, Larry would not appear to be transferring anything personally. It should be noted, however, that it may be argued that Larry is giving up (or at least not objecting to) the loss of future growth with respect to his one-third common share interest. While the U.S. gift tax does apply to indirect transfers, in the absence of donative intent and any act of participation in the decision, the second freezing of the company should have no U.S. gift tax implications to Larry.

2. U.S. Income tax issues

More problematic for Larry is his exposure to the U.S. "anti-deferral" rules that are implicated both under the current structure and under the proposed downstream freeze. U.S. Congress may be viewed as not only xenophobic but also paranoid where its taxpayers have interests in foreign corporations or foreign trusts. In short, the tax laws' goal is to tax passive income earned by such entities either on a current basis or tax it later as though it had been earned on a current basis. There are three basic

---

[91] Treas. Reg. Section 20.0-1(*b*).

corporate anti-deferral statutory sanctions, discussed briefly below. The foreign trust paradigm is summarized at the end.

U.S. citizens, U.S. permanent residents ("green card" holders, as in Larry's case), and persons who satisfy the substantial presence test[92] must report their worldwide income to the U.S. All U.S. income taxpayers are subject to the anti-deferral regimes.

Controlled Foreign Corporation ("CFC")

A foreign corporation is a CFC if "U.S. shareholders" own more than 50% of the total combined voting power or more than 50% of the total value of the stock in the foreign corporation on any day during the corporation's tax year.[93] For this purpose, "U.S. shareholders" are U.S. persons owning, directly or indirectly, 10% or more of the total combined voting power of the foreign corporation.[94]

If a foreign corporation is a CFC for an uninterrupted period of 30 days or more during the tax year, every U.S. shareholder (as defined above) who owns stock in the corporation on the last day of the year must include in gross income: (i) the shareholder's *pro rata* share of the corporation's "Subpart F income", and (ii) the shareholder's *pro rata* share of the corporation's earnings invested in U.S. property.[95]

Subpart F income includes various types of income, the most common of which is certain passive income such as dividends, interest, rents, royalties and annuities,

---

[92] A. Substantial Presence Test

    I. Is present in the U.S. for at least 31 days during current year; and

    II. Is present on at least 183 days within the last 3 years (including the current year.

      (a) 183-day test = days present in the current year plus $\frac{1}{3}$ days present in preceding year plus $\frac{1}{6}$ days present in 2nd preceding year. If total of these days equals 183 days or more, then 183-day test is met and individual is a U.S. resident assuming he was present in the U.S. for at least 31 days in the current year.

      (b) If present in the U.S. for less than 4 30-day months in each of the 3 years, test is not met.

      (c) "Present" means physically present at any time during the day. There are exceptions to this rule (i.e., for students).

      (d) Allows individual to get income in January without tax in U.S. or Canada.

  B. Closer Connection Exception. If a Canadian meets substantial presence test, he can still be a nonresident if he:

    I. was present in U.S. for less than 183 days for the current year;

    II. had a "tax home" in a foreign country; and

    III. had a "closer connection" to the same foreign country than to the U.S.

      (1) Tax Home — Regular or principal place of business or if there is none, the TP's regular place of abode (regularly resides). If neither, must be in existence for entire current year.

  C. Treaty Relief. If the 183-day threshold was met, then a Canadian may still avoid U.S. taxation by making the "centre of vital interests" Treaty election.

[93] I.R.C. §957(a).

[94] I.R.C. §951(b).

[95] I.R.C. §951(a).

and gains from the sale or exchange of property giving rise to the foregoing types of income.[96] Certain amounts are excluded from Subpart F income, including certain rents and royalties derived in the active conduct of a trade or business, and certain dividends, interest, rents, and royalties received from related corporations.[97] There is also an exclusion for Subpart F income subject to high foreign taxes. To qualify for this exclusion, the income must be subject to an effective rate of income tax imposed by a foreign country greater than 90% of the maximum U.S. corporate tax rate, which is currently 35%.[98] U.S. shareholders of CFCs generally are not taxed currently on non-Subpart F income or on Subpart F income in excess of the foreign corporation's earnings.

Another consequence to U.S. shareholders of CFCs is that gains recognized on the sale or exchange of CFC stock may be taxed as a dividend to the extent of the earnings and profits attributable to such stock and subject to the ordinary income tax rates, rather than the lower capital gains rates.[99]

Even if Larry receives shares in Hoots-Paw outright, the ownership of his family members will <u>not</u> be attributed to him because none of them is a U.S. taxpayer. Accordingly, under no foreseeable circumstances will Hoots-Paw be a CFC.

Foreign Personal Holding Company ("FPHC")

☞ **The FPHC rules have been repealed for foreign corporations with tax years beginning after 2004. The following is included for purposes of addressing compliance issues arising prior to 2005.**

A foreign corporation is an FPHC if: (i) at any time during the tax year, more than 50% of the total combined voting power or more than 50% of the total value of all classes of stock in the corporation is owned, directly or indirectly, by five or fewer U.S. persons, *and* (ii) at least 60% (50% after the first year that the corporation is an FPHC) of the corporation's gross income is foreign personal holding company income ("FPHCI").[100]

FPHCI includes (i) dividends, interest, royalties and annuities; (ii) rents (unless such rents constitute 50% or more of the foreign corporation's total gross income); (iii) gains from the sale or exchange of stock or securities (unless the foreign corporation is a regular dealer in stock or securities); (iv) gains from commodity transactions; (v) certain income from estates and trusts; (vi) amounts received under personal service contracts; and (vii) amounts received as compensation for the use of the foreign corporation's property.[101]

---

[96] I.R.C. §954(*c*)(1).

[97] I.R.C. §954(*c*)(2), (*c*)(3).

[98] I.R.C. §954(*b*)(4).

[99] I.R.C. §1248.

[100] I.R.C. §552(*a*).

[101] I.R.C. §553(*a*).

There is a special look-through rule for certain dividends and interest received from a related person. "Related person dividend or interest" is treated as FPHC income only to the extent it is attributable, under the look-through rules, to income which would be FPHC income in the hands of the related person. The term "related person dividend or interest" means any dividend or interest received from a corporation (other than an FPHC) that is related to the recipient, organized in the same country as the recipient corporation, and having a substantial part of its assets used in its trade or business located in that same country.[102]

Each foreign corporation must be tested separately under the FPHC rules. Accordingly, Hoots-Paw and Expensife both must be analyzed separately. However, as long as Hoots-Paw owns at least 50% of the value of Expensife, dividends actually paid by Expensife to Hoots-Paw count as <u>active</u> income to Hoots-Paw. The administrative practice, therefore, should be to ensure that the passive income earned by Hoots-Paw's investments (other than the Expensife stock) be less than the dividends received from Expensife. It should also be noted that the sale of Expensife results in FPHC income.

If a foreign corporation is an FPHC, U.S. persons owning shares in the corporation generally must include in gross income, as a deemed dividend, their pro rata share of the corporation's undistributed taxable income (not just FPHCI) for the year.[103]

Larry's discretionary interest in the current trust, or even the proposed one, will be sufficient to have some ownership interest in Hoot-Paw. Because FPHC family attribution is not determined on the basis of family members' U.S. status, Larry will meet the FPHC ownership threshold. Therefore, up to 2005, Hoots-Paw and its subsidiaries must be monitored to determine whether there is FPHC income as long as Larry remains a Trust beneficiary or owns shares outright.

Passive Foreign Investment Company ("PFIC")

A foreign corporation is a PFIC if it satisfies an income test or an asset test. Under the income test, a foreign corporation is a PFIC if at least 75% of its gross income for the taxable year is passive income under Section 954(c) of the Code.[104] This income generally includes dividends, interest, royalties, rents, annuities, and gain from the sale or exchange of property giving rise to the foregoing types of income.

Under the asset test, a foreign corporation is a PFIC if at least 50% of the assets held by the company during the taxable year produce passive income.[105] For purposes of applying the asset test, publicly-traded corporations generally must use fair market value as the basis for measuring assets.[106] Non-publicly-traded corporations

---

[102] I.R.C. §552(c).

[103] I.R.C. §551(b).

[104] I.R.C. §1297(a)(1).

[105] I.R.C. §1297(a)(2).

[106] I.R.C. §1297(f)(1)(A).

may use fair market value or adjusted basis for measuring assets, except that non-publicly-traded corporations which are also CFCs must use adjusted basis.[107] In testing for PFIC status, various "look-through" rules may apply.

The PFIC regime does not tax U.S. persons currently on income of the foreign corporation (unless a QEF election is made as described below). Instead, U.S. persons are taxed upon receipt of "excess distributions". Excess distributions include both: (i) gains recognized on the sale or deemed disposition of PFIC stock, and (ii) actual distributions made by the PFIC, but only to the extent that the total distributions received in the tax year exceed 125% of the average actual distributions received in the preceding three years.[108] Once determined, an excess distribution is allocated rateably to each day in the U.S. shareholder's holding period for the stock.[109] Amounts allocated to the current tax year and the pre-PFIC holding period (if any) are taxed as ordinary income in the current year.[110] Amounts allocated to the PFIC period (other than the current tax year) are not included in income but are subject to tax at the highest U.S. ordinary income tax rate, plus an interest charge to reflect the tax deferral (the "deferred tax amount").[111]

Since there is no ownership threshold, Hoots-Paw, and its subsidiaries, must be monitored for the PFIC asset or income tests as long as Larry has an interest in the Trust or receives shares directly.

QEF Election

One possible way for a U.S. investor to avoid the excess distribution regime is to make an election known as a QEF election. If such election is made, the investor will be required to include in his gross income each year his pro rata share of the PFIC's ordinary income and net capital gain for the year. The QEF election must be made by the due date for filing the U.S. investor's tax return for the first year to which the election applies. However, if the election is not made for the first year that the corporation was a PFIC, the election will not achieve avoidance of the "excess distribution" regime; rather, the stock will continue to carry "PFIC taint" and be subject to the excess distribution rules upon a sale of the stock. Thus, it may be important for a QEF election to be in effect for all years that a corporation was a PFIC. This may be difficult for investors who learn that the company was a PFIC in a prior year. However, the investor may have the option of filing a retroactive QEF election.

The investor may make a retroactive QEF election if the failure to file a timely election was because the investor reasonably believed that the company was not a PFIC. There are two regimes under which the U.S. investor may make a retroactive election — (1) the protective regime and (2) the consent regime.

---

[107] I.R.C. § 1297(*f*)(2).

[108] I.R.C. § 1291(*a*)(2), (*b*).

[109] I.R.C. § 1291(*a*)(1)(A).

[110] I.R.C. § 1291(*a*)(1)(B).

[111] I.R.C. § 1291(*a*)(1)(C).

Under the protective regime, the investor must (1) have reasonably believed as of the election due date that the foreign corporation was not a PFIC, and (2) file a protective statement in which the investor describes the basis for its reasonable belief and which extends the statute of limitations for the assessment of taxes under the PFIC rules. Special rules apply for certain qualified shareholders who own less than 2% of the vote and value of each class of stock of the foreign corporation — who are not required to satisfy the reasonable belief requirement to preserve the ability to make a retroactive election — and can make a retroactive election for any open tax year in their holding period.

3. Comments on the U.S. treatment of the Reorganization

As noted under the U.S. corporate anti-deferral rules discussion, analyses of the Canadian corporation's activity must be done under U.S. tax principles. It is important that the exchange qualify as a "reorganization" under Code Section 368(a)(1)(E). If it does not, it could give rise to a capital gain to Hoots-Paw (as a deemed sale of its old common shares) that could cause Hoots-Paw to become a PFIC, that in turn could cause a portion of the deemed gain to be currently taxable to direct or indirect U.S. shareholders such as Larry.

The exchange of old common shares for new preferred shares by Hoots-Paw should qualify as a reorganization under 368(a)(1)(E) (a "recapitalization") if certain requirements are met. It should be possible to meet these requirements, except that one such requirement needs special attention. Because the new preferred shares will be retractable, they will generally be considered to be "non-qualified preferred shares" under the U.S. tax laws. In general, the receipt of such shares in an otherwise tax-free reorganization gives rise to current U.S. tax because the shares are treated as "boot". U.S. taxpayers are generally required to recognize gains in an otherwise tax-free exchange to the extent they receipt "boot" in the exchange.

However, in the context of a recapitalization, there is an exception to this rule under 354(a)(2)(C)(ii). Under this exception, non-qualified preferred shares are generally not treated as boot if the corporation whose shares are being exchanged is considered a "family corporation" under 447(d)(2) for the five years prior to the exchange and the three years following the exchange. A corporation is considered a "family corporation" if at least 50% of the voting stock and at least 50% of all other classes of stock are owned by members of the same family. Family members include an individual and his siblings, ancestors and lineal descendants and spouses of the foregoing. Thus, in our case study, it is important that the family members continue to own at least 50% of the stock of Expensife and Hoots-Paw for at least three years following the exchange.

4. Foreign Trust Anti-Deferral Regime

A foreign trust is generally taxed as a non-resident of the United States, so the trust itself is subject to U.S. tax only if it has income from U.S. sources or U.S. business activities. U.S. grantors or beneficiaries of a foreign trust may, however, be subject to U.S. income tax on the earnings of the trust under certain circumstances. In contrast, the worldwide income of a domestic trust is subject to U.S. income tax.

The issue of whether the domestic trust itself, or its grantor or beneficiaries, is the taxpayer responsible for U.S. income tax on the trust earnings depends initially on the identity of the grantor and the types of powers the grantor has with respect to the trust.

There is a two-part "objective" test for determining whether a trust is foreign or domestic for U.S. income tax purposes. A trust satisfying both parts of the test is a domestic trust, whereas a trust that fails <u>either</u> (or both) parts is a foreign trust.

A trust satisfies the first test, referred to as the "Court Test", if a court within the United States is able to exercise primary supervision over the administration of the trust. A court is "able to exercise primary supervision" over the trust if it has or would have the authority under applicable law to render orders or judgments resolving substantially all issues regarding the administration of the trust. The "administration" of the trust includes those duties imposed upon a fiduciary under both the trust instrument and applicable law. The second test, referred to as the "Control Test", is satisfied if one or more U.S. fiduciaries have the authority to control all substantial decisions of the trust. A "fiduciary" includes a trustee and a protector. Clearly, the existing Trust and any proposed trusts will be foreign trusts from Larry's point of view.

A foreign <u>grantor</u> trust funded by someone other than a U.S. person or a beneficiary typically allows U.S. beneficiaries to receive a distribution of current or accumulated income from such a trust without subjecting the U.S. beneficiary to U.S. income tax thereon. Most foreign trusts, however, are non-grantor trusts. Generally, all foreign irrevocable trusts that may benefit persons other than the grantor or the grantor's spouse during the grantor's lifetime are foreign non-grantor trusts. A Canadian testamentary trust is a classic example. The existing Trust is a foreign non-grantor trust.

A U.S. beneficiary of a foreign non-grantor trust generally is taxed on a distribution from such a trust, and an interest charge is imposed as well if a distribution is an "accumulation distribution" (a distribution that is made from accumulated income, rather than current income). This interest charge is designed to penalize the beneficiary because U.S. income tax was not paid in the year when the income was earned. For these purposes, income includes net realized capital gains, even though such gains are allocations to a trust corpus for accounting purposes.

The conversion of capital gain income to ordinary income upon distribution as an accumulation distribution (as opposed to a current distribution) remains in the law. Now that the maximum U.S. capital gains tax rate (15%) is less than one-half of the top ordinary income tax rate (35%), this rule carries significant additional costs.

Compound interest based on the underpayment rate is imposed not only on tax amounts with respect to accumulation distributions made since January 1, 1996, but also on total simple interest for pre-1996 periods, if any. To compute the interest charge, the accumulation distribution is allocated proportionally to prior trust years in which the trust has income, rather than to the earliest of such years.

To date the Trust has received no dividends from Hoots-Paw, common shares of which are its only asset. Therefore, there has been no accumulations to date. Care must be exercised, however, to ensure that none of the proposed transactions trig-gers the deemed realization of a capital gain to the trust under U.S. income tax principles.

If Larry does receive shares of Hoots-Paw as an outright distribution, those shares will not receive a "stepped-up" basis for U.S. income tax purposes despite the Canadian tax that may be imposed.

Canadian Taxation Issues Involving Non-Resident Beneficiaries of a Trust[112]

Denial of Rollover to Larry

The inclusion of Larry, a non-resident of Canada, as a beneficiary of the Trust poses a few problems from a Canadian tax perspective. Notably, the benefit of rolling out the common shares of Hoots-Paw from the Trust to Larry is no longer an option. As noted earlier, a distribution of trust property to the beneficiaries in satisfaction of their capital interests in the trust takes place on a tax-free rollover basis (subsec-tion 107(2)). However, pursuant to subsection 107(5), trusts are prevented from distributing certain types of property on a rollover basis to non-resident capital beneficiaries, including shares of a Canadian controlled private corporation.[113] Therefore, the common shares of Hoots-Paw would be caught by subsec-tion 107(5).[114]

The purpose of subsection 107(5) is to ensure that gains accrued in Canada will be taxed in the resident trust. Where property that runs afoul of subsection 107(5) (such as the common shares of Hoots-Paw) is distributed to Larry, a non-resident, in satisfaction of Larry's capital interest, the Trust is deemed to dispose of and Larry is deemed to acquire the property at its fair market value and Larry is deemed to

---

[112] This section was written by *Samantha Prasad* of *Minden Gross Grafstein & Greenstein LLP.*

[113] Partnerships which are not Canadian partnerships are also caught. Before October 2, 1996, property subject to subsection 107(5) consisted of property which is not taxable Canadian property, "excluded property", or Canadian resource property. "Excluded property" means shares of a non-resident owned investment corporation that does not own taxable Canadian property. Since October 2, 1996, the range of property that cannot be distributed to a non-resident beneficiary on a rollover basis has been extended so as to now include shares of a Canadian controlled private corporation.

[114] This is consistent with changes to the taxpayer migration rules and other provisions that ensure that Canada will only allow ownership of property to pass to a non-resident person (whether by way of an actual transfer or because the person is emigrating from Canada) without immediate tax consequences if, under subsections 2(3) and 115(1) and its tax treaties, it will retain the ability to tax gains thereon at a later date. The property excepted from the deemed disposition on distribution from a Canadian resident trust to a non-resident beneficiary now consists of shares of a non-resident owned investment corporation (whether or not it owns taxable Canadian property, as accrued gains on such shares are not subject to Canadian tax when disposed of by non-residents) and property described in any of paragraphs 128.1(4)(*b*)(i) to (iii), being real property situated in Canada, Canadian resource property (since when the non-resident disposes of such property, he or she will be liable for tax) and timber resource property; capital property used in, eligible capital property in respect of and property described in the inventory of a business carried on in Canada through a permanent establishment in Canada; and an excluded right or interest (defined in subsection 128.1(10) as certain interests in trusts and deferred income streams) i.e., employee stock options and retirement savings in government sanctioned deferred savings plans.

dispose of the capital interest or part thereof at its adjusted cost base.[115] Presumably, the intended result of the provision was that the Trust would be liable for tax on accrued capital gains.[116] But for this provision, the Trust would realize no capital gain on a distribution to Larry, and when Larry disposed of the common shares of Hoots-Paw, he would not be subject to capital gains tax either.[117]

There are, however, certain options that are available to Larry and the Trust in order to plan around the deemed disposition under subsection 107(5). The Trust may either post appropriate security with the CRA or distribute the shares of Hoots-Paw to a Canadian corporation owned by Larry (subject to certain analysis on the ability to do so).

Posting Security

The Trust may elect under subsection 220(4.6) to defer the payment of the resulting tax in respect of the distribution of the trust property (i.e., the common shares of Hoots-Paw) to Larry by providing adequate security with the CRA. Where a valid election is made in prescribed manner, the payment of the tax is effectively deferred, without the imposition of interest or penalties, until the Trust's balance-due day for the year in which the property is subsequently disposed of (presumably, by Larry). The election by a trust must be made, and the security provided, by the trust's balance-due day for the year in which the distribution takes place.[118]

Distribution to Canadian Corporation

Depending on the terms of the agreement setting up the Trust (the "Trust Deed"), consideration may be given to the Trustees distributing Larry's portion of the common shares of Hoots-Paw to a Canadian corporation owned and controlled by Larry. However, the terms of the Trust Deed have to be reviewed to determine whether the Trustees are given the ability to distribute to a corporation owned by Larry. Presumably, the Trust Deed would not include a corporate beneficiary. However, it may be advisable to also review the Trust Deed to determine if there is a clause relating to the payment of income and/or capital to the beneficiaries which might provide for such payment "either to or for the benefit of any one or more of the beneficiaries". Although this clause may not necessarily be needed in terms of being able to distribute to a Canadian corporation where an interest in a trust is assigned to such a corporation by a beneficiary, it may alleviate any possible

---

[115] Canadian trusts which themselves become non-resident after October 1, 1996, suffer a similar deemed disposition.

[116] It is, however, quite possible that the distribution to Larry could mean that the gain resultant from the deemed disposition is paid or payable to the beneficiary receiving the property, subject to an election pursuant to subsection 107(2.11). For further discussion, see ¶317 of *Tax and Family Business Succession Planning*, by David Louis and Samantha Prasad.

[117] Although the common shares of Hoots-Paw are taxable Canadian property, such that there will be Canadian tax liability and Larry would be required to obtain the required section 116 Certificate, Larry could claim treaty protection relating to this tax, subject to the underlying property of Hoots-Paw meeting certain conditions.

[118] Based on the experience of a number of lawyers, due to processing delays by the CRA, the security arrangements will often not be finalized at the time of filing.

concerns that the Trustees may have in distributing to an entity not named as a beneficiary. If the Trust Deed does contain wording to such effect, query whether the inclusion of the words "to or for the benefit of" would include a distribution to a corporation owned and controlled by a beneficiary. Arguably, a distribution to a corporation owned and controlled by Larry could be considered a payment "for the benefit" of Larry.[119] The prevalent view among practitioners appears to be that the phrase "for the benefit of" would include such a distribution to a corporation, or other entity, owned or controlled by a beneficiary. If, however, the Trust Deed does not include such wording, other alternatives may be available that will permit the Trustees to make distributions to a corporation for the benefit of Larry.

Amending the Trust

If concerns remain on the part of the Trustees to distribute to a corporation which has been assigned a beneficial interest in the Trust, and no clause is included in the Trust to give that comfort to the Trustees, one option would be to amend the Trust to provide for the ability to make distributions to a corporation owned and controlled, directly or indirectly, by a beneficiary. In Ontario, however, a trust cannot be amended without a variation order from the Court, unless the trust provides for an amending clause. However, there are certain issues stemming from the provisions of such an amending clause. One issue that has garnered some discussion is a scenario where an amending clause is viewed as being overly broad. While wide powers to add beneficiaries are commonplace in offshore trusts, some commentators have voiced concern that where an amendment is made to a trust on the reliance of an overly broad amending clause, a new trust may be deemed to have been created and the beneficiaries would incur a disposition of their interests in the trust. This would result in the deemed disposition of the trust property by the "old" trust and the acquisition of such trust property by the "new" trust, which would put the Trustees in no better position than before when faced with subsection 107(5). Accordingly, the value of an amending clause has been the subject of some debate. Commentators have suggested that an amending clause should be restrictive in respect of the addition of new beneficiaries. However, query whether such a restriction would be sufficient to protect against the creation of a new trust.[120] Additionally, the amendment to the Trust will include the ability to distribute to a corporation for the benefit of a beneficiary. This might arguably be seen as adding to the list of beneficiaries.

The CRA has indicated that a variation of a trust may result in the creation and resettlement of a new trust if the variation is of a "significant magnitude to cause a fundamental change in the terms of the trust". If, however, the variation affects only

---

[119] There is old case law which would appear to support the argument that if a trust deed were to only include the words "for the benefit of" a beneficiary, such wording would be broad enough on its own to allow trustees to distribute to a corporation owned by a beneficiary. See *Re Moxon's Will Trusts (Downey v. Moxon and others)* [1958] 1 All E.R. and *Re Halsted's Will Trusts (Halsted v. Halsted)* [Chancery Division, April 20, 1937], which both held that the word "benefit" is to be interpreted widely. Danckwerts, J. in *Moxon's Will Trusts* held that the word "benefit" is "the widest possible word which could be employed".

[120] The editorial comment of Q.10 in the 1992 Revenue Canada Round Table discussed the courts' approach to the variation of a trust as follows:

(continued on next page)

the administrative or investment powers, the CRA has indicated that it would not view the variation as a taxable event.

In light of the uncertainty as to the consequences of varying a trust, it may be recommended in the general case to obtain an advance ruling from the CRA to ensure that a new trust is not created as a result of a variance of the trust. However, where a trust already includes the ability to make a payment "to or for the benefit of" a beneficiary, varying the trust to specifically refer to the ability to make a payment to or for the benefit of a corporation wholly owned by a beneficiary may not be of a sufficient magnitude so as to be problematic (although, as noted above, the inclusion of "to or for the benefit of" without a specific reference to a corporation may be sufficient on its own to allow for a distribution to a corporation and arguably would not require the trustees to seek a variance).

Transfer of Trust Interest to a Corporation

The next step would involve Larry rolling his interest in the Trust to a Canadian corporation on a tax-deferred basis pursuant to subsection 85(1). The transaction would appear to come under the umbrella of the rules in subsection 85(1) as it is commonly accepted on basic principles that an interest in a trust is a capital

---

(continued from previous page)

The question of whether a variation of trust which defers the distribution date may have untoward tax consequences has acquired added significance in view of provisions relating to the so-called "21-year deemed disposition rule." In *Murphy v. The Queen*, 80 DTC 6314, a beneficiary of the estate obtained a variation whereby his wife became a beneficiary of the trust, whereupon significant income was paid to the wife instead of the husband. Based largely on this case, commentators have alluded to the possibility that a variation of trust could constitute a disposition nearly always focusing on the beneficiary's interest in the trust, as opposed to a disposition by the trust itself (the former concept was the basis for the department's application of subsection 56(2) in *Murphy*).

U.K. case law has addressed the issue of whether a variation of the trust can create a new trust or a resettlement. A leading U.K. case, *In re Holdmen's Settlement Trusts*, [1968] A.C. 685, involved a situation in which the discretionary period for an income interest was extended by 21 years; a majority of the House of Lords judges were of the view that, under the circumstances, the variation did not create a new trust.

A number of commentators have expressed the view that under the common law variation of trust acts in Canada, a court may only approve a variation of an existing trust but does not have jurisdiction to create a new trust or a "resettlement" of an existing trust.

A more detailed discussion of the effects of a variation of a trust is found in an article by William Innes and Joel T. Cuperfain, "Variation of Trusts: An Analysis of the Effects of Variations of Trusts Under the Provisions of the Income Tax Act", *Canadian Tax Journal*, 1995 Volume 43, No. 1. The authors summarize the main areas of concern for tax purposes as follows:

- the possible application of the attribution rules;

- the possibility that the variation will constitute a resettlement of the trust;

- the possibility that the variation will trigger a disposition of property, either by the trust or by the beneficiaries;

- the possibility that the variation will taint the status of the trust (for example, causing a trust that formerly qualified for graduated tax rates to be taxed at the top marginal rate);

- the impact of various tax pools, including the loss carry-forwards; and

- the possible application of certain benefit conferral provisions (such as subsection 56(2) or 105(1)).

property and, therefore, "eligible property" for purposes of subsection 85(1). Accordingly, the distribution of the Trust property (i.e. common shares of Hoots-Paw) could be made to the Canadian corporation in satisfaction of Larry's entitlement under the Trust. Larry should be aware, however, that the transfer of his Trust interest would necessarily be seen as a disposition of taxable Canadian property. Therefore, Larry would be required to obtain a clearance certificate under section 116.[121]

Unlimited Liability Corporations ("ULCs")

If Larry chooses to transfer his interest in the Trust to a Canadian corporation, it would be recommended that such a corporation be either a Nova Scotia unlimited liability company ("NSULC") formed under the Companies Act (Nova Scotia)[122] ("NSCA") or an Alberta Unlimited Liability Corporation ("AULC") formed under the Business Corporations Act (Alberta)[123] ("ABCA"). Since both an NSULC and an AULC will qualify as a flow-through vehicle for U.S. tax purposes (see discussion below), the transfer of the Trust interest would, arguably, not be taxable in the United States and would enable a tax-efficient structure to be put in place.[124]

Theoretically ULCs provide no limited liability for their members and may be treated as flow-through entities for U.S. purposes, just like a partnership or a limited liability company. However, under the NSCA there is no direct liability of the shareholders to third parties who contract with an NSULC. Liability only arises on dissolution of the NSULC if it has insufficient assets to discharge its obligations.[125] Unlike the NSCA, however, under the ABCA, the Articles of Incorporation of an AULC are required to include reference to the fact that each of the shareholders of the AULC have unlimited liability for any act, liability or default of the AULC and that such liability is joint and several in nature. Consequently, the liability of the shareholders of an AULC arises immediately upon the incorporation of the AULC. Nevertheless, liability of shareholders of NSULCs and AULCs may be limited through the insertion of U.S. C or S corporations.

[121] An additional compliance issue relating to a section 85 transfer involves filing a T2057, which in turn involves determining the fair market value of the transferred property. The fair market value of an interest in trust is not, however, easily determinable. While many practitioners assert that the value of an interest in a discretionary trust may be nominal, the CRA may not agree. In CRA Document No. 2003-0181465, April 3, 2003, the CRA was of the opinion that a reasonable approach would be to value the interest in the trust as if the trust assets were fully distributed equally among all the contingent beneficiaries on the valuation date. The CRA went on to state, however, that where the facts support a finding that one beneficiary has a lesser chance of receiving a distribution from the trust than another beneficiary, it may be appropriate to discount the value of one interest and increase the value of another.

[122] R.S.N.S. 1989, c.81, as amended.

[123] R.S.A. 2000, c.B-9, as amended.

[124] For Canadian purposes, ULCs would be regarded as Canadian corporations and would file Canadian tax returns in respect of their income. However, the ULCs, if controlled by non-residents, such as Larry, will not be entitled to the small business deduction or to refundable dividend tax on hand. As a result, ULCs will be taxable at the top corporate rate net of the corporate tax reduction in section 123.4, excluding the refundable tax on investment income in section 123.3.

[125] There is commentary suggesting that it may be possible for an NSULC to provide in all of its contracts that a creditor's claim shall be limited to the assets of the NSULC and shall not on the dissolution of the NSULC extend to the assets of the shareholders. However, such a clause may jeopardize the NSULC's U.S. status as an unlimited liability entity.

There are other significant advantages that NSULCs have over AULCs. For example, under the NSCA there is no requirement that a majority (or any) of the directors of an NSULC be Canadian residents while, pursuant to the ABCA, an AULC will require at least one-quarter of its directors to be Canadian residents (thus if an NSULC is used, Larry could be the sole director). Another advantage of NSULCs over AULCs is that there is no real solvency test regarding the payment of dividends from an NSULC,[126] whereas AULCs, like all other corporations formed under *Business Corporations Act* statutes, are subject to standard solvency tests in connection with the declaration and payment of dividends. Some other interesting advantages of NSULCs over AULCs include the ability of a subsidiary of a NSCA corporation to permanently own shares in its parent (under the ABCA there are time limits on the ability to have such shareholdings), the ability of an NSULC to issue partially paid shares as well as par and no par shares and arguably less onerous director liability provisions.[127]

On the other hand, there are a number of advantages of using AULCs over NSULCs. For example, AULCs are not subject to any special incorporation or operating fee whereas there is a $6,000 cost of incorporating an NSULC and a $2,000 annual fee to maintain it. In addition, because the AULC legislation in the ABCA is part of a modern *Business Corporations Act* statute similar to most other Canadian corporate statutes, practitioners will tend to be more comfortable with AULCs. In this regard, the ABCA expressly permits, among other things, amalgamations and the continuance of extra-provincial corporations as AULCs and vice versa. To achieve these results under the NSCA will generally require more complex and costly mechanisms, including court approval in situations that many practitioners outside of Nova Scotia may be unfamiliar with.[128]

For U.S. purposes, the "check the box" regulations permit the owner to choose the tax treatment of certain non-U.S. entities as a corporation, or as a partnership or disregarded entity. These regulations include a specific provision that makes it clear that ULCs are not "per se" corporations and can therefore elect their classification

---

[126] Although sections 159 and 160 of Table A of the First Schedule to the NSCA, which deal with the articles of association of an NSULC, provide that no dividends shall be paid except out of a corporation's profits, based on discussions with Nova Scotia counsel, it appears that it is possible to draft articles without these restrictions.

[127] For a much more detailed discussion of matters in respect of NSULCS and AULCs see draft papers #35 and #36 to be published in the *Report of Proceedings of the Fifty-Seventh Tax Conference*, by, respectively, Barry Horne, "The Nova Scotia Unlimited Liability Company: Surf and Turf" and Don R. Summerfeldt, "Alberta Unlimited Liability Corporations — A Corporate and Tax Overview", *2005 Conference Report* (Toronto: Canadian Tax Foundation, 2006).

[128] Some other advantages that AULCs have over NSULCs include the greater scope for giving financial assistance, lower statutory special resolution requirement of 2/3 as compared to 3/4 for NSULCs and greater flexibility in dealing with authorized capital (for example, NSULCs do not permit the creation of share classes with issue of an unlimited number of shares) and paid-up capital (for example, in the event of a tax deferred transfer to an NSULC, there is no direct mechanism to reduce the paid-up capital of the shares to the elected amount).

for U.S. tax purposes.[129] As all members of ULCs will possess unlimited liability, the default U.S. classification for a ULC will be as a "partnership" if it has more than one shareholder and a "disregarded entity" if it has a single shareholder. In either case, the income or losses of the ULC would be flowed through to the U.S. shareholders, i.e., Larry. In lieu of the default classifications, a ULC can elect to be classified as a "corporation" for U.S. income tax purposes, regardless of whether the ULC has one or more than one shareholder.

One of the advantages of having a ULC is that, to the extent that the ULC pays tax in Canada, Larry will be entitled to a foreign tax credit for the Canadian corporate tax when the income is attributed to him. On the assumption that the Canadian tax rates are higher than the U.S. tax rates, Larry's U.S. tax liability should be minimized. However, there may be certain limitations as to the ability to utilize Canadian taxes paid as a U.S. foreign tax credit due to the lack of foreign source income.

Second Estate Freeze — Inclusion of Larry as a Beneficiary of Trust No. 2

The contemplation of a second estate freeze at the Expensife level must also take into consideration the fact that Larry, a potential beneficiary of Trust No. 2, is still a non-resident. Once again, Ben will be faced with the various problematic issues relating to the deemed disposition on the distribution of trust property from Trust No. 2 to Larry. However, in this case, certain preventative measures can be taken to alleviate these tax issues.

The trust deed for Trust No. 2 should, at the outset, include a corporate beneficiary, preferably one which is controlled, directly or indirectly, by a named beneficiary. The beneficiaries of Trust No.2 could, therefore, include "a corporation, the majority of whose shares, having full voting rights in all circumstances, are held directly or indirectly, by means of a trust or otherwise, exclusively by or for the benefit of any one or more of the issue of Ben Lewis at the time of a proposed or actual distribution, payment, allocation, division or any other benefit to such corporation".[130]

---

[129] IRC reg. section 301.7701-2(*b*)(8)(ii)(A) provides the following exception from automatic treatment as a corporation: "With regard to Canada, any corporation or company formed under any federal or provincial law which provides that the liability of all of the members of such corporation or company will be unlimited".

[130] Note, however, that the inclusion of such a corporate beneficiary could trigger certain affiliation rules which may have negative tax consequences.

Double Tax and Post-Mortem Tax Planning[131]

Of Death and Taxes and Even More Taxes

In a world without tax professionals (and family law legislation), Ben's ultimate death would give rise to a number of significant tax consequences.[132] In particular, upon his death he would be deemed to have disposed of all of his capital properties for their fair market value. Given the assets that will form his estate ("Assets") — e.g., low cost base Hoots-Paw freeze shares and an investment portfolio of low cost base assets,[133] this would result in him being deemed to have realized significant capital gains immediately before his death under paragraph 70(5)(*a*).[134] If there is a silver lining to this particular tax consequence (i.e., the deemed disposition), it is that the subsequent owners of the Assets, initially his estate, will be deemed by paragraph 70(5)(*b*) to receive the properties at their fair market value (i.e., the estate will acquire high cost base assets).

Unfortunately, due to the nature of the Assets, being mostly corporate shares, there is an inherent risk that, if the Assets are liquidated, double tax will arise. The reason for this is that, although Ben's death will increase the cost base of the Assets in the hands of the estate, it will have no impact on the underlying assets owned by the corporations in which his estate owns shares (or the paid-up capital of those shares). As a result, under the ordinary rules of taxation, if any of the corporations sell or in any manner transfer any of their low cost base assets or, pursuant to subsection 69(4), if any of the corporations distribute such assets to the estate, they will realize or be deemed to realize capital gains. Furthermore, if the corporations cancel or redeem the estate's shares, the estate will be deemed to receive a dividend under subsection 84(3) to the extent that the value of property received by the estate exceeds the paid-up capital of the shares. Therefore, in a worst case scenario, taxes could be payable at the personal level (i.e., by Ben), the corporate level and the estate level.

Since significant taxes will be payable on Ben's death, there is a very real possibility that the estate will have to liquidate the Assets to have funds to pay these taxes. As a result, there may be a real risk of "double tax".[135]

---

[131] This section was written by *Michael A. Goldberg* and *Samantha Prasad* of *Minden Gross Grafstein & Greenstein LLP*.

[132] To a large extent, the discussion below ignores the existence of Ben's life insurance policy. The impact of life insurance on post-mortem planning is explored in Joel Cuperfain's section "Insurance Planning", which is found later in the case study materials. The discussion also ignores the impact of U.S. taxation issues on post-mortem planning, which is the subject of Edward Northwood's paper found earlier in these case study materials.

[133] Although the Expensife shares will also form part of the estate, since they have nominal value and will result in no material tax consequences, no further reference to them will be made in this portion of the case study.

[134] If Ben's estate is left to a spouse trust for Anne-Marie then the capital gains that would otherwise arise on Ben's death would be deferred until Anne-Marie's death. Spousal trusts are discussed in more detail below under the sub-heading "Double Tax and Spouse Trusts" on p. 273.

[135] Even if the estate did not require cash to pay its tax bill, since the freeze shares might be redeemed at some future point in time, planning to avoid double taxes should still be considered.

There are a number of factors that may reduce or effectively eliminate some of the risks referred to above. In the context of the publicly traded portfolio, by its very nature, there will ordinarily be a market for the shares in the portfolio and, as a result, the estate should be able to sell its shares to a third party with no additional tax consequences.[136]

Assuming that there will be no market for the low paid-up capital Hoots-Paw freeze shares, Hoots-Paw's underlying low cost base assets may have to be sold to generate cash to fund the taxes payable as a result of Ben's death. Since Hoots-Paw is a Canadian controlled private corporation ("CCPC"), any capital gains realized by it from such sales will create surplus accounts (refundable dividend tax on hand ("RDTOH") and capital dividend accounts ("CDA")) which will permit the freeze shares to be redeemed in a manner that should effectively integrate the corporate level tax and the estate level tax.[137] Thus, the multiple levels of tax referred to above should be effectively limited to two levels of tax — the capital gains triggered by Ben's death and the integrated corporate level capital gains and the estate level deemed dividend triggered by redeeming the freeze shares to pay Ben's death taxes.

The picture of the Hoots-Paw double tax situation described so far has omitted one factor that may prove to be very useful to combat the double tax effect. The redemption of freeze shares[138] will be a disposition[139] to Hoots-Paw[140] for proceeds of disposition of nil.[141] Since the Hoots-Paw shares will have a high cost base, their disposition will ordinarily give rise to capital losses, unless the losses are reduced

---

[136] This might not be true if the shares are not heavily traded, the estate owns restricted shares or even if the estate owns a large enough block of shares so that a sale by it could affect the market.

[137] CDA can be distributed to the estate on a tax-free basis. Taxable dividends paid by Hoots-Paw will enable Hoots-Paw to receive a refund of refundable taxes that it previously paid to the extent of its RDTOH account. The double tax discussion regarding Hoots-Paw's freeze shares may be equally applicable to a redemption or cancellation of publicly traded shares except that these integration concepts will not work as efficiently, since the rules governing the creation of surplus accounts apply differently to non-CCPCs. A detailed discussion of these rules is beyond the scope of this case study.

[138] As the freeze shares were issued in 1985, they are grandfathered from the taxable preferred share rules (Parts IV.1 and VI.1 of the Act), subject to any action which might trigger a deemed event of reissuance pursuant to paragraph (*e*) of the definition of the term, "taxable preferred share" in subsection 248(1). If this were not the case, the interaction of the taxable preferred share and "stop-loss rules" in subsection 40(3.6) may raise some complexities.

[139] Paragraph (*b*)(i) of the definition of "disposition" in section 54.

[140] Subsection 84(9).

[141] Paragraph (*j*) of the definition of "proceeds of disposition" in section 54.

pursuant to certain stop-loss rules found in subsections 40(3.6)[142] and 112(3) to (3.32).[143]

In the ordinary situation, the estate will not have capital gains of its own, and these losses may go unused for a period of time or even indefinitely. This is particularly unfortunate, given that the deemed disposition of Ben's Hoots-Paw shares on his death will likely be equal to or nearly equal to the capital losses realized by the estate upon the redemption of those same shares.[144]

And there's the rub! Without proper tax planning to either utilize these losses or to find a way to eliminate the corporate and estate level taxes, multiple layers of taxes could be payable as a result of Ben's death.

Avoiding Double Taxes

The strategies available to assist Ben and his estate to avoid having to pay double taxes fall into two basic categories — strategies that will enable Ben's estate to apply its capital losses against the capital gains resulting from Ben's death using the "subsection 164(6) procedure", and strategies that minimize or eliminate taxes at both the corporate (Hoots-Paw) and estate levels, the "paragraph 88(1)(*d*) bump procedure". If the corporation's assets are cash or other high cost base assets, it will be unnecessary to eliminate corporate level taxes and, as a result, it will be possible to use a third procedure that will be referred to as the "pipeline procedure".

Subsection 164(6) Procedure

The primary objective of the subsection 164(6) procedure is to trigger capital losses in the estate during its first taxation year[145] so that the capital losses can be treated as though they were realized in the year of Ben's death.[146] Ordinarily, where an estate owns shares in a private corporation such as Hoots-Paw, the capital losses

---

[142] See below under the sub-heading "The Stop-Loss Rules" on p. 280.

[143] These rules most commonly apply to restrict capital loss claims to the extent that capital dividends have been paid in respect of a particular share. However, an estate is granted some relief from these rules under subparagraph 112(3.2)(*a*)(iii) which effectively permits the estate to receive a capital dividend equal to the *lesser* of $^1/_2$ of the capital losses otherwise realized and the capital gains realized by the decedent as a result of the deemed disposition immediately prior to his death. A detailed discussion of these rules is provided in Joel Cuperfain's section "Insurance Planning", which is found later in the case study materials.

The stop-loss rules in paragraphs 40(2)(*f*) and (*g*) may also be relevant.

[144] This will be true for many decedents and their estates.

[145] Ordinarily one year from the date of death of a decedent but the estate may elect to shorten this period.

[146] The capital losses will be subject to ordinary tax rules in respect of capital losses (i.e. it can be carried back three years), though carrying it forward will be of no assistance. However, by virtue of subsection 111(2), allowable capital losses realized in the year of death may be applied to offset all income, not just taxable capital gains, in that year as well as in the immediately preceding year. The benefit provided under subsection 111(2) will be reduced on a dollar-for-dollar basis to the extent that the capital gains exemption of a decedent has been claimed.

(continued on next page)

will be triggered by the corporation purchasing the shares for cancellation or, as will be the case with the Hoots-Paw shares, redeeming them.

Although it may be possible to completely offset the capital gains realized by Ben upon his death using this method,[147] the redemption of the low paid-up capital freeze shares will give rise to the estate being deemed to receive a dividend that will be nearly identical to the capital gains that will be offset using this procedure.[148] As a result, this procedure will eliminate the double tax by converting the capital gains on death into a deemed dividend. Since capital gains in Ontario are currently taxed at lower tax rates than dividends this conversion will often be tax-inefficient.[149]

Another objective that is often associated with the subsection 164(6) procedure is that it may permit a corporation such as Hoots-Paw to increase the cost base of its assets without creating any material net additional combined tax liability for the estate and the corporation.[150] As discussed earlier, the sale of Hoots-Paw's underlying low cost base assets will trigger capital gains that will create surplus accounts which will enable Hoots-Paw to distribute its corporate assets on the redemption of the freeze shares in a tax-effective manner.[151] If Hoots-Paw's underlying assets already had a high cost base, the effectiveness of the subsection 164(6) procedure would depend on whether Hoots-Paw already had surplus accounts that would permit it to redeem the freeze shares in a tax effective manner.

Even if the estate did not require cash to pay its tax bill, it might still be advisable to utilize this procedure to bump the cost base of Hoots-Paw's underlying assets. For example, low cost base assets of Hoots-Paw could be transferred by Hoots-Paw to a subsidiary[152] under subsection 85(1). Under this provision Hoots-Paw

---

(continued from previous page)

Subject to certain restrictions, an election under subsection 164(6) can also be used to treat terminal losses deductible by the estate under subsection 20(16) to have been deducted in the terminal period return by a decedent.

[147] The actual results will depend on the tax characteristics of the properties of a decedent in any particular situation.

[148] This will be true for many decedents and their estates.

[149] Subject to the existence of CDA and/or RDTOH in Hoots-Paw, which, in some circumstances could actually make the deemed dividend more tax-efficient than capital gains treatment. Where non-residents, particularly those who are resident in countries that have signed tax treaties with Canada, are beneficiaries of the estate, it may be possible to take steps to make distributions even more efficient. For example, where possible, it may be advisable to distribute CDA dividends received by the estate out to Canadian residents such as Robin and Alan, who will pay no tax on such distributions. Ordinary taxable dividends could be distributed to non-residents such as Larry. Such dividends will be subject to treaty withholding rates of 15% and, so long as the various passive investment rules that may apply to Americans do not apply to such dividends, the withholding tax may completely offset the ordinary tax on dividends of 15% in the United States. Care must be taken when pursuing these types of strategies since there are a number of cross-border traps and tricks that could catch the unwary.

[150] The discussion assumes that recapture will not be realized as a result of this step. If recapture is realized then there may well be some additional net tax liability to the estate and the corporation.

[151] If a corporation that is not a CCPC is being wound-up, the distribution may not be as tax efficient.

[152] A new corporation might be formed for this purpose.

and the subsidiary would elect a transfer price so that the cost base of the assets are "bumped" to their fair market value. Capital gains would be triggered creating surplus accounts that would permit the freeze shares to be redeemed in a tax-efficient manner.

The discussion so far has assumed that Hoots-Paw has no pre-existing surplus accounts. If Hoots-Paw has pre-existing surplus accounts and, in particular, if those surplus accounts include significant RDTOH balances,[153] then the deemed dividend arising from this procedure may enable the corporation to effectively use those balances. This potential advantage of the subsection 164(6) procedure is not available under the paragraph 88(1)(*d*) procedure or the pipeline procedure since those procedures do not generate deemed dividends and, as a result, under those procedures RDTOH may become trapped at the corporate level.

☞ **As delineated in the introduction, Hoots-Paw is the corporate owner of an insurance policy for the joint and last survivor of Ben and Anne. This may generate CDA and, as such, may make a subsection 164(6) procedure advantageous since, to the extent of the CDA,[154] the insurance policy will reduce the tax exposure on the deemed dividend. However, it is quite possible that, due to the nature of the insurance policy (i.e., as joint and last survivor in respect of spouses who may well end up being divorced), the capital dividend account may not materialize on Ben's death.[155]**

In order for the subsection 164(6) procedure to be effective, it is critical that the capital losses be realized in the first taxation year of the estate and that the election is made in a prescribed manner and within the prescribed time.[156] Although paragraph 164(6) contains a provision that would require the estate to file an amended terminal return for Ben in order to be able to take advantage of the subsection 164(6) procedure, in the past the CRA has administratively accepted that as long as the terminal year return for a decedent such as Ben had not already been filed and the filing due date had not passed, then the subsection 164(6) election could be filed with the terminal return. However, if the terminal return is filed before the T3 return

---

[153] Unlike CDA balances which may be repaid free of tax, RDTOH balances require the payment of a taxable dividend.

[154] Subject to the stop-loss rules in subsection 112(3.2).

[155] This idea is briefly discussed in more detail in Joel Cuperfain's section "Insurance Planning", which is found later in the case study materials. As noted above, the bump of corporate owned assets may itself produce surplus accounts — i.e., RDTOH and CDA. However, assuming the insurance payable on Ben's death generates $5,000,000 of CDA, any attempt to distribute additional pre-existing CDA may potentially trigger the stop-loss rules in subsection 112(3.2).

[156] Although it is possible to late-file the election pursuant to the operation of subsection 220(3.2) and regulation 600, the Minister has considerable discretion regarding the acceptance or rejection of the election as well as the waiver of interest and penalties.

for the estate, the CRA will not process the loss carry-back until after the estate's T3 return has been assessed so that the claim can be verified.[157]

Prior to the enactment of new subsection 40(3.61), unless Hoots-Paw was wound-up, as opposed to Hoots-Paw merely redeeming the freeze shares, the stop-loss rules in subsection 40(3.6) represented a significant impediment to taking advantage of the subsection 164(6) procedure.[158] In particular, if a taxpayer (i.e., the estate) disposing of the shares of a corporation (such as on a redemption) would be affiliated[159] with the corporation immediately after the disposition then subsection 40(3.6) would deny the losses realized on the disposition. Consequently, if subsection 40(3.6) were to apply, then the subsection 164(6) procedure would not eliminate double tax as Ben's estate would not be able to claim capital losses itself — and, accordingly, could not elect to have capital losses claimed on Ben's terminal tax return.

Fortunately, in the course of amending the interaction of the affiliated person rules in section 251.1 with trusts ("Affiliation Amendments"),[160] subsection 40(3.61)

---

[157] See CRA Form T4013, *T3 Trust Guide — 2003* at page 25.

[158] Pursuant to subsection 69(5), subsection 40(3.6) does not apply where a corporation is wound-up.

[159] The affiliated person rules, which trigger various stop-loss rules in the Act, are found in section 251.1. A brief discussion of these provisions as they relate to Ben's estate in the context of subsection 40(3.6) is set out below.

> Pursuant to paragraph 251.1(1)(*a*) an individual can only be affiliated with him- or herself and the individual's spouse (Bill C-23, which received Royal Assent on June 29, 2000, has extended the benefits and liabilities associated with an individual's status under the former "spouse" definition in subsection 252(4) to an individual involved in a same-sex relationship) but with no other individual. Therefore siblings cannot be affiliated.

> Pursuant to paragraph 251.1(1)(*b*), a person and a corporation will only be affiliated if the corporation is controlled by the person, by an "affiliated group" of persons, or by the spouse of a person or by a spouse who is a member of an affiliated group of persons. There are also detailed rules concerning the affiliation of two corporations, a corporation and a partnership and two partnerships in paragraphs 251.1(1)(*c*), (*d*) and (*e*), respectively.

> The meaning of "controlled" is broader than mere voting control and includes *de facto* control. According to this test, control of a corporation could exist if a person has any direct or indirect influence that, if exercised, would result in the person having factual control over the corporation, regardless of whether or not the person is able to exercise voting control over the corporation.

[160] Bill C-33, which received Royal Assent on May 13, 2004, S.C. 2005, c. 19, s. 54. The Affiliation Amendments were enacted to specifically deal with the affiliation of trusts and estates and their beneficiaries and trusts and estates to one another. For purposes of the discussion that follows, the terms estate and estates may be used as a proxy for the terms trust or trusts and the terms executor or executors may be used as a proxy for the terms executor or executors.

(continued on next page)

was enacted[161] with the intent of effectively exempting estates from the application of subsection 40(3.6) to the extent that an election is made under subsection 164(6).[162] Subsection 40(3.6) and the Affiliation Amendments are generally applicable at any time after March 22, 2004. However, the scope of the subsection 40(3.61) exemption appears to be too narrow in that the exemption does not appear to apply to alter ego trusts and joint spousal or common-law partner trusts as those terms are defined in subsection 248(1) or to spousal trusts.[163]

(continued from previous page)

The basis for affiliation between a person and an estate is set out in new paragraph 251.1(1)(*g*), which deems a person and an estate to be affiliated where the person is a majority-interest beneficiary of the estate or is affiliated with such a person. The term "majority-interest beneficiary" as well as a number of other provisions are defined in new subsection 251.1(3). A beneficiary will be a majority-interest beneficiary at any particular time if the beneficiary together with all person's affiliated to the beneficiary hold either an income interest or a capital interest having a fair market value in excess of, respectively, 50% of the fair market value of all income interests in the estate or 50% of the fair market value of all capital interests in the estate. Subparagraph 251.1(4)(*d*)(i) deems discretionary powers to receive income or capital to be fully exercised in favour of each beneficiary of an estate. Consequently, in a garden variety discretionary *inter vivos* trust each beneficiary will usually be deemed to be entitled to 100% of the income or capital of the trust and will be a majority-interest beneficiary of the trust affiliated with the trust. Since interests in estates tend to be fixed as opposed to discretionary, subparagraph 256.1(4)(*d*)(i) will tend not to be as problematic in the estates arena.

The basis for affiliation between two estates is set out in new paragraph 251.1(1)(*h*), which deems two estates to be affiliated with one another where contributors are affiliated and where a majority-interest beneficiary of each estate, majority-interest beneficiary of one estate and a majority-interest group of beneficiaries of another estate or two majority-interest groups of beneficiaries are affiliated with one another. Pursuant to new subparagraph 256.1(4)(*d*)(iv), blood, marriage, common-law partnership and adoption are all taken into account for purposes of determining whether contributors are affiliated with one another. The term majority-interest group of beneficiaries is defined in subsection 251.1(3).

The Affiliation Amendments have made the role of the executors irrelevant for purposes of the affiliation rules. In particular, paragraph 251.1(4)(*c*) deems the relationship of executors to a corporation irrelevant to the affiliated person rules.

Based on informal discussions with the Department of Finance, we understand that the Affiliation Amendments are not intended to be a comprehensive regime to deal with estates and the affiliated person rules. In particular, the Department of Finance regards estates as persons and, as such, an estate and a corporation may still be affiliated pursuant to paragraph 251.1(1)(*b*).

[161] S.C. 2005, c. 19, s. 13(1).

[162] There appear to be certain technical deficiencies in the wording of subsection 40(3.61) which may make the provision inapplicable in certain situations. A discussion of these deficiencies is beyond the scope of this case study. Based on discussions with members of The Joint Committee on Taxation of The Canadian Bar Association and The Canadian Institute of Chartered Accountants ("Joint Committee"), we understand that Finance is aware of these technical issues and intends to remedy them.

[163] For more information on this issue see the January 19, 2005 submission of the Joint Committee.

Double Tax and Spouse Trusts

In this portion of the case study it is assumed that Ben and Anne-Marie are now married and that Ben's will provides for the freeze shares to be left in a spouse trust for Anne-Marie.[164]

Many of the concepts relating to the subsection 164(6) procedure apply in the same manner to Anne-Marie's spouse trust as they would to Ben's estate. On the death of the surviving spouse, Anne-Marie, her spouse trust will be deemed to have disposed of all of its capital properties.[165] In order to offset the capital gains arising from this deemed disposition it will normally be desirable for the spouse trust to realize offsetting capital losses.

However, since the capital gains and capital losses will both be realized by the same entity, the spouse trust, it will be possible to create the tax consequences associated with the subsection 164(6) procedure in an estate situation without filing a subsection 164(6) election. Moreover, the spouse trust will not be able to take advantage of the subsection 40(3.61) exemption to subsection 40(3.6), as set out above. While the submission of the Joint Committee recommends changes that would remedy this deficiency, at the time of writing it is unknown whether the Department of Finance will make the requested changes. Until such changes are made, it will continue to be necessary for tax planners to consider taking steps to trigger capital losses in a manner that will avoid the application of subsection 40(3.6) altogether.[166]

The capital gains and capital losses created in Anne-Marie's spouse trust will be governed by the normal provisions of the Act in respect of capital transactions. For example, if the capital losses are incurred in the same taxation year as the capital gains, they must be offset against the capital gains. Alternatively, if the capital losses are incurred in a subsequent year, they could be carried back and applied against the capital gains. Accordingly, in the ordinary case, the capital losses could be generated up to three taxation years after the year in which the surviving spouse passes away.

An issue arises as to whether the terms of a spouse trust permit the trust to continue after the death of the surviving spouse. If Anne-Marie's spouse trust calls for a mandatory distribution of all of its property immediately following her death, then there will be no assets remaining in the spouse trust that can be used to create capital losses to offset the capital gains realized in the spouse trust upon her death. It might be possible to take steps to create capital losses in the hands of the residuary beneficiaries in connection with the distributed trust property. However, there is no specific provision such as subsection 164(6) that will allow these capital losses to be applied against the capital gains realized in the spouse trust.

---

[164] It should be kept in mind that pursuant to section 16 of the *Succession Law Reform Act (Ontario)*, marriage will revoke any existing wills unless a declaration is made in the will that the will is being made in contemplation of marriage.

[165] See subparagraph 104(4)(*a*.1)(iii).

[166] A discussion of such measures is beyond the scope of this case study.

Very little has been written about this issue, although it was raised in an August 11, 1997 Technical Interpretation.[167] To avoid this risk, Anne-Marie's spouse trust should be designed so that its terms permit it to continue for a period after her death (once Anne-Marie is deceased the trust will become an ordinary testamentary trust rather than it continuing as a spousal trust) so that the trustees will have an opportunity to undertake appropriate tax planning steps before distributions are made to the residuary beneficiaries.

Another issue that should be considered when drafting spouse trusts is whether the terms of the spouse trust will allow the spouse trust to redeem any shares that are trust property. Conventional wisdom suggests that this could be a significant problem. For example, if Ben's freeze shares were left to Anne-Marie's spouse trust such that upon her death their distribution to the residuary beneficiaries of the trust *in specie* would be mandatory, then prior to making distributions to the residuary beneficiaries, it would *not* be possible to offset the capital gains realized in the trust upon Anne-Marie's death by creating capital losses using subsection 164(6)-type procedures.[168]

Paragraph 88(1)(d) "Bump" Procedure

Another tax planning tool that can be used to reduce or eliminate the potential double tax on Ben's death is the paragraph 88(1)(d) bump procedure.

The paragraph 88(1)(d) bump procedure will have no impact on a decedent's deemed disposition on death. Its primary objectives are to enable the cost base of certain non-depreciable capital properties of a corporation[169] to be bumped so that such properties can be distributed to a shareholder, in this case an estate that holds high cost base shares, without adverse tax consequences to either the corporation or the estate.

There are three basic steps that are ordinarily used to implement the paragraph 88(1)(d) bump procedure. These steps are illustrated using Ben's situation; however for purposes of the illustration, it is assumed that the estate is the sole shareholder of Hoots-Paw.

1. Ben's estate will sell its Hoots-Paw high cost base freeze shares to Holdco in exchange for a promissory note. Notwithstanding the low paid-up capital of the freeze shares, due to their high adjusted cost base, paragraph 84.1(1)(b) should not apply to deem the estate to realize a dividend.

2. Hoots-Paw will be amalgamated or wound-up into Holdco. Ordinarily this amalgamation or wind-up would proceed on a tax deferred basis under subsection 88(1) and after the amalgamation or wind-up, Holdco would

---

[167] See CRA Document Number 9714075, August 11, 1997.

[168] However, this problem may be addressed by applying the strategy described earlier involving subsection 107(2.001).

[169] These are discussed in more detail below.

own low cost base non-depreciable assets.[170] However, since the Hoots-Paw shares that Holdco owned had a high cost base, Holdco will make a designation to bump the cost base of the low cost base assets, in this case the Trés Expensife Freeze shares, that it receives from Hoots-Paw under paragraph 88(1)(*d*) to the maximum extent possible.

The use of paragraph 88(1)(*d*) will be restricted to non-depreciable capital assets of Hoots-Paw that were continuously owned by Hoots-Paw since its last change of control. Pursuant to paragraph 88(1)(*d*.3), the last change of control of Hoots-Paw will be deemed to have occurred on Ben's death.[171] Some other factors that may impact on the ability to maximize the bump under paragraph 88(1)(*d*) are as follows:

- the total available bump will be reduced by the amount of the cash on hand in Holdco and the net tax cost of the assets of Hoots-Paw immediately before Hoots-Paw is wound-up;[172]

- Holdco will only be able to add an amount to its cost base of a particular non-depreciable capital property to the extent necessary to bring the cost base of the property up to the property's fair market value determined as at the date on which Holdco last acquired control of the subsidiary,[173] which in the present case will be the date of Ben's death;

- the total of amounts added to all non-depreciable capital properties may not exceed Holdco's "loss" on the shares of Hoots-Paw;[174] and

---

[170] In order for subsection 88(1) to apply, Holdco must own at least 90% of the issued shares of each class of shares of Hoots-Paw. If this is not the case then the paragraph 88(1)(*d*) bump procedure will not be available. Reorganizing Hoots-Paw to meet this criteria may be costly. Alternatively, Ben's children could transfer their Hoots-Paw common shares to Holdco in exchange for shares of Holdco on a tax deferred basis. However, involving Ben's children in such tax planning may create its own set of problems.

[171] Would the paragraph 88(1)(*d*) "bump" procedure be available in a spousal trust situation? It is questionable whether a cost base increase would be available to the spousal trust based on the value of non-depreciable capital property on the death of the surviving spouse. Paragraph 88(1)(*d*.3), which allows for this, appears to require that control of a corporation be acquired *as a consequence of the death of an individual.* Query, however, whether there is an acquisition of control under these circumstances, since the spousal trust itself would continue to hold the shares of the corporation in question, both before and after the death of the surviving spouse. In particular, see Document No. 2000-0017625. If, however, the shares were distributed to the residuary beneficiaries, it may well be arguable that paragraph 88(1)(*d*.3) would apply because, in this case, control would be acquired (by the beneficiaries) as a "consequence" of the death of the surviving spouse by virtue of the terms of the will, which would presumably call for a distribution to the residuary beneficiaries as a result of the death of a spouse.

[172] Subparagraph 88(1)(*d*)(i).

[173] Subparagraph 88(1)(*d*)(ii).

[174] Subparagraph 88(1)(*d*)(iii). The 'loss' referred to above is the amount in subparagraph 88(1)(*b*)(ii), less the total of amounts determined in subparagraphs 88(1)(*d*)(i) and (*i*.1).

- a pre-amalgamation or wind-up disposition by Hoots-Paw of assets in respect of which there are accrued gains will generally reduce the amount of the available bump.[175]

  The amount of the bump under paragraph 88(1)(d) will have to be designated by Holdco in its return for the taxation year in which Hoots-Paw is wound-up. There is no prescribed form for this election nor is there a provision in the Act which permits a late filing of this designation.[176]

3. Eventually, the assets of Holdco will be distributed to the estate in satisfaction of the promissory note. So long as each of Holdco's other assets that are distributed have a high cost base, no corporate level taxes will be payable as a result of the distribution. In these circumstances, it should be possible for Holdco to distribute such capital assets to the estate without adverse tax consequences to the estate.

"Pipeline" Procedure

The pipeline procedure may be used to avoid the double tax effect by corporations that already have high cost base properties. This procedure involves a simple reorganization which takes advantage of the high cost base of shares held by the estate to create a pipeline to allow access to these assets, usually on a tax-free basis. The pipeline procedure is similar to the paragraph 88(1)(d) bump procedure; however, under the pipeline procedure, it is not necessary to implement step two of the paragraph 88(1)(d) bump procedure.

Under the pipeline procedure, there is no technical need for Holdco to amalgamate or wind-up Hoots-Paw[177] or make a paragraph 88(1)(d) designation, since the cost base of Hoots-Paw's properties will already be high. Consequently, it will be possible for Hoots-Paw to distribute these properties to Holdco by ordinary intercorporate dividends or deemed dividends without triggering any corporate level taxes in either Hoots-Paw or Holdco. Since subsection 88(1) is inapplicable, it will be possible to implement this procedure even if Holdco does not own in excess of 90% of the shares of all classes of Hoots-Paw.

---

[175] The provisions found in subsection 88(1) are drafted quite broadly and may be interpreted to deny the adjusted cost base bump under paragraph 88(1)(d) in a variety of circumstances that may have been unintended by the Department of Finance. The result is that there is a significant degree of uncertainty as to when property will be treated as ineligible property. This uncertainty is reflected in published Technical Interpretations and ruling requests issued by the CRA (see, for example, CRA Document Number 9727435, August 7, 1998). The CRA has also tried to establish a more narrow administrative practice in *Income Tax Technical News No. 9* based on comments made by the Department of Finance in the Explanatory Notes that accompanied the introduction of paragraph 88(1)(c.3).

[176] The CRA is of the view that the provisions of paragraph 88(1)(d) clearly provide that a designation must be filed in the taxpayer's return of income for the year in which the subsidiary is wound up. (See CRA Document Number 9220205, February 10, 1993.) Based on the decision of the Tax Court of Canada in the case of *Financial Collection Agencies (Québec) v. M.N.R.*, 90 DTC 1040, the CRA's position is that this designation cannot be made retroactively. The courts have held that the words in subparagraph 88(1)(d) are clear and unambiguous and require that the designation must be made in the original return of income which is filed by the taxpayer.

[177] This may be desirable for other reasons.

Hoots-Paw's cash and other high cost base assets could be distributed to the estate using this procedure. Essentially, the estate would sell freeze shares having a fair market value equal to Hoots-Paw's high cost base assets to Holdco in exchange for a promissory note[178] from Holdco that can be repaid to the estate at any time without resulting in adverse tax consequences to the estate or to Holdco. If the estate required repayment of the promissory note, Holdco could direct Hoots-Paw to redeem its freeze shares. The inter-corporate deemed dividend created by the redemption should normally be free of tax.

Choosing Between the Alternatives

The result of implementing the subsection 164(6) procedure is that it may be possible to eliminate the double tax effect, leaving the estate to be taxed on a deemed dividend. The result of implementing both the paragraph 88(1)(*d*) bump procedure and the pipeline procedure is that they may make it possible to eliminate the double tax effect by leaving Ben to be taxed on his terminal period capital gains.

Of the three procedures, the pipeline procedure is by far the easiest to implement. This procedure can be implemented at any time and there are no elections or designations that must be filed. Another advantage associated with the pipeline procedure, which is also available under the paragraph 88(1)(*d*) procedure, is that the capital gains which are taxed under these procedures are now taxed more favourably than dividends. However, both the pipeline procedure and the paragraph 88(1)(*d*) bump procedure will only be available in respect of certain types of assets and may not result in an efficient use of surplus accounts and, in particular, RDTOH balances. As a result, these two procedures may be of limited assistance in certain situations.

It should be noted that the subsection 164(6) procedure, the paragraph 88(1)(*d*) procedure and the pipeline procedure are not mutually exclusive. Therefore, subject to issues such as time limitations, the implementation of any one procedure does not necessarily preclude the implementation of any other procedure.

---

[178] If there are valuation concerns, or if the value of the shares of the deceased's corporation has increased since the date of death, the holding corporation may issue high PUC shares or a combination of shares and a promissory note so that a subsection 85(1) election may be utilized. Section 84.1 should not be applicable because shares of the corporation have a high adjusted cost base for the purposes of section 84.1. However, assuming that the estate and the deceased do not deal at arm's length, section 84.1 should apply in those situations where the cost base was derived from capital gains that accrued prior to 1972 or from the utilization of the capital gains exemption by the deceased or non-arm's length persons.

It has not yet been clearly settled whether an estate and a decedent deal at arm's length. Paragraphs 84.1(2)(*d*) and 251(1)(*b*) appears to indicate that a decedent and an estate do not deal at arm's length. However, it may be argued that those provisions are not applicable because an estate and a decedent do not co-exist. See also *Nichols v. The Queen*, 96 DTC 1652 and CRA Document Number AC58167.

Insurance Planning[179]

Introduction

Life insurance is often viewed as the most tax effective vehicle for ensuring that liquidity will be available to satisfy a number of terminal liabilities including income tax. As described below, with some additional planning Ben will be able to continue to benefit from the existing $5,000,000 corporate owned joint last to die universal life insurance policy notwithstanding his pending separation from Anne. The life insurance will fulfill the dual role of (i) funding terminal tax liabilities and (ii) reducing the total tax payable. The mechanism for achieving this dual role is a strategy commonly referred to as the "50% Solution". In order to understand the mechanics of the 50% Solution it is first necessary to understand the stop-loss rules contained at subsection 112(3.2). However, before addressing the stop-loss rules, consideration must be given to Ben's pending separation and the nature of joint last to die life insurance.

Planning for the Existing Insurance

Joint last to die life insurance is typically recommended in circumstances where two individuals share a common liability which will only arise in the event of the death of the survivor. Such a liability would include, for example, capital gains tax exposure on the deemed disposition of capital property at death in circumstances where the property is bequeathed to a surviving spouse. Joint last to die insurance is recommended precisely because the proceeds are payable at the time they are needed and because the premium cost for joint last to die coverage is significantly less expensive than single life coverage on either of the lives insured.[180] A potential disadvantage of joint last to die insurance can arise in circumstances where there is a marital breakdown. Specifically, the rollover at death is not available for transfers of capital property to a former spouse. To deal with this eventuality, some contracts may allow for "splitting" the policy into individual life coverages. Even if it is possible to split coverage, the tax implications of such action must be considered. Splitting of a policy would likely result in a disposition of the original policy and could give rise to a taxable policy gain.[181]

The specific requirements for "splitting" joint last to die policies will vary from insurer to insurer and from product to product. Typically, in order to split a joint last to die policy, the individuals must establish that they are insurable. As a result of Ben's recent medical diagnosis he is currently uninsurable and, accordingly, splitting the policy will likely not be possible.

---

[179] This section was written by *Joel Cuperfain*, Regional Consultant for *Manulife Financial, Tax and Estate Planning Group.*

[180] By way of example, consider a husband and wife, both of whom are 70 years old and non-smokers. They require $1,000,000 of term to 100 insurance coverage. Based on Manulife Financial's Signet T-100 insurance policy, the annual cost for single life coverage on the husband would be $39,780, single life coverage for the wife would be $32,020 and joint last to die coverage would be $17,770.

[181] See for example Technical Interpretations 2001-0096125, 2000-0021175 and 2002-0127505.

The inability to split the existing coverage leaves Ben with an estate and financial planning dilemma. On the one hand, Hoots-Paw is the owner of a valuable asset in its $5,000,000 joint last to die life insurance policy which has a cash value and will provide significant future benefits. On the other hand, the policy will only pay a death benefit on the death of the survivor of himself and Anne (which, in the current circumstances will likely mean the death of Anne) but on his death he won't be able to take advantage of the spousal rollover of capital property to Anne or a spousal trust for Anne since they will likely not be married at the time. Complicating matters is the fact that Ben is currently uninsurable and post-mortem liquidity will likely be a critical issue for his estate planning.

A possible solution to this conundrum would be for Ben to establish a joint partner trust[182] prior to his separation from Anne. This joint partner trust would own the Hoots-Paw shares. The tax liability associated with the deemed disposition of the Hoots-Paw shares would thus be deferred until the death of the survivor of Ben and Anne and the insurance proceeds from the joint last to die life insurance policy would be available to satisfy the liability at the relevant time. Of course, establishing such a trust in advance of a marital breakdown would raise a number of family law issues; however, for purposes of the discussion which follows, it is assumed that Ben and Anne are able to negotiate the establishment of the joint partner trust as a component of their overall separation agreement. As part of their separation negotiations, the specific entitlements of Ben and Anne to the income of the trust during their lifetimes would be determined as would the rights of the capital beneficiaries (presumably Ben's and Anne's children).

With resolution of the preliminary issue relating to the pre-existing coverage, consideration can turn to the stop-loss rules at section 112.

The Stop-Loss Rules

In order to appreciate the impact of the stop-loss rules released as part of the April 26, 1995 technical amendments, a review of the pre-April 26 regime is in order.

In many cases, before the introduction of the amendments to section 112, corporate owned life insurance was used as the funding mechanism to redeem all of the shares owned by a deceased shareholder from the deceased's estate and thereby avoid the incidence of any tax otherwise payable as a consequence of death.

The strategy is best illustrated by an example. Assume Mr. X had implemented an estate freeze in favour of his daughter. Mr. X owns fixed value preferred shares of XCo with an aggregate redemption amount of $1,000. The adjusted cost base to Mr. X and the paid-up capital of the XCo preferred shares is nominal. Mr. X's daughter owns all the common shares. XCo is the beneficiary of a life insurance policy on the life of Mr. X with a death benefit of $1,000. The adjusted cost basis[183] of the insurance policy is presumed to be nominal. Mr. X is deemed to dispose of the XCo preferred shares for fair market value immediately prior to death and realizes a

---

[182] Within the meaning of subsection 73(1.01).

[183] As defined at subsection 148(9).

$1,000 capital gain. The new adjusted cost base of the preferred shares to Mr. X's estate is thus $1,000. XCo, as the beneficiary of the life insurance policy, receives the $1,000 death benefit tax free and obtains a credit to its capital dividend account of $1,000.[184] XCo then uses the insurance proceeds to redeem the preferred shares from Mr. X's estate and declares that the deemed dividend on the redemption be a capital dividend to the fullest extent possible. The (capital) dividend is received by the estate tax-free. In addition, the redemption constitutes a disposition of capital property.

Under paragraph (*j*) of the definition of "proceeds of disposition" at section 54 of the Act, the adjusted proceeds are calculated by subtracting the amount of the deemed dividend. Thus the adjusted proceeds are deemed to be zero and the estate would realize a $1,000 capital loss. Under subsection 164(6), where the estate realizes such a capital loss in its first taxation year, the loss may be carried back to the terminal return of the deceased. Accordingly, this $1,000 capital loss would be carried back to Mr. X's terminal return and exactly offsets the capital gain arising on the deemed disposition at death. In the result, the estate has $1,000 cash, Mr. X's daughter has obtained sole ownership of XCo and the tax liability is nil. Of course, the liability hasn't "disappeared" but, rather, has been "inherited" by Mr. X's daughter. The adjusted cost base of her shares remains unchanged and she would ultimately pay tax on the gain when she disposes of the shares.

Clearly, the ability to defer the tax liability associated with the deemed disposition at death runs counter to the theory of the Income Tax Act which contemplates a tax liability arising at the time of death. However, the ability to defer the tax liability in the manner described above is a logical extension of the operation of the capital dividend account coupled with the loss carryback rule at subsection 164(6). Indeed, the purpose of subsection 164(6) is to promote integration and prevent the possibility of double taxation that could otherwise arise as a result of the fact that a deceased individual and the estate of such deceased individual are treated as separate taxpayers.

This planning strategy came to an abrupt end on April 26, 1995 with the release of the Technical Bill. Clause 45 of the Technical Bill provided, in part, that where an individual (including an estate) suffers a capital loss on the disposition of shares then the amount of the loss otherwise determined is reduced by the total of all tax-free capital dividends received on the share.

Under the original proposed amendments, the only exception to the stop-loss rule was a *de minimis* provision whereby nominal shareholdings (less than 5%) held for more than 365 days would not have been impacted by the amendments.[185]

In the months (and, indeed, years) following the original proposals, numerous modifications and generous grandfathering relief to the rules were enacted. Since the insurance on the lives of Ben and Anne was acquired prior to April 26, 1995,

---

[184] The actual credit to the capital dividend account would be equal to the proceeds in excess of the adjusted cost basis ("acb") of the policy to the corporation immediately before death. For purposes of this example, it is assumed that the acb immediately before death is nil.

[185] Subsection 112(3.2) *et seq.*

consideration must be given to the grandfathering relief available in respect of the stop-loss rules.

Grandfathering Provisions[186]

The amendments to subsections 112(3) to (7) generally apply to dispositions of shares that occur after April 26, 1995. However, the legislation contains two significant grandfathering provisions that will preserve the old rules for qualifying dispositions of shares owned by an individual on April 26, 1995 (i.e., no reduction to the capital loss and therefore, potentially, no tax to the deceased or the estate). The main areas of grandfathering relief are discussed below.

1. Pre-Existing Agreements

Grandfathering is available for shares that are disposed of pursuant to an agreement in writing made before April 27, 1995. Therefore, a capital loss resulting from a redemption of shares pursuant to such an agreement would fall under the old rules if life insurance funded an existing agreement made on or before April 26, 1995.

Changes to an agreement that existed on April 26, 1995 may cause the shares to lose their grandfathered status. Department of Finance officials have indicated that where an existing agreement is altered to such an extent that it would constitute a new agreement, grandfathering relief under this rule would be lost.[187]

For purposes of this rule it is irrelevant if life insurance was owned as of April 26, 1995. Thus insurance could be acquired at any time to fund the agreement and grandfathering relief would be available.

Based on the available information, there was no agreement in force requiring the redemption of the Hoots-Paw shares on the death of the survivor or Ben and Anne. Accordingly, relief under this rule will not be available.

2. Pre-Existing Insurance

Grandfathering is also available for shares owned on April 26, 1995 where:

(i) the shares were owned on April 26, 1995 by an individual or a trust under which an individual was a beneficiary;

(ii) a corporation was a beneficiary of a life insurance policy on April 26, 1995;

(iii) the taxpayer, or a spouse of the taxpayer, was a life insured under the policy;

---

[186] For a comprehensive review of the grandfathering rules see T.R. Burpee "The New Stop-Loss Rules: Grandfathered Shares" (1998), vol. 46, no. 3 *Canadian Tax Journal*, p. 678. See also Income Tax Technical News Number 12, dated February 11, 1998 and Text of the *CALU Conference for Advanced Life Underwriting Revenue Canada Round Table* held in May 1997 as it relates to the grandfathering provisions of subsections 112(3) to (3.32).

[187] Income Tax Technical News No. 12, dated February 11, 1998.

(iv) it was reasonable to conclude on April 26, 1995 that a main purpose of the life insurance policy was to fund, directly or indirectly, in whole or in part, the redemption, acquisition or cancellation of the shares; and

(v) the disposition of the shares is made by the individual, the individual's spouse, the estate of the individual or the individual's spouse (within the estate's first taxation year) or certain trusts.

Earlier drafts of the legislation had required that a buy/sell agreement be put in place by a certain time in order for this grandfathering provision to apply. This obligation is no longer required.[188]

Clarification of this grandfathering rule has been provided in the explanatory notes to the legislation. First, the shares being disposed of do not have to be shares of the corporation that is the beneficiary under the policy. In other words, the shareholder of Holdco would be eligible for grandfathering in respect of a disposition of shares of Holdco, where there is a redemption buy/sell under which Opco is beneficiary of the insurance and a main purpose of the insurance is to fund a redemption of the shares of Holdco, and the intention is to use the proceeds of the policy (which are paid-up to Holdco) to acquire the deceased taxpayer's shares.

Secondly, the explanatory notes state:

> The shares need not be acquired with the proceeds of the life insurance policy that was in place on April 26, 1995. Therefore, policies may be renewed, converted or entered into after April 26, 1995 without necessarily eliminating the application of these grandfathering rules.

It appears that this provision may have extremely broad application. For example, if the corporation was a beneficiary on April 26, 1995 of a term insurance policy that provided funding for a buy/sell agreement structured as a redemption of shares, the term insurance policy could be converted to a permanent policy without jeopardizing the application of the grandfathering provision. It also appears that additional life insurance coverage or replacement policies may be purchased subsequent to April 26, 1995 to provide buy/sell funding without eliminating the applicability of the grandfathering provisions.

The provision also permits spousal and joint second to die policies where the taxpayer and the taxpayer's spouse are the lives insured.

3. Share Exchange Rules

The legislation provides that where a share has been acquired in exchange for another share under certain specified provisions of the Act (sections 51, 85, 86 or 87), the new share will be deemed to be the same as the old share for purposes of the grandfathering rules. An anomaly exists in the legislation in that this deeming provision only applies to the grandfathering provision where life insurance exists on April 26, 1995, and not where there is an existing agreement in place on April 26, 1995. Therefore, if an individual's shares are grandfathered because a disposition of

---

[188] The December 14, 1995 Press Release and Bill C-69 had indicated that a written agreement must be entered into prior to 1997 in order for grandfathering relief to apply. This date was later extended to April, 1997 and ultimately eliminated altogether.

shares will occur pursuant to an agreement in writing made before April 27, 1995 (with no existing insurance in place on April 26, 1995), any subsequent reorganizations, for example the creation of a holding company, will jeopardize the grandfathering.

While the grandfathering relief is generous, it will not be available in every situation where there is pre-April 26, 1995 insurance. The onus is on the taxpayer to satisfy the "reasonable to conclude" test — that is, the taxpayer must establish that it is reasonable to conclude that one of the main purposes of the insurance on April 26, 1995 was to fund a share redemption. This test could be satisfied in a variety of ways such as by the existence of a shareholders agreement, by a (pre-April 26, 1995) memorandum from the taxpayer's lawyer or accountant describing the purpose of the insurance or even correspondence from the insurance agent to the taxpayer or to the insurance carrier describing the purpose of the policy. Regardless of how the taxpayer establishes the purpose, the fact remains that the obligation is on the taxpayer to provide the evidence as to the purpose of the insurance.

In the current circumstances, there is no evidence as to the purpose of the $5,000,000 joint last to die policy on Ben and Anne. In the absence of any such evidence, it is assumed that grandfathering relief will not be available and alternative planning is required.

50% Solution

Assuming that grandfathering relief is not available, Ben may be able to take advantage of certain of the stop-loss relieving rules — specifically the rule commonly referred to as the "50% solution."

The 50% solution is based on a relieving rule that only applies in the estate context. In simplified terms, the relieving rule generally ensures that the capital loss in the estate is only reduced by the amount by which capital dividends received on the share exceed 50% of the lesser of

(i) the capital gain on the deemed disposition at death; and

(ii) the capital loss in the estate otherwise determined.[189]

As illustrated below, the 50% solution may allow for attractive tax results when an insurance financed corporate share redemption strategy is utilized following the death of a shareholder.

The Planning Strategy

Under the Act an individual is deemed to dispose of all capital property for fair market value immediately before death,[190] or, in Ben's case assuming a transfer of

---

[189] Paragraph 112(3.2)(*a*). Similar rules apply at subsection 112(3.3) for shares acquired by a trust under subsection 104(4) which would be the case where shares are transferred to a qualifying subsection 73(1.01) joint partner trust and are subject to a deemed disposition and acquisition on the death of the surviving spouse.

[190] Subsection 70(5).

Hoots-Paw shares to a joint partner trust, on the death of the survivor of Ben and Anne. The top marginal rate of tax for capital gains in Ontario is approximately 23%.

In the absence of further planning, the future capital gains tax liability on the $10,000,000 capital gain in respect of the Hoots-Paw shares would amount to approximately $2,300,000. However, by taking advantage of certain relieving rules in the Act applicable to corporate owned life insurance, it is possible to use life insurance to decrease the tax liability from $2,300,000 to $1,550,000 and to provide extra cash for Ben's heirs.

Insurance Financed Corporate Share Redemption Strategy

For purposes of this example, it is assumed that Hoots-Paw is the beneficiary of a life insurance policy on the joint lives of Ben and Anne with a total benefit of $5,000,000. Hoots-Paw will redeem the $10,000,000 of freeze shares from the proposed joint partner trust using $5,000,000 cash from the insurance proceeds and $5,000,000 by way of a promissory note. The redemption dividend will be comprised of $5,000,000 of capital dividends and $5,000,000 of taxable dividends. The redemption results in a full $10,000,000 capital loss in the trust. The trust's $10,000,000 capital loss could be carried back to offset the tax liability associated with the deemed disposition on the death of the survivor of Ben and Anne. Only 50% of the dividends ($5,000,000) will be capital dividends. The stop-loss rules will not apply because of the 50% relieving rule discussed previously.

As illustrated at Table 1, the total tax liability has thus been reduced from $2,300,000 to $1,550,000, a tax saving of $750,000 which equals approximately a $^1/_3$ reduction in tax. Further the joint partner trust has $5,000,000 of tax-free insurance proceeds to more than satisfy the $1,550,000 tax liability.

TABLE 1

TAX CONSEQUENCES: CAPITAL GAIN VS. 50% SOLUTION CAPITAL GAINS

Deemed Disposition at Death

Proceeds of disposition	$10,000,000
Capital gain	$10,000,000
Tax at 23%	$ 2,300,000

INSURANCE FINANCED SHARE REDEMPTION STRATEGY

Proceeds of Redemption

Total deemed dividend	$10,000,000
Tax free capital dividend	$ 5,000,000
Taxable dividends	$ 5,000,000
Tax on taxable dividends at 31%	$ 1,550,000
Adjusted proceeds	$ 0
Adjusted cost base to trust	$10,000,000
Capital loss	$10,000,000

The Mechanics

A technical and mechanical issue relating to the payment of the capital dividend should be noted. Specifically, it is not possible to declare part of a dividend to be a capital dividend and part to be a taxable dividend. The full amount of the dividend must be a capital dividend.[191] It is ineffective to simply redeem the shares and declare that the redemption of 50% of the shares is a capital dividend and the balance is a taxable dividend because in that circumstance the 50% relieving rule would only apply to the 50% of the shares redeemed by means of the capital dividend (i.e., the relief would only apply to 50% of 50% rather than the desired 50% of 100%).

One solution is to file a capital dividend election for the full $10,000,000 deemed dividend, and then file another election[192] to treat the portion of the dividend which exceeds the corporation's CDA as a separate taxable dividend. This produces the desired result, although the process is cumbersome. There may also be an issue if the corporation did have $10,000,000 in its CDA at the time, in which case the original election would not have been excessive at all.

Another solution is to increase the paid-up capital of the deceased's shares, as follows:[193]

1. After receipt of the insurance proceeds Hoots-Paw increases its paid-up capital on the preferred shares held by the joint partner trust by $5,000,000. This would be accomplished by means of a director's resolution.

2. The increase in paid-up capital results in a $5,000,000 deemed dividend.[194]

3. The $5,000,000 deemed dividend is elected to be a tax-free capital dividend.

4. The increase in paid-up capital will also increase the trust's adjusted cost base in the shares by $5,000,000, from $10,000,000 (the value as a result of the deemed disposition on death) to $15,000,000.[195]

5. Hoots-Paw will redeem the $10,000,000 of preferred shares. This will result in a deemed dividend equal to the amount of the proceeds of redemption minus the paid-up capital of the shares ($10,000,000 - $5,000,000 = $5,000,000 deemed dividend).

6. This $5,000,000 deemed dividend will be a taxable dividend.

7. The redemption will also trigger capital gains consequences. The adjusted proceeds for capital gains purposes will be equal to the proceeds minus the

---

[191] Subsection 83(2).

[192] Under subsection 184(3).

[193] Note that in implementing this structure it is necessary for the deceased to own shares of a class separate from classes held by the surviving shareholders. This may require a capital reorganization.

[194] Subsection 84(1).

[195] Paragraph 53(1)(*b*).

deemed dividend ($10,000,000 - $5,000,000 = $5,000,000 adjusted proceeds).

8. The capital loss will equal the adjusted proceeds minus the adjusted base of the shares to the trust ($5,000,000 - $15,000,000 = $10,000,000 capital loss).

9. The $10,000,000 capital loss can be carried back to offset the deemed disposition on the death of the survivor of Ben and Anne.

Benefits of this Strategy

In short, this particular planning structure provides the following advantages over a "do nothing" approach:

1. Life insurance provides the cash necessary to satisfy the tax liability.

2. Life insurance reduces the liability from $2,300,000 to $1,550,000.

3. The insurance provides additional cash for Ben's heirs.

4. The tax liability is effectively funded using "cheaper" corporate dollars as opposed to more expensive after-tax personal dollars.

5. No estate assets need be liquidated to fund the tax liability.

Other Considerations

A final comment concerning insurance planning relates to Ben's children. It would be advisable for all of the parties to enter into a shareholders' agreement concerning the future management and control of the corporations. Further, the parties should consider what they wish to happen in the event of the death of one of Ben's children. Specifically, would the shares simply remain in the deceased child's family or should there be a buy-out? If the shares are to be transferred to a spouse or child, consideration should be given to funding the tax liability associated with the shares. If the intent is to purchase the shares from the deceased's estate, consideration should be given to taking out corporate owned life insurance policies on the children to fund this obligation.

Shareholders' Agreement and other Corporate Law Matters[196]

Fact Situation

The 100 common shares of Hoots-Paw are held by the Trust which was established in 1985.

Control of Hoots-Paw will not pass immediately because voting control remains with Ben who holds all of the 10,000 voting freeze shares, but will pass to the children on the death of Ben after which the freeze shares may be redeemed. We can

---

[196] This section was written by *Stephen Witten* of *Minden Gross Grafstein & Greenstein LLP*, based on a paper written and presented by *Hartley R. Nathan* of *Minden Gross Grafstein & Greenstein LLP*.

assume that Ben controls Hoots-Paw and therefore Expensife and eventually some of the siblings will own 100% of the voting shares.

Discretionary Trust

Since the Trust is fully discretionary, the trustees may transfer the 100 common shares to any of Robin, Larry or Alan, or any combination thereof in any proportion they see fit. We can assume that the Trust Indenture provides that they may transfer the assets out of the Trust at any time if all trustees agree. If, in their discretion, they choose to transfer the shares only to Robin or Larry or Alan or any two of them, that would be within their power as set out in the Trust Indenture, subject only to any fiduciary obligations imposed on trustees under trust law.

Based on the facts, both Ben and Anne had historically treated all three children equally. Notwithstanding the fact that Larry no longer works in the family business and appears to have "inflamed" Ben over Desiré Laflamme, I will assume that, in the end, Ben will be persuaded that it is appropriate to treat all children equally and the trustees will not exclude Larry from the distribution. However, the facts raise a number of questions and issues.

Are the Trustees Obliged to Treat the Three Beneficiaries in an Even-Handed Manner upon Distribution out of the Trust?

As noted, the Trust Indenture confers upon the trustees a power which they may exercise at their own discretion. The settlor of the Trust, in this instance, in creating this purely discretionary trust, is attempting to underline that he wishes no interference with the trustees.

A century ago the House of Lords in England established the proposition that absent bad faith (*mala fides*) on the part of the trustees, the court would not control the exercise of an absolute discretion. See *Gisborne v. Gisborne*.[197] However, Canadian case law may be interpreted as broadening this concept. As such, the entire question of the extent to which a court is willing to exercise control over trustees who hold absolute discretion is a difficult issue. There are a number of cases that have considered the matter. One example will suffice. In *Hunter Estate v. Holton*,[198] Steele J. stated:

> Trustees must act in good faith and be fair as between beneficiaries in the exercise of their powers. There is no allegation of bad faith in the present case. A court should be reluctant to interfere with the exercise of the power of discretion by a trustee. I adopt the following criteria in *Re: Hastings-Bass* as being applicable to the court's review of the exercise of such power:
>
> > To sum up the preceding observations, in our judgment, whereby the terms of a trust . . . a trustee is given a discretion as to some matter under which he acts in good faith, the court should not interfere with his action, notwithstanding that it does not have the full effect which he intended, unless (1) what he has achieved is unauthorized by the power conferred upon him, or (2) it is clear that he would not have acted as he did (a) had he not taken into account considerations which he

---

[197] (1877), 2 App. Cas. 300 (H.L.).

[198] (1992), 7 O.R. (3d) 372.

should not have taken into account, or (*b*) had he not failed to take into account considerations which he ought to have taken into account.

It has been said that the grounds on which Canadian courts have used the doctrine of *mala fides* to justify intervention rest on an overriding concern to ensure that the fundamental purpose of the trust is not defeated; therefore the purpose of such discretionary power should be considered when exercised.[199] A more detailed discussion of these cases can be found under the sub-heading *Discretionary Powers* in Howard Carr's section, "Trusts and Fiduciary Issues," which is discussed previously in the case study materials.

Unlike the beneficiary of a fixed trust, the law provides that the beneficiaries of a discretionary trust are not entitled to any specific part of the trust assets until the trustees exercise their discretion in their favour.[200] However, if the trustees bypass Larry in the distribution of the Hoots-Paw shares, there is nothing to prevent Larry from bringing proceedings against the trustees alleging they abused their discretion or that they ignored relevant factors or gave significant weight to irrelevant considerations.

Let us assume, however, that Ben and the other remaining trustee will agree to transfer the 100 shares to the three children equally. Once the shares are distributed out of the Trust, there will be no restrictions on them except for any restrictions imposed on transfers under the Articles.

Should There be a Shareholders' Agreement Entered into Relative to the Common Shares?

In my view, there should be. Shareholders' agreements are generally entered into to set out basic ground rules for ongoing governance of the business and to address the transferability and liquidity available to the shareholders in respect of their shares in a way that provides for orderly "divorce" without resorting to a forced liquidation or other litigious proceedings. More often than not, shareholders' agreements are negotiated among arm's length parties coming together with a

---

[199] Other concepts include failing to give proper consideration to exercising discretion, and whether the exercise is so unreasonable that no honest or fair-dealing trustee would have come to the decision. While Canadian courts have tended to be more aggressive than their English counterparts in interfering with the trustees' exercise of discretion, even where it is "absolute", this tendency is not a universal trait. In the recent case of *Martin v. Banting* ([2001] O.J. No. 510), a decision upheld by the Ontario Court of Appeal, the Court appeared to follow the principle in *Gisborne v. Gisborne* and not interfere with the discretion of the trustees. In *Martin v. Banting*, the plaintiff, Martin, a beneficiary of two discretionary estate freeze trusts, attempted to challenge the exercise of the trustees' discretion in the distribution of the proceeds of the trusts arguing that the trustees relied on irrelevant considerations. Both trustees (his mother and his uncle) exercised their discretion to deny Martin any benefit on the grounds that Martin was ungrateful, lacked integrity and was disloyal to the family. In upholding the trustees' discretion, the Low J. made the following comments:

> Whether the trustees' opinions of the plaintiff's character and conduct were objectively well founded or not is not the issue in the action and is not an issue to be tried. The trustees, in exercising their discretion do not do so in a quasi judicial capacity and the Court does not sit as a Court of Appeal upon the trustees' reasons for exercising their discretion the way that they did. The trustees have no obligation to give reasons in the first instance, and where no *mala fides* is shown, the Court will not interfere.

[200] Oosterhoff, A.H., *Text, Commentary and Cases on Trusts* (Thomson Canada Limited, 1992), p. 105.

common business vision going forward. In a family succession planning context, the owners are being brought together somewhat artificially. In most family situations, the next generation "owners" will likely have differing involvement in the day-to-day business, differing knowledge and understanding of business in general, differing expectations for the future and more likely than not, pre-existing sibling rivalries or tensions that will undermine rational decision making. Therefore, there is a need to create ground rules to balance competing interests in a way that doesn't result in the destruction of either the business or family relationships. A shareholders' agreement can be an important tool for achieving that objective.

When Should a Shareholders' Agreement Be Entered into?

You will recall that the 100 common shares of Hoots-Paw were held by the Trust.

How did the Trust come to acquire these shares?

One way would have been for the settlor, Mr. X,[201] to have subscribed to the shares and have transferred them to the Trust by way of gift. Alternatively, Mr. X could have settled $100 on the Trust which then subscribed for the 100 common shares with the $100. At the time that Mr. X subscribed for the shares, he could have entered into a unanimous shareholder agreement with the freezor Ben imposing suitable provisions. There would be no fiduciary obligation imposed on the settlor that I am aware of if he transfers certain shares to the Trust conditional upon there being a unanimous shareholder agreement controlling or restricting the common shares. On the facts, this clearly was not done here. If there had been such an agreement entered into and it was a "unanimous shareholder agreement", it would bind any transferees by virtue of the provisions of subsection 108(4) of the OBCA which states that "a transferee of shares subject to a unanimous shareholder agreement shall be deemed to be a party to the agreement" as long as there is a reference to this restriction noted conspicuously on the share certificate. Accordingly, if a unanimous shareholder agreement had been entered into and common shares of Hoots-Paw are distributed out of the Trust to the children, they would be bound by restrictions in the unanimous shareholder agreement when the shares are transferred to them.

Alternatively, the trustees could enter into a shareholders' agreement purporting to bind the shares in the hands of the children before the common shares are transferred out of the Trust and just before the mandate of the trustees has ended.

---

[201] The fact situation does not specify the identity of the settler or other mechanics of the freeze. See Joan Jung's section, "The Succession Plan: Income Tax Issues", which is found on p. 223 and, in particular, the discussion under the sub-heading "Reversionary Trust Rules" on p. 232 for comments on the method by which the Trust likely acquired the shares and related income tax considerations.

This could be, however, a matter of some concern. Reference may be made to an article which appeared in *CA Magazine*.[202] The article states in part:

> If trustees are considering ... distribution of trust assets ..., they should be concerned about transferring the trust assets to the beneficiaries without an agreement among them as to their ability to deal with such assets.
>
> An interest in a private company or closely held family business would need a shareholders' agreement to ameliorate the trustees' concerns. The agreement might restrict the sale of shares, provide specific voting rights, prescribe the election of directors, stipulate compensation policy, dividend policy, buy/sell arrangements, succession arrangements and other such matters.
>
> Nevertheless, trustees could be open to attack by a beneficiary at the time the trust assets are distributed if the trustees entered into a shareholders' or other restrictive agreement without the beneficiaries' consent. The beneficiaries could argue that the trustees had exceeded their authority by entering into an agreement designed to remain in effect beyond the period in which the trust property is held by the trustees. The more restrictive the agreement, the more likely it might be set aside. Trustees should try to obtain the consent of the adult beneficiaries or even to have them join in the agreement.
>
> Despite the caveat, trustees should be able to counter any criticism by showing that they acted reasonably and in good faith by entering into the agreement, and that the beneficiary was placed in a stronger, safer position, *vis-à-vis* the other shareholders.
>
> A settlor concerned about what will happen to shares after distribution should state in the trust agreement that the beneficiaries' right to receive shares is contingent on their entering into a shareholders' agreement.[203]

I note from the facts that the other surviving trustee of the Trust is an accountant. Anyone in the position of being a trustee with no financial stake in the trust assets should seek legal advice as to whether to resign before being called upon to exercise discretion in favour of any one or two beneficiaries to the detriment of the third. This is so even though there are indemnities in the Trust Indenture. It would also be appropriate for the trustee to obtain a release from the beneficiaries before distributing the assets out of the Trust. Legal advice should be sought as to the form of release and any other documentation that might be appropriate.

Again, if a unanimous shareholder agreement was entered into and shares are distributed out of the Trust to the children, as noted, they would be bound by restrictions in the unanimous shareholder agreement when the shares are transferred to them.

If the age and sophistication of the parties permits, a further alternative is to design the agreement with input from the first generation and the second generation prior to distribution of the shares and have such agreement signed by the second generation to take effect upon the shares being distributed. In addition to addressing any concerns there may be in having the trustees impose an agreement, the very

---

[202] Alexander, A.E. and Cole, S.R., "Rollouts that Meet the Rules" (October 1991), 124 *CA Magazine* 42 at 47.

[203] The Trust Indenture could contain a provision authorizing the trustees to enter into a shareholders' agreement. The language may need to be more explicit and provide wide discretionary powers for the trustees. It should also be noted that while a court may order the sale or transfer of shares from one spouse to another, it is generally a last resort. The court is instructed by s. 11(1) of the *Family Law Act* (R.S.O. 1990, c. F.3, as amended) that a transfer order should be avoided if it would impair business operations or result in the sale of the corporation. A marriage contract would help.

process of working through what a shareholders' agreement should provide with the input of both generations should better define the potential issues, facilitate solutions to such issues, educate the next generation and hopefully, result in a "buy-in" by the next generation to whatever rules are established in the shareholders' agreement. Inter-generational and intra-generational tensions may make the process difficult even at this early stage, but this is all the more reason to work through the issues before the distribution takes place and while the first generation is still involved. Involving the second generation at this time may also have the added benefit of alleviating any concerns lenders or other "stakeholders" in the business may have in knowing that succession is being planned for in an orderly way.

For What Should the Shareholders' Agreement Provide?

Every family has its own culture and special topics and sensitivities that need to be addressed. The potential for conflict is greater than would normally exist between arm's length business "partners". As noted above, shareholders' agreements typically address governance issues and liquidity issues.

Governance

A shareholders' agreement would address first and foremost the composition of the board of directors. In this instance, one would expect the agreement to address the right of each sibling to be represented on the board of directors, the extent to which any sibling can put forward other nominees in his or her place such as a spouse, and the appropriateness of expanding the board of directors to include "independent directors". Independent directors can play a very significant role in facilitating decision making, help diffuse tensions between family members, act as consensus makers and impose a degree of discipline on management, particularly family management that will help balance the competing interests of those family members who are involved in day-to-day management and those who are not. The agreement would also address what voting majorities are required for key issues, whether it be a simple majority, a super majority of some nature or unanimity. Unanimity generally speaking is a bad policy to adopt for any business where there are several owners. Independent directors who agree with decisions of a majority of the family members reinforce the legitimacy of such decisions without requiring unanimity.

Another key governance area to be addressed in the shareholders' agreement is management. To the extent that it is possible to do so, the chief executive officer of the company going forward should be identified either from within the family or outside the family. The rights of other family members to participate in the business as managers/employees should also be delineated. The agreement should further recognize the principle that family owners who are involved in management are entitled to be compensated in that capacity separate and apart from whatever participation in profits they may be entitled to as owners. The board of directors should serve its proper role in setting compensation levels, dealing with issues of competency, setting the strategic goals and objectives for the business, etc.

In circumstances where some family members are involved in the business day-to-day and some are not, as is the case here, tensions will likely develop over the profit distribution policy of the company. The "passive owners" typically want their interest in the company to generate as much cash to them on an ongoing basis as possible. The "management owners" typically want to preserve as much cash as possible in the business either for purposes of protecting the business, growing the business or simply enhancing their "control". A dividend policy codified in a shareholders' agreement may go a long way to balancing these competing interests. Such a policy might require the payout of a predetermined percentage of profits, unless the board of directors decides otherwise. This would reverse the onus and require the directors to demonstrate in any particular year why the dividend policy should not be followed. Finally, it may be appropriate to provide in the agreement for the appointment of an auditor. Again, in circumstances where there are owners involved in the business and owners who are not involved in the business, the existence of an outside auditor helps legitimize the activities of the owner/managers and gives comfort to the passive owners that there is external scrutiny.

Liquidity

In a family succession planning context, there is often a strong desire to preserve the family ownership of the business for the second generation and potentially for the third generation and beyond. As such, the bias in a shareholders' agreement in this context would typically make it difficult for family owners to sell outside of the family. Notwithstanding this bias, the desire to keep the business within the family should not hold family members hostage to an ownership position that they are not happy with for whatever reason. Therefore, a shareholders' agreement should provide "safety valves". These might include permitting internal transfers among family members subject to rights of first refusal. If the business can afford it, the agreement might also provide a partial redemption mechanism that would allow one or more family members on, say, an annual basis to have the company purchase a small percentage of his or her shares without requiring a sale of the entire interest of such family member(s). The more difficult issue is if a majority of the owners want to sell the business as whole, in circumstances where a minority, typically the management family members, don't want to sell. In that instance, a suitable balance may be to provide that the majority would be required to first offer the business to the minority with predetermined self-financing terms and security and if the minority is not prepared to buy on those terms, then the majority would be free for a period of time to shop the whole company.

Other liquidity considerations that you may want to address include the scope of estate planning that would be permitted *vis-à-vis* the third generation and beyond, the consequences of any marital breakdown among any of the owners, general restrictions on transfer, restrictions on pledging or otherwise encumbering the shares, and so on. In the present fact situation, there may also be an opportunity to provide for different forms of liquidity in relation to other assets that may be bequeathed to the second generation. As an example, an investment portfolio may lend itself to being "split up" among family members so that each family member can acquire ownership of discrete assets. In that respect, you may be able to provide in a shareholders' agreement a mandatory "butterfly" or other distribution mechanism that would permit any one or more of the shareholders to require a "divorce" in relation to the underlying assets. To the extent that there is no business rationale for requiring such assets to be under common ownership, there is no reason why family members should be forced to stay together in respect of the ownership of such assets.

What Rights do Minority Shareholders have? What can a Disgruntled Child do If there is No Shareholders' Agreement in Place?

This is an era in which a minority shareholder has an arsenal of rights and remedies at his or her disposal. Accordingly, Hoots-Paw and its other shareholders must consider the potential risk of exposure to minority shareholder remedies. These include:

(a) The Oppression Remedy

Minority shareholder actions have been commenced by children using the oppression remedy. Ungrateful recipients of common shares have pursued oppression remedies based on the fact that they were not receiving adequate return on their "investment", that is, no dividends having been paid on the common shares. Even though a child paid nothing for his or her investment, the non-payment of dividends may nevertheless be relevant to oppression actions.[204]

In *Mason v. InterCity Properties Limited*,[205] which ended up in the Ontario Court of Appeal,[206] the father had founded a real estate investment company and left the shares to his children equally. One daughter complained that there had been no return to her in respect of the substantial monies which were said to be hers in the company and no participation in how money was being used and/or invested. The court ordered the company to buy out her shares at fair value with no deduction for minority discount.

There are other grounds for pursuing the oppression remedy which could result in a forced purchase of a disgruntled shareholder's shares which in this case could well be Larry. The oppression remedy is his most powerful tool.

He could complain if substantial bonuses were paid out to Ben. This was one of the bases for the court granting an oppression remedy to the complainant in the Ontario Divisional Court decision of *Naneff v. Concrete Holdings Limited*[207] where shareholdings devolved on siblings following an estate freeze. The father, the founder of the business, had intended his sons to have the benefit of the companies, even if one of them failed to stay in the business. The plaintiff, one of the two sons, who ran off with his secretary, was a director and officer of the companies, had worked in the

---

[204] In *Sutherland v. Birks* (2003), 65 O.R. (3d) 812 (C.A.), the Court found that the reasonable expectations of the father in creating a family holding company involved a regular dividend/income policy for the family member shareholders.

[205] Unreported decision of the Ontario High Court (December 10, 1984).

[206] (1987), 59 O.R. (2d) 631.

[207] (1994), 19 O.R. (3d) 691; Varied by the Ontario Court of Appeal, May 16, 1995 (unreported).

companies on a part-time basis during his youth and on a full-time basis throughout his entire adult life. He was involved in the day-to-day operations and management of the business and in the making of executive and ownership decisions. He was viewed and respected by employees and by those who dealt with the companies as an effective owner. When the plaintiff was ejected from the day-to-day operations and effective management of the companies, he commenced an action claiming relief on the basis of oppression. He alleged that he was thrown out of the family business because his parents would not accept the woman he fell in love with and married. The parents contended that the plaintiff's removal was the result of his poor work habits, his lifestyle of excessive drinking and partying and his relationship with a former employee of the companies. The Court allowed the plaintiff's application.

The plaintiff and his younger brother had been led to believe by their parents that they would be co-owners and equal partners of the group of companies and that after the death of their father, they would have complete ownership and control. The reorganization of the companies was carried out in a manner consistent with the concept that the sons would ultimately take over the business and so were the sons' dealings with employees, suppliers and customers. The shareholder's expectation on the part of the plaintiff was, therefore, a reasonable one which had to be taken into account in assessing the conduct of the defendants and their treatment of the plaintiff.

The Court held that the payment of a $1,350,000 bonus to the father, the removal of the plaintiff from his position of employment and from his positions as director and officer of the various companies, and his exclusion from the day-to-day operations and management of the business and from any meaningful participation as a director and shareholder was oppressive. The other family members exercised their powers as directors in an oppressive manner that was unfairly prejudicial to the plaintiff and unfairly disregarded his interests as a shareholder, director and officer. The finding of oppression was upheld by the Ontario Court of Appeal which ordered that the father and brother buy out the complainant's shares — a "standard" remedy in oppression cases. The key question was, "what is the reasonable expectation of the shareholders?".

The *Naneff* decision has been referred to and followed in many cases since 1994.[208]

For a more detailed discussion of the oppression remedy, reference should be made to the materials on *Oppression* written by Howard Carr in "Trust and Fiduciary Issues".

(b) Right of Dissent

Where a corporation undergoes a reorganization or other fundamental change, it may trigger the right of dissent and buy-out which has been successfully used to prevent or delay legitimate corporate activity in the course of a reorganization or to cause shares of a dissenting shareholder to be purchased by the corporation at fair

---

[208] One recent case is that of *Kabutey v. New Form Manufacturing Co.*, [1999] O.J. No. 3635 (Ont. Sup. Ct. of Justice).

market value when the reorganization or other fundamental change was critical. This dissent right arises in a number of situations, such as:

(i) amendment of articles;

(ii) amalgamation;

(iii) continuance of a corporation to another jurisdiction; or

(iv) sale, lease or exchange of all or substantially all of a corporation's assets.

For a more detailed discussion of dissent rights, reference should be made to the materials on *Dissent Rights* written by Samantha Prasad and Glen Lewis in "Trust and Fiduciary Issues".

(c) Audit

Any shareholder could insist on an audit. A shareholder may get some comfort from knowing the financial information of the company is reviewed by an independent third party through the audit inspection rights as long as the shareholder does not consent to exemption of audit.

(d) Investigation

A shareholder could obtain an order for investigation of the corporation[209] if he or she felt there was some impropriety.

(e) Shareholders' Meeting

A shareholder holding 5% or more of the voting shares has the right to requisition meetings of shareholders for any legitimate purpose.[210]

Can a Shareholder Compel the Corporation to Declare Dividends?

It is implied that Ben will leave something to Anne-Marie. Perhaps Ben will leave Anne-Marie a life interest in his estate by way of spouse trust. Let us assume the freeze shares will not be fully redeemed by the time of Ben's death. Accordingly, his estate would control Hoots-Paw. Assume that the freeze shares bear discretionary dividends.

An issue arises as to what extent Anne-Marie can compel the trustees to keep an even hand between the life tenant and the residual beneficiaries. This is a difficult and complex area deserving separate treatment, not for this time. Other problems come to mind — for example, could she compel the trustees to bring proceedings against the corporation to declare dividends? If the estate controls Hoots-Paw, this is more likely to be the case; it may therefore be helpful if thin voting shares are created and willed by Ben to the children directly.

---

[209] See section 105 of the OBCA, and subsection 229(1), CBCA.

[210] See subsection 105(1) of the OBCA and section 143 of the CBCA.

Conclusion

The "family company" which does not have a shareholders' agreement is a ticking time bomb. While Ben still exerts persuasive influence, now is the time to set the tone for the business arrangements between the siblings. The shareholders' agreement is the appropriate framework. Waiting until Ben's death is a recipe for succession problems.

Family Law Considerations[211]

Family law issues must be considered in the context of Ben's intention to divorce Anne and his relationship with Anne-Marie as well as in the context of the distributions from the Trust and the subsequent freeze of Expensife. The following commentary relates to the laws of Ontario, governed by the *Family Law Act*.[212] Family law considerations vary from province to province.

Division of Property Under Ontario's Family Law Act

Before reviewing the specific issues in the case study, the FLA's division of property regime is summarized. Subsection 5(1) provides that when a divorce is granted or a marriage is declared a nullity, or when spouses are separated and there is no reasonable prospect that they will resume cohabitation, the spouse whose "net family property" is the lesser of the two net family properties is entitled to an equalization payment equal to one-half of the difference between the two. Subsection 5(2) provides that when a spouse dies and the net family property of the deceased spouse exceeds the net family property of the surviving spouse, the surviving spouse is entitled to one-half of the difference between the two. The surviving spouse would have to file an election pursuant to the provisions of section 6 in order to claim this equalization payment rather than take his or her entitlement under the will of the deceased or under the laws of intestacy. Finally, subsection 5(3) permits a cohabitating spouse to apply for an equalization payment "if there is a serious danger that [the other] spouse may improvidently deplete his or her net family property".

---

[211] This section was written by *Daniel Sandler*, Professor at the Faculty of Law, University of Western Ontario, London; Senior Research Fellow, Taxation Law and Policy Research Institute, Melbourne; and associated with *Minden Gross Grafstein & Greenstein LLP*, Toronto.

[212] R.S.O. 1990, c. F.3, as amended (the "FLA"). In this section all statutory references are to the FLA unless otherwise noted.

"Net family property" is defined in subsection 4(1) as the value of all property, except certain excluded property, that a spouse owns on the "valuation date"[213] after deducting the aggregate of:

- the spouse's debts and other liabilities on the valuation date; and

- the net value of property other than a matrimonial home, owned by the spouse on the date of marriage, calculated as of the date of marriage.[214]

"Property" is defined broadly in subsection 4(1)[215] and has been held to include an income interest in a trust,[216] a contingent interest in an estate,[217] and a discretionary interest in a trust.[218]

Subsection 4(2) excludes the value of certain property owned by a spouse on the valuation date. Significant among this excluded property are: property, other than a matrimonial home, acquired by gift or inheritance from a third person after the date of the marriage; income from such property if the donor or testator has expressly stated that it is to be excluded from the spouse's net family property; and property, other than a matrimonial home, into which such property can be traced. Property is also excluded if the spouses have so agreed by a domestic contract.

Essentially, where a property is excluded, its value on the valuation date (including any appreciation since the date it was acquired) is not subject to division, whereas a deduction entitles a spouse only to a reduction in determining net family property of the value of such property assuming that it was owned on the date of marriage. Any appreciation in value of such property and any income derived from

---

[213] Defined in subsection 4(1) as the earliest of: the date of separation; the date of divorce; the date that the marriage is declared a nullity; the date a spouse commences an action under subsection 5(3); and the date before the date of death.

[214] The calculation of net family property cannot be less than zero, so that if the net value of property at the valuation date is less than zero, or if the net value of the assets owned at the date of marriage exceeds the net value of assets at the valuation date, net family property will be deemed to be zero (see subsection 4(5)).

[215] "Property" is defined as:

    … any interest, present or future, vested or contingent, in real or personal property and includes,

        (*a*) property over which a spouse has, alone or in conjunction with another person, a power of appointment exercisable in favour of himself or herself,

        (*b*) property disposed of by a spouse but over which the spouse has, alone or in conjunction with another person, a power to revoke the disposition or a power to consume or dispose of the property, and

        (*c*) in the case of a spouse's rights under a pension plan that has vested under clause 20(1)(*a*) of the *Pension Benefits Act*, the employer's contributions to the spouse's pension.

[216] *Brinkos v. Brinkos* (1989), 20 R.F.L. (3d) 445 (Ont. C.A.).

[217] *DaCosta v. DaCosta* (1992), 40 R.F.L. (3d) 216 (Ont. C.A.).

[218] *Sagl v. Sagl* (1997), 31 R.F.L. (4th) 405, additional reasons (1997), 35 R.F.L. (4th) 107) (Ont. C.J. (Gen. Div.)).

such property after the date of marriage is subject to division. Subsection 4(3) provides that the onus of proving a deduction under the definition of net family property or an exclusion under subsection 4(2) is on the person claiming it.

The FLA does provide the court with some discretion to award a spouse more or less than half of the difference between the spouses' net family properties if the equalization payment otherwise determined "would be unconscionable" having regard to certain specified circumstances.[219] However, the Act does not confer any discretion on the courts to include in the valuation of net family property the value of any excluded property.

With this general scheme in mind, the particular facts of the case study can be considered. The general intent in this review is to consider ways in which the impact at the time of death or possible marriage breakdown of any of Ben and his children can be minimized. The facts suggest that Ben is concerned about family law implications of his relationship with Anne-Marie. Ben is also concerned about the state of Robin's marriage to John and about Larry's pending marriage to Desiré. In none of these cases has a domestic contract been completed, nor is one contemplated.[220]

Ben: Divorce, Cohabitation and Possible Remarriage

Ben's most significant assets are the voting freeze shares of Hoots-Paw and a substantial investment portfolio. This discussion is limited to these assets.

The first issue facing Ben is the family law consequences of his pending divorce from Anne, for which he has (surprisingly) not expressed concern. Leaving aside the issues of Anne's interest in the matrimonial home and support payments,[221] Anne will be entitled to an equalization payment under subsection 5(1). The net value of Ben's property on the valuation date (likely, the date of separation from Anne) should be relatively easy to determine, given the nature of Ben's assets: the freeze shares of Hoots-Paw, which have a fixed value of $10 million, and an investment portfolio (which presumably consists of publicly traded securities or other investments with a readily determinable value). However, the net value of his assets on the date he married Anne will be more difficult to determine, particularly 25 years after the fact. When Ben married Anne, he owned all of the common shares of Expensife, a company then in existence for about five years. His other assets at that time were probably minimal. It is in Ben's interest to value the common shares of

---

[219] Subsection 5(6).

[220] The most effective manner of avoiding the impact is for the person concerned to enter into a domestic contract specifically providing for an exclusion from that person's net family property of the specific assets, whether held directly or indirectly, through a trust, or in any manner whatever. The domestic contract should also exclude any income derived from such property, any property into which such property can be traced, and any income from such traced property. There are stringent rules in the FLA that must be complied with in order to ensure that the domestic contract is unimpeachable.

[221] *Family Law Act*, Parts II and III, respectively. For example, under section 24 of the FLA, a court may, by order, direct that one spouse have exclusive possession of the matrimonial home for such period as the court directs.

Expensife to be as high as possible; obviously, the reverse is true for Anne. The onus of proving the deduction is on Ben, under subsection 4(3). However, the fact that he is entitled to a deduction will not be in dispute, thus leaving the matter likely to a battle of valuators if it cannot be agreed upon.[222]

The more interesting question is whether there is anything else that Ben can do in order to minimize the amount of the equalization payment. Nothing prevents a spouse from disposing of property (e.g., by gift or otherwise) as long as the disposition was undertaken in good faith and not for the purpose of defeating a spouse's claim to such property (or an equalization payment based on the value of such property). So, for example, a court will look very closely at a gift or other transfer below market value at a time proximate to the valuation date (e.g., marriage breakdown or death), particularly if there is evidence that the transfer was done in order to remove such property from the transferor's net family property.[223] Thus, it is unlikely that a transfer of the freeze shares of Hoots-Paw and the investment portfolio to his children (or a trust for his children) would defeat Anne's claim (apart from the fact that such a transfer would have undesirable tax consequences to Ben). However, consider the result if Ben transfers the freeze shares and investment portfolio to a joint partner trust (with himself and Anne as the income beneficiaries).[224] It may be possible for Anne to challenge such a transfer as a

---

[222] The onus is certainly on Ben to lead expert evidence of the value of the common shares on the date of marriage. Although there is no onus on Anne to lead contradictory evidence, it may be difficult to impeach Ben's valuation provided that it was done by a credible valuator based on an accurate financial picture of the corporation at the time of marriage.

[223] In *Stone v. Stone* (2001), 55 O.R. (3d) 491 (Ont. C.A.), the court agreed that a husband's outright gift of certain business assets to his children on the eve of his death and without the knowledge of his wife was void against his wife pursuant to section 2 of the *Fraudulent Conveyances Act*. The court disagreed with the trial judge's conclusion ((1999), 46 O.R. (3d) 31 at 53) that the FLA "creates a creditor-debtor relationship which takes the form of a running account which becomes a settled account on separation or death". Rather, according to the Ontario Court of Appeal, the FLA creates a creditor-debtor relationship only on a valuation date (i.e., the time that gives rise to an equalization payment, such as permanent separation, death, or time at which an application is made under section 5(3)), but not prior to such time. In this case, the court concluded (at pp. 501-502) that "[b]ecause [Mrs. Stone] had the right to apply for equalization [pursuant to section 5(3)] at the time of the transfers, but was deprived of her ability to exercise that right by the actions of Mr. Stone and his children, the parties to the transfers, she was a 'creditor or other' within the meaning of [section 2 of the] *Fraudulent Conveyances Act*".

[224] The concept of a "joint partner trust" was first introduced in the December 17, 1999 Notice of Ways and Means Motion. See now subsections 73(1), 73(1.01) and 73(1.02) and related provisions. In order to be a joint partner trust, the trust must satisfy the following conditions:

1. at the time of the trust's creation, the individual settlor was alive and had attained the age of 65;

2. the trust was created after 1999;

3. the settlor or the settlor's spouse was, in combination with the spouse or the settlor, as the case may be, entitled to receive all of the income of the trust that arose before the later to die of the settlor and the settlor's spouse; and

4. no other person could, before the latter of those deaths, receive or otherwise obtain the use of any of the income or capital of the trust.

(continued on next page)

fraudulent conveyance (based on Stone), although the result is less clear because Anne would have an equal interest in the joint partner trust.[225] The transfer to a joint partner trust might give Ben more leverage in negotiating a settlement with Anne.

Ben is contemplating cohabitating with Anne-Marie and possibly marrying her. It is Ben's intention that his assets will ultimately be left to his children. Although his current will leaves his estate to his children, if Ben does marry Anne-Marie, his current will is automatically revoked.[226] It is therefore important that Ben prepare a new will if he marries Anne-Marie in order to avoid dying intestate. In his new will, it is contemplated that Ben will either divide his estate among his children or leave Anne-Marie a life interest in his estate with the remainder interest divided among his children *per stirpes*. In either case, if Ben predeceases Anne-Marie, the issue arises as to whether Anne-Marie has the right to an equalization payment under Part I of the FLA rather than her entitlement (if any) under the will and, if so, the amount of the equalization payment.

The family law implications of cohabitation versus marriage, particularly Anne-Marie's right to an equalization payment in the event that her relationship with Ben breaks down or Ben dies, varies significantly. The right to an equalization payment under Part I of the FLA is available only to a "spouse" as defined in subsection 1(1). Common-law spouses (which now include same-sex partners) are entitled to support under Part III of the FLA, but not to an equalization payment under Part I of the FLA. The fact that Ben and Anne-Marie may live together does not give her rights under Part I of the FLA. In *Nova Scotia (Attorney General) v. Walsh and Bona*,[227] the Supreme Court of Canada dismissed a constitutional challenge by an opposite-sex common law spouse to the definition of "spouse" in Nova Scotia's legislation governing the division of marital property. The definition in the Nova Scotia

---

(continued from previous page)
One benefit of a joint partner trust is that the settlor (i.e., Ben) can transfer property to the trust on a rollover basis.

[225] Careful consideration must be given to the terms of the trust in order to mitigate any argument that the trust was established in bad faith. For example, arm's length trustees should be appointed, both spouses should be given an equal income interest, and the power of encroachment in favour of both spouses should be the same. If the income interests are fully discretionary, with the only proviso being that all income must be distributed annually to the income beneficiaries, a court may not necessarily value the interests of Ben and Anne equally for FLA purposes.

[226] *Succession Law Reform Act*, R.S.O. 1990, c. S.26, section 16. His divorce from Anne does not automatically revoke his existing will. Under section 17 of the *Succession Law Reform Act*, where a person divorces after making a will, the will is declared a nullity to the extent that it includes a bequest to the former spouse, it appoints the former spouse an executor or trustee or it confers on the former spouse a general or special power of appointment, except when a contrary intention appears in the will.

[227] [2002] S.C.R. 325. According to the majority decision, the differing application of the legislation to married persons was not discriminatory because the decision to marry is a personal and fundamental choice and reflects the individual's freedom to choose alternative family forms and the legal consequences that flow therefrom. The reasoning of the majority suggests that a constitutional challenge to the division of property regime might have been successful where the individuals involved did not have the choice to marry (i.e., in the case of same-sex partners).

legislation (and the exclusion from the division of property for non-spouses) was, at that time, similar to that in the FLA.[228] Accordingly, Anne-Marie should be entitled to an equalization payment only in the event that Ben marries her.

Suppose Ben does marry Anne-Marie, creates a new will, as outlined above, and subsequently dies while still married to Anne-Marie. If, in these circumstances, Anne-Marie elects an equalization payment rather than her entitlement under the will, what will she be entitled to? Because the freeze shares of Hoots-Paw would have the same value at the date of marriage and the date of death (assuming that Ben still owns the shares at the time of death), they would not affect the equalization payment. However, Ben's net family property on the valuation date would include any increase in value of his investment portfolio (again, assuming that he still owns the investment portfolio).

As noted above, nothing prevents a spouse from disposing of property by gift or otherwise as long as the disposition was undertaken in good faith and not for the purpose of defeating a spouse's claim to such property (or an equalization payment based on the value of such property). Suppose that (as contemplated above) prior to his divorce from Anne, Ben transfers his freeze shares of Hoots-Paw and his investment portfolio to a joint partner trust, under which he and Anne have life interests and Ben's children are entitled to the capital after the later to die of Ben and Anne. Suppose further that Ben predeceases Anne-Marie (and Anne for that matter) and, under his will, he leaves Anne-Marie with a life interest in his estate. At the valuation date (i.e., the date before the date of Ben's death), Ben would no longer own the freeze shares or investment portfolio; all he would have is an income interest in the joint partner trust. The value of such interest is questionable, particularly if Ben was quite ill prior to his death.

Alternatively, if Ben does not establish a joint partner trust prior to his divorce from Anne, he could establish a joint partner trust shortly after his marriage to Anne-Marie. At that point in time, it is doubtful that Anne-Marie could argue that the establishment of the trust constitutes an improvident depletion under

---

[228] The decision of the Supreme Court of Canada in *Walsh and Bona* was a surprise to virtually all experts in the family law area, who expected the Supreme Court to agree with the Nova Scotia Court of Appeal that the provision was unconstitutional. Three provinces have amended their legislation to extend (or partially extend) the right to an equalization payment (or its equivalent) to common-law spouses. In 2000, Nova Scotia amended its legislation in order to permit same-sex and opposite-sex common-law partners to jointly sign and register a domestic-partner declaration that gives the signatories the same rights and obligations as spouses under various statutes, including the *Matrimonial Property Act*, R.S.N.S. 1989, c. 275, as amended: see Part II of the *Vital Statistics Act*, R.S.N.S. 1989, c. 494, as amended. In 1997, Saskatchewan repealed its *Matrimonial Property Act* and replaced it with the *Family Property Act*, S.S. 1997, c. F-6.3, which defines "spouse" to include both married persons and common-law partners. In 1997, British Columbia amended its *Family Relations Act*, R.S.B.C. 1996, c. 128, adding section 120.1, which permits common-law spouses to enter into an agreement (equivalent to a marriage agreement) to extend the matrimonial property and division of pension entitlement provisions of the statute to them as provided in the agreement. Ontario has not proposed any amendments to the FLA in this respect.

subsection 5(3) (and therefore a fraudulent conveyance). In the event of Ben's death or marriage breakdown, Ben would have an income interest in a joint partner trust (rather than ownership of the assets of the trust) and Anne-Marie would have an identical income interest in the same trust. These equal interests arguably neutralize each other in the context of determining the equalization payment to which Anne-Marie would be entitled. In effect, the joint partner trust should not only eliminate any need to pay Ontario probate taxes at the time of Ben's death, it may also eliminate Anne-Marie's right to an equalization payment *vis-à-vis* the investment portfolio.[229]

Ben's Children: Possible Divorce, Cohabitation, and Possible Marriage

The distribution of the common shares of Hoots-Paw from the Trust and the subsequent freeze of Expensife raises further family law issues for Ben's children, particularly Robin and Larry. Robin and Larry are beneficiaries under a fully discretionary family trust. Since the Trust's settlement, no dividends have been paid to the Trust and no allocations of capital have been made by the Trust.

Robin: Possible Divorce

Robin was married at the time that the Trust was settled. Accordingly, Robin can argue that any shares of Hoots-Paw that she acquires from the Trust are excluded property because they were acquired by gift after the date of marriage. We are not told how the Trust acquired the common shares of Hoots-Paw, and this may be crucial to any claim by Robin that the shares that she receives are excluded property under the FLA. Older estate freezes were often structured with the family trust borrowing money to acquire the common shares of the freeze corporation.[230] If this were the case, it would be extremely difficult for Robin to argue that she acquired the shares of Hoots-Paw by way of gift, even though she paid no consideration for her interest in the Trust. She, through the Trust, did not acquire the shares as a gift. Rather, the Trust paid consideration for the shares. In the absence of a domestic contract that specifically excluded these shares, Robin would have to argue that the distribution of the shares by the Trust to her constituted the

---

[229] It is possible that the transfer of the investment portfolio to an "alter ego trust" would have the same result, although Anne-Marie would not even have an income interest in the alter ego trust. The concern with an alter ego trust is that Ben is the only income beneficiary. If the trustees have a power to encroach on capital in favour of Ben, a family court may include the total value of the corpus of the trust in determining Ben's net family property on the valuation date (i.e., the date before his date of death), rather than including only the present value of his income interest.

[230] For example, the family trust would be settled with a gold coin, which the trust then pledges as security for a bank loan used to buy the common shares. At a later time (e.g., approximately one year after the freeze), the freeze corporation would pay a dividend on the common shares in an amount sufficient to repay the loan plus any accrued interest.

gift and that this gift occurred after her marriage. However, the preponderance of the case law tends to suggest that a gift to a beneficiary of a discretionary trust occurs at the time of the settlement of or other gift of property to the trust rather than at a later time when the beneficiary receives such property from the trust or when the trustees exercise their discretion by allocating income or capital to the beneficiary.[231] It is for this reason that it is now recommended that where married children are to benefit from an estate freeze, the growth shares of the freeze corporation be gifted to the family trust (or directly to the married children) or that the shares be acquired using money gifted to the trust (or children).[232]

Larry: Possible Marriage

Larry presents similar family law issues. He is currently cohabiting with Desiré and intends to marry her in six months. Suppose that at least some shares of Hoots-Paw will be distributed to Larry. If this distribution occurs after Larry marries Desiré, then in determining Larry's net family property at a subsequent point in time, Larry would only be entitled to a deduction of the value of Larry's interest in the Trust at the date of marriage, as opposed to the value of the shares of Hoots-Paw received from the Trust. At the date of marriage, all that Larry has is a fully discretionary interest in a family trust. Even though the common shares of Hoots-Paw had a fair market value of approximately $25 million at this time, it is arguable that Larry's discretionary interest in the Trust has only a negligible value.[233] "Value" is not defined in the FLA, although the majority of cases support a "fair value" concept — the value that is just and equitable in the circumstances — rather than "fair market value".[234]

Only one case has considered the issue of the value of a discretionary interest in the context of an equalization payment under the FLA. In *Sagl v. Sagl*,[235] the Ontario Court of Justice (General Division) accepted counsel for the husband's "compromise submission" under which the value of the discretionary interest in a family trust was determined (both at the date of marriage and the valuation date) by

---

[231] This issue is considered in more detail in Daniel Sandler, "Family Law and the Family Jewels" (1991), vol. 39, no. 3 *Canadian Tax Journal* 513-536. Recent cases under the FLA, such as *Armstrong v. Armstrong* (1997), 34 R.F.L. (4th) 38 (Ont. CJ. (Gen. Div.)) and *Sagl v. Sagl, supra* footnote 8, support this conclusion.

[232] The terms of the trust and the gift should be structured in order to avoid the application of the attribution rules in sections 74.1 through 74.4 and the potential application of subsection 75(2).

[233] In *Leedale v. Lewis*, [1982] 3 All E.R. 808 (H.L.), Lord Scarman indicated (at 818) that a discretionary interest in a family trust "is, according to the evidence (and in common sense), negligible".

[234] See, generally, Stephen R. Cole and Andrew J. Freedman, *Property Valuation and Income Tax Implications of Marital Dissolution* (Toronto: Carswell, 1995).

[235] *Supra*, footnote 8.

dividing the value of the corpus of the trust by the number of discretionary beneficiaries at the two dates. Whether or not this solution will be followed by other courts remains to be seen. The court's approach in *Sagl* is difficult to substantiate as a general principle of trust law,[236] although the result may be considered "just and equitable" in the context of an equalization payment.[237]

---

[236] L.H. Wolfson, counsel for Mr. Sagl, elaborated on the issue in his case comment, "*Sagl v. Sagl:* Valuation of an Interest in a Discretionary Trust under Ontario's *Family Law Act*" (1998-99), 16 *C.F.L.Q.* 521-531. He quotes Hovius and Youdan, who suggest:

> [I]n many cases the extreme difficulty of determining the likelihood of the power being exercised, or the extent of any exercise, and the consequent uncertainty in the value of the interest, will have the result that no value can be put on the property, whether for the purpose of including it in a spouse's net family property or of including it in the value of property owned on the date of marriage.

> [B. Hovius and T.G. Youdan, *The Law of Family Property* (Toronto: Carswell, 1991), at 265.]

Wolfson cites Cullity for the following principles in determining the value of a discretionary interest in a trust:

> For the purposes of the Family Law Act, the circumstances to be considered in valuing an interest that depends upon, or may be affected by, the exercise of a discretion should include ... the intentions of the settlor, the fiduciary responsibilities of the holders of the power, the number of beneficiaries and, perhaps, the manner in which the power has been exercised in the past.

> [M.C. Cullity, Q.C., *Trust Assets in a Family Law Case* (Canadian Bar AssociationOntario, Continuing Legal Education, 2 October 1995), at 17.]

See also Lorne H. Wolfson and Ikka Delamer, "The Valuation of Trusts Under the *Family Law Act*" (2002) vol. 20, no. 2 *Canadian Family Law Quarterly* 97-118 at 105-117. The cases discussed by Wolfson and Delamer indicate that different results may occur in other provinces due to differences in definition of property subject to division (or exclusions therefrom). The decisions also cast some doubt on the correctness of the decision in *Sagl.*

[237] Under section 9, courts have broad discretion in choosing the method of satisfying an equalization payment. An "if and when" order, under which the paying spouse would pay the recipient spouse a portion of any realization from a particular asset, has been used in cases in which the asset in question was difficult to value or where contingencies made it uncertain as to when the paying spouse would receive the asset in question. Under paragraph 9(1)(*d*), the court can order that the paying spouse be trustee for the other spouse to the extent of the other spouse's interest in the asset. This result may be appropriate where the discretionary interest in a family trust represents a significant portion of a spouse's net family property.

Due to the uncertainty involved, it is recommended that the Trust distribute the common shares prior to the date of Larry's wedding.[238] Furthermore, the subsequent freeze of Expensife should take place after Larry's wedding in order to better ensure that Larry's interest in Trust No. 2 (and any assets distributed to him from such Trust) are excluded from his net family property. In this context, a gift should be made of the growth shares of Expensife to Trust No. 2 and to Robin, if she is to receive a direct interest, in order to bolster the position that such shares are excluded from the net family property of Larry and Robin.

Alan

Because Alan is not yet married, there is little that can be done at this time to protect any post-marriage growth of his interests in Hoots-Paw and Expensife from a potential spousal claim. In the absence of a domestic contract, he will be entitled to a deduction of the value of his shares of Hoots-Paw (distributed from the Trust) and the value of his interest in Trust No. 2 in determining his net family property (although determining the latter value may be problematic). In effect, what is not protected is any increase in the value of his shares of Hoots-Paw after marriage (reflecting any increase in the value of the investments, other than the shares of Expensife, held by Hoots-Paw) and the future growth of Expensife reflected in the common shares held by Trust No. 2. In the absence of a domestic contract, consideration should be given to additional planning, such as a further re-freeze, in the event that Alan plans to marry.

---

[238] As noted above, the right to an equalization payment under Part I of the FLA is available only to a married person and not a common-law spouse. The fact that Larry and Desiré have been living together for four years does not give her rights under Part I of the FLA. Of course, the FLA would not govern the relationship of Larry and Desiré if they continue to live in California. California's Family Code is based on property rights ("community property") rather than the sort of debtor-creditor relationship in many other jurisdictions (including Ontario). The Family Code applies only to married persons, not persons in a common-law relationship. Under the Family Code, property excluded from community property ("separate property") includes property owned before marriage, property acquired by gift or inheritance after marriage, and any income from such property (Family Code, section 770). Thus, generally speaking, the growth in value of an asset owned at the time of marriage is excluded from community property, unlike under the FLA. However, there may be circumstances in which a California court might conclude that the increase in value over the course of a marriage of property owned before marriage is, in part, attributable to the work of the spouse non-owner and therefore include the property in community property. For common-law relationships, California courts have developed the concept of "palimony", under which a common-law spouse may acquire property rights if he or she can prove that there was an express or implied contract between the common-law partners through which such rights were acquired. The jurisprudence is generally traced back to the California Supreme Court decision in *Marvin v. Marvin* (1976), 18 Cal.3d 660, 557 P.2d 106.

Appendix A

Checklists

Estate Freeze Checklist

❏ If financing of living expenses requires depletion of capital, ensure that the individual has sufficient capital to meet their cash flow requirements (include additional analysis in Chapter 7).

❏ Is a full or partial freeze of parent's assets desirable?

❏ If a partial freeze is desirable, should parent retain assets personally or should parent acquire common shares in the freeze company?

❏ Have independent formal valuations of the property being transferred been obtained from a qualified appraiser/valuator supporting the fair market value? (Copies should be attached.)

❏ Have the various income attribution rules been considered? (Subsections 75(2), 56(4.1) — 56(4.3), sections 73 — 74.5.)

❏ Where applicable, has an agreement been prepared?

  • Does it contain a price adjustment clause?

  • Have alternatives been considered which might increase the non-share consideration that the person implementing the freeze will receive?

❏ Have family law implications been considered?

❏ Transfer of assets (see Worksheet B, from Appendix D)

  • If property is transferred to a corporation using section 85, is the corporation a taxable Canadian corporation?

  • Is the property being transferred "eligible" property for the purpose of section 85?

  • Is the elected amount within the lower and upper limit?

- Does the corporation have appropriate authorized share capital?

- If unrecorded goodwill or other assets are transferred to the corporation, has a minimum of $1 been elected?

- Have stop-loss rules been considered in respect of transferred assets?

- If accounts receivable have been transferred, has an election under section 22 been considered and has Form T2022 been filed?

- Has Form T2057 been filed?

❏ Internal and Holding Company Freezes

- Have the benefits of a holding company freeze versus an internal freeze been considered, e.g., creditor protection, additional corporations/compliance?

- If there is significant cost base in the pre-existing shares, have the different methodologies been considered in respect of the manner in which the cost base is sequestered? For example, if the freeze is followed by a spin-out reorganization, a stock dividend freeze may ensure that there is minimal loss of cost base.

- If section 86 is used, have the prerequisites been considered, including whether there is a reorganization, shares of all classes are disposed of, shares constitute capital property.

- If a section 87 (amalgamation) or 51 (conversion of shares) is used, ensure that no consideration other than shares is received.

- If a holding company freeze is used, have the effects of section 84.1 been considered, especially if non-share consideration is received?

- Has the capital gains exemption been considered, particularly, crystallization?

❏ Share conditions (see Worksheets C and D in Appendix D)

- Attributes of retractable freeze shares are received as a consideration:

  (a) Are the shares redeemable/retractable based on the FMV of the transferred or exchanged assets?

  (b) Do the shares have priority in the event of a wind-up, liquidation or redemption?

  (c) Do the shares have a non-cumulative dividend right, either fixed or to a ceiling, usually based on the redemption/retraction amount?

  (d) Is there an anti-waiver clause, to the effect that dividends can be paid on one class of shares to the exclusion of another class of shares, which would otherwise have the right to receive a dividend in a particular period?

(e) Is the corporation prohibited from paying dividends on other classes of shares where the dividend would reduce the fair market value of the retractable shares below their redemption amount?

(f) Does the holder of the freeze shares retain the desired voting control?

(g) Are the shares voting on matters related to a change to their rights, preferences, conditions or limitations?

(h) Are there any restrictions on the transferability of the freeze shares (other than as required by corporate law)?

(i) Has consideration been given to segmenting voting rights (e.g., by a separate class of "thin voting" shares)?

- Has an amount been "specified" for the purposes of subsection 191(4)?

- Do the articles of incorporation or amendment provide for adjusting the retraction price, where a price adjustment clause is invoked?

- Have computations of the reduction in paid-up capital been completed?

- (Section 84.1, subsections 85(2.1) and 86(2). Attach work sheets and other supporting calculations.)

- Has the stated capital of the issued shares been limited to the paid-up capital of the shares?

- Has consideration been given to post-mortem procedures to avoid double taxation, including the application of stop-loss rules and the relationship to taxable preferred share rules?

❏ Trusts

- Where a trust will be used to hold property, has consideration been given to having the trust settled and growth shares acquired in a manner to avoid attribution?

- Has the trust been settled with non-income producing property (such as a gold coin)?

- Have contingent beneficiaries been identified who would receive the trust property in the event that the primary beneficiaries are no longer living?

- Has subsection 75(2)/107(4.1) been considered (e.g., is the trust irrevocable)?

- Does the trust prohibit the distribution of income to a designated person (i.e., if the corporate attribution rules may be applicable)?

- Does the trust require that the trustees be residents of Canada?

- Has thought been made to the distribution of growth shares before the 21st anniversary of the trust?

- Is there a shareholders' agreement in place in respect of the family business in the event the family trust is no longer in place?

- Consideration should be given to ensuring the trust is "related" for tax purposes, e.g., to facilitate future spin-outs.

- Has consideration been given to a "bail-out structure", e.g., wherein a freezer is a beneficiary of the trust? If so, consider subsections 75(2) and 107(4.1) carefully.

❏ Other Alternatives

- Is there a method available whereby part of the appreciation of the corporation is diverted back to the Freezor without modifying the corporate structure, i.e. a "melt" (e.g., payment of bonuses, rent, dividends)?

- Is it possible to unwind an estate freeze, i.e. a "thaw", whereby the children or family trust transfers the shares back to the Freezor so that the Freezor may take advantage of the lifetime capital gain exemption, e.g., a "gel" whereby the growth shares are reverted (or "bailed out") to the Freezor by including the Freezor as a discretionary beneficiary?

- Would it be more advantageous to "refreeze", i.e., modify the estate freeze rather than unwind it, e.g., at a lower value, by declaring a stock dividend as a "downstream" freeze, or as a "reverse" freeze?

Checklist for a Subsection 85(1) Rollover

The following checklist, from H. Kellough and P. McQuillan's *Taxation of Private Corporations and Their Shareholders* (3rd ed., Canadian Tax Foundation) is reproduced with permission.

❏ Ensure that real estate is not inventory.

❏ Ensure that capital property that is real estate (or an interest therein or an option thereon) owned by non-residents is not transferred, unless the property is used in a business in Canada and certain other conditions are met (subsection 85(1.2)).

❏ Receivables cannot form part of a section 85 election if they are part of a section 22 election.

❏ Review for fully depreciated assets such as class 12 or class 29, and elect nominal values (for example, $1, but not nil). Farming inventory of a cash-basis taxpayer can be transferred, but within certain limitations (paragraph 85(1)(c.2)).

❏ Review assets transferred for existence of intangibles (for example, goodwill) and elect, in any event, a nominal amount.

❏ Review assets for V-day values to increase elected amounts.

❏ Ensure that the transferee qualifies as a taxable Canadian corporation — that is, it is a company incorporated in Canada or resident here continuously since June 18, 1971, and is not exempt from tax under Part I of the Act.

❏ Ensure that shares are specified as part of the consideration given by the corporate transferee.

❏ Allocate debts transferred to specific assets or prorate to ensure that non-share consideration or "boot" does not exceed elected values.

❏ Where capital property that is real property is transferred by a non-resident, ensure that the specific requirements set out in subsection 85(1.1) are met.

❏ File election (Form T2057 or T2058) by the earliest time at which any of the parties must file a tax return. For a partnership, the relevant taxation year is that of the partners.

❏ The transferor must file the election. Observe the specific requirements and formalities set out in the election forms and in Information Circular 76-19R3, dated June 17, 1996.

❏ When property is held in a co-tenancy, separate elections must be filed.

❏ Ensure that the "boot" does not exceed the elected values or the fair market value of the asset.

❏ Ensure that the consideration received is equal to the fair market value of the property to avoid the benefit provisions of paragraph 85(1)(*e*.2). Consider obtaining a ruling where uncertainty exists.

❏ Consider the use of a price adjustment clause in the agreement of purchase and sale to avoid the application of paragraph 85(1)(*e*.2) or subsection 84(1).

❏ Consider PUC restrictions and a possible grind of PUC under subsection 85(2.1).

❏ Ensure low PUC and high-redemption shares to avoid the adverse effect of section 84.1. Review the jurisdiction of incorporation to ensure that such shares can be created and issued for corporate law purposes.

❏ If the transferor holds pre-1972 shares of the transferee, review the transfer for the effect of change in value of pre-1972 and post-1971 shareholdings on potential future gains from the disposition of shares.

❏ Review fair market value of property transferred in to ensure that:

- PUC and other consideration is not increased over the fair market value (FMV) of property (subsections 85(2.1), 84(1), and 15(1));

- the boot does not exceed the FMV (subsection 15(1) benefit);

- the elected amount does not exceed the FMV (paragraph 85(1)(*c*));

- if the property is depreciable property, the elected amount is not less than the least of the UCC, the cost, and the FMV of property (a similar limitation is applicable to eligible capital property); and

- the paragraph 85(1)(*e*.2) (benefit) is not operative.

Consider also the price adjustment clause in the agreement of purchase and sale and the rights and restrictions attaching to the preferred shares.

❏ Consider the stop-loss rules (e.g., subsections 14(12), 40(3.4), and 40(3.5)).

❏ Review the implications of GST and provincial sales tax. Most provinces provide for tax-free rollovers between related taxpayers where there is at least 95 per cent common ownership.

❏ Review elections under the *Excise Tax Act* to determine whether a transaction may be exempt from the GST. For transfers of real property, ensure that conditions in the ETA section 221 are met for a waiver of the GST.

❏ Provincial land transfer taxes normally will apply. Refer to the relevant legislation for exceptions.

❏ Review CCA requirements. The transferor cannot obtain a CCA claim if the transfer is prior to year-end, but may be able to claim a terminal loss in certain arms length situations. The 50 per cent rule may apply, and the transferee must pro-rate the claim on regulation 1100(1)(*a*) classes if the taxation year is less than 12 months. If only some assets are transferred, consider whether a disproportionate part of UCC can be transferred.

❏ Consider the exclusion of depreciables from election — for example, to escape subsection 85(5) and/or other CCA inheritance provisions.

❏ Ensure that all adjustments in computing the cost amount of an asset are taken into consideration — for example, a subsection 83(1) dividend received on shares or newly aquired liabilities, such as a mortgage.

❏ Review for the existence of rental properties or leasing properties. The transferee may not qualify as a principal business corporation, but the transferor may.

❏ Note regulations 1102(14) and (14.1) respecting retention of pre-existing CCA classes or separate sub-classes, and regulation 1100(19) respecting leasing properties. Note carefully whether a non-arm's length relationship and/or section 85 are prerequisites.

❏ Note the section 22 election in respect of receivables. Review Interpretation Bulletin IT-188R.

❏ If the transferor is a non-resident and the property is shares of a Canadian corporation, review for the application of section 212.1.

❏ Consider the effect on foreign affiliates — for example, regulation 5905(5)(*a*) operates if shares of a foreign affiliate are transferred.

❏ Consider whether section 85.1 applies to the transaction.

❏ If the transferor is a non-resident, consider the section 116 certificate requirement.

❏ If a non-resident is transferring taxable Canadian property to a public company, consider the effect of paragraph 85(1)(*i*), which deems public company shares to be taxable Canadian property.

❏ Consider the necessity of using section 85, if a non-resident has treaty protection concerning capital gains.

❏ With respect to specific assets, consider whether a section 85 election is desirable in the light of

- capital gains to use capital losses; and

- a sale of goodwill to the business and the extraction of the tax-free portion.

❏ Where the receivables give rise to reserves under paragraph 20(1)(*n*) or subparagraph 40(1)(*a*)(iii), a section 85 election will negate the right to take a reserve. Review whether other differences between accounting treatment and tax reporting will create adverse implications (such as warranty reserves).

❏ If debt is issued, consider the thin capitalization rules where the transferor is a specified non-resident (see subsection 18(4)).

❏ Consider the effects of a change in control — for example:

- a deemed year-end;

- a potential loss of capital dividends, if public controls; and

- a loss of net capital loss carryovers and restrictions on non-capital loss carryovers.

❏ Review corporate legal agreements, leases, etc., to ensure that there are no restrictions on transferability.

❏ Consider whether a change in corporate name and style will be necessary.

❏ If non-residents may be involved, ensure that the transfer does not have adverse offshore effects.

❏ Consider whether it is necessary to have a corporation repay any present or future government assistance.

❏ Review for the transferability of all fringe benefit programs, pension plans, etc. Also, advise appropriate government authorities, transfer any insurance policies, etc.

❏ Consider whether the transfer can be regarded as a dividend strip and whether the GAAR may apply. Review subsection 55(2) and section 245.

❏ Review the corporate histories of the purchaser and vendor concerning

- the determination of the PUC of transferred shares regarding section 84.1;

- the existence of a previous PUC deficiency; and

- previous non-arm's length share or asset transfers.

❏ Ensure that all partners have signed the subsection 85(2) election.

❏ File the appropriate Quebec election forms where the corporation is subject to Quebec income tax.

❏ Determine whether the purchase of assets gives rise to Investment Canada implications. If so, obtain the necessary approvals.

❑ Where eligible capital property or depreciable assets are the subject of any election, review the order in which the disposition is to take place (paragraph 85(1)(*e*.1)).

❑ Review the effect on any government assistance programs, if substantial business assets are being transferred.

❑ Ensure compliance with the bulk sales acts of the province(s).

❑ Ensure that the accounting treatment has been thoroughly reviewed, especially where there is a non-arm's length transaction, including step-ups in values on financial statements. Deferred taxes associated with the transferred assets may give rise to accounting complexities.

❑ Are there identical capital properties acquired partly before and partly after V-day that should be elected in two separate elections?

❑ Review the consequences of a different company's carrying on operations:

- the repayment of government subsidies, which will not increase costs of property subsection 13(7.1) and paragraph 53(2)(*k*));

- the loss of ITAR 21 protection for non-government rights;

- the loss of replacement property rollovers;

- Canadian securities and commodities elections (Interpretation Bulletin IT-346R, November 20, 1978);

- a section 34 election;

- scientific research carryovers;

- the capitalization of three previous years' interest (to be made only by the taxpayer who incurred the expense (section 21));

- loss utilization;

- creation of a common interest in rental properties so that the cost is under $50,000; and

- the realization of gains and losses on liabilities (for example, foreign exchange).

❑ Review the general structure of the transaction:

- ensure that the financing arrangements between the transferor and the transferee are structured to ensure maximum tax benefits — for example, if rental or leasing stop-loss rules apply, their effect may be mitigated if the transferor bears the interest costs personally, since additional income will be in the corporation;

- choose assets to create a principal leasing, rental, or farming company;

- consider the effect on non-qualifying and active business tax deductions — for example, ensure that segmentation is necessary;

- consider any possible double taxation resulting from the transfer;

- assess the possibility of trapped losses;

- tailor income flows to maximize the investment tax credit, charitable donations, manufacturing, and production;

- consider other tax rates — provincial, capital, corporate partnership rules, etc.;

- consider year-ends and the effect on tax instalments, etc.

Here are some other additional points that may be taken into consideration:

❏ Consider eligibility for the capital gains exemption, including whether the corporation will qualify as a small business corporation, the capital gains anti-avoidance rules in subsections 110.6(8) and (9).

❏ Consider the effect of the transfer on capital gains status, e.g., if the transferred property is to be sold shortly, or if the shares of the transferee corporation are to be sold (see section 54.2).

❏ Ensure that the elected amount includes acquired liabilities (i.e., a mortgage).

❏ If the eligible property is in the form of a holdback, then ensure that the holdback is included in the taxpayer's income within the required period.

❏ Other assets that are not eligible include:

- a "specified participating interest" — i.e., in a FIE;

- a life insurance policy, and

- a right to income (e.g., a dividend receivable)

❏ If the transferor is paying the transferee corporation to provide services that the transferor had originally agreed to provide, consider filing a subsection 22(24) election.

❏ Consider subsection 85(1.11) with regard to anti-avoidance issues pertaining to foreign resource property.

Appendix B

CRA Documents

Revenue Canada (CRA) Round Table Questions and Answers

The following questions and the CRA's responses have been extracted from CCH Canadian Limited's *Revenue Canada Round Table*.[1]

1980, Q.8 — Transfer of Property to Corporation by Shareholder

Will the CRA consider ruling favourably on a proposed transaction where a taxpayer holding appreciated capital property transfers such property to a corporation on a rollover basis under subsection 85(1) and the acquiring corporation immediately thereafter sells the property at a profit? The issue is whether the profit will still be considered to be a capital gain in the light of the short holding period of the corporation.

Department's Response

Whether or not a particular transaction is of an income nature or a capital transaction is a question of fact and can only be determined upon the review of the facts in a particular case. The fact that capital property has been transferred to a corporation pursuant to subsection 85(1) of the Act and the corporation immediately thereafter sells the property at a profit, will not, by itself, preclude capital gains treatment on the sale. Where it is reasonable to consider, from the particular facts, that the transaction is a capital transaction, the department will generally take this view. Although the department will consider a favourable ruling on a proposed set of transactions such as the above, a specific ruling on whether or not the transaction was of an income nature or a capital transaction cannot be given. This is in line with the exclusion in paragraph 14(g) of Information Circular 70-6R5.[2]

---

[1] For questions pertaining to assets that are eligible for the section 85 rollover, see "Eligible Property" section in Chapter 2 on p. 35.

[2] See also 1986, Q.20; 1984, Q.49; and 1983, Q.24.

1980, Q.14 — Price Adjustment Clauses

(1) Typically, when a corporation acquires property from a shareholder as part of an estate planning transaction and the corporation issues shares to the transferor that are subject to a price adjustment clause, what is the CRA's present policy — should the value of the property transferred ultimately be determined to be different from the nominal value of the shares issued?

(2) Will the CRA permit a corresponding change to be made in the elected amount in respect of property which has been transferred to a corporation subject to an election under subsection 85(1) of the Act at the adjusted cost base estimated by the taxpayer, when there is a subsequent adjustment in the amount of the adjusted cost base of the property transferred?

(3) What is the CRA's policy concerning any subsequent adjustment that may be made in either the number of shares so issued or the price at which they may be redeemed? Would the CRA also comment on the experience of the willingness of taxpayers to give notification of the existence of price adjustment clauses?

Department's Response

(1) When a corporation acquires property from a shareholder as part of an estate planning transaction and the corporation issues shares to the transferor that are subject to a price adjustment clause, we have no policy concerns regarding the nominal value of the shares issued should there be a subsequent change in the determined value of the property transferred. Our concern is to ensure that the price adjustment clause provides for a change in the redemption amount of such shares equal to any change in the fair market value of the property as subsequently determined.

(2) The only circumstance in which an adjustment to the elected amount can be made is set forth in paragraph 18 of Information Circular 76-19R3. The agreed amount expressed in dollars will be adjusted where

(a) taxpayers have indicated on the election form that the amount is the estimated ACB,

(b) the ACB is based on V-day value, and

(c) a reasonable attempt was made to determine V-day value correctly.

It should be noted that the adjustment to the agreed amount would be to reflect the change in the V-day value only. Other errors and omissions would not be picked up in calculating the ACB.

(3) Where an advance ruling request incorporates a price adjustment clause (to provide for the event where the fair market value is finally determined to be different upon reassessment and/or a tax court adjudication), the Department is prepared to issue favourable rulings provided the taxpayers agree to vary their redemption amount of the frozen shares where possible and/or make cash payments — all with retroactive effect to the transaction date (freeze). In our opinion, the cancellation or

issue of additional frozen shares carries with it a host of technical difficulties that are best avoided from the point of view of both the taxpayers and the Department.

We are unable to comment on the experience of the willingness of taxpayers to give notification of the existence of price adjustment clauses. It is the choice of the taxpayers whether or not they agree to the operation of a price adjustment clause. In order for the price adjustment clause to be operative, the Department must be notified by a letter attached to a taxpayer's return for the year in which the property was transferred. This policy is reflected in Interpretation Bulletin IT-169 and, where the taxpayers have not done so, they should inform the Department immediately if they wish to have the clause considered.

In an advance ruling application, a taxpayer may simply state that the transaction is subject to a price adjustment clause. For it to be operative, however, all the terms and conditions of IT-169 must be satisfied.[3]

1983, Q.3 — Issues Concerning Elections

It has been suggested that the Department has changed its assessing practice with respect to section 85 elections in that one district office now "insists on an estimate of fair market value being shown on the election form, otherwise the election will be considered invalid".

Our policy in this respect has not changed. As indicated in paragraph 13 of Information Circular 76-19R3,[4] fair market value at the time of disposition is a requirement of filing elections under section 85 and omission of the required amount will result in an invalid election. This information is essential where late filing penalties, gifting, or possible deemed dividends may be involved. We are now simply enforcing the requirement to eliminate the taxpayer contact that is required if the information is missing. However, as indicated in Information Circular 76-19R3, we do not insist on a precise valuation of the properties transferred. An estimate of fair market value is acceptable, although the basis for the estimate should be retained should it be required by the Department.

Several provisions in the Act provide for elections to be made by a taxpayer in the return of income without any prescribed form or manner for making the election. In these cases, it is the Department's general position that the election should take the form of a letter attached to the return for the year in which the election is made. In the absence of such a letter or some positive evidence in the return that the election is being made, each case will have to be decided on its own merits. The Department will accept that a valid election has been made when the taxpayer's actions clearly indicate the intention to have the elective provision apply. The taxpayer will be expected to confirm his intention in writing when requested to do so.

---

[3] With respect to the second question above, see also 1981, Q.6(1). With respect to the third question, see 1990, Q.58.

[4] IC 76-19R3, Transfer of Property to a Corporation under Section 85, November 13, 1978.

1983, Q.24 — "Section 85 Rolls"

We have been asked to clarify the position given in our response to question 8 of the 1980 Round Table in which we were asked whether we would rule favourably on a proposed transaction where a taxpayer holding appreciated capital property transfers such property to a corporation on a rollover basis under subsection 85(1) and the acquiring corporation immediately thereafter sells the property at a profit. The issue was, of course, whether the profit would still be considered to be a capital gain in the light of the short holding period of the recipient corporation.

Our response was intended to indicate that we were prepared to accept the 85(1) roll and would also accept that the profit would still be a capital gain, despite the short holding period, where the roll was between two sister corporations or a parent and its controlled subsidiary and the ultimate sale was to an arm's length third party. We confirm this position and are now prepared to rule in those specific circumstances.[5]

1984, Q.49 — Capital Property

What is the CRA's present policy with respect to the treatment to be afforded to the income generated in the hands of a company that acquires capital property from an individual who is its controlling shareholder (pursuant to section 85 of the Act) and within a very short time thereafter disposes of said property? Will the property so acquired continue to constitute capital property to the company, and in consequence, will the gains incurred by the corporation upon the disposition of the property be treated as capital gains?

Department's Response

At last year's tax conference, we stated that where the transfer is within a corporate group, we were prepared to accept the transfer pursuant to subsection 85(1) of the Act and to accept that the nature of the property transferred will not have changed solely as a result of the transfer. The department is prepared to accept this general position with respect to an individual who transfers capital property to his or her corporation.

Whether or not the anti-avoidance provisions in the Act would be applicable to any such transfer can be determined only with respect to the facts of the particular case.[6]

1984, Q.78 — Clerical Error — Section 85 Elections

What is a clerical error with respect to section 85 elections, and why is the Department so strict about accepting amended elections?

---

[5] See also 1980, Q.8; 1981, Q.7; 1984, Q.49; and 1986, Q.20.

[6] See also 1980, Q.8; 1983, Q.24; and 1986, Q.20.

Department's Response

It appears that today most of the problems with rollovers are in the following areas:

(1) *Errors in the calculation of the adjusted cost base.* For example, in the case of the omission of tax-free dividends (subsection 83(1)) on the disposition of shares, a taxable capital gain results to the transferor provided the year of the transaction is not statute-barred.

(2) *Estimated Valuation Day values.* Where the elected amount equals V-day value and it is subsequently determined that the V-day value is less, a capital gain will result to the transferor. Paragraph 14 of Information Circular 76-19R3 gives relief, provided the taxpayer has made a reasonable effort to determine V-day value.

(3) *Inadvertent falling into the gifting provision.* Under paragraph 85(1)(e.2) — estate freeze plan — where the fair market value (FMV) of the operating company's common shares exceeds the FMV of the preferred shares, other consideration taken back could result in an increase of the elected amount by this excess and a gift to the common shareholders of the holding company, resulting in a capital gain to the transferor. Relief is provided administratively to increase the redemption value or number of preferred shares taken back, especially where a price adjustment clause was contained in the agreement.

(4) *Late-filed elections.* These will be accepted as valid provided they are filed within three years of the due date of the first election and the applicable amount of the penalty is paid (maximum $4,000). There is no relief.

Revenue Canada was asked if it is willing to give any administrative relief in these matters over and above that already offered in the *Income Tax Act* and Information Circular 76-19R. Revenue Canada generally adheres to the rules provided in section 85 and its position as set out in the above-mentioned circular.

In situations where the tax consequences of an election were unintended and extremely harsh, Revenue Canada is prepared to provide taxpayers with administrative relief only in exceptional circumstances. Any elections that result in inequity or hardship can only be considered on a case-by-case basis.

Once the proposed changes to subsection 85(7.1) are passed, amended elections and elections where the prescribed late-filing period has expired will be accepted by Revenue Canada where it would be just and equitable to do so.

1986, Q.20 — Sale of Shares: Subsection 85(1)

What is the CRA's position regarding shares that are sold soon after their acquisition by a taxpayer, where that taxpayer received the shares as consideration for the transfer of capital property into a corporation pursuant to subsection 85(1)?

Department's Response

Generally, if the sale of the capital property would have been on account of capital, then similarly the sale of the shares will be on account of capital. The nature of the property transferred and the reason for the transfer may, however, indicate that the gain on the share sale is not a capital gain. For instance, if the property transferred is depreciable property, the gain on the sale of the shares may, depending on the circumstances, be on account of income. The line of cases — *Fraser* (*Fraser v. M.N.R.*, 64 DTC 5224 (S.C.C.)), *Belle-Isle* (*Belle-Isle v. M.N.R.*, 66 DTC 5100 (S.C.C.)), and *Gibson Bros.* (*Gibson Bros. Industries Ltd. v. M.N.R.*, 72 DTC 6190 (F.C.T.D.)) could be relevant with respect to the disposition of depreciable property and inventory.[7]

1986, Q.33 — Late-Filed Elections: Subsection 85(7.1), Procedures and Guidelines

Subsection 85(7.1) permits a late-filed election or an amended election where, in the opinion of the minister, the circumstances of a case are such that this would be just and equitable. Would you please outline the procedures that taxpayers should follow to file an election beyond the day that is three years after the day on which the election was required to be made or an amended election? Would you please outline the guidelines the minister uses in determining whether it would be just and equitable to allow a late-filed or amended election?

Department's Response

The filing requirements for elections pursuant to subsection 85(7.1) are basically the same as for elections under subsection 85(1). The completed election Form T2057 is to be filed in duplicate by the transferor at the district office where the transferor would normally file an income tax return and is to be filed separately from any tax return. For such a late-filed or amended election, the transferor is required to pay the relevant estimated penalty with the election before it may be accepted as valid. In addition, a written submission is required from the taxpayer or the taxpayer's representative which sets out the request for the minister's concurrence for the late or amended election, together with the taxpayer's reasons for believing that the subject election should be accepted.

At present, the department is developing some general guidelines as to when such elections would be considered for acceptance. Because of the nature of this matter, however, no guidelines could cover all possible situations, and it will still be necessary to process many elections on a case-by-case basis.

The following examples indicate situations in which elections could be accepted as valid under the above provisions:

(1) "*Late-late-filed*" election (an election filed after the three-year period specified by subsection 85(7)). The relevant property was transferred and the transferor(s) and transferee have accounted for this property in accordance with the rules

---

[7] See also 1981, Q.6(4). A number of Round Table questions have addressed the question of capital gains status in respect of the property which is transferred to a corporation and resold shortly thereafter. See, for example, 1984, Q.49; 1983, Q.24; 1981, Q.6(4); 1980, Q.8. Section 54.2 (added by 1988, c. 55, S. 32(1), applicable with respect to dispositions occurring after 1987) specifies that, where a person has disposed of property that consists of all or substantially all of the assets used in an active business carried on by that person to a corporation for consideration that includes shares of the corporation, the shares shall be deemed to be capital property of the person. For departmental policies thereon, see 1989, Q.13 and 33, 10/15/90. See also 1981, Q.6.

stipulated in the Act since the transaction date; however, the required election form was not filed before the three-year deadline because of inadvertence or misunderstanding on the part of the parties involved or their representatives.

(2) *Amended elections.* The error is a mechanical error that was clearly unintended, as shown by the supporting documents; for example, depreciable property was transferred at net book value instead of the specified undepreciated capital cost.[8]

1990, Q.36 — Subsection 85(6): Taxation Year

According to paragraph 33 of Information Circular 76-19R,[9] the Department accepts that the "taxation year" referred to in subsection 85(6), in the case of a transfer by a partner or proprietor of capital property included in a business, is the calendar year in which the relevant fiscal period of that business ended. IC 76-19R2 cancelled and replaced IC 76-19R. It does not mention this Departmental position. Does it still apply?

Department's Response

This practice no longer applies in order to be consistent with the reporting requirements of the Act for capital dispositions.

1990, Q.37 — Amendment of Section 85 Election

If a section 85 election triggers a capital gain and the agreed amount was established on the assumption that this gain would be eligible for the enhanced capital gains deduction, would the CRA find it just and equitable to permit an amendment under subsection 85(7.1) to reduce the agreed amount if it were subsequently found that the shares transferred did not meet the definition of qualified small business corporation shares?

Department's Response

The CRA's policy concerning the acceptance of an amended election under subsection 85(7.1) is outlined in Information Circular 76-19R.[10] An amended election will generally be accepted under subsection 85(7.1) if its purpose is to revise an agreed amount and if, without this revision, there would be unintended tax consequences for the taxpayers involved.

An amended election will not be accepted if the main purpose of the amended election is:

- to effect retroactive tax planning,
- to take advantage of amendments in the law enacted after the election was filed,

---

[8] See also 1981, Q.6(1); 1980, Q.14.

[9] Information Circular 76-19R, November 13, 1978, cancelled and replaced by IC 76-19R3.

[10] Ibid.

- to avoid or evade tax, or

- to increase the agreed amount in a statute-barred year.

Revenue Canada Round Table Questions and Answers on "Eligible Property"

1981, Q.6 — Section 85

(1) *Erroneous election.* We have seen a number of cases where an erroneous election under subsection 85(1) has been filed. This may be due to an error made in the computation of the adjusted cost base of the property transferred or to a misunderstanding of the mechanics of the rules in subsection 85(1). In some cases, the error is merely a clerical or typographical error. At the 1980 Revenue Canada Round Table, in Question 14, the Department stated that the only adjustment that could be made to the elected amount is as set forth in paragraph 14 of Information Circular 76-19R3, with regard to elected amounts based on an estimate of V-Day value. What is the Department's position as to errors made in the elected amount under subsection 85(1)?

(2) *Subsection 84(1).* On a transfer of property to a Canadian corporation in consideration for shares, which may in many cases be subject to an election under subsection 85(1), a deemed dividend will arise under subsection 84(1) if the paid-up capital of the shares thereby issued exceeds the fair market value of the property acquired by the corporation. In many situations, the value of the property transferred cannot be determined with any certainty. On the other hand, since premiums on the issuance of shares are not recognized in computing paid-up capital, there is a disadvantage in the corporation issuing shares at a premium. Where a *bona fide* attempt has been made to determine the fair market value of the property transferred, a deemed dividend may nevertheless arise under subsection 84(1) if the Department disagrees with the valuation of the property. It has been suggested in some cases that the corporation is permitted to reduce its paid-up capital without payment in order to avoid the application of subsection 84(1). What is the Department's position in this regard?

(3) *Rulings — butterfly transactions.* Under what circumstances will the Department of National Revenue grant rulings to the effect that paragraph 85(1)(*e*.2) of the *Income Tax Act* will not apply to so-called butterflies or spin-off transactions?

(4) *Assets on income account.* It is understood that the CRA may now regard certain shares received by a transferor as consideration for a transfer of assets in respect of which a section 85 election is filed to be assets on income account. Is this true and, if so, would you provide details of this new administrative policy, together with any statutory or jurisprudence authority?

(5) *Know-how.* Depending on the circumstances, amounts paid or received for know-how may be on income or capital account. In particular, an amount paid for know-how may qualify as an "eligible capital expenditure". However, know-how may not be "property" (*Rapistan Canada Ltd. v. M.N.R.*) and, therefore, may not come within the definition of "eligible capital property" found in ITA section 54. How is

know-how regarded by the Department of National Revenue for purposes of the Act and, in particular, for purposes of ITA subsection 85(1)?

Department's Response

(1) The Department's position on errors made in the "agreed amount" in section 85 elections is set out in Information Circular 76-19R. Section 85 elections are monitored closely by the Department to attempt to obtain uniformity in the application of the law. Any elections that result in inequity or hardship can only be considered on a case-by-case basis.

(2) Where, as the result of a disagreement on the fair market value of property subject to an election and transferred under section 85, subsection 84(1) comes into play and the tax consequences so triggered are extremely harsh, the Department is prepared to consider on a case-by-case basis whether administrative relief is warranted.

(3) Where a ruling request clearly states that the provisions of paragraph 55(2)(b) are met, that is, each shareholder receives his *pro rata* share, based on fair market value, of each type of property distributed, the Department will not apply paragraph 85(1)(e.2) of the Act.

(4) The Department has not adopted a new administrative position with respect to the nature of shares received on a sale of assets to a company. The Department is following the principle established in *Fraser v. M.N.R.* and followed in numerous cases since that time. Therefore, where the transfer of assets under section 85 followed by a sale of shares is simply an attempt to convert what would otherwise be an income gain to a capital gain, the profit on the sale of the shares will be considered to be income.

Where the property rolled in is capital property of the transferor, the rollover, in and by itself, does not change the nature of that property.

(5) For the purposes of the Act, amounts paid for know-how that are on account of capital will constitute an eligible capital expenditure.

In *Rapistan Canada Ltd. v. M.N.R.* the Chief Justice of the Federal Court of Appeal states:

> The "know-how" would, however, continue as a capital asset of indefinite duration. It is not however, as such, "property".

As such "know-how" acquired in these circumstances clearly falls within the meaning of "eligible capital expenditure" as defined in subsection 14(5) of the Act, it follows that on a subsequent disposition of "know-how", amounts received for such know-how on account of capital would enter into the calculation of cumulative eligible capital within the meaning of subsection 14(5) of the Act.

The *Rapistan* case, which considered reassessments under the former Act, appears to be inconsistent with the scheme of the amended Act. Therefore, the Department will consider know-how that is of a capital nature as being "eligible capital property" for purposes of the Act.

In order to establish whether amounts paid or received for know-how are on income or capital account, we are of the opinion that the comments contained in paragraph (2.*d*) of Interpretation Bulletin IT-386 continue to be relevant.[11] [12] [13]

1984, Q.48 — Rollover of Inventory

Subsection 85(1) of the Act prohibits the rollover of inventory that is real property to a taxable Canadian corporation but permits the rollover of capital property, which can include an interest in a partnership that carries on a real estate development or construction business. What is the Department's practice with respect to a rollover under subsection 85(1) of such a partnership interest with underlying real property inventories?

Department's Response

The practice of the Department is to accept that a partnership interest in a partnership, the underlying property of which is real property inventory, is not in itself inventory of real property. Therefore, we accept that a capital property that is an interest in such a partnership can be transferred pursuant to subsection 85(1).

It is, however, also our opinion that in a particular set of circumstances it will be a question of fact whether there is a transfer of partnership interest.[14] [15]

1986, Q.50 — Interests in Partnerships: Section 85

Do all interests in partnerships constitute capital property or an interest in the underlying assets? Will an interest in real property that is inventory be eligible for a subsection 85(1) transfer if the interest in the real property is held through a partnership?

Department's Response

This question was answered at the 1984 tax conference. An interest in a partnership is not considered to be an interest in its underlying assets for purposes of section 85. An interest in a partnership could be held by its owner as capital property or inventory, depending on the circumstances. An interest in a partnership with

---

[11] With respect to the second question above, reference should be made to subsection 85(2.1) and section 84.1, which may limit the paid-up capital in respect of shares received as consideration for transferred property. With respect to the first question above, see also 1980, Q.14 and 1986, Q.33. Reference should also be made to paragraph 85(7.1)(*b*) where the Minister may permit an election to be amended.

[12] With respect to the fourth question above, see also 1989, Q.13; 1986, Q.20; 1984, Q.49; 1983, Q.24; 1980, Q.8.

[13] With respect to the Department's response to the third question, the section reference should be paragraph 55(3)(*b*).

[14] See Information Circular 88-2, paragraph 22 with respect to application of subsection 245(2) to a transfer of land inventory to a partnership pursuant to subsection 97(2) followed by a transfer of the partnership interest to a corporation under subsection 85(1).

[15] See also 1990, Q.35; 1989C, Q.10; 1986, Q.50.

assets that include an inventory of real property would be eligible for a subsection 85(1) transfer. A determination of whether a partnership exists has to be made on the basis of the facts of each case.[16] [17]

1986, Q.54 — Canadian Resource Properties

Is an interest in a partnership that owns Canadian resource properties considered to be a "Canadian resource property" for purposes of a section 85 election as well as the successor and second successor elections found in the Act?

Department's Response

It is the department's position that an interest in a partnership, the underlying property of which consists of Canadian resource property, is not a Canadian resource property for purposes of either a section 85 election or the successor and second successor provisions.[18]

1988, Q.24 — Seismic Data

Assume that a taxpayer has acquired certain seismic data and has properly deducted the cost thereof as a Canadian exploration expense (CEE) pursuant to section 66.1 of the Act. If the taxpayer sells the seismic data under a subsection 85(1) election, should he treat the seismic data as a Canadian resource property within the meaning of subsection 66(15) as a capital property or as an eligible capital property?

Department's Response

Assuming that the taxpayer in the above circumstances has acquired seismic data, the cost of which is in fact CEE, the taxpayer would be prohibited from rolling such seismic data pursuant to a subsection 85(1) election. Seismic data can be the subject of a subsection 85(1) election only if they are an inventory item.

1989C, Q.10 — Partnership Interest Held by Non-Resident

A non-resident owns an interest in a partnership whose assets consist primarily of real property. In the CRA's view, would the partnership interest held by the non-resident be "eligible property" as defined in subsection 85(1.1)?

---

[16] See Information Circular 88-2, paragraph 22 with respect to application of subsection 245(2) to a transfer of land inventory to a partnership pursuant to subsection 97(2) followed by a transfer of the partnership interest to a corporation under subsection 85(1).

[17] See also 1990, Q.35; 1989C, Q.10; 1984, Q.48.

[18] The successor and the second successor elections, previously found in subsections 66(6) and (7) (Canadian exploration and development expenses), subsections 66.1(4) and (5) (Canadian exploration expenses) and subsections 66.2(3) and (4) (Canadian development expenses), were repealed by 1987, c. 46, and were substantially replaced with new section 66.7.

Department's Response

As indicated in our response to question 50 of the 1986 round table, it is the Department's view that an interest in a partnership is not considered to be an interest in its underlying assets for the purposes of section 85. Thus a partnership interest owned by a non-resident will normally be eligible to be transferred under section 85, notwithstanding that the assets of the partnership consist primarily of real estate. However, where the formation of the partnership and the transfer of the land held by a non-resident are undertaken to circumvent the prohibition in section 85, subsection 245(2) would likely apply.[19]

1990, Q.35 — Transfer by a Non-Resident

Real property, an interest therein, or an option in respect thereof that is owned by a non-resident person (other than a non-resident insurer) does not qualify as "eligible property", as defined in subsection 85(1.1), for the purposes of an election pursuant to subsection 85(1). Does a non-resident's interest in a partnership the assets of which are primarily real property qualify as "eligible property" for the purposes of subsection 85(1)?

Department's Response

This question was answered at the 1986 tax conference. It is the Department's view that, for purposes of section 85, an interest in a partnership is not considered to be an interest in its underlying assets. Therefore, an interest in a partnership held by a non-resident as capital property would qualify as "eligible property" under paragraph 85(1.1)(a), notwithstanding the fact that the assets of the partnership consist primarily of real property.

However, if a partnership is formed as one of the steps in a series of transactions that is designed to circumvent the provisions of subsection 85(1.1), the provisions of section 245 could apply.[20]

---

[19] See also 1990, Q.35; 1986, Q.50; 1984, Q.48.

[20] See also 1989C, Q.10; 1986, Q.50; 1984, Q.48.

"Eligible Property" — Other CRA Documents

The following are technical interpretations and other documents pertaining to "Eligible Property", selected from CCH Canadian's loose-leaf service, *Window on Canadian Tax*:

Eligible Property — Cumulative Dividends

It is the CRA's view that the right to a cumulative dividend that is in arrears is not a separate property from the share itself. Where a share that has a cumulative dividend in arrears is transferred to a corporation under section 85, it is the share that is an "eligible property" under section 85. Similarly, where the share is exchanged for another class of shares in a reorganization of capital to which subsection 86(1) applies, the transfer of the cumulative dividend that is in arrears would not represent a transfer of a separate property. A share "represents a bundle of rights, privileges, restrictions, and conditions attached to the share under the articles of incorporation of the issuing corporation. The right to the accrued cumulative dividends would be just one of the bundle of rights that would be attached to a particular share".

The transfer of the share to a corporation would not result in a deemed payment of the cumulative dividend in arrears. However, where the purpose of the transfer is to allow dividends to be paid on another class of shares, subsections 56(2), 86(2), or 245(2) may apply.

[Technical Interpretation, Reorganizations and Foreign Division, September 1, 1994, CRA File Number 9413775.]

Eligible Property — Royalty for Know-How

In order for section 85 to apply to the transfer of property to a corporation, the property must be an "eligible property" as defined in subsection 85(1.1). It is the CRA's view that a royalty for know-how, i.e., the right to receive income, is not a capital property or an eligible capital property where there is no underlying right to the property that created the income.[21] However, where the taxpayer also owns the underlying property which gives rise to the rights to receive income, the CRA has stated that it is arguable that the rights to income, in such a case, may constitute capital property for purposes of the Act.[22] The CRA also stated in that Technical Interpretation that, alternatively, since the rights to receive income relate to the taxpayer, an argument could be made that such rights are in respect of a business and therefore qualify as eligible capital property or that the rights are inventory in respect of the taxpayer's business. A natural resource royalty, on a Canadian resource property, is an "eligible property" as defined in subsection 85(1.1). A natural-resource royalty would therefore be eligible to be transferred to a corporation under subsection 85(1).

---

[21] See *Evans v. M.N.R.*, 60 DTC 1047 (S.C.C.), and *Asamera Oil (Indonesia) Limited v. The Queen*, 73 DTC 5274 (F.C.T.D.).

[22] Technical Interpretation, Document No. 9502507, March 28, 1995.

[CRA Round Table, Canadian Petroleum Tax Society, June 6, 1994. CRA File Numbers: 9410840 & 9502507.]

Eligible Property — Copyrights

The CRA held that subsection 85(1) would apply to the transfer by the individual to Bco of his copyrights and of his right to receive royalties from Aco.

[Technical Interpretation, March 23, 2005, CRA File Number 2002-0149781R3.]

Eligible Property — Holdbacks and Unapproved Billings

In order to have section 85 apply to a transfer of property to a corporation, the transferred property must be "eligible property" as defined in subsection 85(1.1). Where accounts receivable are transferred to a corporation, an election under section 22 will often be made.

Where a contractor includes in income approved progress billings, the CRA is of the view that unapproved progress billings and unapproved holdbacks may be transferred to a corporation under section 85 as capital property. The elected amount in respect of the property can be a nominal amount of $1.

The CRA indicated that subsection 56(4) could apply to the unapproved progress billings and unapproved holdbacks which would require that the amounts be included in the transferor's income. Since the income from the unapproved progress billings and unapproved holdbacks would not be from a source that is property, the exclusion from the application of subsection 56(4) would not apply. However, where the transferee includes the amounts in its business income, the department would generally not apply to the provision.

[Technical Interpretation, Reorganizations and Foreign Division, February 3, 1994, CRA File Number 9237475; Technical Interpretation, Reorganizations and Resources Division, April 17, 2002, CRA File Number 2001-0097463; Technical Interpretation, Reorganizations and Resources Division, February 16, 2004, CRA File Number 2003-0054091E5 (in French).]

Undivided Interest in the Property of a Partnership

The CRA has stated that where a partnership has dissolved and each partner's interest in the property of the partnership is received on such dissolution pursuant to subsection 98(3), the partner's undivided interest would be eligible property for the purposes of subsection 85(1.1).

[Technical Interpretation, Tax Ruling, Resources, Partnerships and Trust Division, October 25, 2000. CRA File Number 2000-0028423.]

Transfer of Farm Inventory to Corporation

The CRA was asked to comment on the transfer of the inventory by a farmer to a corporation under section 85. The inventory involved was wheat, which had a current market value of $2 per bushel. However, under the Gross Revenue Insurance

Program ("GRIP") of the province of Manitoba, the farmer was guaranteed a price of $4 per bushel. The correspondence implies that the farmer used the cash basis and therefore the cost of the inventory was nil, since the cost would be deductible in the year incurred.

It was the CRA's view that the farmer could elect under section 85 to transfer the wheat inventory to his corporation at any amount between nil and $2.00 per bushel. As the farmer had not purchased the wheat, paragraph 85(1)(*c.*2) would not apply. If the wheat was still in the ground, there is no discussion as to how the number of bushels being transferred would be determined; with an appropriately worded agreement, however, this could presumably be determined after the fact.

The GRIP amount was, in the CRA's view, a separate property that was an income amount similar to an account receivable which could not be transferred to a corporation by a cash-basis farmer. This position is consistent with the comments in Interpretation Bulletin IT-433R, Farming or Fishing — Use of Cash Method, and is based on the CRA's view that an income amount is not an "eligible property" under subsection 85(1.1). It should also be noted that subsection 28(5) would apply to include, in income, any amount received in respect of a debt owing to the taxpayer, which effectively negates the use of a section 22 election where receivables are sold by a cash-basis farmer.

As the GRIP amount was payable to the farmer rather than the corporation, the CRA was of the view that an assignment of the right to the amount, to a corporation, would be subject to subsection 56(4) and would be included in the taxpayer's income. Technically, subsection 56(2) might also apply to the amount.

The CRA was also of the view that any shares or debt of the corporation received in respect of the GRIP amount would be a security received in satisfaction of an income debt within the meaning of subsection 76(1), which could also include the amount in income.

As noted in the CRA's correspondence, subsection 4(4) should apply to prevent double taxation of the GRIP amount.

[Technical Interpretation, Reorganizations and Foreign Division, December 3, 1993. CRA File Number 9200995.]

Life Insurance Policy Cannot be Rolled Over on a Tax-deferred Basis

The CRA is of the view that an interest in a life insurance policy cannot be transferred to a corporation on a tax-deferred basis under subsection 85(1) or to a partnership under subsection 97(2).

An interest in a life insurance policy is not

(i) "eligible property" for the purposes of subsection 85(1.1), because the insurance premiums are not eligible capital expenditures;[23]

---

[23] See paragraph 3 of IT-143R3, Meaning of Eligible Capital Expenditure.

(ii) a property that is described in subsection 97(2); or

(iii) capital property, because of the specific exclusion in subparagraph 39(1)(*a*)(iii) and the definition of capital property in section 54.

[Memorandum, Legislative and Intergovernmental Affairs Branch, May 11, 1992. CRA File Number 9211270.]

Transfer of a Professional Business to a Corporation

The CRA will recognize that a corporation is carrying on a professional practice if provincial law or the regulatory body for the particular profession does not provide that only individuals may practice the profession and if the activities of the corporation and its relationship to its employees and clients are similar to those associated with a corporation carrying on a business.

It is the CRA's opinion that where an individual carrying on a profession has made an election under section 34 to exclude work in progress from income, the work in progress is "eligible property" as defined in subsection 85(1.1). This reasoning appears to be based in part on the premise that work in progress is "inventory".[24] If the work in progress is transferred to a professional corporation, its cost amount for purposes of any subsection 85(1) election made in respect of the transfer is nil.[25]

Also, the CRA expressed the view that unbilled disbursements are costs incurred in the year to earn income from the practice and are not "eligible property" as defined by subsection 85(1.1).

[Technical Interpretation, Reorganizations and Non-Resident Division, August 15, 1991.]

Capitalization of Debt — Interaction of Subsection 80(1) and Subsection 85(1)

According to the CRA, a receivable that is a capital property is an "eligible property" under subsection 85(1.1) and may be the subject of a subsection 85(1) election if transferred to the debtor corporation for shares. However, the CRA also feels that section 80 could apply to the debtor corporation if the fair market value of the shares is less than the principal amount of the debt. There may also be situations when the CRA would take the position that the general anti-avoidance rule in section 245 should apply.

[Technical Interpretation, Reorganizations and Non-Resident Division, December 3, 1990.]

---

[24] See paragraph 4(f) of IT-291R3, Transfer of Property to a Corporation under Subsection 85(1).

[25] See paragraph 18 of IT-457R, Election by Professionals To Exclude Work in Progress from Income.

Appendix C

External Articles

Transfers to Corporations and the Stop-Loss Rules — Article

The following is an article by Michael Goldberg and Samantha Prasad of Minden Gross Grafstein & Greenstein LLP, which appeared in the August 2001 edition of CCH Canadian's TAX NOTES.

"Sometimes a Loss Is Not a Loss"

Prior to transferring any depreciable or non-depreciable property it is important to consider whether the transaction is or has previously been subject to a stop-loss rule under the *Income Tax Act*[1] in order to determine the tax consequences of the transaction. Given current economic conditions, these rules warrant a closer look.

Disposition of Non-Depreciable Capital Property Other Than by an Individual

If a corporation, trust or partnership disposes of non-depreciable capital property at a loss and, during a specific time period that begins 30 days before the disposition and ends 30 days after the disposition, the transferor or an "affiliated person"[2] has acquired and continues to own that property, an identical property or an option to acquire such properties at the end of the time period,[3] the stop-loss rules found in subsection 40(3.4) will apply. The effect of these stop-loss rules is that

---

[1] All statutory references are to the *Income Tax Act* (Canada).

[2] An individual can be affiliated with him- or herself and the individual's spouse but with no other individual. A person and a corporation will only be affiliated if the corporation is controlled by the person or the person's spouse, or by an "affiliated group" of persons of which the person or the person's spouse is a member. There are also detailed rules concerning the affiliation of two corporations, a corporation and a partnership and two partnerships. See subsection 251.1.

[3] See subsections 40(3.3) and (3.5).

333

the loss will be deferred until such time as the property or an identical property is no longer owned by the transferor or an affiliated person.[4]

Disposition of Non-Depreciable Capital Property by an Individual

Similar to the above stop-loss rules, where an individual disposes of non-depreciable capital property at a loss and, during the same time periods set out above, the transferor or an affiliated person has acquired and continues to own that property, an identical property or an option to acquire such properties at the end of the time period,[5] the disposition will be subject to the stop-loss rule found in subparagraph 40(2)(g)(i).[6] The effect of this stop-loss rule differs from the subsection 40(3.4) stop-loss rules in that the individual's loss is denied rather than deferred. However, the amount of the loss denied under subparagraph 40(2)(g)(i) is added to the cost base of the property acquired by the transferee (see paragraph 53(1)(f)). Therefore, assuming that there is no change in value, the loss disallowed to the individual would be allowed to the transferee upon a subsequent disposition of the property by the transferee to an unaffiliated person.

The distinction between the tax treatment of losses stopped under these two provisions may present tax planners with both opportunities and pitfalls. For example, an individual may choose to trigger subparagraph 40(2)(g)(i) by transferring shares to his spouse that have unrealized losses so that she can sell the shares and trigger the losses herself. On the other hand, a corporation seeking the same result could not use the stop-loss rule in subsection 40(3.4) to achieve the same result, since the losses would be trapped in the transferor corporation.

Disposition of Depreciable Property

If a corporation, trust or partnership disposes of depreciable property at a loss and, on the 30th day following the disposition, the transferor or an affiliated person has acquired and continues to own that same property or an option to acquire that property, the stop-loss rules found in subsection 13(21.2) will apply. The effect of these stop-loss rules is similar to the stop-loss rules in subsection 40(3.4) in that the loss will be deferred until such time as that property or an option to acquire that property is no longer owned by an affiliated person. However, if capital cost allowance has previously been claimed, the capital cost of the property will be ignored and the stop-loss rule will only apply to the extent that the undepreciated capital cost ("UCC") exceeds the proceeds of disposition in respect of the property.

Up until recently, no stop-loss rules applied to deny losses of individuals in connection with the disposition of depreciable property. Recent changes to subsection 13(21.2) expand these stop-loss rules to be applicable to individuals after November 30, 1999, subject to limited grandfathering. As a result, an individual is no

---

[4] Subsection 40(3.4) contains a number of rules that may apply to deem property to no longer be owned by an affiliated person.

[5] See section 54 — definition of "superficial-loss".

[6] Paragraph 40(2)(g) contains a number of other stop-loss rules that may be relevant to individuals. In particular, a loss resulting from a disposition of property to an RRSP or other similar plans will be denied.

longer able to dispose of depreciable property to a spouse in order to trigger a terminal loss.

Valuation Issues

Sometimes following a disposition of depreciable or non-depreciable capital property it will be determined that the property has been overvalued and the transaction should have taken place at a loss (or the loss should have been greater than expected). If the disposition took place between affiliated persons, one of the stop-loss rules described above may be applicable. As is illustrated in the three examples set out below, in this situation the nature of the consideration received by the transferor may have a considerable impact on the tax consequences associated with the disposition.

(1) If the consideration received by the transferor (i.e., a promissory note or preferred shares) does not contain a price adjustment mechanism (or contains an improperly drafted price adjustment mechanism) then, since the value of the consideration received by the transferor and the proceeds of disposition will not adjust to equal the fair market value of the property, the transferor will not realize a loss and the stop-loss rules will not apply. However, pursuant to paragraph 69(1)(*a*), the capital cost of the property in the hands of the transferee will be deemed to be equal to the fair market value of the property and not the fair market value of the consideration received by the transferor. As a result, the transferor will not be entitled to claim the loss and the transferee will not be entitled to add the amount of the denied loss to its capital cost. To make matters even worse, the transferor may also be deemed to receive a benefit to the extent that the fair market value of the consideration received exceeds the fair market value of the property transferred by the transferor to the transferee.

(2) If the consideration received by the transferor is subject to an effective price adjustment mechanism, then, since the value of the consideration received by the transferor and the proceeds of disposition will automatically adjust to equal the fair market value of the property, the transferor will realize a loss and the stop-loss rules will apply. Since the value of the consideration received will automatically adjust to equal the fair market value of the property, neither paragraph 69(1)(*a*) nor subsection 15(1) will be applicable under this scenario.

(3) If the consideration received by the transferor includes common shares, then the applicability of the stop-loss rules will depend on whether or not other common shares of the transferee corporation are issued and outstanding. If the transferee corporation does not have other issued and outstanding common shares, the stop-loss rules will apply in a manner similar to that in scenario number (2) above, since the value of the common shares will automatically adjust to equal the fair market value of the property transferred to the corporation. However, if there are other issued and outstanding common shares, then the application of these stop-loss rules may lead to unexpected results that are beyond the scope of this article.

It should be noted that if the subsection 13(21.2) stop-loss rules are applicable, sections 85 and 97 will not apply. As a result, it will be necessary to consider the nature of the consideration received (as above) in order to determine the tax consequences of the disposition.

Summary

As a result of the recent collapse of stock markets and the loss of value of many other assets, dispositions of depreciable and non-depreciable capital properties at a loss are likely to become much more commonplace. Unfortunately, the tax consequences of such transactions may be impacted by the various stop-loss rules discussed throughout this article and, unless these rules are considered in advance, unintended tax consequences may arise.

Double Tax Issues — Article

The following article is by Michael Goldberg and Samantha Prasad (both of the Toronto law firm, Minden Gross) and is a general discussion of double tax exposure as a result of the death of a shareholder of a corporation, as well as post mortem tax planning strategies that may apply. This article is based on "Post-Mortem Planning", which appeared in the November 2001 issue of TAX NOTES.

For a more detailed discussion of double taxation on death and post-mortem tax planning to deal with this problem, including post-mortem strategies, reference should be made to CCH's *Wealth Management Guide for Accountants*.

When a loved one passes away, income tax should be the last thing you have to worry about. We only wish that the government could have been more sensitive to this situation. Sadly, some key tax planning opportunities may be missed unless certain reorganizations are completed within the first year after death. Worse still, these can be extremely complex, thus necessitating professional attention within a few months after death.

Post-mortem tax planning is most critical when assets pass to another generation. Unless there is careful attention to tax planning at this point, not only can there be a costly tax bill as a result of the demise itself, but also, and worse still, there is a possibility for certain double tax effects, where assets are held in a corporation (or partnership). These effects can be quite complex, but let us try to explain how the problem arises. Generally speaking, where a closely-held corporation is involved, death results in a "deemed sale" of its shares at their market value when they are bequeathed to another generation, which will usually give rise to a taxable capital gain in the decedent's final tax return. The good news is that the estate/beneficiaries will then have an increased cost base in respect of these shares — again, based on market value at death, but here's the problem — there is no compensating increase at the corporate level. In other words, there is neither an increase to the tax cost of the assets held by the corporation, nor is there any enhancement in the ability to distribute the underlying assets of the corporation on a tax efficient basis. This sets the stage for double tax — once when the shares pass between generations, and a second time when the company's assets themselves are sold or distributed.

We should note that this problem does not depend on prior estate freezing or other estate planning; it is endemic to any "ordinary" situation where shares of a closely-held company pass between generations. *Double tax issues should be addressed whenever there is capital gains tax resulting from shares of a closely-held corporation passing to another generation.*

In most cases, the double tax effects can be mitigated; however, as stated previously, one of the key techniques may necessitate the completion of a complex reorganization within the first year after death, hence the necessity for immediate attention.

Post-Mortem Strategies

Basically, there are three strategies available to minimize the double tax effect:

1. *"Pipeline"*. The first, and simplest, is what we call the "pipeline" strategy. In this case, the increased cost base to the estate/beneficiaries resulting from the terminal period capital gain is used as a mechanism to provide a "pipeline" to extract assets from the corporate level on a tax effective basis. This may typically involve transferring the shares of the decedent's corporation to a holding company. As we said, the strategy is fairly straight-forward and, better yet, need not be completed in a rush. However, it is typically advantageous when the beneficiaries are looking to access cash or other "tax paid investments" from their corporation. In some circumstances, particularly with affluent families, this may not be a priority; in others, the company's assets may have a deferred tax exposure so that the "pipeline" procedure may be of little or no benefit.

2. *Increase in tax cost of company's assets.* The second technique involves the transfer of the deceased's shares to a holding company, followed by a dissolution of the decedent's corporation into the holding company. Under these circumstances, it is possible to increase the tax cost of certain underlying assets of the decedent's corporation, based on the tax cost to the estate of the shares themselves. Unfortunately, though, the ability to do this is usually limited to what tax advisors call "non-depreciable capital property" — the value of land (but not buildings), or equity held by the decedent's corporation — say, a portfolio share investment, mutual funds, or a major holding in another company. Accordingly, this technique applies only in limited circumstances.

3. *Reacquisition of shares — the "redemption manoeuvre".* The last post-mortem strategy is usually the most complex; ironically, it must be done within the first year of the decedent's estate. In essence, the procedure involves the redemption (reacquisition) of some or all of the shares of the corporation which were formerly held by the decedent. The effect of the reacquisition tends to create taxable dividends to the estate, combined with a capital loss, with the latter applied to reduce the decedent's capital gains[7], so the manoeuvre essentially replaces the terminal period capital gain

---

[7] This occurs pursuant to subsection 164(6) of the Act; accordingly the "redemption manoeuvre" is referred to by tax advisors as the "subsection 164(6) procedure".

with a dividend to the estate.[8] Besides this, the redemption manoeuvre will typically involve the disposition of underlying assets owned by the corporation, thus having the extra effect of increasing the tax cost of these assets, so as to reduce or eliminate future double taxation.[9]

This alternative becomes more attractive if the corporation has special surplus accounts (notably capital dividend or refundable dividend tax on hand accounts) that can reduce the effective taxation on the dividend to the estate that we just mentioned. If the redemption manoeuvre involves the disposition of corporate level assets, this itself may generate such surpluses, making the manoeuvre more tax effective; in other cases, there may be pre-existing surplus balances, e.g., from previously earned investment income or corporate-owned life insurance payable on the death of the decedent.

In summary, situations in which the "redemption manoeuvre" may be advantageous include the following:

- Where the tax cost of the underlying corporation's assets is significantly less than their market value, and a sale of the assets is foreseeable.

- The corporation has pre-existing surplus balances (e.g., it has previously earned investment income, capital gains, or has received insurance proceeds), or will generate the surplus accounts through a disposition of corporate level assets as part of the redemption manoeuvre.

The terms of the will as well as the selection of executors may be important in terms of facilitating post-mortem tax planning to occur. In a freeze-type situation for example, where executors are also beneficiaries, recent CRA Technical Interpretations appear to suggest that appointing at least two executors can simplify post-mortem tax planning. In addition, where the will utilizes a "spouse trust" — par for the course for more affluent clients — the spouse trust should provide for a "lagged distribution" on the death of the surviving spouse, rather than an immediate distribution to the residual beneficiaries.

---

[8] At time of writing, dividends are taxable at higher rates than capital gains (about 8% higher in Ontario); accordingly, the manoeuvre is somewhat less desirable than it was before the capital gains rates were reduced last year. For example, if the redemption of shares *vis-à-vis* the estate were simply in the form of a cash distribution from the corporation, the "pipeline" procedure we described earlier would be preferable, since it leaves the decedent's terminal period capital gain "as is", rather than effectively converting this gain to a dividend taxable at higher rates.

[9] Similar procedures are available where shares of the corporation have been left to a spouse under a qualifying spouse trust and the surviving spouse passes away. In this case, however, the ability to do this procedure may be restricted if the will itself calls for a mandatory distribution of assets at the death of the surviving spouse. For this reason, it is advantageous for the will to provide that the assets can be retained in the estate after the death of the spouse. If this is done, the reorganization can be completed within three years of the year in which the spouse passes away, rather than the first year of the estate.

U.S. Income Tax Considerations for Canadians — Article

The following article is by Mr. Allan Tiller of Chamberlain, Hrdlicka, White, Williams & Martin, of Houston, Texas, a member of MERITAS Law Firms Worldwide. It summarizes the basic U.S. tax considerations that might arise from a freeze structure. This article appeared in the March 10, 2005 issue of TAX TOPICS *as part of the Estate Planning in the 21st Century series and was co-edited by Michael Atlas, David Louis and Brian Nichols.*

U.S. Income Tax Concerns of Canadian Expatriates Holding Canadian Corporate Stock

High levels of cross-border mobility for individuals between the United States and Canada is hardly news anymore, 9/11 notwithstanding. There are thousands of Canadian citizens or former Canadian citizens living in the United States, many of whom brought with them stock (shares) in Canadian corporate entities or who suddenly find themselves owners of such stock as the result of the death of a parent or other loved one or a distribution from a trust. Whether as a result of becoming a U.S. resident or citizen while holding such shares, or by receiving such shares after having become a U.S. citizen or resident, they all face a bewildering array of U.S. income tax laws — and associated reporting forms — governing "U.S. persons" who own stock in a "foreign" (non-U.S.) entity.[10]

When is a Canadian a "U.S. person"?

A Canadian citizen or resident enters a brave new world when he or she attains the status of a "U.S. person" for U.S. income tax purposes. Regardless of that person's status under Canadian law, he[11] becomes a U.S. person for U.S. income tax purposes if he becomes either a U.S. citizen (which does not necessarily require relinquishment of Canadian citizenship) or a U.S. "resident alien". In turn, a "resident alien" is an individual who either is a permanent resident of the United States, sometimes referred to as a holder of a "green card", or who has crossed the "substantial presence" threshold set forth in the U.S. *Internal Revenue Code* ("the Code"), essentially a day-counting test.[12] A rough rule of thumb is that if an individual spends more than 120 days within the United States each year on an ongoing basis, he will be a resident alien.[13] A person who is a resident of both the United States and

---

[10] This article addresses only U.S. income tax. There are also important considerations under the U.S. gift and estate tax, which are not addressed in this article. Also not addressed are state income tax regimes, but these generally are piggy-backed onto the federal income tax, adding percentage points to the marginal rates of taxation.

[11] The masculine pronouns are used throughout this article for efficiency, but of course are intended to be gender-neutral.

[12] Section 7701(*b*) of the U.S. Federal *Internal Revenue Code* of 1986, as revised (all section references herein are to this Code, except that "Reg. Sec." refers to sections of the Internal Revenue Service regulations).

[13] The threshold is 183 days, but the rule counts not only all of the days of the year for which residency is being determined but also $^1/_3$ of days of presence in the immediate preceding year and $^1/_6$ of the days of presence in the second preceding year, assuming the inapplicability of several significant exceptions. Sec. 7701(*b*)(3).

Canada under their respective rules may not be treated as a U.S. person for certain U.S. income tax purposes if, under the so-called "tie-breaker" rules of the income tax treaty between the United States and Canada,[14] he has closer ties to Canada than to the United States. The rules discussed below presume the status of "U.S. person" for the individual in question, referred to here as a "Canadian expatriate".

U.S. rules regarding the nature of the Canadian entity

The first step in determining what U.S. rules will apply to a Canadian expatriate in the United States is to determine the nature or character of the Canadian entity in which he holds an interest. For the most part, a foreign (non-U.S.) entity in which an individual holds an interest will be characterized for U.S. income tax purposes as either a "corporation" (also called an "association"), a "partnership", or an extension of the individual himself (a "disregarded entity"). With few exceptions,[15] Canadian stock companies will be treated as "corporations" for U.S. income tax purposes, and Canadian partnerships will be treated generally as partnerships under U.S. law unless an election is made under the so-called "check-the-box" regulations[16] to treat the partnership as a corporation. However, it is rarely advantageous to treat a Canadian partnership as a corporation for U.S. income tax purposes; partnership status allows Canadian losses to "flow through" (be attributed) to the Canadian expatriate where they can offset taxable income from other sources on the expatriate's U.S. tax return. Likewise, Canadian income taxes can be attributed to the expatriate for purposes of the U.S. foreign tax credit, whereas the Canadian taxes paid by a corporation (other than the Canadian withholding tax on dividends[17]) cannot be taken into account by the expatriate for purposes of the credit.[18]

Main U.S. tax concerns with respect to owning shares in Canadian corporations: The Anti-deferral rules

When a Canadian expatriate finds himself holding shares of a Canadian corporation, he has special U.S. income tax concerns other than just reporting the receipt of dividends from the corporation as income and claiming a foreign tax credit for any Canadian withholding tax. Of particular concern are the U.S. anti-deferral rules, in particular the so-called "subpart F" rules, also sometimes called the "controlled foreign corporation" ("CFC") rules,[19] and the "passive foreign investment company",

[14] Article IV, paragraph 2, of the Convention Between the United States of America and Canada with Respect to Taxes on Income and Capital.

[15] A Nova Scotia unlimited liability company being the most notable.

[16] Treas. Reg. Secs. 301.7701-2 and 301.7701-3.

[17] Under Article X of the Treaty, the Canadian withholding tax on dividends made from a Canadian corporation to a U.S. individual, including a Canadian expatriate, is limited to 15%.

[18] Only corporations, and only those corporations that own at least 10% of the stock of the foreign dividend paying corporation, can enjoy the U.S. foreign tax credit for corporate level foreign taxes paid by the foreign dividend paying corporation. Section 902.

[19] Sections 951 through 964, contained in Subpart F of Part III of Subchapter N of Chapter 1 of the Code.

or "PFIC", rules.[20] In general, the subpart F rules are the principal anti-deferral rules applicable to closely-held non-U.S. companies in which U.S. persons, including resident aliens, own a majority interest (and therefore can control dividend distributions), while the PFIC rules come into play when the non-U.S. company is not majority-owned by U.S. persons.[21]

As is apparent from the explanation of these rules below, the PFIC rules and even the subpart F rules can conceivably also apply to publicly-held corporations but rarely do because of the active nature of their income and the broad distribution of their stock. In contrast, the PFIC rules can, and often do, apply to non-U.S. mutual funds that are structured as corporations because such funds predominately earn "passive" income, that is, income from investments rather than from direct active business activities.

The Subpart F rules

When applicable, the subpart F rules essentially have the effect of attributing certain kinds of income of a foreign corporation, called "subpart F income",[22] currently to its U.S. shareholders as "ordinary" income (to the extent of their pro rata ownership of the corporation), even though the corporation has not yet declared or paid a dividend with respect to that income. Thus, there is no deferral of U.S. taxation by using a foreign corporation to earn those types of income. However, later when the corporation does declare and pay an actual dividend, the income is not taxed again to the U.S. shareholders.[23]

The rules generally look to two basic factors: (i) the level of U.S. ownership, and (ii) the type of income and investments that the foreign corporation makes. With respect to ownership, the subpart F rules generally apply (with exceptions for insurance related activities) only if the foreign (non-U.S.) corporation is more than 50% owned, in either voting power or value, by U.S. persons who each own at least 10% of the voting stock of the corporation. Such a corporation is referred to as a "controlled foreign corporation" ("CFC"). A Canadian corporation can inadvertently be converted into a CFC if, whether or not known to the other shareholders, one of the shareholders crosses the threshold of "resident alien", either by obtaining U.S. permanent residence or by exceeding the number of days necessary to satisfy the "substantial presence" test referred to above. CFC status can occur even though one or more of the shareholders are non-U.S. citizens who are claiming the benefit of the "tie-breaker" residency rules in the U.S.–Canada or other income tax treaty, since the

---

[20] Section 1291 through 1298.

[21] The *American Jobs Creation Act* of 2004 eliminated, effective generally beginning January 1, 2005, two other anti-deferral regimes which had already been largely superseded by the subpart F and the PFIC rules: the deemed dividend "foreign personal holding company" rules of old Sections 551 through 558 and the "foreign investment company" rules of old Section 1246, which converted gain from the sale of stock of a "foreign investment company" into ordinary income.

[22] Section 952.

[23] Section 959.

IRS asserts that such a person is nevertheless a "U.S. person" for purposes of the subpart F rules.[24]

Once a Canadian corporation has the status of a CFC, the focus turns to the type of income earned by the corporation, generally called "subpart F income" as noted above. Very generally, the rules most often apply to two basic types of income: (i) passive income such as interest, dividends, capital gains, rents, and royalties, called "foreign personal holding company income", with certain significant exceptions,[25] and (ii) active business income earned in transactions involving related persons, called "foreign base company sales income" in the case of the sale of goods[26] or "foreign base company services income" in the case of the provision of services.[27] There are other special rules for oil-related income, banking and financing businesses, and the insurance business,[28] and there is also a special rule with respect to investments (including certain loans) by the foreign corporation in or to related persons in the United States, creating taxable income to U.S. shareholders even when the income invested was not otherwise subpart F income.[29]

An important exception (among others) to the subpart F rules, and particularly applicable to Canadian corporations, is the so-called "high tax" exception. Under this exception, income that is otherwise subpart F income will not be treated as such (and thus there is no deemed income to the U.S. shareholders) if such income "was subject to an effective rate of income tax imposed by a foreign country [Canada] greater than 90% of the maximum rate of tax specified in section 11" (the U.S. federal corporate tax rate, presently with a maximum marginal rate of 35%).[30] For this purpose, Canadian provincial income taxes are taken into account along with the Canadian federal income tax.[31] In many or most cases, because of the high combined federal/provincial income tax rates in Canada, this exception will prevent the immediate inclusion of subpart F income in the taxable income of a Canadian expatriate who is a U.S. shareholder in the corporation. Nevertheless, the expatriate must still report the income and his ownership in the Canadian corporation on a

---

[24] Treas. Reg. Sec. 301.7701-b(7)(a)(3).

[25] Section 954(c).

[26] Section 954(d).

[27] Section 954(e).

[28] Section 954(f) through (i). A category for shipping income was removed in the *American Jobs Creation Act* of 2004.

[29] Section 956.

[30] Section 954(b)(4).

[31] While there is no direct authority to this effect with respect to subpart F, IRS regulations do state that, for purposes of the U.S. foreign tax credit, the income taxes of provinces and other "political subdivisions of any foreign state" are treated the same as national income taxes. Reg. Sec. 1.901-2(g)(2).

special annual information reporting return,[32] and submit a statement claiming the benefit of the high tax exception.[33]

The PFIC rules

As indicated above, the PFIC rules generally step in where the subpart F rules leave off, that is, when the U.S. ownership thresholds of subpart F have not been exceeded, either because all U.S. persons combined do not own more than 50% of the corporation or because the U.S. ownership is so disbursed that all of the 10%-or-more shareholders, if any, do not hold more than 50%.[34] However, like the subpart F rules, the PFIC rules apply only to corporations, since only corporations offer the opportunity of tax deferral by the delay of dividending foreign income that is not otherwise subject to U.S. income tax.

Where applicable, the PFIC rules do not cause immediate deemed income to the U.S. shareholders of undistributed corporate earnings like the subpart F rules; rather, they allow deferral to take place (since the U.S. shareholder(s) may not have enough control to force a dividend) but then impose two charges for the benefit of the tax deferral: (i) characterization of all income, including otherwise tax-advantaged long-term capital gain,[35] as dividend income taxed at "ordinary" rates (rather than capital gain rates), and (ii) the imposition of an interest charge on the amount of income that is U.S. tax deferred.[36] Generally, these penalties are imposed at the time that income is recognized by the shareholder, i.e., upon an actual dividend[37] or upon the shareholder's sale of his stock (or redemption of the stock). Unlike the subpart F rules which apply only to certain defined categories of "subpart F income", the PFIC rules generally apply to all of the PFIC's income, not just the passive income.

A non-U.S. corporation is a PFIC in any year in which either: (a) 75% or more of the corporation's gross income that year is the same kinds of passive income that is treated as subpart F income (with certain modifications), or (b) the "average

---

[32] A U.S. person reports his ownership interest in a controlled foreign corporation with a special IRS form, Form 5471, Information Return of U.S. Persons with Respect to Certain Foreign Corporations, which is filed annually with the IRS's Philadelphia Service Center as well as with the person's individual income tax return (Form 1040) which is filed at the appropriate regional IRS service centre. To the extent that a U.S. person owns more than 50% of the stock of a foreign corporation, the U.S. person is considered to own a financial interest in any bank accounts held by that foreign corporation and the U.S. person will be required to file Treasury Department Form TD F 90-22.1 with the Treasury Department's office in Michigan in order to avoid severe penalties.

[33] Reg. Sec. 1.954-1(*d*)(5).

[34] The PFIC rules can apply to a CFC that also meets the definition of a PFIC, but only with respect to U.S. shareholders to whom the subpart F rules do not apply because the shareholders do not own at least 10% of the voting stock.

[35] Long-term capital gain is generally taxed at the maximum rate of 15% when earned by individuals, as opposed to the maximum "ordinary rate" for individuals of 35%.

[36] Section 1291.

[37] Penalized dividends are only those that are so-called "excess" dividends, that is, dividends that exceed 125% of the average distributions over the preceding three years. The purpose is to not penalize dividends that take out annual earnings currently.

percentage of assets" held by the corporation over the year that either produces passive income or is held to produce passive income is 50% or more of the corporation's total assets.[38] Once a corporation attains the status of a PFIC, the corporation remains a PFIC with respect to those shareholders for all subsequent years unless the shareholder makes an election in the year that PFIC status ceases to recognize his gain in his stock of the corporation and subject the gain to the PFIC penalties.[39] In any case, any U.S. person, including a Canadian expatriate as defined in this article, who owns even a single share in a Canadian corporation that meets the definition of a PFIC must comply with annual reporting requirements distinct from the subpart F reporting requirements.[40]

The PFIC penalties can be avoided if the shareholder makes a special election to treat the foreign corporation as a "qualified electing fund", or "QEF", and if the corporation complies with certain reporting requirements,[41] the result of which is immediate inclusion in the shareholder's taxable income of his share of corporate earnings, although he can elect to defer (with an interest charge) the imposition of tax on such income.[42] Such an election would at least preserve the character of long-term capital gain, but it is not full pass-through treatment which would allow the pass-through of losses or the attribution of Canadian taxes to an individual for purposes of the U.S. foreign tax credit.[43]

Unlike the subpart F rules, there is no high tax exception under the PFIC rules. Thus, with respect to a corporation in a high tax jurisdiction such as Canada, it may be advantageous that the corporation be a CFC with respect to a 10%-or-more U.S. shareholder (the CFC rules trump the PFIC rules where both apply[44]) and therefore avoid the imposition of an interest charge notwithstanding the deferral of U.S. income taxation.

Share ownership through trusts

Often, the shares of non-U.S. companies that might subject the Canadian expatriate owner to the subpart F or PFIC anti-deferral rules are not held directly by the expatriate but by trusts that he has either established or of which he is a beneficiary. Such a dual-level structure introduces not only the complexity of two distinct anti-deferral regimes applicable to trusts, but also the complexity of coordinating the trust anti-deferral rules with the corporate anti-deferral rules discussed above.

Very generally, the trust anti-deferral rule is very simple if the trust is a "grantor trust" with respect to the expatriate; there is no deferral at the trust level, but instead,

---

[38] Section 1297.

[39] Section 1298(*b*)(1).

[40] A U.S. person must annually report using Form 8621, Return by a Shareholder of a Passive Foreign Investment Company or Qualified Electing Fund.

[41] Sections 1293 and 1295.

[42] Section 1294.

[43] See footnote 9.

[44] Section 1297(*e*).

all of the trust's income is immediately attributed to the expatriate in his capacity as the grantor, or in some cases as a beneficiary.[45] A "grantor trust" is one with respect to which the grantor (or beneficiary) retains or is granted one of any specified economic interests or powers of control over the trust, such as a power to revoke the trust or to change beneficiaries.[46] If a foreign trust is created by a U.S. person, including a Canadian expatriate, and if the trust has U.S. beneficiaries, the trust is a "grantor trust" in any event, regardless of the presence of any of the tainting powers described in the rest of the grantor trust rules.[47]

In contrast, if the trust is not a grantor trust (a "non-grantor trust"), such as if the U.S. grantor has died or if the trust were settled by a non-U.S. person who retained no tainting powers,[48] the trust anti-deferral rules are a good deal more complicated. In general, trust income is not attributed to the grantor but rather to the beneficiaries, and while income is not attributed immediately to any beneficiary, complex "throwback" rules apply to ensure that a beneficiary who does receive a distribution pays tax on trust income at a rate that is not significantly lower than the beneficiary's average rate over the previous five years,[49] and an interest charge is generally imposed on the amount of income tax deferred by not making distributions currently.[50]

With respect to income earned by trust-owned corporations, both the grantor trust and the non-grantor trust anti-deferral rules generally apply only with respect to actual dividends paid to the trust, and so the trust anti-deferral rules can generally be avoided by simply deferring the payment of dividends to the trust until such time as a distribution from the trust is intended. There still remains, however, the possible applicability of the corporate anti-deferral rules described above, notwithstanding that the corporation (foreign corporation) is owned indirectly through a trust. Very generally, the corporate anti-deferral rules contain the following stock ownership attribution rules with respect to trust-owned shares of a foreign corporation:

a. subpart F:

    (i) *grantor trust* — the stock of any trust-owned corporation is treated as owned by the grantor (or by any beneficiary who is treated as an owner of trust assets under the grantor trust rules);[51]

---

[45] Section 671 through 679.

[46] Ibid.

[47] Section 679.

[48] Trusts settled by non-U.S. persons can also be grantor trusts, but only under circumstances more limited than if the grantor were a U.S. person. See Section 672(f).

[49] Sections 666 and 667.

[50] Section 668. Probably the best way to understand the throwback rules and the interest charge is to attempt to complete the throwback computation in IRS Form 3520, Part III, which also contains a "default" computation if the beneficiary does not have sufficient information on the trust's history of income and distributions.

[51] Reg. Sec. 1.958-2(c)(1)(ii)(b).

(ii) *non-grantor trust* — stock owned, directly or indirectly, by or for a trust (other than a qualified 401(*a*) retirement trust) is treated as owned by the trust beneficiaries in proportion to their "actuarial interests" in the trust.[52] Determining an "actuarial interest" is often easier said than done, such as when distributions are entirely in the discretion of the trustee over whom the beneficiary has no control. There is no deeming that any discretion of the trustee has been exercised fully in favour of the beneficiary, since to do so in the case of multiple contingent beneficiaries would result in multiple attribution of the CFC's income, and to individuals who may never receive any portion of the CFC's income.

b. the PFIC rules:

(i) *grantor trust* — although neither the PFIC Code sections nor the IRS regulations explicitly state so, it is clear that any stock of a PFIC owned by a grantor trust will be treated as owned by the grantor (or beneficiary) to whom the trust's income is attributed under the grantor trust rules;

(ii) *non-grantor trust* — the PFIC attribution rule as applicable to non-grantor trusts is no less ambiguous than the subpart F attribution rule; stock owned by a trust is treated as owned "proportionately" by its beneficiaries.[53]

In the absence of more specific guidance (none of which is anticipated in the near future, unless by a court), the corporate anti-deferral rules in the context of a corporation owned by a non-grantor trust seem to be possibly applicable only under circumstances in which income of the trust-owned corporation has either been actually paid to a U.S. beneficiary or clearly set aside for his benefit. Even this result could be harsh, with the current imposition of tax on deemed income under subpart F or interest charges under the PFIC rules even though the beneficiary has no power to compel a distribution of the income. In any event, the resolution of this issue must await another day.

General Observations Regarding the U.S. Anti-Deferral Regimes

The above explanation of the subpart F rules and the PFIC rules may appear, to the uninitiated, as complex and confusing, but this discussion is only a brief summary of the rules. The full breadth and complexity of the rules and their interaction can be breathtaking. Suffice at this point to make the following few observations:

(i) if a Canadian expatriate owns a majority interest in a Canadian corporation, he will be exposed to the subpart F rules and, therefore, will have at least special reporting requirements annually (and perhaps cause others to be subject to either the subpart F or the PFIC regimes);

(ii) if the Canadian expatriate owns less than a majority interest, he needs to know the nature of the entire ownership of the corporation and of the

---

[52] Reg. Sec. 1.958-2(*c*)(1)(ii)(a).

[53] Sec. 1298(*a*)(3), Proposed Reg. Sec. 1.1291-1(*b*)(8)(iii)(C).

nature of all of the income of the corporation in order to determine whether or how the subpart F rules and/or the PFIC rules apply to him;

(iii) generally, if the corporation is earning mainly passive investment income, the expatriate will have to examine carefully the status of the corporation and of his own stock ownership to determine whether he has to make a "QEF" election and other elections under the PFIC rules to ameliorate the worst effects of those rules;

(iv) regardless of the applicability of the U.S. anti-deferral rules, it is highly unlikely that a Canadian corporation could offer any significant tax deferral benefit because of the high Canadian income tax rates, and so the problems of dealing with the U.S. anti-deferral rules, which are primarily aimed at tax haven operations, are largely for naught other than avoiding penalties;

(v) to add insult to injury, while the United States recently (2003) adopted a rule which significantly reduces the rate of tax (at least until 2008) on dividends paid to individuals by most domestic (U.S.) corporations and by many foreign corporations — called "qualified foreign corporations" — and while Canadian corporations generally meet the requirements of a qualified foreign corporation,[54] the reduced rate does not apply to distributions from a PFIC or to the inclusion of income under subpart F;[55]

(vi) except to the extent that payments can be made out of the Canadian corporation that are deductible under Canadian law, such as compensation payments to the Canadian expatriate, there will be two-tier taxation of the Canadian corporation's income, first by Canada at the corporate level and then by the United States at the shareholder level when dividends are paid to the expatriate or income is attributed to him under subpart F, with no credit in the United States for the Canadian taxes paid (except the Canadian withholding tax on dividends); and

(vii) if the Canadian expatriate is the beneficiary of a trust that owns a Canadian corporation, he may find himself taxable on all or a part of the corporation's income even though he has no access to such income.

One final observation, and perhaps the most important one to a Canadian expatriate in the United States who finds himself holding stock of a Canadian corporation, is that he will need a good U.S. tax attorney from time to time, and a good U.S. tax accountant all of the time.

---

[54] Because there is a "comprehensive income tax treaty with the United States which the Secretary [the IRS] determines is satisfactory for purposes of this paragraph and which includes an exchange of information program". Section 1(*h*)(11)(C)(i)(II). The U.S.–Canada treaty has proved "satisfactory". Treasury Notice 2003-69.

[55] Although the new qualified dividend rate, which in most cases is 15%, does apply to actual dividends from a controlled foreign corporation, subpart F inclusions always are computed before taking into account actual dividends, and so subpart F earnings never get the chance to qualify for the 15% tax rate. This leaves only actual dividends from non-subpart F income (or subpart F income that qualifies for an exemption) qualifying for the lower rate. IRS Notice 2004-70, 2004-44 I.R.B. 724 (11/1/2004).

Change of Trustees — Article

A new issue pertaining to replacement of trustees has emerged by virtue of a recent CRA technical interpretation. In the following article, David Louis summarizes the problem. David Louis, J.D., C.A., is a tax partner at Minden Gross, a member of MERITAS Law Firms Worldwide. Special thanks to Professor Daniel Sandler.

Change of Trustees = Tax Disaster?

The CRA recently released a Technical Interpretation[56] that could have widespread repercussions to practitioners involved in administration of trusts and estates. The "Technical" canvasses whether control of a corporation is acquired when a trustee of a trust that controls a corporation is replaced. The Technical's short answer: with the *possible* exception of situations where the replacement trustee is related to the pre-existing trustees, yes.

The Technical itself deals with *inter vivos* trusts. While it may be somewhat unusual for such a trust to control a corporation, it would seem that the same result would occur where there is a replacement of executors of an estate, in which a control situation is much more likely.

Because of the importance of the Technical, we have reproduced it below in its entirety; Situation 1 highlights the difficulty. Essentially, the CRA's position (which is based on *M.N.R. v. Consolidated Holding Company Limited*, 72 DTC 6007 (SCC)) is that, in the absence of evidence to the contrary, the CRA considers there to be a presumption that all of the trustees of a trust constitute a group that controls the corporation. It would follow from this that the replacement of a trustee would constitute an acquisition of control.

The situation of concern in the Technical itself is the effect of an acquisition of control on losses. However, an acquisition of control also triggers a year end of the corporation. Besides having to file a tax return, a deemed year end may have a number of other important consequences, including various limitation periods (e.g., the "179-day rule" for bonuses), filing deadlines for various tax elections, shareholder loan repayment deadlines, etc. Besides the impact on non-capital losses, a change of control could affect a number of other tax accounts.

Assuming that the Technical applies equally to estates, it seems to depart from a pre-existing benign administrative policy, as expressed in older technical interpretations as well as Interpretation Bulletin IT-302R3, paragraph 10, which indicates that:

Where an executor, administrator or trustee of an estate controls a corporation, it is a question of fact as to whether there is an acquisition of control of the corporation when there is a change of the executor, administrator or trustee. For purposes of paragraph 256(7)(*a*), where the executor, administrator or trustee is replaced as a result of that person's death or inability to fulfill his or her functions, the control of the corporation will be regarded as remaining unchanged. However, a change in executor, administrator or trustee together with a substantial change in the

---

[56] Doc. No. 2004-0087761E5, May 24, 2005.

ownership of the beneficial interest in the estate will be considered an acquisition of control of the corporation.[57]

In contrast, in the Technical, the CRA concludes that: "it is our view that a change in any of the trustees would result in a new group controlling Lossco and, subject to the provisions of paragraph 256(7)(*a*), an acquisition of control of Lossco".

Subsection 256(7) contains a number of "saving provisions" applicable to the change of control rules; unless one fits squarely into one of these, an acquisition of control will occur. While Situation 2 in the Technical deals with an amalgamation, which would be governed by the saving rule in paragraph 256(7)(*b*), it seems to me that the usual saving provisions in this sort of situation are clauses 256(7)(*a*)(i)(A) and (B), which deem control not to have been acquired solely because of the acquisition of shares of any corporation by a particular person who is related either to the transferor or to the particular corporation immediately before the time.[58] However, it is not completely clear whether these provisions can be relied on where the trustees of a trust or executors of an estate are simply replaced.[59]

The spectre of trustee replacement and its potential of adverse tax consequences is, of course, commonplace. Suppose, for example, there are three executor siblings of an estate that control a corporation. One of the siblings dies or resigns and is replaced by a non-related individual (this may often be a lawyer, accountant or other professional advisor). Based on the Technical, it would appear that this would constitute an acquisition of control.[60]

Obviously, the adverse tax consequences resultant from a change of trustees is inappropriate. Clearly, what is called for is a change in legislation to address this problem, perhaps the adoption of a provision similar to paragraph 256(1.2)(*f*) for the purposes of the acquisition of control rules.

Without this, the Technical greatly restricts the pre-existing administrative largesse, with fundamental and serious implications in many situations.

---

[57] The pre-existing administrative policy was based upon wording of subsection 256(7) which was altered in the December 1992 Technical Amendments.

[58] Per paragraph 251(2)(*b*), such a person will be related to a corporation if: (i) he or she is a person who controls the corporation, if it is controlled by one person; (ii) is a member of a related group that controls the corporation; or (iii) is any person related to a person described in (i) or (ii).

[59] See also Heather L. Evans, "Recent Developments in the Taxation of Owner-Managed Businesses", 93 OC 8:30, in which the issue of trustee replacement is discussed, including two technical interpretations with a more benign policy: Doc. No. 9307165, July 28, 1993, and Doc. No. 9319425, August 6, 1993. However, the latter indicates that paragraph 256(7)(*a*) has no direct application as it envisages an acquisition (etc.) of shares of the corporation. The author observes:

> While the comments with regard to the application of subsection 256(7) may be well-founded, the position regarding the acquisition of control in the circumstances described above would appear to have no basis in law and simply represents an administrative concession of uncertain application.

[60] Because the replacement trustee is unrelated to the siblings, he or she would not fit within the exceptions of clauses 256(7)(*a*)(i)(A) or (B), if applicable. Consideration might be given to not replacing the trustee in these circumstances. Query, however, the consequences if there are a number of unrelated trustees, e.g., Trustees A, B, and C, and one of them resigns or dies and is not replaced. Would there be an acquisition of control by a group — i.e., Trustee A and B? Doc. No. 9307165 seems to suggest that this may be the case.

Reversionary Trust Review — Article

The following is an article by Robert Spenceley, MA, LLB, which appeared in the December 2005 edition of CCH Canadian's newsletter THE ESTATE PLANNER

Attribution under Subsection 75(2)

Very basically, subsection 75(2) of the *Income Tax Act* provides for the attribution of income and capital gains derived from trust property where the property was received by the trust from the person and can revert to that person (or pass to other persons determined by that person). Subsection 75(2) may apply to any *inter vivos* trust that does not fall within the statutory exceptions set out in subsection 75(3).[61]

In certain circumstances, the application of subsection 75(2) may be inconsequential or even desired. The danger lies in *inadvertently* falling within the purview of subsection 75(2); in which case, the tax consequences can be quite severe. Aside from attribution under subsection 75(2) itself, subsection 107(4.1) precludes a rollout to beneficiaries of capital property of a trust to which subsection 75(2) applies (or has applied). A notable aspect of subsection 75(2) is that, in contrast to many of the other attribution rules, which explicitly or implicitly incorporate an intention on the part of the taxpayer to reduce or avoid tax and/or benefit a non-arm's length person, subsection 75(2) may apply even where the trust was established for strictly non-tax planning purposes. And the fact that subsection 75(2) may apply where tax planning is not the order of the day probably increases the risk of inadvertently falling within its provisions. Therefore, it is imperative that subsection 75(2) be considered in planning and implementing an *inter vivos* trust. More particularly, the provisions of subsection 75(2) should be considered in determining:

- the identity of the settlor;

- the identity of the trustee(s);

- the identity of the income and capital beneficiaries;

- the manner in which trustees are to reach decisions; or

- what (if any) power should be retained by the settlor (or any other contributor to the trust).

---

[61] The trusts exempted by subsection 75(3) include: trusts governed by registered pensnion plans; employee profit sharing plans; registered supplementary unemployment benefit plans; RRSPs; deferred profit sharing plans; registered education savings plans; registered retirement income funds; employee benefit plans; retirement compensation arrangements; and related employee segregated fund trusts. Paragraph 75(3)(*d*) refers to prescribed trusts, although currently there are no trusts prescribed in the Regulations for this provision. Draft legislation, most recently republished July 18, 2005, proposes to add new paragraph 75(3)(*c.2*), which is intended to ensure that subsection 75(2) does not apply to property held by a "60-month immigration trust", *viz.*, a trust in respect of which all of the contributors are recent immigrants to Canada (i.e., none of the contributors to the trust has been resident in Canada for more than 60 months).

The following provides an overview of some of the issues to be considered in making such decisions.[62]

The Trap — Key Words

Subsection 75(2) reads as follows:

> Where, by a trust created in any manner whatever since 1934, property is held *on condition*
>
> > (a) that it or property substituted therefor *may*
> >
> > > (i) revert to the *person* from whom the property or property for which it was substituted was *directly or indirectly received* (in this subsection referred to as the person), or
> > >
> > > (ii) pass to persons to be determined by the person at a time subsequent to the creation of the trust, or
> >
> > (b) that, during the existence of the person, the property shall not be disposed of except with the person's *consent* or in accordance with the person's *direction*,
>
> any income or loss from the property or from property substituted for the property, and any taxable capital gain or allowable capital loss from the disposition of the property or of property substituted for the property, shall, during the existence of the person while the person is resident in Canada, be deemed to be income or a loss, as the case may be, or a taxable capital gain or allowable capital loss, as the case may be, of the person.

Italics have been added above to highlight aspects of subsection 75(2) that make it a particularly expansive provision and thereby increase the scope for taxpayers to inadvertently fall within its purview.

"Or property substituted therefore"

The property to which subsection 75(2) applies includes "substituted property", as defined by subsection 248(5). Subsection 248(5) provides that where one property is disposed of or exchanged and a second property is acquired in substitution for the original property and that second property is disposed of or exchanged and a third property is acquired in substitution for the second property, the third property is deemed to have been substituted for the original property. This deeming rule will apply to a fourth property acquired in substitution for the third property and so on, such that no matter how many substitutions are made, the property owned at any particular time is deemed to have been substituted for the original property.

"May"

Subsection 75(2) will apply whenever, under the terms of a trust, there is the possibility that trust property could revert to the person who contributed it, even if the possibility of reversion is remote. It may apply, for example, where the contributor has no more than a contingent capital interest under a "disaster" clause. The CRA has made the following comment on the word "may":

---

[62] For a more detailed discussion, see Brenda L. Crockett, "Subsection 75(2): The Spoiler", *Canadian Tax Journal* (2005) Vol. 53, No. 3, pp. 806–830. See also M. Elena Hoffstein, "Tips & Traps: Issues in Estate Planning", *Estates and Trusts Forum 2001*, pp. 1–40. Reference may also be made to Interpretation Bulletin IT-369R, Attribution of Trust Income to Settlor.

The word "may" implies that the subsection applies even though there is only a possibility that the property reverts to the transferor. We would like to stress that the condition found in subparagraph 75(2)(a)(i) of the Act does not refer to the notion of control or certainty in order to be met.[63]

Accordingly, the CRA concluded that subsection 75(2) would apply where a taxpayer transferred property to a trust, under the terms of which the taxpayer's spouse was given a power of appointment exercisable through the spouse's will. Accordingly, the spouse would determine the beneficiaries who would share in the assets of the trust at the spouse's death. The assets of the trust would not become the assets of the spouse's estate. Rather, the assets of the trust would be distributed to the persons chosen by the spouse through the exercise of the power of appointment given to the spouse in the trust indenture. Since the contributor could be so chosen, subsection 75(2) applied. (The CRA went on to state that, where the terms of the power prevented the donee of the power from appointing the transferor, subsection 75(2) would not apply because the property could not return to the contributor through the operation of the trust.)

"Directly or indirectly"

Not only will subsection 75(2) apply where the meeting of its conditions is only a hypothetical possibility, the contribution triggering it may be direct or indirect. Therefore, it would apply where property is transferred to a taxpayer who thereafter (perhaps years later) establishes a trust naming the transferor as a beneficiary (and perhaps only a contingent beneficiary at that). It is not hard to imagine how such a circumstance might arise. Say, for instance, Parent gives Child a property which, a number of years later, Child transfers to an *inter vivos* family trust, the primary beneficiaries of which are Child's spouse and children, but the terms of which name Parent as a contingent residual beneficiary. In such circumstances, subsection 75(2) applies to attribute any income, loss, etc., from the property to Parent.

"Received"

Unlike most of the attribution rules, subsection 75(2) can apply even where the property was transferred to the trust for fair market value consideration (or where the property can pass back to the transferor for fair market value consideration).[64] The word "received" is very broad and subsection 75(2) does not qualify it by reference to "for inadequate consideration" or any other such phrase.

"The person"

Generally, it is the settlor who transfers property to a trust to which subsection 75(2) may apply. However, subsection 75(2) is worded such that it may apply to any person from whom property is received by the trust and not just the settlor. By virtue of the definition of "person" in subsection 248(1), this may include a corporation or another trust.

---

[63] Doc. No. 2002-0162855, April 25, 2003.

[64] Doc. No. 2004-0086941C6, October 8, 2004.

"Consent", "direction"

Typically, the settlor of an irrevocable trust will retain some control over the assets of the trust by being one of its trustees. The CRA is of the view that subsection 75(2) may apply where:

- the transferor has the ability to select beneficiaries, including the beneficiaries among a predetermined class, to whom property will pass; and

- the transferor has retained the right to veto distributions of trust property to beneficiaries.

To avoid the application of subsection 75(2), the settlor should not be the sole trustee. Where, as is common, three trustees are appointed, the settlor should not have a veto. The trust indenture should specify that decisions are to be made by a majority vote. In the absence of such a clause, trust law requires decisions to be unanimous, which would mean the trust property could not be dealt with without the consent of the settlor-trustee. Although two relatively recent CRA technical interpretations (see the discussion of "Co-Trustees" below) have cast some doubt on the issue, it has generally been understood that the presence of such a veto would cause subsection 75(2) to apply. Notwithstanding the leniency expressed in these documents, it should be borne in mind that: these documents are not binding on the CRA; the latter frequently revises its positions; and the precise interpretation to be given these two particular technical interpretations is subject to question. Accordingly, it remains prudent for the settlor not to be the sole trustee, for him or her not to have a veto, and for decisions to be made by a majority of at least three trustees.

Even where it is provided that decisions are to be made by a majority of three trustees and the settlor does not have a veto, a *de facto* veto may arise in certain circumstances such as when a non-contributing trustee resigns before he or she can be replaced. This would leave the settlor-trustee with a veto until a replacement trustee was appointed and, even though the situation could be quickly corrected, the temporary nature of the veto would not stop subsection 75(2) from applying. (The significance of even the temporary application of subsection 75(2) will become clear when subsection 107(4.1) is considered.) To preclude such an eventuality, the trust indenture could stipulate that, while the settlor-trustee is one of fewer than three trustees, all discretionary distributions and dispositions are to be suspended until a third trustee is appointed.

Restrictions on the Application of Subsection 75(2)

It will be apparent from the above that subsection 75(2) is broadly worded and may apply in many seemingly innocent situations. However, the terms of this provision and the CRA's administrative position in regard thereto indicate some significant restrictions on its scope and impact.

Loans

In Interpretation Bulletin IT-369RSR (paragraph 1, replaced by the special report), the CRA states that: "A genuine loan to a trust would not by itself be considered to result in property being 'held' by the trust under one or more of these conditions (i.e., would not by itself result in the application of subsection 75(2)), if the loan is outside and independent of the terms of the trust." Therefore, based on the CRA's administrative discretion, a loan to a trust will not attract the application of subsection 75(2), although a sale or gift to a trust would. Of course, the loan must be "genuine" and its terms not so generous as to constitute a disguised gift. Also not to be overlooked is the requirement that "the loan is outside and independent of the terms of the trust", which is to say, at least, the making of the loan should not be reflected in the drafting of the trust.

Second Generation Income

As is generally the case with other attribution rules, subsection 75(2) does not apply to second-generation income. Therefore, for example, as the CRA puts it in Interpretation Bulletin IT-369R (paragraph 6), "if the property received from a person is money which is deposited by the trust into a bank account, the interest on the initial deposit will attribute to that person but interest on the interest left to accumulate in the bank account will not attribute." As noted above, subsection 75(2) applies to "substituted property". Thus, while subsection 75(2) does not apply to attribute second-generation income, it does apply to second- (and subsequent) generation capital gains.

Income Beneficiaries

If the settlor/contributor is an income beneficiary under the trust, subsection 75(2) will not normally apply unless, for example, there is a power to encroach upon the trust capital for the benefit of the income beneficiary. The terms of any trust can deny the settlor access to the capital of the trust. It it is interesting to note, however, that doing so becomes problematical in the case of an alter ego trust. The rub is that a trust will not qualify as an alter ego trust if anyone other than the settlor has access to the capital (or income) of the trust during the lifetime of the settlor. Therefore, for an alter ego trust to avoid subsection 75(2) the entire capital of the trust will have to be completely inaccessible during the lifetime of the settlor.

Reversion by "Operation of Law"

The CRA has consistently held that the reversion of property contemplated by paragraph 75(2)(*a*) would not include the situation "where the property may revert to the person by operation of law only, e.g., a total failure of the trust for lack of beneficiaries, and not pursuant to any condition under the trust indenture".[65] This creates the possibility of planning for reversion by the operation of law.

Contributor Inherits Property from Spouse's Estate

As noted above, it is the CRA's view that subsection 75(2) could apply where an individual transferred property to a trust for the benefit of the individual's spouse where the disposition of the trust's assets would be determined by the spouse through his or her will. As the settlor could reacquire the property under the terms of the spouse's will, it was the CRA's view that subsection 75(2) could apply.

---

[65] Doc. No. 2002-0116535, February 19, 2002.

Nonetheless, the CRA has said that, as it sees it, subsection 75(2) would *not* apply where the spouse's estate acquires the property and the spouse could potentially — through his or her will — leave that property to the settlor of the trust.[66] In brief, then, if the trust indenture grants a power of appointment to be exercised via the will of the beneficiary, subsection 75(2) applies (unless the power of appointment is suitably limited); but, if the property becomes part of the beneficiary's estate (again to be distributed pursuant to his or her will), it will not.

Transfer of Property from Reversionary Trust to New Trust

The CRA has expressed the view that, where property of a trust to which subsection 75(2) applied is transferred to a new trust, the terms of which would avoid the provision, subsection 75(2) would not apply to the new trust solely because the provision applied to the first trust.[67]

Business Income

Subsection 75(2) does not apply to business income or losses of a trust (see Interpretation Bulletin IT-369R (paragraph 5)). However, capital gains or losses arising in regard to business property are attributed to the contributor.

"In Existence" and "Resident in Canada"

Subsection 75(2) applies "during the existence of the person while the person is resident in Canada". It, therefore, will not apply on the death or emigration of a contributor. However, note that, although any income, gain and loss in respect of property received from a person is attributed by subsection 75(2) to that person only during a period when that person is resident in Canada, its application does not depend upon the person having been resident in Canada at the time the property was received by the trust.

Given the requirement that the person be in "existence" for it to apply, subsection 75(2) will not apply to a deceased testator. And, given that a testamentary trust is defined in subsection 108(1) in such a manner that it ceases to be such if anyone other than the deceased contributes to it, subsection 75(2) can have no application to testamentary trusts.

Applies on a Property-by-Property Basis

Where subsection 75(2) applies, "any income or loss from the property or from property substituted for the property, and any taxable capital gain or allowable capital loss from the disposition of the property or of property substituted for the property" is attributed to the person who contributed it. What is attributed then is only the income, loss, etc. of the specific property (i.e., the property contributed by a

---

[66] Doc. No. 2002-0139205, July 22, 2002.

[67] Doc. No. 2001-0067955, January 3, 2002. The CRA noted in the same document that, in its view, where subsection 75(2) applied to the first trust, the rollover under subsection 107(2) would not apply to the transfer of property to the new trust unless one of the conditions in paragraphs 107(4.1)(c) and (d) is not met. Otherwise, subsection 107(4.1) applies to deny the rollover under subsection 107(2), and subsection 107(2.1) would apply to the disposition of property by the first trust.

person to whom it may revert) and not that of the assets of the trust as a whole. Accordingly, in and of itself, the attribution of income under subsection 75(2) may not be of great importance.

Determination of the Quantum of Capital Distributions

The CRA has indicated that subsection 75(2) may not apply where the person from whom the property was received by the trust cannot determine the identity of the beneficiaries but can only determine the quantum of the trust property to be distributed to the beneficiaries which have already been identified by the trust.[68] However, it added that, if the power to determine the quantum of the trust property is such that it results in the power to determine the beneficiaries to whom the property will pass, subsection 75(2) would apply. (For example, this situation may occur, if the settlor retains the possibility to identify which property can be distributed to a beneficiary or if he or she retains the possibility to fix the quantum (for example, in allocating nothing to a beneficiary) so that he has retained the possibility to identify the beneficiary.)

Co-Trustees

As noted above, in recent years the CRA has moved away from the position that subsection 75(2) will necessarily apply where the settlor (or other contributor) has what amounts to a veto. Most recently, the CRA has stated:[69]

> Generally speaking, when no specific provision is made in a trust indenture as to the way in which the trust's property must be administered, the administration of this property is subject to the standard terms in the trust indenture. In this case, the fact that an individual from whom the trust received property is a co-trustee of the trust with one or more individuals and the trustees, decisions must be made by a majority or unanimously does not in and of itself mean that paragraph 75(2)(b) I.T.A. applies.

Also in 2004, the CRA commented as follows:[70]

> When the settlor is one of two or more co-trustees acting in a fiduciary capacity in administering the trust property and there are no specific terms outlining how the trust property is to be dealt with, but rather the property is subject to standard terms ordinarily found in trust indentures, we accept that paragraph 75(2)(b) will generally not be applicable.

Similarly, in an earlier document,[71] the CRA opined that:

> Our current position is that where a person contributes property to a trust and is one of two or more co-trustees acting in a fiduciary capacity in administering the trust property and there are no specific terms outlining how the trust property is to be dealt with, but rather the property is subject to the standard terms of the trust, paragraph 75(2)(*b*) may not be considered applicable.

The CRA's current position appears to be that a trust will not necessarily be subject to subsection 75(2) where a contributor is a trustee and decisions are to be

---

[68] Doc. No. 9213965, August 11, 1992.

[69] Doc. No. 2004-0086921C6, October 8, 2004.

[70] Doc. No. 2003-0050671E5, April 5, 2004.

[71] Doc. No. 2000-0042505, April 30, 2001. In the same document, the CRA made a corresponding statement re paragraph 75(2)(*a*).

made unanimously, so long as the trustees are required to deal with the property pursuant to "standard terms ordinarily found in trust indentures" or their fiduciary duties. Yet, this attitude toward co-trustees is hard to square with the CRA's long-standing position that subsection 75(2) necessarily applies to a sole trustee who has contributed property to the trust.[72] While practitioners no doubt welcome an accommodating approach from the CRA, they may have misgivings about relying too heavily on its current administrative largesse. As one commentator has put it:[73]

> The CRA's recent reassurances in respect of co-trustees aside, if a contributor of property is also a trustee it seems prudent to continue the practice of using a minimum of three trustees with decisions to be made by a simple majority vote, except where doing so would be entirely impractical and where all possible negative consequences have been fully analyzed.

Denial of Tax-Deferred Roll-out Where Subsection 75(2) Applies

The application of subsection 75(2) may be temporary and pertain to only a relatively minor contribution; however, even in such circumstances, due to its interaction with subsection 107(4.1), the application of subsection 75(2) can have momentous tax consequences.

One of the most valuable features of a personal trust[74] is its ability to transfer property to its capital beneficiaries on a tax deferred "rollout" basis. Pursuant to subsection 107(2), a distribution in satisfaction of a beneficiary's capital interest will generally occur without triggering adverse tax consequences. Therefore, for instance, to avoid the deemed disposition that normally takes place on the 21st anniversary of a trust, it is usually advisable to roll out the capital property to the beneficiaries sometime prior to this date. The interaction of subsection 75(2) and subsection 107(4.1) puts an end to this happy arrangement. In brief, where subsection 75(2) applies to a trust, or has ever applied to it, the subsection 107(2) rollout will not be available.

Subsection 107(4.1) is intended to remove the tax advantage in creating a trust under which the settlor holds capital property which will appreciate in value for a period during which such property could revert to the settlor or pass to people to be determined by the settlor in the future. As a result of subsection 107(4.1), the settlor cannot cause the trust property to be distributed on a tax-free basis to persons chosen by him or her subsequent to the creation of the trust. Subsection 107(4.1) reads in part as follows:

> Subsection (2.1) applies (and subsection (2) does not apply) in respect of a distribution of *any property* of a particular personal trust or prescribed trust by the particular trust to a taxpayer who was a beneficiary under the particular trust where
>
> (a) the distribution was in satisfaction of all or any part of the taxpayer's capital interest in the particular trust;
>
> (b) subsection 75(2) was applicable *at a particular time* in respect of *any property* of
>
> (i) the particular trust,

---

[72] See for instance, Doc. No. 2001-0110425, June 20, 2002.

[73] Brenda L. Crockett, *supra*, note 2, at p. 812.

[74] As defined in subsection 248(1), a personal trust is essentially either a testamentary or *inter vivos* trust all the beneficiaries of which received their interests as gifts.

The words that make this provision particularly expansive have been italicized. Two aspects of this provision are particularly noteworthy:

- The denial of the 107(2) rollout applies to all the property of the trust and not just the property subject to subsection 75(2).

- For subsection 107(4.1) to apply, it is enough for subsection 75(2) to have ever applied to the trust. It does not matter, if at the time of the distribution, 75(2) no longer applies to any property then held by the trust. Therefore, whereas a subsection 75(2) problem can be rectified more or less simply, a subsection 107(4.1) problem is permanent.

Prior to a 2001 amendment, paragraph (*b*) of subsection 107(4.1) read "subsection 75(2) was applicable *at any time* in respect of any property of the trust,"; as quoted above, it now reads "subsection 75(2) was applicable *at a particular time* in respect of any property of". This would appear to be the case of a distinction without a difference. The fact remains that, where subsection 75(2) has ever applied to any of the property of the trust none of the property of the trust may be rolled out under subsection 107(2).

It is interesting to note that when subsection 107(4.1) was introduced in 1988, there were no grandfathering provisions, with the result that trusts that were in existence at that time could be subject to it due to the application of subsection 75(2) at some earlier time in the life of the trust. This retroactive aspect of subsection 107(4.1) can be very problematic since, before 1988, some trusts (established, for example, in the course of an estate freeze) may have been purposely formulated with the knowledge that subsection 75(2) would apply, i.e., because the settlor wanted a high degree of control of the trust assets and because there was little downside prior to subsection 107(4.1).

The effect of subsection 107(4.1) is that, where it applies to exclude subsection 107(2),[75] subsection 107(2.1) applies instead, with the result that:

- The trust is deemed to have disposed of the property distributed to the beneficiary for proceeds equal to its fair market value at the time of distribution. As a result, the trust will realize a capital gain or loss at the moment of distribution. In addition, the trust may realize profits or losses in respect of inventory, and recapture or terminal losses in respect of depreciable property.

- The beneficiary is deemed to have acquired the trust property at a cost equal to its fair market value.

In this light, not only should subsection 75(2) be considered in establishing a trust (choosing the trustees, etc., as noted above); given its interaction with subsection 107(4.1), anytime an *in specie* distribution of assets to a beneficiary in satisfaction of his or her capital interest in the trust is considered, it will be necessary to review the history of the trust to determine if subsection 75(2) ever applied to it.

---

[75] The rules in subsection 107(2.1) will not apply to a disposition of property by a reversionary trust which takes place after the death of a settlor. Nor do they apply where the trust property was transferred to a spouse or common-law partner of the settlor on a rollover basis under subsection 73(2). In these two circumstances, the rollover provisions of subsection 107(2) remain available.

Conclusion

Clearly, subsection 75(2) may apply to trusts that are not normally thought of as "reversionary trusts", with potentially serious tax consequences. Subsection 75(2) is worded in such a way that it is hard to delimit the precise parameters of its potential application and there is effectively no case law to assist in this task. Subsection 75(2) received some consideration in *Fraser v. The Queen*, 91 DTC 5123, Federal Court-Trial Division, but only in a peripheral way. In this case, the taxpayer was one of 94 taxpayers who had purchased units in an investment vehicle holding a pooled fund of mortgages managed by a professional brokerage firm. The Minister characterized this vehicle as a trust, and disallowed the deduction by the taxpayer personally of losses sustained. Having lost the argument that the relationship was one of agency rather than trust, the plaintiff switched track and argued that, if it was a trust, subsection 75(2) applied to allow the flow through of the losses from the trust to her. Reed J. made short shift of this argument; however, his cursory comments on subsection 75(2) provide little general illumination as to its application, not surprising given the peripheral relevance of subsection 75(2) to the facts of the case. In particular, his comment at p. 5130 that "subsection 75(2) anticipates a situation in which the whole corpus of the trust is capable of reverting to the settlor (75(2)(a)) or where the corpus during the life of the trust remains under the control of the settlor (75(2)(b))" seems inexact.

Given the lack of guidance from the courts, technical interpretations issued by the CRA take on added interest and should be considered in reviewing a trust in regard to subsection 75(2) — even if they are not binding. A few of the more notable of these documents have been cited above.

Appendix D

Estate Freeze Worksheets

Details of Property to be Frozen

Worksheet A

	Date of Acquisition	Acquired From	Adjusted Cost Base	Fair Market Value	Paid-up Capital
Shares and Securities[1]					
Non-Depreciable Capital Prop.[1]					
Depreciable Property[2]					
Other Property[3]					

[1] If property has been acquired prior to V-day (December 31, 1971; December 22, 1971 for publicly traded securities; ITAR 24) or acquired in a non-arm's length transaction, subsection 84.1(2) may apply to restrict the amount of non-share consideration if the property is transferred to a corporation. For property owned on June 18, 1971 or acquired in a non-arm's length transaction from a person who owned the property on that date, refer to ITAR 26 when computing the adjusted cost base. Additional information and calculations should be attached, where appropriate.

[2] The "cost amount" of depreciable property of a prescribed class is essentially the proportion of the undepreciated capital cost of the class that the cost of the property is to the cost of all property of the class. Refer to the definition of "cost amount" in subsection 248(1) of the Income Tax Act for the adjustments required. If the property was acquired prior to V-Day, refer to the Income Tax Application Rules. Additional information and calculations should be attached, where appropriate.

[3] Refer to the definition of "cost amount" in subsection 248(1). Attach additional information and calculations.

361

Transfer of Property to a Corporation Using Section 85

Worksheet B

Property Transferred				Non-Share Consideration			Shares				Total Consideration
Description	Fair Market Value[4]	Cost Amount	Paid-up Capital[1]	Elected Amount[2]	Description	Fair Market Value	Adjusted Cost Base[3]	Description	Fair Market Value[4]	Adjusted Cost Base[3]	Fair Market Value[4]	Adjusted Cost Base[3]

[1] Where the property transferred are shares of a connected corporation (see section 84.1)

[2] The elected amount cannot be less than the lesser of the fair market value and the cost amount of the property transferred, and cannot be greater than the fair market value of the property transferred. Generally, the elected amount should equal the cost amount of the property transferred.

[3] The adjusted cost base of the consideration received is equal to the elected amount. The elected amount is allocated first to any non-share consideration (paragraph 85(1)(f)), secondly to preferred shares (paragraph 85(1)(g)), and then to any common shares (paragraph 85(1)(h)) received as consideration; where the consideration consists of more than one of any particular type, the adjusted cost base is allocated based on the relative fair market value. Where applicable, supplementary calculations should be attached.

[4] The fair market value of the total consideration should not exceed the fair market value of the property transferred.

Paid-Up Capital Reduction — Worksheet C

Subsection 85(2.1)

Section 85(2.1) applies when property is transferred to a corporation using section 85. The provision does not apply if either section 84.1 or section 212.1 applies.

Reduction in paid-up capital — share consideration:

	Description	Stated Capital	Reduction In Paid-up Capital $(A-B) \times (C \div A)$	Paid-up Capital
Class	_____	_____ C	_____	_____
Class	_____	_____ C	_____	_____
Class	_____	_____ C	_____	_____
Class	_____	_____ C	_____	_____
Total		_____ A	_____	

Adjustment for no share consideration:

Corporation's cost of property, determined under subsection 85(1) or (2) (elected amount)   _____

exceeds

Fair market value of non-share consideration:

Description	Fair Market Value
_____	_____
_____	_____
_____	_____
_____	_____
	_____

EXCESS   _____ (B)

Paid-Up Capital Reduction — Worksheet D

Section 84.1

Section 84.1 applies when there is a non-arm's length transfer of the shares of a corporation, the "subject corporation", to another corporation, the "purchaser corporation" and, immediately after the transfer, the "subject corporation" and the "purchaser corporation" are "connected" (see subsections 186(4) and 186(2)).

Reduction in paid-up capital — share consideration:

	Description	Stated Capital	Reduction In Paid-up Capital $(A-B)\times(C\div A)$	Paid-up Capital
Class	_____	____ C	_____	____
Class	_____	____ C	_____	____
Class	_____	____ C	_____	____
Class	_____	____ C	_____	____
Total		____ A	_____ F	

Amounts from attached worksheet

B _____

D _____

E _____

Deemed Dividend:

(_____ A + _____ D) - (_____ E + _____ F) = _____

Maximum allowable amount (E) and excess (B) non-share consideration (D):

(I) Paid-up capital of subject shares (84.1(1) - B(i) of formula) ========== (i)

(II) Adjusted cost base of subject shares _____

  Adjustment under 84.1(2)(a) for shares acquired prior to 1972:

    Adjusted cost base computed without reference to ITAR 24(3) and ITAR 26(7) - (84.1(2)(c)(E) _____

    Dividends received which the corporation has elected under 83(1), 84.1(2)(c)(ii) _____

    Total/adjustment ========== _____

  Adjustment under 84.1(2)(a.1) for shares acquired subsequent to V-day, which were acquired in a non-arm's length transaction or a share substituted for a share acquired prior to 1972:

    (i) For shares or substituted shares owned by taxpayer or non-arm's length person at the end of 1971:

      (A) Fair Market Value, ITAR 24, 84.1(2)(a.1)(i)(B) ==========

      exceeds

      (B) Actual Cost — January 1, 1972 ITAR 26(13) _____

      (C) Dividends received, on which the corporation has elected under subsection 83(1) _____

       ==========

      Excess/adjustment ========== _____

    (ii) For shares acquired after 1972, the amount of capital gains exemption previously claimed by the taxpayer or a non-arm's length person (84.1(2)(a.1)(ii) _____

     ========== (ii)

Greater of (I) and (II) _____ (E)

exceeds

Fair market value of non-share consideration received _____ (D)

Excess ========== (B)

TOPICAL INDEX